How to Read Church History
Volume 2

The Crossroad Adult Christian Formation Program

The Crossroad
Scripture
Study Program

How to Read the Old Testament
How to Read the New Testament

The Crossroad
Theology and Church
History Study Program

How to Read Church History: Vol. 1
How to Read Church History: Vol. 2
How to Understand the Creed
How to Understand Church and Ministry in the U.S. Experience

The Crossroad
Christian Living
Study Program

How to Understand the Liturgy
How to Understand the Sacraments
How to Understand Marriage
How to Understand Morality and Ethics

Crossroad
Special Interest
Courses

How to Understand Islam
How to Read the World
How to Understand God
How to Read the Church Fathers
How to Read the Apocalypse

Some "How To..." texts, and accompanying study guides, may be in preparation. For complete up-to-date information, please write: The Crossroad Publishing Company, 370 Lexington Avenue, New York, NY 10017.

Jean Comby with Diarmaid MacCulloch

How to Read Church History

Volume 2

From the Reformation to the present day

CROSSROAD · NEW YORK

This printing: 2004

The Crossroad Publishing Company
16 Penn Plaza, 481 Eighth Avenue, New York, NY 10001

Translated by Margaret Lydamore and John Bowden from the French
Pour lire l'Histoire de l'Église Tome 2
published 1986 by Les Editions du Cerf
29 bd Latour-Mabourg, Paris

with additional material by Diarmaid MacCulloch

Nihil Obstat: Rev. Anton Cowan
Censor

Imprimatur: Rt. Rev. John Crowley, VG
Bishop in Central London
(sic), 17 October 1988

Drawings by Liliane Piorkowski

Additional drawings by Rachel Bowden

Printed in the United States of America

Library of Congress Cataloging in Publication Data

Comby, Jean.
How to read church history.

Translation of: Pour lire l'histoire de l'Eglise.
Includes bibliographies.
Contents: v. 1. From the beginnings to the fifteenth century.
— v. 2. From the Reformation to the present day.
1. Church history. 2. Catholic Church—History.
I. Title.
BR145.2.C6513 1985 270 85-11040
ISBN 0-8245-0722-3 (v. 1)
ISBN 0–8245–0908–0 (v. 2)

Contents

Introductory Note vii

For Further Reading ix

11 Renaissance and Reformation 1

I Europe at the Time of the Renaissance 2
II The Reformers 8
III Religious Confessions in Europe 19

12 The Catholic Renewal 23

I Catholic Reform in the Sixteenth Century 24
II The Religious Flowering of the Seventeenth Century 34
III Internal Conflicts and Crises 38

13 The British and North American Experience 46

I Reformations of the Sixteenth Century 46
II The Seventeenth Century: Toleration out of Conflict 54

14 The Evangelization of the World 64

I The Great Missionary Enterprises of Modern Times 65
II Across the Continents 70
III Missions from the European Perspective and the Crisis of the Eighteenth Century 84

15 New Worlds: Britain and North America 87

I The Industrial Revolution 87
II English Churches in the Eighteenth Century 88
III Catholicism in Ireland 92
IV The Evangelical Revival 94
V The 'Awakenings' in America 98

16 The Church in the Age of Enlightenment and Revolution 101

I Changes in the Eighteenth Century 102
II The Revivals in Protestantism and in the Eastern Churches 106
III The Shock of the Revolution 111

17 Restoration and Liberalism 122

I Restoration 123
II God and Freedom 128
III The First Vatican Council 134

18 The British Experience 138
I The Fortunes of Church Establishments 139
II English Churches beyond the Establishment 148
III A New Outlook to Face 152

19 Secularization, the Defence of Religion and Pluralism 156
I Across Europe up to 1914 157
II French Catholics and the Third Republic 159
III From the First World War to the 1930s 162

20 A Worldwide Christianity 169
I The Beginning of the Missionary Revival in the Nineteenth Century 170
II Across the Continents 174
III Missions after the First World War 185

21 The Weight of Modernity 189
I Christians in Industrial Society 190
II The Difficult Confrontation between Catholic Tradition and Modern Science 195
III The Hesitant Beginnings of Ecumenism 202

22 From the Second World War to the Council 210
I Christians in the Second World War 211
II The Religious Repercussions of Political Events in the Post-War Period 215
III Pastoral and Theological Dynamism 220

23 The Church of Vatican II 224
I Vatican II 225
II The More or Less Unforeseen Results of the Council 233
III Disillusionment and Hope 236

Chronological Tables 242

Introductory Note

This book follows directly on from Volume 1 of *How to Read Church History*. That is why the numbering of the chapters and of the boxes take up where Volume 1 left off. The book keeps to the same principles as the preceding volume, and you should look at the introduction to that for a guide to reading and work plan.

From the sixteenth century onwards, church history developed some new characteristics. The Latin church and the Eastern church had already been following different paths for several centuries. With the Reformation, it was the Latin church which split up into several rival confessions; at the same time, in the wake of the great voyages of discovery, the gospel was proclaimed throughout the world. In a period when nation states were establishing themselves and when absolutism was supreme, church history often became the history of national churches, even within Catholicism. In a study as short as this it is not always easy to take account of all these aspects. As far as possible we have tried to find room for all the Christian confessions and the new churches overseas. Equally, we have tried not to limit this religious history to Western Europe. However, authors always speak from a specific context, and the book will necessarily have the local limitations of those who have produced it.

The sheer number of events makes it impossible to tackle everything. Choices have been made, and events and figures which some will think important have been left out. Readers and group leaders will find further help in the books mentioned in the bibliography which follows and those at the end of each chapter.

For Further Reading

The books listed here cover the period from the Reformation onwards. Some of the multi-volume series begin at the earliest days of Christianity; details of volumes on pre-Reformation history appear in *How to Read Church History*, Volume 1. Only those titles are listed here which are in series or cover the subject-matter of more than one chapter. For works relating to particular periods see the lists at the end of the relevant chapter.

1. Multi-volume series

The Pelican History of the Church, Penguin Books
O. Chadwick, *The Reformation*, 1964
G. R. Cragg, *The Church and the Age of Reason*, 1966
A. R. Vidler, *The Church in an Age of Revolution*, 1977
S. C. Neill, *A History of Christian Missions*, revised edition 1986

The Christian Centuries, Darton, Longman and Todd and Paulist Press.
Vol.5. R. Aubert et al., *The Churches in a Secularized Society*, 1978
(Vols.3 and 4 have not appeared)

History of the Church, ed. Hubert Jedin, Herder and Herder and Burns and Oates 1981
Vol.5 *Reformation and Counter-Reformation*
Vol.6 *The Church in the Age of Absolutism and Enlightenment*
Vol.7 *The Church between the Revolution and Restoration*
Vol.8 *The Church in the Age of Liberalism*
Vol.9 *The Church in the Industrial Age*
Vol.10 *The Church in the Modern Age*

2. Some important single-volume histories

K. Aland, *A History of Christianity*, Volume 2. *From the Beginnings to the Reformation*, Fortress Press 1986
John Bossy, *Christianity in the West 1400–1700*, Oxford University Press 1985
J. Derek Holmes and Bernard W. Bickers, *A Short History of the Catholic Church*, Burns and Oates 1985
Paul Johnson, *A History of Christianity*, Penguin Books 1984
Diarmaid MacCulloch, *Groundwork of Church History*, Epworth Press 1987

3. Histories of the Churches in England

John Bossy, *The English Catholic Community 1570–1850*, Darton Longman and Todd 1975
Rupert Davies, A. Raymond George and Gordon Rupp (eds.), *A History of the Methodist Church in Great Britain*, four volumes, Epworth Press, 1965–1988
David Edwards, *Christian England*, Volume 2, *From the Reformation to the Eighteenth Century*, Fount Paperbacks 1984

–, *Christian England*, Volume 3, *From the Eighteenth Century to the First World War*, Fount Paperbacks 1985
Edward Norman, *Church and Society in England. 1770–1970*, Oxford University Press 1976

4. Histories of the Churches in America

S. E. Ahlstrom, *A Religious History of the American People*, Yale University Press 1972
R. T. Handy, *History of the Churches in the United States and Canada*, Oxford University Press 1977
M. E. Marty, *Pilgrims in Their Own Land: 500 Years of Religion in America*, Little, Brown 1984

For further information about all the questions in this book the indispensable guide is F. L. Cross and E. A. Livingstone (eds.), *The Oxford Dictionary of the Christian Church*, Oxford University Press ^{2}1974. J. C. Brauer (ed.), *The Westminster Dictionary of the Christian Church*, Westminster Press 1971, offers a different perspective.

Geographical information and pictures relating to this period are contained in Henry Chadwick and G. R. Evans (eds.), *An Atlas of the Christian Church*, Macmillan 1987. See also E. S. Gaustad, *Historical Atlas of Religion in America*, rev. ed. Harper and Row 1976

11

Renaissance and Reformation

End of the Fifteenth and the Sixteenth century

The Creation of Adam, Michelangelo. Ceiling of the Sistine Chapel.

The end of the fifteenth century witnessed the appearance of modern nations which sought to be free from the powers of the past: the papacy and the Germanic empire. This resulted in a profound cultural renewal which has been called the Renaissance. The invention of printing allowed the wide dissemination of both the sacred and the secular works of the past. By returning to the sources, the texts of the Bible and the church fathers, a number of people sought to purify the church from the excrescences which had grown up over the centuries. Many worn-out ecclesiastical institutions no longer met up to the expectation of Christians. And so, at the beginning of the sixteenth century, there was a sudden upsurge of people determined to bring about reform in the church. Unfortunately, as a result of misunderstandings and violence on both sides, this reform burst apart the Western church. At the close of the sixteenth century the new aspects of the religious geography we have inherited were taking shape.

I · Europe at the Time of the Renaissance

1. The birth of modern states

France, England, Spain

Several European countries took the shape of states in the modern sense: they had powerful sovereigns, with money and armies. The Hundred Years War, which ended in 1453, defined the respective territories of the kingdoms of France and England. In France, the kings affirmed their authority throughout their domains. In 1516, by the Concordat of Bologna, King Francis I obtained from Pope Leo X the authority to appoint all bishops and abbots in the kingdom, which gave him considerable power over the Church of France. England was still only a small kingdom, but one of its sovereigns, Henry VIII (1509–1547), played a prominent role in the politics and religion of Europe. The marriage between Isabella of Castille and Ferdinand of Aragon in 1469 set the seal on Spanish unity. The capture of Granada, the last Arab outpost, in 1492, marked the end of the *reconquista* (recapture) and final unification of Spain. The 'catholic sovereigns' took the interests of the church to heart and set them alongside those of the state. In 1478 they reorganized the Inquisition; this became a national institution which they utilized to their profit. The court was merciless in hunting down heretics, Moslems and Jews who were more or less converted.

Northern and eastern Europe

Poland, a large kingdom with ill-defined frontiers which stretched from Lithuania to the Ukraine and whose political framework was weak, was the front line of Latin Christianity over against the Orthodox Christian world. The Russian sovereigns in Moscow, Ivan III (1462–1504) and Ivan IV ('The Terrible', 1530–1584), looked on themselves as the heirs of Constantinople. Moscow was the third Rome. They had little to do with Western Europe.

From the time of their capture of Constantinople in 1453, the Turks had been continuing their advance into the heart of Eastern Europe, subjugating the people of the Balkans, who were Orthodox Christians, and periodically threatening the Christian West: Hungary, Austria, etc. Under the Turkish régime the Greek church undoubtedly retained its administrative structures: the inviolability of the Patriarch of Constantinople and the bishops who exercised civil authority over all Christians in the Ottoman Empire, albeit in dependence on the Sultan. However, Christians were living in a ghetto. They were forbidden to evangelize the Moslems. Corruption was rife when it came to choosing religious leaders; sultans made and unmade patriarchs, who succeeded one another at an ever-increasing rate. The Patriarch of Constantinople ended up by recognizing the autocephaly (independence) of the Russian church and himself consecrated the first Patriarch of Moscow in 1589. On the other hand, however, he tried to Hellenize the other churches of the empire – Serbia, Bulgaria, Romania – and keep them under strict control.

The Germanic Holy Roman Empire

The emperor, who was elected by the seven elector princes, did not have much authority over a number of German principalities, which were virtually independent. However, since 1438 the emperor had always been chosen from the Austrian house of Habsburg. In 1519 the new emperor Charles V inherited lands of the Habsburgs, the domain of Burgundy and the kingdom of Spain. If we add to this the colonies conquered by Spain in the new world, we can see how Charles V was able to dream of world-wide domination. However, he came up against both his neighbour the King of France and the papacy.

The papacy

After the Great Schism and the conciliar crisis (see Volume 1, Chapter 10), the papacy had lost some of its prestige. The popes were Italian princes who became more and more involved in the affairs of Italy, which had become a battle-ground between France and the Habsburgs. The popes favoured their families, nephews and natural children. The lavish entertainments of the Roman court sometimes turned into orgies under Alexander VI Borgia (1492–1503), who bought his election, and with his children Caesar and Lucretia was widely talked about. Pope Julius II (1503–1513) rode to the attack against enemy towns, helmeted and in armour. By their role as patrons, and their commissioning of buildings and paintings, these popes were also behind the artistic and literary revival, the Renaissance.

2. The renewal of literature, arts and sciences

Educated men in the middle of the sixteenth century were aware that a deep cultural renewal had come about in the course of a few decades. As one of them said: 'In one century, we have seen more progress made by men of science than our ancestors saw throughout the preceding fourteen centuries.'

While it was not a radical break with the Middle Ages, the Renaissance rediscovered antiquity in all its forms: literature, arts and sciences. In an Italy which was closer to its Latin past, educated people had a passionate interest in the ancient literature which was lying dormant in the monasteries. Byzantine scholars like Bessarion fled from Constantinople, bringing numerous Greek manuscripts to the West. The invention of printing by Guthenberg in the middle of the fifteenth century revolutionized the communication of thought. Works formerly restricted to the privileged few became widely available: editions of books by ancient secular

Julius II (from the Vatican).

143

The Renaissance popes

In his *In Praise of Folly* (1511), Erasmus makes Folly describe in an amusing and ironical way the failings of the men of his time, great and small, particularly the men of the church.

If the sovereign pontiffs who are in Christ's place tried to imitate him in his poverty, his works, his wisdom, his cross and his scorn for life; if they meditated on the name Pope, which means Father, and on the title Most Holy that they are given, would they not be the most wretched of men? Does not he who uses all his resources to purchase this dignity not then have to defend it by sword, poison and violence? How many advantages would be lost were wisdom one day to enter into them? And not even wisdom, but just one grain of the salt Christ talked about: so many riches, honours, trophies, offices, dispensations, taxes, indulgences; so many horses, mules, guards and so many pleasures . . . They would have to be replaced by vigils, fasts, tears, prayers, sermons, study and penance – a thousand tedious inconveniences. And do not let us forget this: what would become of so many writers, copyists, notaries, advocates, promoters, secretaries, muleteers, ostlers, innkeepers, go-betweens (I would use another word, but let us not damage our ears!)? This vast multitude would be reduced to starvation.

Erasmus, *In Praise of Folly*, LIX.

writers, by the church fathers, Bibles, spiritual works. The first books to be printed were mostly religious ones. A passion for knowledge and action was evident everywhere: the encyclopaedic knowledge of the humanists and the boundless prowess of the *condottieri* and the *conquistadores*.

Humanism and Christian faith

The humanist, the Renaissance man *par excellence*, drew on good sources to direct his life and guide his fellows. If the inspiration of certain humanists, like Machiavelli (1469–1527) in his work *The Prince*, was pagan, the majority of them remained Christians, anxious that their work should be for the betterment of the church and the faithful. Thomas More (1478–1535) was one of the more attractive of the Christian humanists. An 'uncloistered' Christian, a good family man, Chancellor of England, Thomas More was a model of patience and kindness. His book *Utopia*, written in 1516 – More coined the word that

The religion of Erasmus

Erasmus pinned all his hopes on a better knowledge of scripture. Not only is it necessary to rediscover the original text, Hebrew, Greek and Latin, but it is necessary to translate the Bible into all languages. Scripture contains the true wisdom of life, the philosophy of Christ accessible to all men.

What audience did Christ himself have? Was it not a mixed crowd which contained the blind, the lame, beggars, tax-collectors, centurions, workers, women and children? Can he complain at being read by those by whom he wanted to be understood? In truth, the labourer will read his writings; the artisan, too, the thief, the prostitute and the pimp, will read him and even the Turks. If Christ did not prevent them from hearing his words, I will not prevent them from reading his books.

Christ desires his philosophy to be spread as widely as possible. He died for all and he wants to be known by all. This goal will be achieved if his books are translated into every language of every country or if, thanks to the princes, the people are taught the three languages (Hebrew, Greek and Latin) in which this divine philosophy was founded.

Finally, what indecency is there in reciting the gospel in one's native language, the tongue which everyone understands: the French in French, the English in English, the German in German, the Indian in Indian? It seems to me far more indecent and even ridiculous that uninstructed people and women should sing the psalms and Sunday prayer, like parrots, in Latin, without understanding what they are saying!

Erasmus, 'Note to the reader' in his *Paraphrases of St Matthew* (1522).

Erasmus by Holbein the Younger.

Printer's works.

gives it its title (it means 'No place') – is a light-hearted criticism of the political and religious society of his time. Steadfast in his convictions, his loyalty to the Roman Catholic Church led More to his martyrdom.

Erasmus of Rotterdam (1469–1536)

Erasmus, the 'prince of the humanists', is a complex and subtle figure. The illegitimate son of a priest, a religious and a priest in his turn, an enthusiast for ancient literature, he left his monastery to travel extensively in Europe to meet humanists and to look for manuscripts: he lived in France, in England, in Italy, and in Germany, and he died in Basle. He was involved in prolific correspondence with people of all kinds (humanists like More, princes, bishops, and so on). In his most famous work, *In Praise of Folly* (1511), Erasmus held forth on the folly of the world. In this way he offered a biting satire on all classes of society, with criticism of the ecclesiastical world taking pride of place. He

145

The return to scripture should allow a religious purification and a practical Christianity which rejects otiose theological speculation. Erasmus tells his friend Jean Carondelet, in January 1523, how he understands the links between scripture, dogma and theology.

The ancient writers of the church philosophized on divine things only with extreme sobriety. They did not dare to affirm anything which was not clearly declared in the letters whose authority is sacrosanct for us . . . Let us forgive the men of old who gave their definitions only grudgingly. But the rest of us have no excuse for raising so many inquisitive questions and defining so many things which are of no use for salvation.

Is it impossible to be united to the Trinity without being capable of explaining the distinction between the Father and the Son or between the Spirit and the other two persons? What matters, that to which we have to apply all our energies, is to purge our soul of passions: envy, hatred, pride, greed, concupiscence. Unless I have a pure heart, I shall never see God. Unless I forgive my brother, God will not forgive me . . . We shall never be damned for not knowing whether the principle of the Holy Spirit is single or double; but we shall not escape damnation unless we try to possess the fruits of the Spirit, which are love, joy, patience, goodness, gentleness, faith, modesty, continence . . . The essence of our religion is peace and concord, and we can only easily maintain this on condition that we define a very small number of dogmatic points and leave everyone the freedom to form his own judgment on the majority of problems.

The true science of theology consists in not defining anything that is not indicated in the scriptures. And it is seemly to communicate these very indications simply and in good faith. Nowadays appeal is made to an ecumenical council to decide on many problems; but we would do much better to postpone them until the day when we see God face to face.

At one time faith consisted more in life than in the profession of articles of faith. Little by little it became necessary to impose dogmas; but there were not many of them and they had a quite apostolic simplicity. Subsequently, because of the disloyalty of the heretics, scripture was submitted to a more rigorous examination. The symbol of faith began to be found more in writings than in hearts. Articles accumulated; sincerity decreased. The doctrine of Christ, which initially rejected all wars of words, sought protection from the schools of philosophers; that was the first step in the decline of the church. Then riches increased, and that led to violence. The instrument of imperial authority in church affairs impaired the sincerity of faith. Religion became simply sophistic argument. And the church was inundated with a myriad of articles. From there things moved on to terror and threats. By force and by fear we are trying to make people believe things that they do not believe, to make them love what they do not love, and to compel them to understand what they do not understand. Constraint cannot bring people together in sincerity; and Christ only accepts the voluntary gift of our souls.

Letter from Erasmus to Jean Carondelet, Archbishop of Palermo, 5 January 1523.

writes in the same vein in his *Colloquies*, which consist of conversations between often ridiculous characters. Much more important was Erasmus' work as an editor. He published a large number of ancient authors, particularly church fathers, with different European printing houses, his most famous critical edition being that of the Greek New Testament in 1516. Erasmus also wrote treatises on a variety of subjects: Christian education, marriage, war and peace, the Lutheran crisis.

Erasmus' intention throughout his work was to 'regenerate humankind by purifying religion and baptizing culture'. He wanted first to renew  theology by going back to the sources, i.e. to the original text of scripture and the church fathers who allowed a good interpretation of scripture. He thought that theology should have only one aim, the discovery of Christ, and he had no time for pointless disputes which did not contribute anything to the conversion of humankind. The gospel ought to be accessible to everyone and in (145) all languages: people would find wisdom by which to live in the Sermon on the Mount. A return was needed to an inward religion purified of its many excesses and ready to welcome all the good that was to be found among the ancient authors. Finally, 'religion is none other than a true and perfect friendship'.

Erasmus wanted to base a political system on the gospel. Christian princes ought to be trained in this direction. Erasmus proved to be a vigorous champion of peace. It was scandalous that Christians fought one another. If men could start (146) a war, they should also stop it. Christian solidarity ought to favour arbitration. Erasmus exercised a great influence on all those who wanted a peaceful reform of the church. But soon violence gained the upper hand. An opponent of over-simple attitudes, Erasmus could not be a leader of men.

The militant for peace

Erasmus can also be indignant that a pope should be a warrior and passionately calls on Christians to make peace.

What is there in common between the helmet and the mitre? Or between the cross and the sword? Between the sacred book of the gospel and the shield? Bishop, you who hold the place of the apostles, how do you dare teach people war?

Julius (Pope Julius II) *excluded from Heaven* (1514).

Certain truths approved by some do not cross the sea: certain others do not cross the Alps; finally, others do not get further than the Rhine . . . Flags bear the sign of the cross; impious mercenaries, paid to perpetrate murder and brigandage, bear the cross before them, and the cross, which is the one thing that should have dissuaded people from war, becomes its symbol. Mass is said in either camp. Is anything more monstrous?

(Peace is speaking) I call on you princes, you priests, you bishops. I call on all you who glory in the title of Christians to conspire with one accord and with all your might against war . . .

Erasmus, *The Plaint of Peace, decried and hunted on all sides by all nations* (1517).

147

A church to reform

Imprecations of the Dominican Savonarola against the sinful church

With his fiery preaching, Girolamo Savonarola set about reforming the morals of the people of Florence and violently attacked the abuses of the papacy (we are in the time of Alexander VI). The people were won over to begin with, but political circumstances and religious rivalries turned them against him and he was burned at the stake on 23 May 1498.

Savonarola by Fra Bartolomeo. San Marco, Florence.

Come here, infamous church, and listen to what the Lord tells you: I have given you this fine raiment and you have made yourselves idols with it. You have nourished your pride with your precious vessels. You have profaned the sacraments by simony. Your luxury has made you a disfigured harlot. You are worse than a beast; you are an abominable monster. At other times you would at least have blushed for your sins, but now you do not even have this shame. At other times, if priests had sons they called them their nephews; now they no longer have nephews – just sons. You have built a house of debauchery, you have transformed yourselves from top to toe into a house of infamy. What does she do, this public woman? Sitting on the throne of Solomon she makes signs of all who pass by; anyone who has the money enters and does whatever he pleases. But anyone who desires the good is thrown out. So it is, prostituted church, that you have uncovered your shame in the eyes of all the universe, and your poisoned breath rises up to heaven. On all sides you have exposed your immodesty.

3. A church which did not live up to Christian expectations

The optimistic view of some humanists could not conceal the deep anxiety in the air at the end of the fifteenth century. Speculations on the Apocalypse were rife, and the imminent end of the world was continually being announced. Anxiety over their salvation gnawed at Christians who were caught between an all-powerful God who made arbitrary choices and the threat of an ever-present Satan. In fact the Renaissance coincided with a resurgence of witch-hunting. Innocent VIII, a sorry pope in every respect, gave official sanction to witch-hunting in his bull *Summus desiderantes* (1484). The pope described the evil spell of 'familiar spirits', incubi and succubi, and called for their repression. He charged two Dominicans with this task and in 1487 they produced the *Malleus Maleficarum, The Hammer of the Witches*, a handbook on demonology and the procedure for extracting confessions. The hunting down of warlocks and above all witches was to last until the middle of the seventeenth century. The number of men and women who were burnt at the stake during those two centuries has been put at one hundred thousand.

In search of good shepherds

What was the answer to this anxiety? It was sought in devotion to the Virgin Mary – this was when the cult of the rosary was developed – in pilgrimages, in indulgences. It could also be sought in a deepening of personal religion, in reading the scriptures, in the practice of confession. But there was no confidence in the church as an institution. Many priests did not live up to the exacting expectations of the faithful, not so much through their bad behaviour as through their ignorance. Interested only in the revenues from their dioceses, many bishops accumulated episcopal sees in which they did not reside. The papacy could not be relied on to correct these abuses. Constantly on the look-out for money for their building programmes, including that of the basilica of St Peter, and their banquets, the popes gave dispensations in respect of residence and authorizations for the accumulation of sees for a financial consideration: they sold indulgences.

Criticisms and demands for reform

Today we are surprised at Erasmus' ironical view of the abuses of the church and at the vehemence of Savonarola, who for several years (1494–1498) exercised a moral dictatorship over Florence. He thundered against Alexander VI's abuse of the papacy, announced divine punishment and imposed a monastic austerity on the Florentines.

147

From time to time Christians, princes, called a reform council. In 1512 Julius II opened the Fifth Lateran Council, which deplored the abuses and spelt out a reform programme, but nothing came of it. The Lateran Council concluded on 16 March 1517. On 31 October of the same year Luther nailed up his ninety-five theses against indulgences in Wittenberg.

II · The Reformers

In the Western church, 'reform' has become synonymous with 'break'. A division is always an unfortunate occurrence and one looks to see what caused it and who was responsible. It has often been said that there have been so many abuses in the church that some people, despairing of ever seeing any change, have left it. But most people today recognize the deep spiritual causes of the Reformation. The Reformation arose from the piety of the late Middle Ages and its passionate quest for the Jesus of the Gospels. For a long time it was difficult to speak calmly of the reformers, and particularly of Luther. In the eyes of Protestants he was a 'humble doctor', 'an angel raised up by providence to fight the Antichrist of Rome'. For Catholics he was nothing but a coarse individual, a drunkard, a liar and a sensualist who left the church only so as to be free to gratify his baser instincts.

Over several decades opinions have been converging. Today everyone thinks of Luther as a man of faith who was motivated by a truly religious spirit. No Catholic would deny the deficiencies and the misunderstandings in the Roman Catholic Church; at the same time, Protestants admit Luther's personal shortcomings: a violent temperament, obstinacy and a certain fondness for beer.

Luther

The discovery of mercy

It was at the end of his life that Luther related what he regarded as his basic experience: salvation by faith alone. Many historians think that the event should be dated at the end of 1514.

Luther preaching in the church of Wittenburg, an open Bible in front of him. After Lucas Cranach.

I had burned with desire to understand a term used in the first chapter of the Epistle to the Romans, where it is said: 'The justice of God is revealed in the Gospel', since until then my dreams were troubled. I hated this word 'the justice of God' since the habitual usage of the doctors had taught me to understand it in philosophical terms. By it I understood that justice which they call formal or active, that by which God is just and which impels him to punish sinners and those who are guilty.

Despite the irreproachable character of my life as a monk, I felt that I was a sinner before God: my conscience was extremely disturbed, and I was by no means certain that God was appeased by my satisfactions. Moreover, I did not love this just and vengeful God. I hated him, and if I did not blaspheme in secret, I was certainly indignant and murmured violently against him. I said: 'Is it not enough that he condemns us to eternal death because of the sin of our fathers, and that he makes us undergo all the severity of the law? Must he increase our torment by the gospel and even announce his justice and his wrath there?' I was beside myself, my conscience was so violently upset, and I ceaselessly puzzled over this passage from St Paul in the ardent desire to know what Paul had meant by it.

Finally God took pity on me. While I was meditating, day and night, and examining the implications of the words 'The righteousness of God is revealed in the gospel, as it is written: the righteous shall live by faith', I began to understand that the righteousness of God here means the righteousness which God gives and by which the righteous lives if he has faith. So the meaning of the phrase is that the gospel reveals to us the righteousness of God, but this is the passive righteousness by which God in his mercy justifies us by means of faith, as it is written: the righteous shall live by faith. Immediately I felt myself reborn, and I seemed to have entered the broad gates of Paradise itself. From then on all scripture seemed different to my eyes. I ran through the texts as my memory recalled them and noted other terms which had to be explained in similar fashion, like the work of God, i.e. the work which God accomplishes in us, by which he gives us the strength, the wisdom by which he makes us wise: the salvation, the glory of God. Formerly I had detested this term 'the righteousness of God', but now I loved and cherished so sweet a saying.

Luther, *Preface to his Works* (1545).

1. Luther's approach

31 October 1517 is kept as the date of the birth of the Reformation, but what happened on that day was the culmination of something that began a long time before. Luther recounts his career in the works that he wrote at the end of his life, and undoubtedly his story is somewhat biassed. Martin Luther was born in 1483 in Eisleben in Saxony into a family of petty-bourgeois who were almost peasants. In the course of a rough childhood he listened with terror to stories of demons and witches. In 1505, in the grip of a powerful emotion, and fearful of dying and bringing damnation on himself, he entered the monastery of the Reformed Augustinians of Erfurt. There he led the austere life of a good monk and became a priest. He was entrusted

Luther's ninety-five theses (31 October 1517)

Luther published his theses on the eve of All Saints and All Souls days, when many Christians wanted to acquire indulgences for their dead.

1. Our Lord and Master Jesus Christ, in saying 'Repent ye, etc.', meant the whole life of the faithful to be an act of repentance.

4. And so penance remains while self-hate remains (i.e. true interior penitence); namely right up to entrance into the kingdom of heaven.

8. The canons of penance are imposed only on the living, and nothing ought to be imposed on the dying in accordance with them.

27. Those who assert that a soul straightway flies out (of purgatory) as a coin tinkles in the collection-box, are preaching an invention of man.

50. Christians must be taught that if the pope knew the exactions of the preachers of indulgences he would rather have St Peter's basilica reduced to ashes than built with the skin, flesh and bones of his sheep.

62. The true measure of the church is the sacrosanct gospel of the glory and grace of God.

From H. Bettenson (ed.), *Documents of the Christian Church*, OUP [2]1963, 186–91.

Faith and works

By his faith the believer has been restored to Paradise and created anew: he has no need of works to achieve righteousness (grace); but in order to escape idleness, to employ and conserve his body, he has to perform the works of freedom of which he is aware, with no other intention than that of pleasing God.

That is why both these affirmations are true: 'Good works do not make a man good, but a good man does good works. Evil works do not make a man evil, but an evil man does evil works.' So it is necessary for the substance itself, or the person, to be good before any good work. It is as Christ says: 'A bad tree does not produce good fruits; a good tree does not produce evil fruits.'

The Freedom of the Christian (1520).

Luther burning the papal bull *Exsurge Domine*.

Luther before the Diet of Worms, 18 April 1521

In spite of all the threats that weighed on him, including that of death. Luther affirmed that he was bound by his conscience and by the word of God.

Unless I am convicted of error by the testimony of scriptures or (since I put no trust in the unsupported authority of pope or of councils, since it is plain that they have often erred and often contradicted themselves) by manifest reasoning, I stand convicted by the scriptures to which I have appealed, and my conscience is taken captive by God's word. I cannot and will not recant anything, for to act against our conscience is neither safe for us, nor open to us. On this I take my stand. I can do no other. God help me. Amen.

Bettenson, *Documents*, 201.

with teaching a course in holy scripture at the University of Wittenberg. In spite of his rigorous adherence to the rule, he did not find peace of mind. Concupiscence and a proneness to sin were always there. According to the theology of the time, God does what pleases him, saving some and damning others. One day Luther found an answer to his anguish while reading the Epistle to the Romans: 'Man is justified by (148) faith apart from the works of the law' (Rom. 3.28). A man is not saved by his efforts, but God makes him righteous by God's grace alone. Man goes on being a sinner, but God comes to save him in his despair. So Luther found joy and tranquility.

Indulgences

The matter of indulgences afforded Luther the occasion for making his discovery known. The Dominicans preached an indulgence (remission for the living and for the dead of punishment incurred by sin) throughout Germany to cover the expenses of the Archbishop of Mainz, who had to pay tax because he had accumulated three sees, and to help in the building of the basilica of St Peter in Rome. According to one preacher: 'Another soul to heaven springs when in the box (149) a shilling rings.' Incensed, Luther attached ninety-five theses to the door of the castle church at Wittenberg. It was at once a protest and an invitation to a debate with the university teachers. Luther rejected the false security which indulgences gave. Christians could not buy the grace freely given by God. Luther's attack on the papacy was never anything but restrained, and he never dreamed of a break with Rome. His theses enjoyed a huge success throughout Germany and Europe; Erasmus warmly approved of them.

Towards the break

Luther was accused at the Court of Rome. For three years, members of his order and envoys from Rome tried to get him to recant what he had said. But the dispute had aroused German nationalism. Luther was seen as the champion of a people wearied by the mercenary behaviour of the Roman court and by the accumulation of church property in Germany. Luther defined his thinking in the three important Reformation writings of 1520: *Address to the Christian Nobility of the German Nation*, *The Babylonian Captivity of the Church* and *The Freedom of the Christian*. He called (150) for a council to be held, while affirming that a council could be wrong. Luther's standpoint hardened: 'I am on the point of no longer doubting that the Pope really is antichrist', he said in 1519. In June 1520 the papal bull *Exsurge* condemned forty-one of Luther's propositions. He was given two months in which to submit. On 10 December 1520 Luther solemnly burnt the bull. In January 1521 he was excommunicated. Summoned to the Diet of Worms, the assembly of the princes of the empire, to appear before the emperor Charles V, Luther upheld his stand- (151) point, affirming that he was bound by scripture and by his own conscience. He was anathematized by the empire and had to go into hiding (May 1521). During his exile he translated the Bible into German.

The trade in indulgences in Rome.

The Peasants' War, or, Different interpretations of scripture

The poor German peasants rose against the nobles in the name of the gospel. Luther, somewhat conservative in the social sphere, was frightened by such a reading of scripture. He wanted to calm things down, but when he did not succeed, for fear that his message would be distorted, he called on the nobles to exterminate the peasants without mercy. At their head they had a priest who was an enthusiast for the Lutheran reform, Thomas Müntzer. Müntzer saw the gospel as a message addressed to the poor, and felt that the doctors, like Luther, had monopolized it and the nobility had distorted its meaning. Müntzer was captured and tortured, and beheaded in 1525.

Thomas Müntzer (1490–1525)

Poor people in need are deceived in an unspeakable way. With all their words and all their actions the doctors see to it that the poor man, preoccupied with his concern for food, cannot learn to read, and they have the impudence to preach that he must allow himself to be flayed and plucked by the tyrants. So when will he be able to learn to read?

The doctors turn scripture into a covering which prevents the true nature of the Christian faith from shining in the eyes of the whole world. Nevertheless, even someone who has never seen the Bible or heard speak of it, would not be in any less of a position, thanks to the true teaching of the Spirit, to have an authentic faith, of the kind that those had who wrote holy scripture without the help of any book.

That is why it is necessary to put down the mighty, the proud and the impious from their thrones because they are in themselves and throughout the world an obstacle to the true and holy Christian faith which seeks to spread throughout the world in all its original authentic nature. If only the poor censured peasants knew that, how it could benefit them! God scorned the great lords like Herod, Caiaphas and Annas and welcomed to his service the humble like Mary, Zachariah and Elizabeth . . . They were not the bigwigs with prestigious titles which the church of the impious possesses today.

The filthy source of usury, of theft and brigandage, is our princes and lords, who appropriate all creatures: the fish in the water, the birds in the air, the plants in the earth – all must belong to them (Isaiah 5.8). After that they proclaim the commandment of God among the poor and say: 'God has ordained: thou shalt not steal . . . Anyone who commits the least crime must be hung', and Dr Liar (Luther) says 'Amen'.

Sleep calmly, my dear chunk of meat! If the devil has to eat you (Ezekiel 24.3–13) I would prefer it to be in the pan and the oven (what a sweet smell!) in your pride by the divine wrath (Jer. 1.13) than by your stewing in your own juice. But your meat is that of an ass; you would take a long time to cook, and the dish would be leathery for the milk teeth of your friends.*

*The reference is to Luther.

Luther

My lords, abate your pride somewhat and mitigate your tyranny, so that the people has some air and space to live. Peasants, allow yourselves also to be advised and abandon some of your articles which go too far and demand too much; settle this matter in accordance with human right and justice, if not in a Christian fashion.

Exhortation to Peace (1525).

Let him who can strike, strike. You rush at a mad dog and kill him; otherwise, he kills you and a whole country with you. That is a terrible thing. They hide their crimes under the cloak of the gospel. Let authority do its duty. Wherever the peasant does not heed reason, let the authority seize the sword and strike. Every prince here is a servant of God. The time of mercy is past; it is the time of the sword and of anger.

What a strange time it is in which a prince can gain heaven by shedding blood, as others gain it by their prayers! Do not forget that among these peasants there are a large number of misguided souls who are dragged along by force. At all costs they must be delivered and saved. That is why you must strike and slaughter. If you lose your life, you are happy, and could not desire a better death.

Against the murdering and pillaging peasants (1525).

Troubles and controversies

Germany was divided into those for and against Luther, but those who were for him had many different motivations. The nobles hurled themselves into the fray over church lands; the poor peasants rose up against the lords who exploited them in the name of the equality of men before God. It was a horrifying war (1524–1525). Luther was disturbed because all these people claimed (152) to be acting in accordance with the Word of God. As he was unable to calm the peasants, he called on the lords to massacre the rebels. Thomas Müntzer defended them and violently attacked Luther. During the same years Luther broke (153) with Erasmus, who did not accept his pessimistic conception of human beings and their freedom. Finally, in 1525, Luther married a former nun, Katherine von Bora, 'to flout the devil and his scales . . . and all those who are mad enough to forbid priests to marry'.

Lutheran doctrine and the Lutheran church

Luther had no intention of founding a new church. He thought that by returning to the gospel the church would reform itself. But divergences in the interpretation of scripture and extremist movements led him to some doctrinal definitions and to a minimal organization. In 1529 Luther published a Lesser and Greater Catechism, the first examples of a literary genre which was destined to have a great success.

For Luther everything began from his fundamental experience. Conscious of being basically sinners, human beings discover from scripture that salvation comes to them from God through faith alone. God does everything and they do nothing. Good works do not make people good, but once people have been justified by God they do good works. So Luther turned his back on everything in tradition which denied the pre-eminence of scripture and faith. He rejected what appeared to him to be a means, a claim on the human side to deserve salvation: the cult of the saints, indulgences, religious vows, those sacraments which are not attested in the New Testament. Anything not explicitly set out in scripture was worthless. All that counted was the universal priesthood of the faithful. The church, the community of believers, an invisible reality, had no business to give itself an external organization and to possess property.

In practice Luther retained two sacraments, baptism and eucharist, and admitted the possibility of confession. The eucharist was to be celebrated in German. He rejected talk of sacrifice in connection with the eucharist, but firmly maintained the real presence. He gave an important place to choral singing. The proclamation of the Word of God and the celebration of the sacraments did necessitate a minimum of organization. The princes, who held a power which came from God, were entrusted with this. So Luther, who radically rejected ecclesiastical power, considerably reinforced the power of the princes over the church. The Lutheran churches became national churches, the organization of which varied from one state to another.

2. A rash of reformers

Luther had his own disciples such as Melanchthon (1497–1560), 'the gentle Philip'. But at the same time as Luther, a number of reformers arose throughout Germany and Switzerland. Almost all of them were priests, and many of them monks. If on the whole they agreed with Luther over faith and scripture, their differences were to prove important in their conceptions of the eucharist. Luther broke with several of them on this subject. Bucer (died 1551) established the Reformation in Strasbourg, Oecolampadius (died 1531) in Basle and Osiander (died 1552) in Nuremberg.

154

Calvin: The Institutes of the Christian Religion

Following the custom of the French Reformation theologians, in 1536, in Basle, Calvin published in Latin a small volume which summed up the major features of his theology. The work was expanded and translated into French in Geneva in 1541. Successive editions, constantly enlarged down to the last one in 1559, in four volumes, make the work the theological *summa* of Reformed Protestantism.

Calvin.

In all acts of life we must consider our vocation

Finally, this point is to be noted; the Lord bids each one of us in all life's actions to look to his calling. For he knows with what great restlesness human nature flames, with what fickleness it is borne hither and thither, how its ambition longs to embrace various things at once.

Therefore lest through our stupidity and rashness everything be turned topsy-turvy, he has appointed duties for everyman in this particular way of life. And that no one may thoughtlessly transgress his limits, he has named these various kinds of living 'callings'. Therefore each individual has his own kind of living assigned to him by the Lord as a kind of sentry post so that he may not heedlessly wander about through life.

Institutes III, X, 6

The distinction between the invisible church and the visible church

Holy Scripture speaks of the church in two ways. Sometimes by the term 'church' it means that which is actually in God's presence, into which no persons are received but those who are children of God by grace of adoption and true members of Christ by sanctification of the Holy Spirit. Then, indeed, the church includes not only the saints at present living on earth, but all the elect from the beginning of the world.

Often, however, the name 'church' designates the whole multitude of men spread over the earth who profess to worship one God and Christ. By baptism we are initiated into faith in him, by partaking in the Lord's Supper we attest our unity in true doctrine and love; in the Word of the Lord we have agreement, and for the preaching of the Word the ministry instituted by Christ is preserved. In this church are mingled many hypocrites with the good . . .

Just as we must believe, therefore, that the former church, invisible to us, is visible to the eyes of God alone, so we are commanded to revere and keep communion with the latter, which is called church in respect to men.

The marks of the visible church

From this the face of the church comes forth and becomes visible to our eyes. Wherever we see the Word of God purely preached and heard, and the sacraments administered according to Christ's institution, there, it is not to be doubted, a church of God exists (cf. Eph. 2.20). For his promise cannot fail: 'Wherever two or three are gathered in my name, there I am in the midst of them' (Matt. 18.20).

The church universal is a multitude gathered from all nations; it is divided and dispersed in separate places, but agrees on the one truth of divine doctrine, and is bound by the bond of the same religion.

Under it are thus included individual churches, disposed in towns and villages according to human need, so that each rightly has the name and authority of the church.

Institutes IV.1, 7 and 9.

Texts taken from Library of Christian Classics XX, translated F. L. Battles, SCM Press and Westminster Press 1966, 724, 1021–3.

Zwingli (1484–1531), the 'third man' of the Reformation

Zwingli by Hans Asper.

Zwingli has been given this title in relation to Luther and Calvin. A humanist, a disciple of Erasmus, the priest of Glaris in Switzerland, Zwingli travelled with his flock, who were mercenaries in the papal service, during the Italian wars. As vicar of Zurich, he imposed the Reformation on the city: this involved the secularization of the convents, the liturgy in German, the destruction of statues. Less stamped by a personal experience than Luther, he was more concerned to build up a church in accordance with the gospel and free his people from foreign dependence. He did not hesitate to call for the use of force against his opponents. Anabaptists who refused to allow their children to be baptized were drowned. Zwingli opposed Luther on the eucharist, in which he saw only a symbolic presence of Christ. The sacraments were only memorials, simple promises. Baptism was not effective in itself. It indicated that God had made his choice. Some Swiss cantons were opposed to the spread of the Reformation and civil war broke out. Zwingli died in battle when he went out with the Zurich troops. The Zwinglian reform had an influence on Berne and on the whole of Switzerland. Many Swiss churches have followed Zwingli in celebrating the Last Supper only four times a year.

3. Calvin and the French Reformation

With John Calvin (1509–1564) we embark on the second generation of the Reformation, a period of consolidation rather than creation. Calvin was not a priest, like the majority of the first Reformers, but a layman. Moreover, while the first Reformers came from Germany, with Calvin the Reformation became French.

In France, reform in the wider sense had become the preoccupation of several groups, of which the best known is that of Meaux, centred on its bishop William Briçonnet (he died in 1534), his vicar-general Lefèvre d'Étaples (1450–1536), a humanist and translator of the New Testament, and Margaret of Navarre, sister of King Francis I. A Lutheran was burnt in Paris in 1523. At first the king proved relatively tolerant, but the 'placard affair', posters attacking the mass and fixed on the very door of his room (1534), whipped up his rage and sparked off a general campaign against religious dissidents: many were burned. The French innovators had their martyrs: in Calvin they were about to find their theologian.

John Calvin (1509–1564)

Calvin, who came from Noyon in Picardy, studied letters and law. When he began to take the Christian life seriously – what he called his 'conversion' – it was with Reformation ideas. About the time of the 'placard affair' he left Paris, travelled through France, and became a theologian in the service of the French Reformation. Having settled at Basle, in 1536 he published the *Institutes of the Christian Religion*, in Latin, to provide the French with sound doctrine and to uphold the memory of the martyrs. The work was translated into French in 1541 and went through several editions, each time expanded. After a first short stay in Geneva (1536–1538) he spent three years in Strasbourg looking after French refugees. Reluctantly, in 1541 he gave way to pressing demands from the citizens of Geneva that he return there, and there he remained until his death in 1564. In organizing the church in Geneva Calvin set up a model which was to become widespread in Europe and throughout the world.

0
500 km
ICELAND
NORWAY
SCOTLAND
Oslo
SWEDEN
Stockholm
Edinburgh
IRELAND
Armagh
Riga
York
DENMARK
Copenhagen
ENGLAND
London
Königsberg
Amsterdam
Canterbury
POLAND
Wittemberg
LITHUANIA
Cologne
Paris
Prague
La Rochelle
FRANCE
Basle
Munich
Vienna
Zurich
Geneva
Lyons
TRANSYLVANIA
Milan
Venice
HUNGARY
Toulouse
Genoa
PORTUGAL
Lisbon
Madrid
Rome
SPAIN
Athens

Catholics

Lutherans

Reformed/
Calvinists

Anglicans

Hussites

Orthodox

Moslems

The Religious Confessions at the End of the Sixteenth Century

(155)

The four ministries of the church

Calvin, who had been banished from Geneva in 1538, returned there in 1541 at the urgent request of the people of Geneva. His condition was that the church should be organized strictly, and this organization was codified in the *Ecclesiastical Ordinances* of 1541.

There are four orders of ministry which our Lord instituted for the ministry of his church: first the pastors, then the doctors, then the elders and finally the deacons.

As for the pastors whom scripture sometimes also calls elders and ministers, their office is to proclaim the word of God, to teach, admonish, exhort and rebuke, both in public and in private, to administer the sacrament and to administer brotherly correction with the elders and stewards.

Now so that there should be no confusion in the church, no one may enter on this office without vocation. Here three things must be considered, namely the examination, which is the most important; after that it is appropriate to institute the ministries, and thirdly it is good to observe that ceremony or mode of procedure for introducing them into office.

The proper office of doctors is to instruct the faithful in sound doctrine, so that the purity of the gospel is not corrupted either by ignorance or by bad opinions. However, as things are at present arranged by this we understand help and instruction to preserve the doctrine of God and concern that the church is not ravaged by the fault of pastors and ministers – to use a more intelligible word, we call it the order of schools.

The office of elders is to take charge of the life of the individual, to admonish in love those whom they see failing or leading a disordered life, and where it is their role, to report to the community, which will be deputized to make fraternal corrections along with others.

There were always two kinds of deacons in the early church, one deputized to receive, dispense and conserve goods for the poor, both daily alms and possessions, rents and pensions, and the others to care for and tend the sick, and to administer the allowance of the poor, a custom which we still observe. For we have bursars and hospitallers.

Ecclesiastical Ordinances of Geneva (1541).

Geneva, the church town

Similar to Luther's in its basic intuitions, Calvin's doctrine is much more systematic and has particular emphases. Equal emphasis is given to scripture and to faith. Calvin was seized by the sovereignty of God (*soli deo gloria*, 'to God alone the glory') and strongly stressed the fall of man after the original sin. We ought all to be damned, but almighty God saves those whom he has chosen. That is predestination, often thought to be the distinguishing feature of Calvinist doctrine. Calvin set out a practical moral code which is the way of confirming the adoption through which God has accepted us as his children. This moral code is a social one because man is a 'social creature'.

In order to affirm his faith, man needs an external aid – the church. While constantly speaking of the invisible church, from the very beginning Calvin laid stress on a visible church in the form of the local community. The real church is 'where the Word of God is preached with purity and the sacraments administered'. The sacraments are the outward sign of God's grace towards us and the confirmation of our faith. Baptism is the sign of the forgiveness of sins. Calvin vigorously defended infant baptism. As for the eucharist, the Last Supper, Calvin's teaching differed from that of Luther and Zwingli: Christ gives himself to us at the moment when we receive the bread and wine.

The church was to be organized along strict lines, as disorder is an insult to Christ, the head of the body which is the church. The *Ecclesiastical*

(155)

Ordinances of 1541 set out the principles of the church of Geneva. This organization derived from scripture, but also from the personality of Calvin, who was influenced by his study of the law and his knowledge of the writings of Plato. There were four orders of ministry: pastors, doctors, elders and deacons. Church life was governed by a consistory made up of pastors and twelve elders chosen by the authorities. The consistory had oversight of everything in the church, and the civil powers undertook to implement its decisions. In principle there was a clear distinction between civil and ecclesiastical powers, but they were closely linked because the state intervened in the nomination of ministers and the consistory was an expression of civil power. It was Calvin's ambition to build up the Christian city of Geneva. Church people were judged by their activity in the state. Mediaeval Christianity was not far away!

Petty rules dictated the whole way of life of the citizens of Geneva. Many were condemned to death. Personal quarrels were common. Rather more seriously, the doctrinal conflicts took a dramatic turn when Michael Servetus was burned at the stake in 1553 for having denied the Trinity.

The influence of the Calvinist Reformation

The foundation of the Academy of Geneva in 1559 by Theodore of Beza contributed to the influence of the Calvinist Reformation. It offered a complete education, from elementary to advanced level, and many foreigners went there to study theology, going on to take charge of Reformed churches in the Calvinist tradition. In this way Calvin gave both world-wide recognition and authority to the Reformation. Many churches were to borrow elements from the church of Geneva, particularly Presbyterianism (i.e. church government by elders) and the local community with its four ministries. Moreover, in proposing a way of life based on the gospel in the world as it is, and restoring a theological status to material life, Calvin created a particular type of person and civilization. He broke away from mediaeval perspectives by regarding lending at interest as legitimate. Because of this some historians have seen him as an initiator of capitalism.

III · Religious Confessions in Europe

During the sixteenth century, Christianity split into a number of different churches. A new religious landscape took shape, but its outlines were not fixed definitively until the seventeenth century, after the Thirty Years War which ended in 1648.

1. Germany and Northern Europe

For a long time the emperor Charles V clung to the hope of rebuilding the unity of the empire. One after the other, and sometimes at the same time, he envisaged the calling of a General Council (cf. Chapter 12), friendly discussions, and armed combat. Catholic princes, and princes who supported the Reformation, organized themselves into opposing forces ready for civil war. The Diet of Speyer in 1526 had allowed the princes freedom of reform in their dominions. A new Diet of Speyer in 1529 withdrew this concession. The princes who had chosen to follow the Protestant Reformation made a solemn protest at this, hence the name Protestants, which from then on was the general title for the Reformers separated from Rome. In 1530 Charles V tried to sort out the religious question by persuasion, at the Diet of Augsburg. He asked the various parties to present their doctrines. In the name of the supporters of Luther, Melanchthon drew up a memorandum which under the title the Augsburg Confession remains the point of reference for all Lutherans. Melanchthon showed himself to be a moderate, and took care to keep the most contentious questions in the background.

The Lutheran expansion continued. It became necessary to wage war on splinter groups, like that of the Anabaptists of Münster (1535), who wanted to establish a kingdom of Christ founded on the Apocalypse, in which communism and polygamy were practised. No action, whether civil war or the colloquia which began with the Council of Trent, succeeded in bringing about peace and religious unity. Moreover in 1555 the religious peace of Augsburg took note of the confessional division of Germany. To the princes alone was given the freedom to choose their confession: *cuius regio, eius religio*, literally 'of whom the region, of him the religion'. Subjects had to abide by their prince's choice or go into exile.

The Scandinavian sovereigns (Sweden in 1527 and Denmark and Norway in 1537) opted for Lutheranism. This had little effect upon the people: few changes were made and on the whole the old customs were retained.

2. The British Isles

A matrimonial affair was the origin of the conflict between the kingdom of England and the papacy. Because Henry VIII was unable to get

The execution of Thomas More

In spite of all the pressures from his friends and family, Thomas More refused to recognize Henry VIII as the supreme head of the Church of England. The aged Chancellor was executed on 6 July 1535. He kept his sense of humour to the last.

Sir Thomas More, as one that had been invited to some solemn feast, changed himself into his best apparel. Which Master Lieutenant espying, advised him to put it off, saying that he should have it was but a javill.

'What, Master Lieutenant?' quoth he, 'shall I account him a javill that will do me this day so singular a benefit? Nay, I assure you, were it cloth of gold, I should think it well bestowed on him, as Saint Cyprian did, who gave his executioner thirty pieces of gold.'

And so was he by Master Lieutenant brought out of the Tower, and from thence led towards the place of execution. Where, going up the scaffold, which was so weak that it was ready to fall, he said merrily to the Lieutenant: 'I pray you, Master Lieutenant, see me safe up, and for my coming down let me shift for myself.'

Then desired he all the people thereabout to pray for him, and to bear witness with him, that he should now suffer death in and for the faith of the holy Catholic Church. Which done, he kneeled down, and, after his prayers said, turned to the executioner with a cheerful countenance, and said unto him: 'Pluck up thy spirits, man, and be not afraid to do thine office: my neck is very short, take heed, therefore, thou strike not awry, for saving of thine honesty.'

So passed Sir Thomas More out of this world to God, upon the very same day which he most desired.

The Mirror of Vertue in Worldly Greatness or the Life of Sir Thomas More Knight by William Roper

the pope to annul his marriage to Katherine of Aragon, which had not given him a son, he sought the annulment from the English clergy and proclaimed himself head of the Church of England (Act of Supremacy, 1534). Those who (156) wanted to remain loyal to Rome – Thomas More, Bishop Fisher and many others – were executed. However, Henry VIII retained the essentials of the Catholic faith in the Six Articles of 1539. Thanks to the fact that the young king Edward VI (1547–1553) was a minor, Calvinist ideas crept into the 1549 *Book of Common Prayer* and the Forty-Two Articles of 1552. When Mary Tudor (1553–1558), daughter of Henry VIII and Katherine of Aragon, became queen (1553–1558), she restored Catholicism and went on to carry out more than two hundred executions, which earned her the title Bloody Mary. Elizabeth I (1558–1603) was the real founder of Anglicanism. She took the title 'Supreme Governor of the Realm in Matters Spiritual and Temporal', restored the Prayer Book of Edward VI and promulgated the Thirty-Nine Articles defining Anglican belief. Anglicanism proved to be a compromise: a theology very close to neighbouring Calvinism which maintained traditional forms like the episcopate and liturgical vestments. Both Catholic and Protestant dissidents were mercilessly persecuted.

Scotland adopted Calvinism. The Scottish Reformed Church (Presbyterian) was given official status in 1560. Its main organizer was John Knox (1513–1572), who had paid several visits to Geneva and had been influenced by Calvin. Ireland steadfastly refused the Reformation which England wanted to impose on her.

3. France

The policy of the kings fluctuated. The advantages of the Concordat of Bologna persuaded them to be faithful to Rome. After the 'placard affair' (see above, p. 15), repression of heretics became increasingly severe. In 1545 the Vaudois

Henry VIII by Hans Holbein.

of Provence who had rallied to the cause of the Reformation were massacred. Reformed Churches were set up in several French towns. In 1559 the Synod of Paris brought together representatives of about fifty churches. They drafted the *Discipline* and *Confession of Faith* of the Reformed Churches in France, and in 1571 the Synod of La Rochelle revised and formally ratified these foundation texts.

Meanwhile the Reformed, known as Huguenots*, formed themselves into a political party ready to defend their freedom by force of arms. In a conciliatory gesture the regent Catherine de Medici and the chancellor Michel de l'Hôpital allowed certain freedoms to the Huguenots by the Colloquy of Poissy in 1561 and the Edict of Saint-Germain in 1562. However, the massacre of Protestants at Wassy in 1562 marked the beginning of the wars of religion, which were to last until 1598. The most bloody of these episodes was the St Bartholomew's Day Massacre on 24 August 1572. While claiming to be foiling a Protestant plot, Catherine de Medici killed off the Huguenots in Paris. Her example was followed in numerous towns in France, and there were scores of thousands of victims. King

*Huguenots: from a German word denoting 'confederates', used of citizens of Geneva who were fighting the Duke of Savoy.

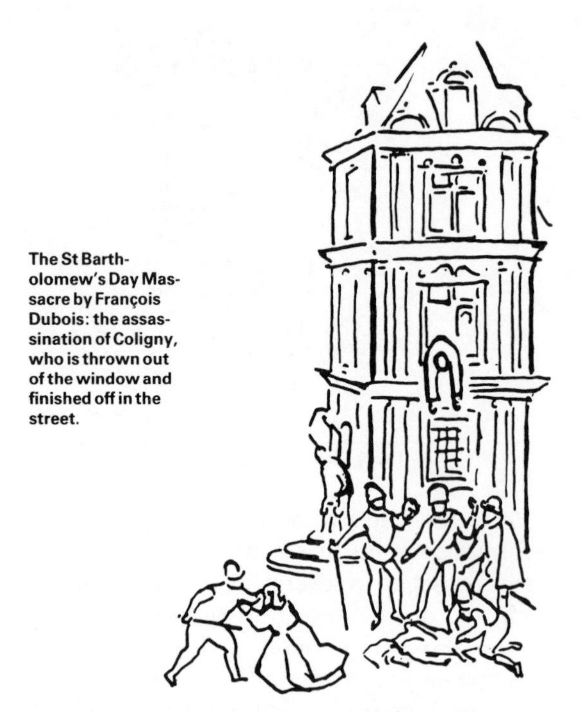

The St Bartholomew's Day Massacre by François Dubois: the assassination of Coligny, who is thrown out of the window and finished off in the street.

Henry IV, who had renounced Protestantism, restored peace by signing the Edict of Nantes in 1598. This was in the nature of a compromise which many people thought would be temporary. Freedom of conscience was recognized: freedom of worship was allowed with certain restrictions. Legal guarantees were granted to Protestants, who were given places of asylum defended by their own troops.

4. The new religious geography

To complete this tour of Europe we must turn to the Low Countries of the Habsburgs, which had been in the hands of Philip II of Spain since 1555. In 1561 the Calvinists there issued a Confession of the Low Countries, and in the name of the King of Spain the Duke of Alba led a bloody repression. In the northern provinces the Protestants formed a free state around William of Orange (the Silent): the United Provinces. These are the present-day Low Countries. Ancient European Christendom thus split up into a number of churches opposed to Rome: Lutheran or Evangelical, Calvinist or Reformed. The Roman Church, drastically cut back, was about to react by attempting to reform itself; some Catholic princes even threw themselves into an attempt to regain ground by force of arms. All this activity is sometimes called the Counter-Reformation.

For further reading

O. Chadwick, *The Reformation*, Penguin Books 1964

A. G. Dickens, *Reformation and Society in Sixteenth Century Europe*, Thames and Hudson 1966

J. C. Huizinga, *The Waning of the Middle Ages*, Penguin Books 1955

Alister McGrath, *The Intellectual Origins of the European Reformation*, Blackwell 1987

B. M. G. Reardon, *Religious Thought in the Reformation*, Longmans 1981

R. W. Scribner, *The German Reformation*, Macmillan 1986

Roland Bainton, *Here I Stand. A Biography of Martin Luther*, Lion Publishing 1983

M. Bainton, *Erasmus of Christendom*, Scribner 1969

F. Wendel, *John Calvin*, Fontana Books 1963

G. R. Potter, *Zwingli*, Cambridge University Press 1976

E. G. Rupp, *Patterns of Reformation*, Epworth Press 1969

J. M. Todd, *The Reformation*, Darton, Longman and Todd 1972

G. H. Williams, *The Radical Reformation*, Weidenfeld and Nicolson 1962

12

The Catholic Renewal

Sixteenth and Seventeenth centuries

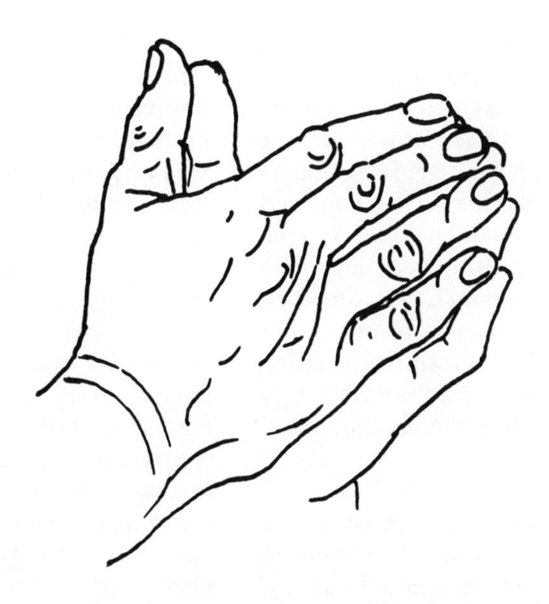

The hands of St Joseph from the central panel of a nativity on the Partinari triptych of Hugo van der Goes (Musée des Offices, end of the fifteenth century).

Parallel to the Protestant movement, a desire for reform became apparent in the Roman Catholic Church. The first steps were taken by those in orders, by some pious laymen and sometimes by bishops. Finally, after much difficulty, the papacy succeeded in calling a general council at Trent in 1545. It was eighteen years and many interruptions later before the council came to an end, and its decisions were only slowly put into effect. In France no action was really taken until the seventeenth century. Then that traditional church was brought into being, the features of which have been retained until recent times. But to say the least, this classical Catholicism has been shaken by numerous crises and conflicts.

I · Catholic Reform in the Sixteenth Century

1. Reform by church members themselves

If religious fervour and disquiet prompted the activity of those reformers who separated from Rome, they were also responsible for a number of attempts at reform within the Roman Catholic Church itself. These efforts often began from the grass roots. Franciscan piety gave birth to a new religious order, the Capuchins, in 1526. The Oratory of Divine Love, a kind of brotherhood which brought together laymen and priests, spread through several Italian towns at the beginning of the sixteenth century. Its members prayed together and looked after the poor and sick. Some bishops were associated with it. One of them, Ghiberti, who died in 1543, and who had belonged to the Roman Curia, devoted himself completely to his diocese of Verona. For fifteen years he worked to reform it, insisting both on dignity in worship and that the clergy stay in residence and be intellectually trained.

Regular clergy

In 1524 another member of the Oratory, the priest Cajetan of Verona, founded a society of priests, the Theatines, who combined the everyday apostolate with the regularity of the religious life. This was the starting point for the regular clergy, a new form of priestly and religious life the most famous representatives of which were the Jesuits, founded by the Spaniard Ignatius of Loyola (1491–1556). Converted after being wounded in battle, he related his personal experience in the *Spiritual Exercises*, which he

commended to those whom he met during his travels, and in particular to the companions he gathered around him in Paris in 1534 (the vow of Montmartre). In 1540 the group became the Society of Jesus. By making a fourth vow of

obedience to the pope the Jesuits demonstrated their willingness to respond to all the needs of the church of their time. They were active in teaching, founding numerous colleges, and in spiritual matters and in foreign missions. By the time Ignatius died they already numbered a thousand.

2. The Council of Trent

'The whole world is shouting Council! Council!', the papal nuncio was saying at the time when Luther was appearing in Worms before Charles V (1521). For a long time the popes had been reluctant to call a council. The continuous wars between the emperor and the king of France made the meeting difficult. Pope Adrian VI (1522–1523), a Dutchman and the last non-Italian pope before John-Paul II, recognized the faults of the Roman Church but did nothing about them. His successor Clement VII allied himself with Francis I; the imperial forces, some of which were Lutheran, sacked Rome in May 1527; there followed seven days of pillage, rape and sacrilege which some saw as the judgment of God. Pope Paul III (1534–1549) had a doubtful past. Converted as time went on, he decided to call a council and drew up a plan for reform with some remarkable cardinals: Contarini, a Venetian humanist; Sadolet, Bishop of Carpentras; the Englishman Reginald Pole, and so on. But the hope of a Reformation in the spirit of Erasmus evaporated. The prevailing attitude was defensive. In 1542 the pope reorganized the Roman Inquisition, which took the name of the Holy Office (nowadays it is called the Congregation for the Doctrine of the Faith), to arrest the spread of heresy: the Master General of the Capucins went over to the Reformed side! In the end the Council managed to open at Trent on 13 December 1545.

The Jesuits

The extraordinary development of the Society of Jesus was the result of the personality of its founder, Ignatius of Loyola, who left his followers two 'instruments' of great effectiveness: the *Spiritual Exercises* and the *Constitutions*. The *Exercises* have contributed to the training not only of Jesuits but also of a large number of other Christians. The *Constitutions* organize the order into a centralized and authoritarian monarchial structure around the Master General and the pope. The Jesuits sought to be the servants of the church *par excellence.*

(157) Spiritual Exercises

1. The name 'Spiritual Exercises' means every form of examination of conscience, of meditation, contemplation, prayer (vocal and mental) and the spiritual activities mentioned later. Going for long and short walks and running are physical exercises; so we give the name of spiritual exercises to any process which makes the soul ready and able to rid itself of all irregular attachments, so that, once rid of them, it may look for and discover how God wills it to regulate its life to secure its salvation.

365. To arrive at complete certainty, this is the attitude of mind we should maintain: I will believe that the white object I see is black if that should be the decision of the hierarchical Church, for I believe that linking Christ our Lord the Bridegroom and His Bride the Church, there is one and the same Spirit, ruling and guiding us for our souls' good.

The Spiritual Exercises of St Ignatius Loyola, translated by Thomas Corbishley SJ, Anthony Clarke 1963, 12, 122.

(158) Fundamental rule of the Jesuits (1540)

Whoever wishes to enter our society, that we desire to be called the Society of Jesus, to bear arms for God, and to serve only Jesus Christ Our Lord and the Roman Pontiff, his Vicar upon earth, must, after making a solemn vow of perpetual chastity, offer himself to be part of a Society chiefly instituted to work for the advancement of souls in life and Christian doctrine, and for the propagation of the faith, by public preaching and the ministry of the Word of God, by the Spiritual Exercises and by works of charity, especially teaching the catechism to children and those who are not instructed in Christianity, and hearing the confessions of the faithful for their spiritual consolation . . .

As to the right of command, that shall belong entirely to the General . . . Although we have learned from the gospel and the orthodox faith and make profession that we believe firmly that all the faithful of Jesus Christ are subject to the Roman Pontiff as to their leader and to the Vicar of Jesus Christ, in order that the humility of our society may be even greater, we have come to believe that it would be very useful, in addition to this bond common to all the faithful, to commit ourselves further by a particular vow. So, whatever the present Roman Pontiff and his successors command us concerning the good of souls and the propagation of the faith, we are committed to carry out without hesitation or excuse, in whatsoever country he may send us to, whether among the Turks or other infidels, even in India, or among the heretics and schismatics, or among the faithful of whatever kind.

St Ignatius of Loyola (from a manuscript in the Bibliothèque nationale).

The proceedings of the Council

The town of Trent, lying in the valley of the Alto Adige in the heart of the Alps, had been demanded by Charles V as the meeting place. In this imperial city with an Italian culture they were hoping for the Germans to come. At the opening there were only 34 participants to represent the universal church, which numbered 500 bishops. During the course of the Council the number grew somewhat to reach a maximum of 237 during the last meetings. For the most part the fathers of the Council were from Mediterranean countries. Italians alone often made up three-quarters of the gathering. The French did not come in any numbers until the end. Trent represented an extreme concession by the southerners to avoid a bad attendance by people from the north, but the people from the north did not come. It would be wrong to envisage the Council of Trent as being similar to what we know of Vatican I or Vatican II. Ambassadors and princes  spoke, parties were given, there were disputes over points of precedence: rumours of epidemics and wars caused panics.

The Council was presided over by the papal legates. They could not take any important decisions without consulting the pope. Three attempts were necessary to see the Council through to a conclusion. Under Paul III it met from 1545 to 1547 at Trent, then it moved to Bologna, where nothing was accomplished. Pope Julius III reconvened the Council at Trent from 1551–1552. Some Protestant delegates came as well this time. Pope Paul IV (1555–1559), a headstrong old man, decided to reform the church without recourse to a council by his own methods, primarily the Inquisition and the destruction of pernicious books (the Index). The persecution of heretics even affected cardinals. The works of Erasmus were burned. The translation of the Bible was forbidden. Pope Pius IV decided to reconvene the Council (1562–1563). Cardinal Morone, one of the victims of Paul IV, brought the assembly to a successful conclusion. On 3 and 4 December 1563 the fathers present approved all the decisions taken since 1545. The Cardinal of Lorraine led eleven acclamations and the company parted, hugging one another in tears of joy.

A ball at the Council

The Council of Trent was not just an assembly of bishops discussing the reform of the church. Such a gathering posed a large number of problems relating to lodging, provisioning, domestic matters, policing and so on. Ambassadors were there. Festivals were organized, like this ball, which some people did not like:

The Cardinal of Trent, Cristoforo Madruzzo, had great feasting in his palace for the marriage of a certain nobleman which was celebrated there. Among other things, after the banquet, there was a ball in the presence of a large gathering of noble ladies. As it is the custom of the country to invite all the guests at the banquet to dance, and the Cardinal had welcomed to his table the bishops of Feltre, Agde, Clermont and so on, the official secretary, Pighino, and the procurator fiscal of the Council, all were able to take part in the dancing. And the Cardinal wanted to honour them in that way. That evening he invited the Archbishop of Palermo and several bishops to supper, and invited them to open the ball, with himself at the head. And all this took place very honourably, with seemly modesty and Christian charity.

Journal of the Council
by Secretary Massarelli,
3 March 1546.

The decisions of the Council

160 No council had ever achieved so much. It defined a large number of points of dogma which had never been precisely defined in the past and demanded reforms in all the areas of pastoral care. Many of the texts of the Council were the fruit of long reflection, like those which dealt with justification and the collaboration of God and humanity in salvation. Other texts were more marked by anti-Protestantism. Certain practices were condemned just because they were in use among Protestants, for example liturgy in the vernacular. Among the pastoral decisions made, the request for the founding of seminaries was to have far-reaching consequences for the future of the church.

The Council of Trent, after a contemporary engraving.

Definitions and decisions of the Council of Trent

As a rule, in each area the Council set out an explanation which was often followed, in the case of dogmatic definitions, by condemnations of the opposing view. In most cases we can see that Protestant affirmations were being attacked.

On Holy Scripture and tradition

The Holy Council, following the example of the orthodox Fathers, receives and venerates with equal pious affection and reverence, all the books both of the New and the Old Testaments, since one God is the author of both, together with the said traditions, as well those pertaining to morals, as having been given either from the lips of Christ or by the dictation of the Holy Spirit and preserved by unbroken succession in the Catholic Church.
(Fourth session, 8 April 1546, 61 voters.)

On justification

If anyone says that man can be justified before God by his own works, which are done either in the strength of human nature or through the teaching of the law, apart from the divine grace of Jesus Christ, let him be anathema.

If anyone says that the free will of man, moved and aroused by God, does not co-operate at all by responding to the awakening call of God, so as to dispose and prepare itself for the acquisition of the grace of justification, nor can it refuse that grace, if it so will, but it does nothing at all, like some inanimate thing, and is completely passive, let them be anathema.
(Sixth session, 13 January 1547, 70 voters.)

On the sacraments

If anyone says that the sacraments of the new law were not all instituted by Jesus Christ, or that there are more or less than seven, or that any of the seven is not truly and strictly speaking a sacrament, let them be anathema.
(Seventh session, 3 March 1547, 73 voters.)

On the eucharist

If anyone denies that in the venerable sacrament of the eucharist the whole Christ is contained under each species and in each separate part of each species,

→

→

and in each separate part of each species, let them be anathema.
(Thirteenth session, 11 October 1551, 54 voters.)

On the mass

If anyone says that the rite of the Roman Church in which part of the canon and the words of consecration are recited in a low voice, must be condemned, or that the mass may only be celebrated in the vulgar tongue, let them be anathema.
(Twenty-second session, 17 September 1562, 183 voters.)

On the priesthood

If anyone says that there is no visible and external priesthood in the New Testament, or that there is no power to consecrate, to offer the true body and the true blood of the Lord and to forgive or retain sins, but only a function and a simple ministry of the preaching of the Gospel; or that those who do not preach are no longer priests, let them be anathema.
(Twenty-third session, 15 July 1563, 237 voters.)

On the foundation of seminaries

Unless young people are well educated, they can easily be led astray towards the pleasures of the world. Also, unless they are trained in piety and religion at the tenderest age, when vicious habits have not yet entirely taken hold of them, it is impossible for them to persevere in a perfect fashion in church discipline without very great and special protection from Almighty God. The Holy Council therefore ordains that all cathedral churches, metropolitan churches and others superior to them, each according to its means and the size of its diocese, shall be required and obliged to nurture and bring up in piety a certain number of children of the city, the diocese or (if there are not enough of them) the province and to train them in church discipline, in a college which the bishop shall choose for this purpose close to the churches or in another suitable place.
(Twenty-third session, 15 July 1563, 237 voters.)

On marriage

If anyone undertakes to contract marriage other than in the presence of the parish priest or some other priest authorized by the parish priest or the ordinary, and before two or three witnesses, the Holy Council declares them absolutely incompetent to make a contract of this kind and declares that such contracts are null and void.
(Twenty-fourth session, 11 November 1563, 231 voters.)

A selection of texts from the Council, including the first four quoted above, can be found in H. D. Bettenson, *Documents of the Christian Church*, OUP [2]1963.

How the popes applied the decisions of the Council

The Council had left it to the pope to carry out its decisions. Pius IV published the decrees officially and drew up rules for their implementation. Pope Pius V (1566–1572), a one-time Inquisitor, who was canonized, made his priority the fight against heretics and Turks (the Battle of Lepanto, 1571). One after the other he published *The Roman Catechism**, sometimes called the Catechism of the Council of Trent, the *Roman Breviary* and the *Roman Missal*, which has just come into fashion again! To guard against liturgical anarchy the pope imposed a uniform text for the mass and decreed that all liturgies which had been in use for less than two centuries should be suppressed. The oldest (those of Milan, Lyons, the Dominicans) could be preserved. Gregory XIII (1572–1593) reformed the calendar by omitting eleven days in 1582 (4–15 October) so that the seasons could get back to their rightful dates. He founded a number of colleges and seminaries, including the Gregorian university, and introduced permanent nuncios alongside the sovereigns. Sixtus V (1585–1590) set up a central government for the church in the

**The Roman Catechism* is not a manual for children. It is a work intended for priests, to help them in preaching and teaching the catechism to children.

form of fifteen Roman *congregations*, kinds of ministries to help the pope in the government of the church and the Papal States. The cardinals, whose number had reached seventy, were distributed amongst these congregations. Finally, in 1614 Paul V (1605–1621) published the *Roman Ritual*: texts and rules to follow when celebrating the sacraments.

The basilica of St Peter at the accession of Sixtus Quintus; the base of the dome followed a plan by Michelangelo.

Rome smartened itself up and took its place at the head of the Roman Catholic world. The cupola of the basilica of St Peter was finished in 1590. During the following century, with the construction of the colonnade, Bernini was to give the building and its surroundings their final profile. The 'holy' years of 1575 and 1600 proved a great success.

How the decisions of the Council were implemented in Catholic countries depended partly on the good will of the sovereigns. Philip II of Spain quickly accepted the decisions of the Council but reserved his royal prerogative. Elsewhere there was marked reluctance. In Germany, the emperors would have liked permission for priests to marry. In France, thinking that the Council would undermine their powers, the kings refused to publish its decisions.

3. Catholic Reform and the Counter-Reformation

The Council became absorbed into church life thanks to a certain number of people who devoted all their energies to it. It was a question of suppressing abuses, teaching Christians and training the clergy. But at the same time there was a desire to wage wars on the Protestant Reformation and to regain lost ground, sometimes by armed force. That is why one can talk of both Catholic Reform and the Counter-Reformation. The different aspects are intermingled.

Jesuit church, Rome; façade constructed in 1594.

Peter Canisius and Charles Borromeo

They were in the case of Peter Canisius (1521–1597), a Dutch Jesuit who travelled tirelessly throughout Europe and especially the Germanic countries to achieve Catholic reform. He was the (161) adviser to princes and bishops and gave pride of place to religious education, founding numerous colleges and publishing several catechisms which enjoyed a prodigious success (there were 550 editions, lasting until quite recently). In Milan, Charles Borromeo (1538–1584) was a model bishop along Tridentine lines. He led an extremely austere life, called provincial councils and diocesan synods, and founded colleges and seminaries. His devotion at the time of the plague in 1576 made a great impression. His decisions published in the *Acts of the Church of Milan* and in his *Instruction to Confessors* circulated throughout Catholic Europe.

St Charles Borromeo, by de Crespi.

(161)

How to Fight Heresy

Ignatius of Loyola, here loyal to the spirit of his time, gives Peter Canisius, the emperor's adviser, energetic advice on combating Protestant heresy in Austria.

Once a man has been convicted of heretical impiety or is strongly suspect of it, he has no right to any honour or riches: on the contrary, these must be stripped from him. To make a few examples by condemning some to death or exile along with the confiscation of their goods, will show that one is taking religious affairs seriously, and the remedy will be all the more effective. If public professors or administrators at the University of Vienna or the other universities have a bad reputation in relation to the Catholic faith, they must be deprived of their degrees.

All heretical books must be burned or sent beyond all the provinces of the kingdom. This is appropriate treatment for the productions of heretics, even if their content is not heretical, as with the grammar, rhetoric or dialectic of Melanchthon. It is necessary to be able to exclude them as a sign of antipathy to the heresy of their author.

Ignatius of Loyola to Peter Canisius, 13 August 1554.

The flowering of spirituality and the rise of the religious orders

In Spain, ever watchful to guard against any infiltration of heresy, the Inquisition hunted down the *alumbrados* (the illuminated) and at the same time censured a certain number of members of religious orders. But freedom from religious wars allowed a flowering of spirituality and the development of religious orders. Teresa of Avila (1515–1582), having struggled slowly through the degrees of the mystical life, in 1562 founded the first Reformed convent of Carmelites at Avila and then, up to the time of her death, travelled round Spain setting up convents of Carmelites and Reformed Carmelites with the help of John of the Cross (1542–1591). The latter, in the midst of real persecutions, gave expression to his spiritual experience in poems which are masterpieces of Spanish literature.

In Rome, Philip Neri (1515–85) who, in his

The walls of Avila.

Teresa of Avila (1515–1582)

The beauty of Christ

After a vision of Christ there remained with me an impression of his exceeding great beauty, which I have preserved to this very day. And if one single vision sufficed to effect this, how much greater would be the power of all those which of his favour the Lord has granted me! One very great benefit which I received was this. I had a very serious fault, which led me into great trouble. It was that, if I began to realize that a person liked me, and I took to him myself, I would grow so fond of him that my memory would feel compelled to revert to him and I would always be thinking of him without intentionally giving any offence to God, I would delight in seeing him and think about him and his good qualities. This was such a harmful thing that it was ruining my soul. But when once I had seen the great beauty of the Lord, I saw no one who by comparison with him seemed acceptable to me or on whom my thoughts wished to dwell. For if I merely turn the eyes of my mind to the image of him which I have in my soul, I feel I have such freedom that from that time forward everything I see appears nauseating to me by comparison with the excellences and glories which I have seen in this Lord. Nor is there any knowledge of any kind of consolation to which I can attach the slightest esteem by comparison with that which it causes me to hear a single word coming from that divine mouth – and more wonderful still is it when I hear many. And unless for my sins the Lord allows this memory to fade, I consider it impossible for me to be so deeply absorbed in anything that I do not regain my freedom when I run once more in thought, even for a moment, to this Lord.

St Teresa of Avila, *Life*, Chapter 37, in *The Complete Works of St Teresa of Jesus*, ed. Allison Peers, Sheed and Ward 1946.

163

John of the Cross (1542–1591)

The Fountain

John of the Cross composed this poem at Toledo in the darkness of the dungeon in which the opponents of the reform of Carmel had imprisoned him. The theme of the night often returns in John. It symbolizes faith, the way of encounter with God.

How well I know the fount that freely flows
Although 'tis night.

The eternal fount its source has never show'd,
But well I know wherein is its abode,
Although 'tis night.

Its origin I know not – it has none:
All other origins are here begun,
Although 'tis night.

Detail from the Apocalypse by El Greco.

I know that naught beside can be so fair,
That heaven and earth drink deep refreshment there
Although 'tis night.

Well know I that its depths can no man plumb,
Nor, fording it, across it hope to come,
Although 'tis night.

Never was fount so clear, undimm'd and bright:
From it alone, I know, proceeds all light,
Although 'tis night.

Rich are its streams and full – this know I well
They water nations, heavens and depths of hell,
Although 'tis night.

Yea, more I know: the stream that hence proceeds,
Omnipotent, suffices for all needs,
Although 'tis night.

From fount and stream another stream forth flows,
And this, I know, in nothing yields to those,
Although 'tis night.

The eternal fount is hidden in living bread,
That we with life eternal may be fed,
Although 'tis night.

Detail from El Greco's Resurrection of Christ (Prado museum).

Call'd to this living fount, we creatures still
Darkly may feed hereon and take our fill,
Although 'tis night.

This living fount which is so dear to me
Is in the bread of life, which now I see,
Although 'tis night.

Complete Works of Saint John of the Cross, ed. E. Allison Peers, Vol.II, Burns and Oates 1935, 431f.

imaginativeness and lack of interest in structures, was the exact opposite to Ignatius of Loyola, brought together in an informal way both laity and priests who prayed, sang, wrote commentaries on the scriptures, studied church history and devoted themselves to the service of the sick and to pilgrims. This was the Oratory, and the link which bound its members together was born of 'mutual affection and daily converse'. The group, whose members included such illustrious names as the historian Cardinal Baronius, gained a following outside Rome and even Italy.

All over the place, the religious orders underwent a phenomenal development. Under the direction of remarkable Master Generals, the Jesuits passed the 10,000 mark in 1600 and 15,000 in 1650. By the beginning of the seventeenth century the Capucins numbered 20,000. This can be seen as a sign of religious fervour. But the growth of clergy in Spain (200,000 by 1650) also indicated an escape from work in a country where only the clergy and the army were held in any esteem. In many of the towns of Europe, the multiplication of religious houses brought about a growth in the amount of church property, which worried the city authorities.

When it came to the restoration of primitive discipline among the women's orders, all attempts at renewal came up against opposition from Rome and the bishops. The only options open to a woman were 'a cloister or a husband'. Because of this the Ursulines of Angela Nerici (1535) and the followers of François de Sales and Jeanne de Chantal continued to be enclosed. Mary Ward, the founder of the English Ladies, suffered terrible trials, including seclusion, because she tried to hold out for her order's work of pastoral care and teaching.

The birth of modern Catholicism

The Council of Trent gave the church the make-up which it has kept until recently. 'Catholic' was now used to denote a particular group of Christians distinct from Protestants and Orthodox. The Catholic Church came out of the Council with stability and hierarchy and with the pope as its focal point. The Council brought about a harmonious integration of the past with the present, but kept silent in the face of many new problems, including economic and social changes.

Ecstasy of St Teresa by Bernini (1645–1652), Santa Maria della Vittoria, Rome.

Mass to music (Counter-Reformation).

II · The Religious Flowering of the Seventeenth Century

1. Religion and politics

In this century of absolutism, both Catholic and Protestant sovereigns expected in their own countries to rule over all the institutions, including the churches. Religion had to serve their political interests, and they did not flinch even in the face of the most startling contradictions. France continually allied itself with the Protestant princes except the Turks in order to fight against the emperor and the king of Spain, champions of Catholicism. But within the kingdom of France the treatment of Protestants went from bad to worse.

The Thirty Years War (1618–1648)

The emperor had not given up hope of re-establishing Catholicism uniformly throughou his realms. The refusal of concessions to the Protestants of Bohemia unleashed the hostilities of the Thirty Years War. At first victorious, Ferdinand II issued the Edict of Restoration (1629), enforcing the restoration to the Catholics of the ecclesiastical property which had been confiscated in 1552. The Protestants made an alliance with Sweden and France. The conflict, which spread throughout Europe, ended with the treaties of Westphalia in 1648. Protestants found themselves in the same position as they had been in 1618. Calvinism was recognized in the empire. Pope Innocent X protested against the religious clauses of the treaties, but from then on the papacy was excluded from international political decisions.

Glimmers of tolerance and timid ecumenism

During the course of the century there had been some peaceful souls, albeit few in number, who had laboured to bring Christians of different confessions together. Particularly memorable are the exchanges of which the philosopher Leibniz (1646–1716) was the prime instigator. As a first step, Spinola, a Franciscan bishop and friend of the Emperor Leopold I, came to an agreement with a Lutheran abbot from Hanover, Molanus, and with Leibnitz. A basic text was drawn up in 1683: *Rules for the General Reunion of Christians*. During the second stage the French Bishop of Meaux, Jacques Bossuet, and Leibniz exchanged a copious correspondence (1691–1694). Leibniz wanted the Council of Trent to be suspended in expectation of a new general council. He had no means of gaining a hearing. Bossuet thought that Leibniz should become a Catholic while the latter wanted Bossuet to recognize more than one Christian sensibility.

The political and religious problems of the Orthodox churches

The Orthodox churches were spread over three political areas: the kingdom of Poland (Ukraine), the Russian empire and the Ottoman empire. Try as they might, the different churches found it very difficult to maintain a communion of faith and liturgy. The Poles tried to win the Slavs, who used the Byzantine rite in their kingdom, back to allegiance to Rome. The union of Brest-Litovsk in 1596 produced a Uniate church with Kiev as its metropolis. Uniate is the name for those Eastern churches allied to Rome which keep their traditional customs in the matter of language, liturgy and the marriage of priests.

Since the intellectual centres had disappeared in the Ottoman empire and were barely developed in the Russian empire, several religious leaders of Orthodoxy came into being in the West and were more or less stamped by the doctrines of the Reformation or Tridentine

Catholicism. Violent doctrinal clashes developed. Cyril Lukaris, Patriarch of Constantinople, in 1629 proposed a profession of Calvinist faith which led to numerous protests and condemnations. In an opposite direction Peter Mogila, Metropolitan of Kiev, was inspired by Tridentine doctrine in his 1640 confession and his 1645 catechism, while rejecting papal primacy and the *filioque*. The confession of Dositheus of Jerusalem (1672) is along the same lines. It should be added that the intervention of Western ambassadors, Catholic and Protestant, at Constantinople in the affairs of the Orthodox Churches were often unfortunate. In particular the French ambassador was in favour of the action of Catholic missionaries. When these were unable to convert the Moslems, they tried to make the Orthodox, whom they considered schismatics, into Catholics.

In the Russian empire Nikon, Patriarch of Moscow (1652–1658), undertook to reform certain practices in the Russian church to bring it in line with the rest of Greek Orthodoxy. In this way he provoked the schism (Raskol) of several million Old Believers. The vehement protests of their leader Petrovich Avvakum (1620–1682) led him to the stake. The schism has lasted right down to the present day.

The Turkish threat

The naval victory of the Catholic fleets over the Turks at Lepanto in 1571 did not have the results expected from it, apart from the development of devotion to the rosary. The Turks continued their advance into the Greek islands – Crete was taken from the Venetians in 1669 – and threatened south Poland and the Austrian states. Every day at noon, in the German states, the 'Turkish bell' was rung. Pope Innocent XI (1676–1689) engaged in feverish diplomatic activity to form an alliance against the Turks, and financed it principally himself. On 12 September 1683 King John Sobiesky, at the head of the Polish and imperial troops, forced the Turks to raise the siege of Vienna. A general offensive followed in which Budapest and Belgrade were recaptured. The Christian populations experienced great relief, which expressed itself in the flourishing of baroque art throughout this part of Europe.

2. New bishops and new priests

In the face of royal ill-will, the French bishops decided in 1515 to put the decrees of the Council of Trent into practice. Many of the bishops undertook a pastoral reform which influenced the entire spectrum of Christian life. Among the best-known we should note Cardinal de la Rochefoucauld, Bishop of Senlis, and Alain de Solminihac, Bishop of Cahors from 1636 to 1659. Spiritual directors encouraged a new type of priest who would reform the Christian people. In a more discreet way, many women also had their place in this renewal.

François de Sales (1567–1622)

François de Sales, Bishop of Geneva-Annecy, was inspired by the example of Charles Borromeo. He had a great influence on the spirituality of lay people as well as on that of priests and religious through his two works *Introduction to a Devout Life* (1608) and *Treatise on the Love of God* (1616). Salesian piety is characterized by an optimistic humanism and a simple and evangelical style of preaching.

164

The 'French school' of spirituality

Pierre de Bérulle (1575–1629), with the help of Madame Acarie, introduced reformed Carmelite piety into France. Aware of the grandeur of the priesthood he founded a company of priests, the Oratory (1611), to pay homage to the priesthood of Jesus and restore the state of the priesthood. As secular priests, the Oratorians put themselves at the service of the bishops. Several heirs of Bérulle spread his spirituality, each one adding his own original touches. All were preoccupied

All Christians are called to holiness where they live

François de Sales was one of the first to propose a spirituality for the laity starting from their state of life. Compare this with what Calvin says about vocation (cf. p.14).

St Francis de Sales.

It is my intention to instruct those who live in the towns, in households and at the court, who by their condition are obliged to outward appearance to live a common life and who often, because they suppose that it is impossible, do not even want to think of the enterprise of a devout life.

True and living devotion, O Philotheus, presupposes the love of God; it is none other than a true love of God. In so much as it gives us the strength to do good, it is called charity; but when it has attained to the degree of perfection in which it not only makes us do good but also makes us act carefully, frequently and promptly, then it is called devotion.

Devotion must be practised differently by the gentleman, the artisan, the valet, the prince, the widow, the daughter, the married woman. And not only that; the practice of devotion must be accommodated to the strength, the concerns and the duties of each individual . . . It is a mistake, a heresy, to seek to ban the devout life from the company of soldiers, the workshop of artisans, the court of princes and the household of married couples . . . Wherever we may be, we can and should aspire to the perfect life.

François de Sales, *Introduction to the Devout Life* (1629).

with evangelization by popular missions and were interested in the training of priests. John Eudes (1601–1680) founded a congregation and developed the cult of the heart of Jesus. This devotion took a more feminine form with Marguerite-Marie Alacoque (Paray-le-Monial 1673). Jean-Jacques Olier (1608–1657) founded the Society of Priests of Saint-Sulpice for the training of the clergy. Vincent de Paul (1581–1660), 'the great saint of the great century', had left the Landes for Paris to make his fortune in the church. Little by little he became aware of the needs of the Christian people. In a more pragmatic spirit – 'Let us go to God with kindness and holiness, and let us work' – he founded the Congregation of Mission (Lazarists) for the evangelization of the countryside and the Daughters of Charity to serve the poor (1633).

The founding of seminaries

All these figures were concerned with the training of priests. There was still no single condition for admission to the priesthood. There were various initiatives. In his parish of Saint-Nicolas du Chardonnet, Adrian Bourdoise trained candidates on the job, so that they learned how to look after a church and celebrate with dignity. In his eleven-day retreats for ordinands Vincent de Paul offered the essentials of theology and of ministry. He proposed a kind of permanent training of clergy in his 'Tuesday Lectures'. Then he collected the candidates for the priesthood together in a college for a longer stay. Seminaries proper grew up gradually in the middle of the century. They were only established in all the dioceses at the end of the seventeenth and

The training of clergy: progressive demands

Vincent de Paul gave future priests training in a retreat lasting eleven days. Little by little the demands became greater. Seminaries were founded. Here are some decrees issued by the archbishops of Lyons.

1657: *We decree that those desirous of being promoted to holy orders shall come to this city for sufficient time to be instructed in Monsignor's seminary and to stay there the number of days it has pleased him to ordain for each order, namely: twelve days for the sub-diaconate, ten days for the diaconate and fifteen days for the priesthood.*

1663: Foundation of the Seminary of St Irenaeus of Lyons

We have created a seminary to serve to instruct the clergy of our diocese, to train in the piety and competence required by the dignity and importance of so holy a calling those who aspire to this profession, and to perfect those who are already engaged in it, by retreat, spiritual conversations, lectures and exhortations . . . Finally, it is to be a holy school in which one can learn virtue, the practice of the sacraments and ceremonies of the church, and all that is required of persons who wish to employ themselves in the sanctification of the people . . .

1694: *No one shall be admitted to the sub-diaconate who has not spent six months in one of our seminaries in Lyons: three months before presenting himself for the diaconate and three months also before receiving the order of priesthood . . .*

beginning of the eighteenth centuries. The bishops entrusted the direction of their seminaries to Oratorians, Sulpicians, Lazarists, Eudists. The length of stay there varied. From a few months it went to a year towards the end of the seventeenth century and to two years during the eighteenth century. Moral and religious training was the first concern, then studies. The seminaries helped to train the type of priest which is still familiar today; a man set apart from the world by his dress and way of life, who celebrates mass daily, says his breviary and is conscientious over his pastoral duties.

(165)

3. The transformation of Christians

The Protestant Reformation, like the Council of Trent, was the starting point of an in-depth evangelization of all Christians. The better-trained clergy, but also the educated laity, sometimes formed into societies like the Society of the Blessed Sacrament, wanted to alter the religion of the people to conform to that of the élites. That involved the rejection of popular religious practices which had come down from the mists of time. Christianity had the garb of pre-Christian religions. The sacraments were often viewed in an animist mentality as being in some way magical. Satan continued to be active: he was associated with the old religious depths which had to be fought against. In 1634 in Loudun some Ursuline nuns, possessed by the devil, accused their priest Urbain Grandier of having bewitched them and he was burned at the stake. With some development of a critical spirit, however, interest in the devil began to retreat.

Bishops, priests and pious laity, then, with the support of the civil authorities, determined to drive home the creed, cause Christian morality to be practised, make a division between the secular and the sacred, work out a proper liturgy and get it into regular use.

The means used

The religious and public authorities took measures against the folk festivals, such as itinerant festivals celebrating patron saints, St John's fire, etc. Some people resisted this and sometimes went on celebrating them in secret without the participation of the clergy. At the beginning of the seventeenth century the parochial missions made up for the deficiencies of the secular clergy. These were concerted efforts which went on for several weeks, organized by religious or members of priests' associations.

In their parishes, priests tried to put Christian practices on a regular basis: baptism during the three days which followed the birth of a child, confirmation at the time of the bishop's visit, Easter communion, for which the absentee rate was virtually nil in certain country districts. Solemn communion spread gradually. Attendance at the Sunday mass became increasingly obligatory, but the faithful did what they felt like during the mass: saying prayers, telling their rosaries. The priest spoke to the faithful in their own language only when addressing them directly: for the prayers, the notices and the sermon after the Gospel. Certain Jansenist priests gave more place to French. Eucharistic devotion lay less in frequent communion than in adoration of the blessed sacrament and in Holy Day processions.

Catechisms and schools

Christians had to be taught from their childhood. It was one of the priest's tasks to teach children, and also uneducated adults, every Sunday. Very soon, every bishop introduced a catechism manual into his diocese. Sunday catechism proved to be insufficient. So that the poor could have access to general and religious instruction, generous Christians founded a number of small free schools within the parish structure. To complete this picture of Christian fervour, mention must be made of the large number of brotherhoods of piety and charity such as the Ladies of Charity, started by Vincent de Paul. However, the great preachers of the time scarcely touched on the question of social responsibility when speaking to high-ranking congregations, but contented themselves with inviting them to give alms.

All these things helped to bring about that unanimous Christianity which lasted until quite recently, and to which we sometimes look back with nostalgia.

III · Internal Conflicts and Crises

The Council of Trent did not solve all the theological problems raised by the Reformation. Discussions went on and on. The biblical tradition began to be confronted with the first scientific research and discoveries. Theologians who had played an important part in the Council from then on formed a new power in the church. A new theological genre, controversy, developed, as much among Catholics as among Protestants. The master of the genre was the Jesuit and Cardinal Robert Bellarmine (1542–1621), who held the chair of controversial theology in Rome: 'to arm the soldiers of the church for the war against the powers of darkness'. Furthermore, religious conflicts always had a political dimension.

1. The first clash between science and biblical tradition

The Copernican revolution

Bellarmine intervened in two important cases of this fear of heresy which haunted the minds of the Counter-Reformation, the condemnations of Giordano Bruno and Galileo. The Polish canon Copernicus had overturned the traditional conception of the world in a work dedicated to the Pope, *The Revolution of the Terrestrial Orbs* (1543): it is not the sun which revolves around the earth but the earth which turns on itself and around the sun. Half a century later, there was a great upset in Rome when Copernican heliocentrism was taken up by Giordano Bruno and then by Galileo. For Roman Catholic theologians, but also for Protestants, the Copernican system went against statements in scripture (Ecclesiastes 1.4 and Joshua 10.12–13): had not Joshua stopped the sun in its course? It is true that Bruno drew from Copernicus conclusions which were very remote from Christianity and he was accused of having given up his religious vows. After a trial lasting seven years, he was burned in Rome in 1600. Some years later, Galileo was able to say that in the Bible 'the intention of the Holy Spirit is not to show us how the heavens move but how we get to heaven'; the condemnation of heliocentrism was no less in 1616. Copernicus' work was put on the Index of banned books 'until such time as it is corrected'! The second condemnation of Galileo in 1633 was more serious; the scholar ended his life under house arrest. This was the beginning of a misunderstanding between church and science which was only going to increase.

Galileo by Sustermans.

The beginnings of critical exegesis

Commentaries on and translations of the Bible grew in number. Alongside books of apologetics and spirituality the first 'scientific' studies began to appear in the works of the Dutch Jewish philosopher, Spinoza (*Tractatus theologico-politicus*, 1670) and the French Oratorian Richard Simon (1638–1712) (*Critical History of the Old Testament*, 1678; *Critical History of the Text of the New Testament*, 1689). Richard Simon is one of the fathers of biblical criticism. For the first time he raised the problem of the nature of inspiration.

The beginning of critical exegesis

Moses cannot be the author of all the Pentateuch

It is not difficult to produce evidence that Moses is not the sole author of all the Pentateuch in the form in which we have it today. For example, are we to say that Moses is the author of the last chapter of Deuteronomy in which his death and burial are described? I know that Josephus and Philo resorted to prophecy on this occasion, but one cannot believe them here any more than one can believe the other Jews who attribute all the law to Moses in order to make it more authentic . . . There is an infinity of duplications in the Pentateuch which do not seem to come from Moses but rather from those who collected the sacred scriptures together, and who brought together several readings and explanations of the same words . . . To the number of these revisions or repetitions we can add the account of the flood . . . These repetitions are even more frequent in Exodus and Leviticus than in Genesis . . . The diversity of style which we meet in the books of Moses also seems to be an indication that they have not all been written by the same author.

Richard Simon, *Histoire Critique du Vieux Testament*, 1678.

He compared the versions of the Bible in the various ancient languages and demonstrated the impossibility of seeing Moses as the sole author of the Pentateuch. But he remained an isolated figure in the Catholic world. Bossuet succeeded in obtaining the condemnation and destruction of the *Critical History*, and also Simon's expulsion from the Oratory.

A theological course at the Sorbonne in the fifteenth century.

The sources of theology

In an attempt to reply to certain malicious historical accounts by Protestants, Catholic scholars did a good deal of work in the scientific presentation of the sources of theology. The Belgian Jesuit John van Bolland (died 1655) has given his name to a systematic publication of the lives of the saints (The Bollandist Society). The Benedictines of the Congregation of Saint-Maur (Maurists) with their centre at the abbey of St-Germain des Prés published numerous editions of the fathers and sources of French history. The most remarkable of the Maurists was Mabillon (died 1707), founder of diplomacy (critical study of manuscripts).

2. Jansenism

Freedom and grace

Jansenism had its origins in the theological debate of the Reformation: what are the respective places of grace and freedom in the salvation of humankind? A powerful Augustinian tradition emphasized grace and predestination at the expense of human freedom. The arguments of Baius, a theologian from Louvain, which were of this kind, were condemned in 1567. On the other hand, Jesuits like the Spaniard Molina struggled to safeguard the place of freedom by putting forward the idea of a grace sufficient to bring about a state of human freedom.

Jansenius

Jean Duvergier de Hauranne, abbot of Saint-Cyran (1581–1643), and his friend Jansen (Jansenius), later Bishop of Ypres in the Spanish Low Countries (Belgium), concerned themselves with a renewal of the church by a return to the church fathers, with a marked preference for St Augustine. Saint-Cyran became the spiritual director of the reformed convent of Port-Royal and of the large Arnauld family: Angélique Arnauld was abbess of Port-Royal. Saint-Cyran opposed the politics of Richelieu, who had him imprisoned. Jansenius put forward his arguments on grace in a posthumous work, the *Augustinus* (1640). Basing himself on St Augustine, he displayed a deep pessimism in respect of human nature, fallen through original sin. Antoine Arnauld and Port-Royal spread the thought of these two figures in their absence. In his work *Frequent Communion* (1643) Arnauld, by his demands, restricted the receiving of communion and stirred up the opposition of the Jesuits.

167

The first crisis

The opponents took the argument to Rome, which condemned five propositions drawn from the *Augustinus* (1653). The quarrel continued

Jansenism

Sin, grace and predestination are the great themes of Jansenism. Saint-Cyran does not talk about predestination very differently from Calvin.

Predestination is none other than the eternal love which God bears to certain children of Adam, having seen them all fall into damnation by the sin of their father. Some he leaves in sin and ordains for them none other than the hell which they have deserved. But for the others, for the sake of the love that he bears willingly, he ordains the eternal bliss of paradise, as for his children and his friends.

Here you see the obligation which those who have been saved have to God, for having separated them before they were born from the company of other men with whom they were in the same damnation.

Port Royal.

Those who have entered the church after having heard the preaching of the word of God and having received baptism, which are the two prime means by which we must be holy, not knowing whether they are of the number of those whom God has loved eternally, must not disquiet themselves, but simply do precisely what God has ordained for them by Jesus Christ to save them.

unabated between the representatives of the two conceptions of Christian life, the Jansenists and the Jesuits. The Jansenists affirmed that the five propositions did not come from Jansen. Blaise Pascal (1623–1662) in *The Provincials* (1656–1657) came to the assistance of the Jansenists by openly attacking the lax morality of the Jesuits. Having refused for a long time to sign a formulary, in 1668 the Jansenists accepted a compromise. The provisional peace favoured the expansion of the influence of Port-Royal. In 1670 Pascal's *Pensées* were published, notes which he had prepared for an apologia for Christianity in the face of the unbelievers of his time. The 'gentlemen' of Port Royal were also teachers and scholars.

The second crisis

The Jansenist conflict broke out again at the end of the century with the publication of the *Moral Reflections* of the Oratorian Quesnel (1695). The Jansenists gave the appearance of being political opponents; their leaders took refuge in enemy Holland. In 1709 Louis XIV had the monastery of Port-Royal destroyed, imprisoned many Jansenists and obtained from the pope the condemnation of 101 propositions of Quesnel by the bull *Unigenitus* (1713). However, Jansenist opposition was kept up throughout the eighteenth century.

Jansenism has remained synonymous with an

The second Jansenist crisis

The bull *Unigenitus* of Pope Clement XI (1713) condemned 101 propositions drawn from the *Moral Reflections* of the Jansenist Oratorian Pasquier Quesnel. The bull condemned not only theological opinions, but also the Jansenist desire for a return to the earliest church and for all Christians to be able to read the Bible directly.

The following propositions of Quesnel were condemned:

80. The reading of holy scripture is for all.
81. The sacred obscurity of the word of God is no reason for the laity not to read the scriptures.
82. Christians must sanctify the Lord's Day by pious reading, in particular by reading the holy scriptures. To seek to divert them from reading these scriptures is to be condemned.
83. It is an illusion to persuade oneself that the knowledge of the mysteries of religion must not be communicated to women by the reading of the holy books. The abuse of scripture and the birth of heresy does not arise out of the simplicity of women but out of the proud knowledge of men.
85. To take the New Testament out of the hands of Christians or to keep it closed by telling them how they must understand it is to close the mouth of Christ to them.

We declare, condemn and censure the propositions cited above as being false, misleading, objectionable, offensive to pious ears, scandalous, pernicious . . . reviving various heresies and in particular those which are contained in the famous propositions of the Jansenists . . .

austere and passionate Christianity. Some Jansenists proposed a liturgy more acceptable to the people through the use of the vernacular and a church where priests and laity, as opposed to bishops, would have more of a place. The Jansenists had been witnesses to the rights of conscience against reasons of state. However, there were those who thought that their narrow-mindedness was perhaps the reason for a waning of religious enthusiasm.

3. The revocation of the Edict of Nantes

Louis XIV was concerned to restore religious unity to his kingdom in accordance with the principle 'one God, one king, one law, one faith'. He thought that this would stand him in good stead with the pope at the time of the conflict over the Regale, the claim by kings to the revenue of bishoprics and abbeys when vacant. He applied the Edict of Nantes in an increasingly restrictive way in order to force the people of the 'supposedly Reformed religion' (religion prétendue réformée = RPR) to convert to Catholicism: restrictions on worship, prohibitions on certain professions, and so on. A conversion office was set up. The dragonnades (billeting of troops on the Reformed) increased the number of forced conversions. The king, pretending to believe that there were no longer any Protestants in France, revoked the Edict of Nantes in 1685, thus gratifying the wishes of all the clergy of France. For all that, however, the RPR did not disappear. Many Protestants (200,000?) left France for the united provinces, Hessen and Brandenburg. The next generation rebelled in the Cévennes (the Camisards, 1702) and organized the desert church (Antoine Court, 1715).

169
170

The effectiveness of the Dragonnades

Since persuasion and financial aids to convert (the Conversion Fund) proved to be of limited effect, in 1681, and above all in 1685, administrators had the idea of billeting troops on the Protestants. This practice was known as the Dragonnades, and led to violence. A large number of Protestants became 'New Catholics', to the satisfaction of public opinion generally.

Satisfaction of the Bishop of Grenoble, Étienne Le Camus

We have seen almost all the alleged Reformed Christians of the Dauphinate converted to the Catholic religion with such ease and rapidity that although one could say that the fear of disobeying the king and incurring his indignation was a major contributory factor, it has to be acknowledged that God played a part and that his almighty hand miraculously supported the good intentions of His Majesty. Finally, almost fifty thousand Huguenots counted in the Dauphinate were converted in a month, and not a single one of those who claimed to support this religion had the steadfastness even to rise above the loss of some worldly goods which might have ensued from giving lodging to these warlike men, much less to endure martyrdom . . . Finally, Montpellier, Lunel, Nîmes, and the majority of other towns in the Languedoc recanted. Nothing in the world could be more glorious for our great king, nor a greater merit towards the church and the Holy See, for in three months there was no longer any Huguenot practice or Calvinist religion in France.

Revocation of the Edict of Nantes

Fortified by the many bulletins of victory which arrived from all sides, in October 1685 Louis XIV revoked an Edict of Nantes which had apparently been robbed of its force by the Edict of Fontainbleau.

At the present we see with the just recognition which we owe to God that our concerns have achieved the end that we had in view, since the better and greater part of our subjects professing that religion which claims to be Reformed (RPR) have embraced the Catholic religion. And since the execution of the Edict of Nantes and all that was ordained in favour of the so-called Reformed religion (RPR) has been of no effect, we have judged that we could do nothing better entirely to obliterate the memory of the troubles, the confusion and the evils that the progress of this false has caused in our kingdom and has given rise to this edict . . . than to revoke entirely the so-called Edict of Nantes.

2. We forbid our subjects who belong to the so-called Reformed religion (RPR) to continue to meet to practise the said religion in any house or other place.

8. With regard to children who are born to those of the so-called Reformed religion (RPR), it is our will that they should be baptized by the parish priests. We instruct the fathers and mothers to send them to the churches for that purpose, on pain of a fine of five hundred pounds . . .

4. Quietism, or the calling into question of mysticism

Although mysticism has always had an important place in the Christian tradition, it has often met with suspicion. It has been accused of undervaluing the incarnation and the humanity of Christ, of veering towards pantheism or of justifying loose morality even in sexual matters. The condemnation of the *alumbrados* in Spain pointed to such deviations, real or imaginary. At the beginning of the seventeenth century, France, too, underwent a 'mystical invasion' (Bérulle, Madame Acarie, Marie of the Incarnation, the Ursulines) which died away in the second half of the century.

Abandonment, or pure love

A Spanish priest, Miguel de Molinos (1628–1696), had a great success in Rome with the publication of *The Spiritual Guide* (1675), which outlined a mysticism of abandonment and acquired contemplation. He played down the role of good works and asceticism. In 1687, after a lengthy trial, he was condemned to life imprisonment for heresy and immorality. His guilt was Quietism: the word derives from quietude, or repose.

Jeanne Guyon (1648–1717), unhappy in her family life and then in her marriage, discovered the mystical tradition of annihilation inherited from the French school and of abandonment to

171

Quietism

To its opponents, Quietism was the doctrine of abandonment to God and passivity verging on pantheism, indifference to prayer, the sacraments, good works and even morality. The work of Fénelon was condemned in 1699.

Madame Guyon (1648–1717)

At the moment of which I have spoken my prayer was empty of all forms, types and images . . . It was a prayer of faith which excluded all distinction, for I did not have any view either of Jesus Christ or of the divine attributes: all was taken up into a fragrant faith, in which all distinctions disappeared, to give place to the love of loving with a wider love, without any motive or reason for loving . . . Nothing took place in my head; it was rather in the most intimate depths of my being. If anyone were to ask me why I loved God, whether it was because of his mercy, his goodness, I would not know what they were saying to me. I knew that he was good, full of mercy, that his perfections delighted me, but I did not think at all of myself in loving him. I loved him and burned with his fire, because I loved him; and I loved him in such a way that I could love only him; but in loving him I had no motive but himself. All that called itself interest, recompense, was painful to my heart. O my God, if only I could understand the love with which you have possessed me from the beginning!

Autobiography of Madame Guyon.

Fénelon (1651–1715)

The passive state of which all the mystical saints have spoken is passive only to the degree that contemplation is passive, that is to say, that it does not exclude peaceable and disinterested actions but only activity or actions which are restless and fussy in our own interest. The passive state is that in which a soul, no longer loving God with a mixed love, performs all its deliberate actions with a will which is full and efficacious, yet tranquil and disinterested. At one time it performs simple and distinct acts that are called quietude or contemplation; at another time it performs distinct acts of virtue in conformity with its state. But whether it be the one or the other, it performs them in an equally passive way, that is, a way which is peaceful and disinterested.

Fénelon, *Explanation of the Maxims of the Saints on the Inner Life.*

the love of God. A widow, she spread her message in the course of her travels in the Dauphinate, the Savoy and Italy, and in 1684 published *A short and very easy guide to praying that all can practice and in so doing arrive at a high perfection* (1684). In this 'mission' she was associated with a Barnabite priest, Père François Lacombe. Sordid slander linked with malicious gossip led to Lacombe's being imprisoned for seventeen years and sinking into madness, and to a first arrest for Madame Guyon from which she was rescued by Madame de Maintenon, the wife of Louis XIV, in 1688. Madame de Maintenon put Madame Guyon in touch with Fénelon. In this way he discovered the mystical life, of which he had hitherto been ignorant.

The conflict

Madame de Maintenon was soon anxious about the influence her mystical friend might be having on the young girls in her house at Saint-Cyr. She was fearful of losing the royal favour by having dealings with Quietism, which had been condemned. With the support of Bossuet, who was impervious to mysticism, the king's wife quarrelled with Madame Guyon and Fénelon, who refused to say anything at all against Jeanne Guyon. The latter was imprisoned in secret for ten years (1695–1705). In order to justify his spiritual ideas, Fénelon composed the *Explanation of the Maxims of the Saints on the Interior Life* (1697), referring to the traditional authors: 'All interior paths lead towards pure and disinterested love. This pure love is the highest degree of Christian perfection. It is the end of all the roads which the saints know.' The pressures of Bossuet and Louis XIV ended up in the condemnation by Rome of twenty-three propositions of Fénelon's work (1699). The censors believed that in Fénelon they had found confirmation of indifference towards retribution or divine punishment. Fénelon submitted, and devoted himself entirely to his job as Archbishop of Cambrai.

172

Catholic reform had succeeded only too well. In a society which prized order, there was no longer any place for anyone who went beyond what was reasonable, or overstepped a strict boundary. Like folk religion, mysticism had become suspect.

Medal of Louis XIV struck in 1669 on the occasion of the peace of Clement IX. The crossed insignia of the pope and the king (key, sceptre and orb) represent the union of the two societies, civil and ecclesiastical, under the inspiration of God.

For further reading

Geoffrey Barraclough, *The Medieval Papacy*, Thames and Hudson 1968

J. Delumeau, *Catholicism from Luther to Voltaire*, Burns and Oates 1976

A. G. Dickens, *The Counter Reformation*, London 1968

D. Evenett, *The Spirit of the Counter Reformation*, Cambridge 1968

H. Jedin, *Crisis and Closure of the Council of Trent*, Burns and Oates 1967

M. Mullett, *The Counter-Reformation*, Methuen 1985

A. D. Wright, *The Counter-Reformation*, Weidenfeld and Nicolson 1982

13

The British and North American Experience

Sixteenth and Seventeenth Centuries

I · Reformations of the Sixteenth Century

1. Henry VIII and the break with Rome

In 1509, Henry VIII succeeded to the throne of a country which could consider itself one of the brighter spots in the Western church. England and Wales, contained within the two ecclesiastical provinces of Canterbury and York, were famed in Europe for the piety of their people; their king could look back on at least a century of good relations between the pope and the English crown. Bishops were generally conscientious, although quick to take offence at criticism of the church structures, and often prevented from directly supervising their diocese by duties as royal civil servants. Numbers in the monasteries and friaries had kept up since a great slump in the aftermath of the Black Death (1347–9), and the life of the parish churches flourished. Altogether there was much that was good, much that was indifferent, but little that was catastrophic in the life of the English church.

Nevertheless, the king who had been brought up as a conventionally pious son of the church was to lead his realm out of communion with Rome. Reasons of state and the king's obsession with getting his own way were more important than theology; Protestantism came in once the decision had been made. The problem lay in Henry's yearning for a legitimate son; his wife

Katherine of Aragon had presented him merely with one surviving daughter, and he was terrified for the future political stability of his realm. By the 1520s he had convinced himself that he must divorce his wife on moral grounds, because she had first been the wife of his deceased elder brother. The pope had good reasons for refusing to grant a divorce on these grounds, and was also under pressure from Katherine's nephew, the Holy Roman emperor. For all Henry's bluster and frenzied European-wide diplomatic manoeuvrings, matters were at a standstill until a new royal minister, Thomas Cromwell, persuaded the king to act on his long-standing belief that a king of England had no superior under God. If this was so, he had no need to go kow-towing to the pope for a divorce.

With Cromwell planning the details of the new policy, matters moved swiftly during the 1530s. The English Parliament was used to make a complete break with Rome, the decisive step being the parliamentary Act of Supremacy of (173) 1534. Opposition was confused and rebellions unsuccessful; a handful of leading men, including the great writer who briefly served as Henry's Chancellor, Sir Thomas More, were executed for refusing to accept the break with Rome. Nevertheless, Protestantism was in a peculiar position throughout the king's reign; the king detested it, particularly Lutheranism, and always considered himself a good Catholic. Even though he let Cromwell carry out a campaign which dissolved all English monasteries, producing a vast financial windfall for the Crown from their lands and property, he never condemned the monastic life, and would not allow the English clergy to marry.

Cromwell also succeeded in getting a century-old ban on publishing the Bible in English officially reversed in 1537, yet he himself was executed on charges trumped-up by his conservative political enemies in 1540. (174)

Despite the great setback for Protestant advance which Cromwell's downfall represented, the king could not uproot Protestantism in England. Popular English opposition to papal power and to the traditional theology which it represented went as far back as the fourteenth century and the movement known as Lollardy, inspired by the teachings of John Wyclif (see Vol. 1, p.183). The mediaeval English church had made a good job of crushing Lollardy among the influential and prominent, but Lollard ideas obstinately survived in small and secretive communities; some Lollard groups lasted long enough to feel a new excitement when they heard of the teachings of Martin Luther in the 1520s. At the same time, several young clerics, particularly in the two English universities of Oxford and Cambridge, became interested in Lutheranism. One in particular, William Tyndale (1494?–1536), was inspired to produce a new translation of the Bible in English, which became the basis for subsequent English translations including the Bible which Cromwell persuaded Henry VIII to authorize, and later still, the Authorized Version of 1611.

However, Tyndale was to die an exile from Henry VIII's England, arrested and executed as a heretic by the agents of the Holy Roman emperor. After Cromwell's death, the only prominent Protestant cleric to hang on to a position of importance in England was the Archbishop of Canterbury, Thomas Cranmer (1489–1556), for whom Henry never lost his personal affection. Otherwise Henry's last years were a time of uncertainty and frequent danger for English Protestants, many of whom remained in exile.

2. English religion in flux 1547–1559

A Protestant Reformation only began in earnest on the old king's death in 1547; for reasons which are still not entirely clear, he had allowed his son Edward to be brought up under the influence of devout Protestants, and it was Protestant noblemen who dominated policy in the reign of this boy-king Edward VI (1547–1553). Now Protestant theologians were given an increasingly free hand to transform Henry's still Catholic church, notably Archbishop Cranmer, who in successive

The Henrician Reformation

The Act of Supremacy of 1534

An extract from the preamble to the Act, which takes the line that Parliament is merely recognizing something which was already a fact.

Albeit the King's Majesty justly and rightfully is and oweth to be the supreme head of the Church of England, and so is recognized by the clergy of this realm in their Convocations; yet nevertheless for corroboration and confirmation thereof, and for increase of virtue in Christ's religion within this realm of England, and to repress and extirp all errors, heresies and other enormities and abuses heretofore used in the same, Be it enacted . . . that the King our sovereign lord, his heirs and successors kings of this realm, shall be taken, accepted and reputed the only supreme head in earth of the Church of England . . . any usage, custom, foreign laws, foreign authority, prescription or any other thing or things to the contrary hereof notwithstanding.

Text taken from G. R. Elton, *The Tudor Constitution*, CUP 1968, 355–6.

Henry VIII.

Cromwell and the reading of the Bible

Cromwell used the wide powers given him by the king to issue orders to all the English clergy in 1538; they included the following. Note the way in which Protestant leaders were already becoming alarmed at what people might read into the biblical message!

Item, that you shall provide on this side the feast of Easter next coming, one book of the whole Bible of the largest volume, in English and the same set up in some convenient place within the said church that you have cure of . . . Item, that you shall discourage no man privily or apertly [secretly or openly] *from the reading or hearing of the said Bible, but shall expressly provoke, stir, and exhort every person to read the same, as that which is the very lively word of God, that every Christian man is bound to embrace, believe, and follow, if he look to be saved; admonishing them nevertheless, to avoid all contention and altercation therein, and to use an honest sobriety in the inquisition of the true sense of the same, and refer the explication of obscure places to men of higher judgment in Scripture.*

Text taken from H. Bettenson, *Documents of the Christian Church*, OUP 1963, 231–2.

Thomas Cromwell.

revisions (1549 and 1552) produced a Prayer Book for the new church written in majestic English. It has been the basis of Anglican Prayer Books ever since.

Edward's reign was cut short when he died of tuberculosis, and in a swift *coup d'état*, his Catholic elder sister Mary (Katherine of Aragon's daughter) asserted her place as rightful queen.

The English Prayer Book

Extracts from the Preface to the 1549 Prayer Book, repeated in all subsequent versions including that of 1662. Note the emphasis on a new uniformity through the realm, and that implicitly, Latin could be used if those present understood it.

There was never any thing by the wit of man so well devised or so surely established, which (in continuance of time) hath not been corrupted: as (among other things) it may plainly appear by the common prayers in the church, commonly called divine service: the first original and ground whereof if a man would search out by the ancient fathers, he shall find that the same was not ordained, but of a good purpose, and for a great advancement of godliness . . .

. . . here you have an order for prayer . . . more commodious, both for the shortness thereof, and for the plainness of the order, and for that the rules be few and easy. Furthermore, by this order, the curates shall need none other books for their public service, but this book and the Bible: by the means whereof, the people shall not be at so great charge for books, as in time past they have been.

And where heretofore there hath been great diversity in saying and singing in churches within this realm: some following Salisbury use, some Hereford use, some the use of Bangor, some of York, and some of Lincoln: now from henceforth, all the whole realm shall have but one use.

. . . Though it be appointed in the afore written preface, that all things shall be read and sung in the church, in the English tongue, to the end that the congregation may be edified: yet it is not meant, but when men say Matins and Evensong privately, they may say the same in any language that they themselves do understand.

Cranmer, burnt at the stake.

Reactions to the new Prayer Book varied. In the West Country there was an almost immediate rebellion, and the rebels published demands which made clear their detestation of it:

We will have the Mass in Latin as was before, and celebrated by the priest without any man or woman communicating with him.

. . . We will not receive the new service because it is but like a Christmas game; but we will have our old service of matins, Mass, evensong and procession as it was before; and we Cornishmen, whereof certain of us understand no English, utterly refuse this new English.

Text quoted in F. Rose-Troup, *The Western Rebellion of 1549*, London 1913, 220–1.

The Elizabethan Settlement

(176) The Act of Uniformity of 1559

This restored a version of Edward VI's second English Prayer Book of 1552. The clause about ornaments quoted last, rather puzzlingly gave a date before the publication of the 1549 Prayer Book; this was to cause trouble later.

Where at the death of our late sovereign lord King Edward the Sixth there remained one uniform order of common service and prayer and of the administration of sacraments, rites and ceremonies in the Church of England . . . the which was repealed and taken away by Act of Parliament in the first year of the reign of our late sovereign lady Queen Mary, to the great decay of the due honour of God and discomfort to the professors of the truth of Christ's religion: Be it therefore enacted by the authority of this present Parliament that the said statute of repeal . . . shall be void and of none effect from and after the feast of the Nativity of St John Baptist next coming [29 August 1559] *. . . and that if any manner of person . . . shall . . . use any other rite . . . or shall preach, declare or speak anything in the derogation or depraving of the said book or anything therein contained . . .* [he shall suffer forfeiture of a year's income and six months' imprisonment for a first offence, one year's imprisonment and loss of office for a second and loss of office and imprisonment for life for a third offence] *. . . provided always and be it enacted that such ornaments of the church and of the ministers thereof shall be retained and be in use as was in the Church of England by authority of Parliament in the second year of the reign of King Edward the Sixth until other order shall be therein taken by the authority of the Queen's Majesty . . .*

Text quoted in Elton, *The Tudor Constitution*, 401–3.

(177) Some of Elizabeth's Protestant clergy were unhappy with the caution that her new government showed in bringing forward the Protestant Reformation: even some who would accept bishoprics from her and have to defend the new arrangements. Here is the future Bishop of Salisbury, John Jewel, writing in 1559 to his friend Peter Martyr, an Italian theologian in Switzerland, after returning to England from his refuge from Queen Mary in Zurich:

And what, after all, can I write to you? For we are all of us hitherto as strangers at home. Return then, you will say, to Zurich. Most earnestly do I wish, my father, that this may some time be possible: . . . O Zurich! Zurich! how much oftener do I now think of thee than ever I thought of England when I was in Zurich! . . . As to religion, it has been effected, I hope, under good auspices, that it shall be restored to the same state as it was during your latest residence among us, under Edward. But, as far as I can perceive at present, there is not the same alacrity among our friends, as there lately was among the papists . . . The scenic apparatus of divine worship is now under agitation; and those very things which you and I have so often laughed at, are now seriously and solemnly entertained by certain persons (for we are not consulted), as if the Christian religion could not exist without something tawdry.

. . . Others are seeking after a golden, or as it rather seems to me, a leaden mediocrity; and are crying out, that the half is better than the whole.

Text abbreviated from *Zurich Letters* Vol. 1, Parker Society 1842, 23.

This meant an emphatic reaction against Protestantism, but to most people's surprise, Mary I insisted on taking this as far as a full return to Roman obedience. She also insisted (to the increasing unease of her advisors) on encouraging local magistrates and the national courts to hunt out and even execute obstinate Protestants: Cranmer was among more than two hundred who died in this way, leaving the Queen with the lasting nickname of 'Bloody Mary'.

Mary might have got over the unpopularity of her policies and succeeded in giving a firm foundation to restored traditional Catholicism had she not had an even briefer reign than Edward VI; she died of cancer in 1558. Her successor and half-sister Elizabeth was the daughter of Henry VIII's second wife Anne Boleyn, for whom he had divorced Katherine of Aragon. As she was a living symbol of Henry's breach with Rome, it was more or less inevitable that Elizabeth should form a group of advisors committed to a Protestant shape to the church, and they steam-rollered a new Settlement of Religion through the English Parliament in 1559. 

3. The Elizabethan Settlement

The Elizabethan Settlement produced a curious hybrid of a church; it had no links with Rome, it restored the 1552 English Prayer Book and

Puritanism and Catholic recusancy

Puritan clergy organize themselves

Some clergy and gentry decided to work semi-secretly for change in the church within the structure, quietly founding groups for regular co-operation. Here one group of clergy seeks to recruit a member from another (June 1587). The 'exercises' mentioned were a form of theological seminar.

Whereas (beloved brethren) at the time of the last Parliament order was taken by consent of many of our godly brethren and fellow labourers assembled at London that all the ministers which favoured and sought the reformation of our church should sort themselves together to have their meeting to confer about the matters of the church, besides such exercises as should most make for their profiting every way; it was further advised that none should assemble above the number of ten, and therefore they which exceeded that number should sort themselves with others of their brethren next adjoining, where defect was. According hereunto, we your brethren, whose names are underwritten, have had our meeting so often as our troubles would give us leave; but find, in regard to the smallness of our number, and distance of place, that we stand in need of further aid of some to be adjoined unto us. Whereupon, understanding that God hath blessed you with store, we are constrained to make suit unto you that you would of your abundance supply our want. And namely, considering that our beloved brother Mr Newman is one who may be profitable unto us, and in place most fit, in respect of you and us, our earnest desire is that you would yield this benefit unto us . . . The Lord our God and the merciful Father multiply his graces upon us that, according to the manifold wants of his church, and the times wherein we may live, we may be enabled unto that high and mighty service He hath called us unto . . .

A puritan.

Text quoted in H. C. Porter (ed.), *Puritanism in Tudor England*, Macmillan 1970, 241–2.

The troubles of a Catholic priest

Roman Catholic families and the roving priests who served them often faced grave danger from Elizabeth's government, and sometimes through traitors in their own midst. Here is the account of Fr John Gerard, SJ, of a narrow escape in 1594, just before he was indeed caught by government agents:

On Easter Monday we rose earlier than usual for Mass, for we felt there was danger about. As we were preparing everything for Mass before daybreak we heard, suddenly, a great noise of galloping hooves. The next moment, to prevent any attempt at escape, the house was encircled by a whole troop of men. At once we realized what was afoot. We barred the doors: the altar was stripped, the hiding-places opened and all my books and papers thrown in. It was most important to pack me away first with all my belongings . . . [A search for Gerard's hiding-place went on in the house for four days; but without success; the government agents left.] *The doors of the house were then barred and the mistress came to call me out. Like Lazarus, who was buried for four days, I came forth from what would indeed have been my tomb if the search had continued a little longer. I was very wasted and weak with hunger and lack of sleep. All that time I had been squatting in a very confined space. While the search was on the mistress of the house had eaten nothing whatsoever, partly because she wanted to share my discomfort and find out by testing herself how long I could live without food, but chiefly to draw down God's mercy upon me and upon herself and her whole family by fasting and prayer. When I came out I found her face so changed that she looked a different person; and had it not been for her voice and her dress I doubt whether I would have recognized her.*

Text from P. Caraman (ed.), *The Autobiography of John Gerard*, Longmans 1951, 58–63.

allowed the clergy to marry, and all its senior clergy were firmly committed to Protestant theology, many of them enthusiastic for Calvinism. The Queen was named Supreme Governor of the Church (not Supreme Head, like Henry VIII and Edward VI, because many would have found it scandalous for a woman to bear such a title). Yet the ancient threefold Catholic order of bishop, priest and deacon was also retained, and the Prayer Book contained many ceremonies which well-informed Protestants regarded as offensive Catholic survivals. Even some of Elizabeth's first bishops were unhappy with the Settlement, and few thought that it would last long without alteration. Yet the queen refused to allow any significant change, and the choice for English Protestants was either to accept an imperfect church to carry forward their mission, or to carry on vainly protesting. Those who continued expressing their disapproval of the Settlement were nicknamed Puritans; they included many nobility, gentry and clergy. A few took their disapproval further (much to Puritan dismay) and formed their own congregations separate from the established church: these were the Separatists, of whom Robert Browne (*c.*1550–1633) was a leading figure.

Others, particularly among the gentry, found it impossible to accept the Elizabethan Settlement because they felt that it betrayed Catholicism. After a decade of indecision, many of them started refusing to go to the official churches, and therefore acquired the name Recusants (Latin *recusare*, to refuse). They turned to Rome for help; from 1574, a steady stream of priests trained on the Continent started arriving in England to minister to them, and if possible to promote the cause of Catholicism. The government passed legislation making it treason even to enter the realm in this way, and many clergy and a few lay people, more than three hundred in all, were executed as a result. Despite this

179 persecution, a minority Catholic community loyal to Rome maintained a precarious existence throughout England.

4. The Reformation in Scotland

In the sixteenth century, Scotland was still a proudly independent kingdom, generally on bad terms with its English neighbour. Its pre-Reformation church organization was chaotic, largely thanks to the self-interested manipulation of church revenues and offices by the Scottish nobility. English invasions under Henry VIII and Edward VI only added to the confusion, and it did not greatly help the cause of Protestant Reformation in Scotland when the English began to support Scottish Protestants against their French-backed Catholic opponents. However, the Protestant leader John Knox (*c.*1513–72), who had strong connections both with England and with Calvin's Geneva, eventually built up a strong party among leading Scottish aristocrats, and through them, he was able in 1560 to construct a thoroughgoing Genevan Settlement

The Scottish Reformation

John Knox returned to Scotland from continental exile in 1559, and was soon plunged into civil war with the Catholic forces led by the Queen Regent, Mary of Guise. Here is his own description, in an exultant letter of June 1559 to a friend in Geneva, of the mounting chaos in eastern Scotland:

. . . The queen and her council made promise that no person within Saint Johnston [Perth], *neither yet of these that assisted them, should be troubled for any thing done either in religion, either yet in down casting of places,* [wrecking churches and monasteries] *till the sentence of the estates in Parliament had decided the controversy, and that no bands of French soldiers should be left behind the queen and council in the town, and that no idolatry should be erected, nor alteration made within the town. But after she had obtained her desire, all godly promises were forgotten; for the Sunday next after her entering, mass was said upon a dyeing table (for you shall understand all the altars were profaned); the poor professors* [i.e. Protestants] *were oppressed; when children were slain, she did but smile, excusing the fact by the chance of fortune . . . This cruelty and deceit displeased many that before assisted her with their presence and counsel; and among others, the earl of Argyll and the prior of St Andrews left her, and joined themselves to the congregation openly . . . At their command I repaired to them at St Andrews . . . in the meantime came the Bishop of St Andrews to the town, accompanied with a great band of warriors, and gave a straight commandment, that no preaching should be made by me . . . assuring the lords that if they suffered me to preach that twelve haquebuts* [guns] *should light upon my nose at once. O burning charity of a bloody bishop! But as that boast did little affray me, so did it more incense and inflame with courage the hearts of the godly, who with one voice proclaimed that Christ Jesus should be preached in despite of Satan . . .*

In the meantime . . . the Abbey of Lindores, a place of Black Monks, [Benedictines] *. . . we reformed, their altars overthrew we, their idols, vestments of idolatry, and mass books, we burnt in their presence, and commanded them to cast away their monkish habits. Divers Canons of St Andrews have given notable confessions, and have declared themselves manifest enemies to the Pope, to the Mass and all superstition. Thus far hath God advanced the glory of his dear Son among us . . . for now forty days and more hath my God used my tongue, in my native country, to the manifestation of his glory. Whatsoever now shall follow as touching my own carcass, his holy name be praised . . .*

From text in T. McCrie, *Life of John Knox*, Edinburgh 1839, 172, 486–7.

of the Scottish Church, complete with a Confession of Faith, *Book of Discipline*, and an Anglo-Swiss liturgy called the *Book of Common Order*. Church organization was presbyterian, with the office of bishop keeping the most shadowy of survivals within the system; monastic life was allowed to wither away and monastic property gradually confiscated. Catholic opposition to this was hampered by the political incompetence of the Catholic Mary Queen of Scots (1542–87; not to be confused with the English Queen Mary I), and when she was deposed in 1567, Knox's settlement was triumphant. Catholic survival was confined to the remotest parts of the kingdom. Mary's successor was her infant son, who became King James VI; as he grew up, he willingly embraced Calvinism and accepted the broad outlines of the 1560 Reformation.

II · The Seventeenth Century: Toleration out of Conflict

1. The beginnings of Anglicanism: the English Civil Wars

It is difficult to know when we can begin applying the term 'Anglican' to the Church of England which emerged from Elizabeth I's 1559 Settlement. Most of those committed to it during her reign would merely have thought of themselves as part of the international Protestant world; but by the end of the century, a small but growing group particularly among the church's clergy were beginning to prize the special features which the Settlement had preserved: its links with the past, particularly its retention of the historic episcopate. It was this group which first deserves the label Anglican. One of the chief writers to express such a point of view was Richard Hooker (*c.*1554–1600), who framed a majestic justification for the Church of England's position in his eight books of *A Treatise on the Laws of Ecclesiastical Polity*. A younger generation of clerics, including a future Archbishop of Canterbury, William Laud (1573–1645), went further than Hooker in emphasizing that their church was as Catholic as the Roman church, even though its Supreme Governor was the king and not the pope. They were the first people to represent what would come to be called the High Church viewpoint within Anglicanism.

During the seventeenth century, through many struggles, Anglican clergy and sympathizers would come to dominate the Church of England and impose their identity on it, at the cost of alienating many who at the beginning of the century were happy enough to be part of the national church. High church Anglicans like William Laud first came to positions of influence in the church in the reign of James I, that son of Mary Queen of Scots who had been King James VI of Scotland, but who succeeded peacefully to the English throne as well on the death of Queen Elizabeth in 1603. However, James retained his old sympathy for Calvinist theology (which high churchmen increasingly abhorred), and it was only in the reign of his son Charles I (1625–49) that high churchmen gained the leading place in royal counsels; Laud became Archbishop in 1633.

This shift in the leadership of the church baffled and infuriated more traditionally Protestant clergy and laypeople, but it was Charles' political incompetence which led to his downfall and the temporary overthrow of Elizabeth's Church Settlement. The flashpoint came with his tactless attempt to impose similar institutions of church government and a prayer book very like the English liturgy on the Church in Scotland; his father had been much more cautious and subtle in efforts to bring change in Scotland. Now the Scots leadership exploded in fury and in 1639–40 defeated successive English armies, leading in turn to a storm of indignation in England against the king's mismanagement. The king continued to mishandle the situation to such an extent that by 1642 open warfare had broken out between him and a substantial section of his parliament; not only that, but the opposition were determined to purge the Church of Charles' High Church supporters and even, with Scots Presbyterian encouragement, to abolish the office of bishop. Charles had forced Puritans who had once been content to be members of the national church to become its enemies.

81

A complicated series of Civil Wars followed throughout the British Isles, in the course of which Charles was defeated; a radical element in the army eventually forced his execution (1649), the abolition of the monarchy and the destruction of Elizabeth's 1559 Church Settlement. The Interregnum ('time between the reigns') began. The way seemed open for an entirely fresh start in church and state, and in this atmosphere of disruption and high excitement, many sects felt that they represented the coming of the new Jerusalem. However, the most powerful commander in the army, Oliver Cromwell (1599–1658), steered a more moderate course; he had masterminded the king's execution and detested episcopacy, but he also disliked the highly-structured Presbyterian system which the Scots wanted to see set up in England, and he mistrusted the wilder religious leaders.

Under Cromwell's rule, the English church became dominated by Independency; in effect it became a vast collection of parishes, each with a certain amount of freedom to organize religious life as it chose, and with the minimum of central direction. Most of those who wished to worship in 'gathered congregations' separate from the parochial system were able to do so: for instance, strict Independents (those who would later be known as Congregationalists), and Baptists. Wilder sects, such as the Quakers (the common nickname for the Society of Friends), greatly alarmed moderate Puritans by their enthusiastic behaviour, and suffered official and unofficial persecution. Yet those loyal to the defeated and destroyed Anglican system were treated with reasonable tolerance, while English Roman Catholics found themselves better treated than for nearly a century, even though they had supported the king against parliament in the Civil Wars. The same could not be said of Irish Roman Catholics; in the course of his campaigns in Ireland, Cromwell allowed his armies to carry out some horrific massacres of Catholics, which have never been forgotten there.

182

2. Restoration and the 'Glorious Revolution'

Cromwell's problem was that he never found a satisfactory way to govern England once the monarchy was destroyed, and after his death in 1658, the country began sinking into political chaos. Once more an army commander intervened: George Monck (1608–70). Monck correctly diagnosed the popular longing for the return of the Stuart royal family after a decade of uncertainty, and by masterly use of the troops under his command, he ended the Interregnum and in 1660 Charles I's exiled eldest son was restored as King Charles II. In this Restoration, Monck co-operated with political leaders who favoured a Presbyterian system for the church, but the remarkable part of this Restoration was that it brought a return of the Anglican leadership, swept to power on a wave of popular

(181)

The Civil War

Anger against High Churchmen

Sir Benjamin Rudyerd was no revolutionary, for he was to fight for the king in the Civil War. But it is a proof of the anger which Laud's policies had raised among ordinary English gentlemen like Rudyerd that in 1640 he could deliver a speech in the House of Commons, bitterly attacking the Laudian clergy's divisive actions in the church:

We well know what disturbance hath been brought upon the church for vain, petty trifles . . . We have seen ministers, their wives, children and families undone, against all law – against conscience – against all bowels of compassion – about not dancing upon Sundays. What do these sort of men think will become of themselves when the master of the house shall come, and find them thus beating their fellow-servants? These inventions are but sieves made on purpose to winnow the best men, and that's the devil's occupation. They have a mind to worry preaching; for I never yet heard of any but diligent preachers that were vexed with these and the like devices . . . They would evaporate and dispirit the power and vigour of religion, by drawing it out into some solemn, specious formalities – into obsolete, antiquated ceremonies, new furbished up . . . they have so brought it to pass that, under the name of Puritans, all our religion is branded; and, under a few hard words against Jesuits, all popery is countenanced. Whosoever squares his actions by any rule, either divine or human, he is a Puritan. Whoever would be governed by the King's laws, he is a Puritan. He that will not do whatsoever other men would have him do, he is a Puritan. Their great work, their masterpiece, now is, to make all those of the religion to be the suspected party of the kingdom . . .

Richard Baxter.

nostalgia for the church of the 1559 Settlement. Naturally they and those who had fought and suffered for Charles I had many old scores to pay off; and the Settlement of religion which they constructed made virtually no concessions to the Presbyterian leaders.

The Act of Uniformity of 1662, enforcing the use of a new Book of Common Prayer based on the Elizabethan book, completed this Settlement, and resulted in over two thousand clergy leaving the national church because they could not accept the new arrangements; English Dissent was born. Permanent groups took shape out of the rather confused groupings of the Interregnum: Presbyterians, Baptists, Congregationalists, Quakers. In the Established Church, High Churchmen seemed to have triumphed, and many Dissenters faced harsh persecution from Charles II's officials. However, there was to be a new crisis when Charles II died in 1685 and his brother became King James II of England. James had been converted to Roman Catholicism, and soon made it clear, to the horror of Anglicans and Dissenters alike, that he wished to promote the

(182) A jaundiced view of Interregnum sects

Richard Baxter (1615–91) was a saintly clergyman who came to be a champion of Presbyterianism during the Civil War. It is interesting to see how much he deplored the more extreme sects which emerged; modern historians have suggested that the Ranters were more a product of the worried imaginations of people like Baxter than a real identifiable group! The 'Familists' mentioned were an earlier sectarian group. The Quakers would survive as a much less aggressive denomination, even though Baxter thought that many of them were 'Papists' (i.e. Roman Catholics) in disguise.

The third sect were the Ranters. These also made it their business, as the former, to set up the light of nature under the name of Christ in Men, and to dishonour and cry down the Church, the Scripture, the present ministry, and our worship and ordinances; and called men to hearken to Christ within them. But withal they conjoined a cursed doctrine of libertinism, which brought them to all abominable filthiness of life. They taught as the Familists, that God regardeth not the actions of the outward man, but of the heart, and that to the pure all things are pure (even things forbidden). And so, as allowed by God, they spake most hideous words of blasphemy; and many of them committed whoredom commonly, insomuch that a matron of great note for godliness and sobriety, being perverted by them, turned so shameless a whore that she was carted in the streets of London . . .

And that was the fourth sect, the Quakers, who were but the Ranters turned from horrid profaneness and blasphemy to a life of extreme austerity on the other side. Their doctrines were mostly the same with the Ranters. They make the light which every man hath within him to be his sufficient rule, and consequently the Scripture and ministry are set light by; they speak much for the dwelling and working of the Spirit in us, but little of justification and the pardon of sin, and our reconciliation with God through Jesus Christ; they pretend their dependence on the Spirit's conduct, against set times of prayer and against sacraments, and against their due esteem of Scripture and ministry; they will not have the Scripture called the Word of God; their principal zeal lieth in railing at the ministers as hirelings, deceivers, false prophets, etc., and in refusing to swear before a magistrate, or to put off their hat to any, or to say 'You' instead of 'Thou' or 'Thee', which are their words to all . . . Many Franciscan friars and other Papists have been proved to be disguised speakers in their assemblies, and to be among them, and it's like are the very soul of all these horrible delusions . . .

The Autobiography of Richard Baxter, Dent, Rowman and Littlefield 1974, 73–4.

Roman Catholic cause in his kingdoms. As politically inept as his father Charles I, within three years he had even alienated the fervently loyal high churchmen, and when a small group of English politicians invited his Dutch Protestant son-in-law William of Orange to mount an invasion to overthrow him, few people were prepared to stand up and resist William. James fled the country, even failing to do this properly at his first attempt. In a curious but in practice very successful constitutional improvisation, William and his wife Mary (James' daughter) became joint sovereigns, and the 'Glorious Revolution' of 1688–9 was complete.

Such had been the breadth of national Protestant support for the overthrow of James that it was clear that Anglicans would have to modify their aggressive attitude to the Protestant Dissenters. Even James had tried to promote toleration of Dissent as part of his plans to help his fellow Roman Catholics, and so the new régime would have to try to do at least as much. In the event, high church pressure limited what could be done; but at least the Act of Toleration (1689)

183

The Glorious Revolution

The diarist John Evelyn (1620–1706) was a devout Anglican, whose record of events leading up to the Act of Toleration reveals the sort of Anglican suspicions of Dissenters which prevented any fuller reunion of the Church of England through the 'Bill of Comprehension' which he mentions. It also shows how unhappy many Anglicans were about the legality of James II's overthrow. The Archbishop of Canterbury, William Sancroft, eventually refused to swear loyalty to the new régime.

12 February 1689. I went with the Bishop of St Asaph to visit my Lord of Canterbury at Lambeth, who had excused himself from officiating at the Coronation, which was performed by the Bishop of London, assisted by the Archbishop of York. We had much private and free discourse with his Grace concerning several things relating to the Church, there being now a bill of comprehension to be brought from the Lords to the Commons . . . We discoursed likewise of the great disturbance and prejudice it might cause, should the new oath, now on the anvil, be imposed on any, save such as were in new office, without any retrospect to such as either had no office, or had been long in office, who it was likely would have some scruples about taking a new oath, having already sworn fidelity to the government as established by law. This we all knew to be the case of my Lord Archbishop of Canterbury, and some other persons who were not so fully satisfied with the Convention making it an abdication of King James, to whom they had sworn allegiance . . .

Scotland declares for King William and Queen Mary, with the reasons of their setting aside King James, not as abdicating, but forfeiting his right by maladministration; they proceeded with much more caution and prudence than we did, who precipitated all things to the great reproach of the nation, all which had been managed by some crafty ill-principled men. The new Privy Council have a Republican spirit, manifestly undermining all future succession of the Crown and prosperity of the Church of England, which yet I hope they will not be able to accomplish so soon as they expect, though they get into all places of trust and profit.

The Diary of John Evelyn, Dent 1907, Vol.2, 300–1.

184 Non-Juring spirituality

Among the Anglican Non-Jurors was the former Bishop of Bath and Wells, Thomas Ken (1637–1711). A man of deep spirituality and an inspired writer of hymns, his broad Catholic piety can be gauged from this Marian hymn:

Her virgin eyes saw God incarnate born,
When she to Bethl'em came that happy morn;
How high her raptures then began to swell,
None but her own omniscient Son can tell.

As Eve her fontal sin reviewed,
Wept for herself and all she should include,
Blest Mary with man's Saviour in embrace
Joyed for herself and for all human race.

All Saints are by her Son's dear influence blest,
She kept the very Fountain at her breast;
The Son adored and nursed by the sweet Maid
A thousandfold of love for love repaid.

Heaven with transcendent joys her entrance graced,
Next to his throne her Son his Mother placed;
And here below, now she's of heaven possest,
All generations are to call her blest.

gave Dissenters the right to build their own places of worship and form congregations under official licence. This meant that they would preserve their identity, although for half a century they experienced little growth and formed quite a small proportion of the population.

In another religious direction, a by-product of the Glorious Revolution was the separation of several hundred High Church clergy and some lay sympathizers from the official church; although they had detested what James II had done, they felt that their oath of loyalty to him was too sacred to break in order to acknowledge William and Mary as lawful. More followed suit when James II's second daughter Queen Anne died in 1714, and James' Catholic son was excluded from the British throne in favour of the Protestant Hanoverian prince George. They formed a Non-Juring church (so called because of their refusal to swear the new oaths) which, although very small in numbers, was of considerable influence through the theological and spiritual writings of its members, particularly William Law (1686–1761). In Scotland, all the bishops became Non-Jurors (1690), which meant that their Presbyterian opponents took over the running of the state church. The Church of Scotland has been Presbyterian ever since.

184

3. British religion in a new setting: North America

In the next chapter we describe the way in which the Catholic church embarked on a truly worldwide mission during the sixteenth century. Part of that mission was pursued through the French settlements of North America, particularly in what is now Canada; equally, the Spanish missionary effort pushed northwards from South America into the southern regions of the modern USA. However, North America became dominated by colonies initiated in the British Isles. A witness of this is how persistent a 'White Anglo-Saxon Protestant' ethos has been in the leadership of the United States, even although the USA has become far more diverse in its population.

Permanent colonies in North America arrived later than the founding of Spanish and Portuguese colonial empires to the south. Northern European nations, particularly the English and the French, regularly frequented those coasts for fishing during the sixteenth century, but the first permanent settlement was not established until 1607. This colony, Virginia, was established by a commercial company from London, and had a clergyman of the Church of England serving it; Virginia remained dominated by Anglicanism. Very early on, in 1619, the colony began the practice of importing Africans for labour in the fields: at first as indentured servants, like some Englishmen, but very quickly as slaves for life. The dreadful trade in black slaves and the society which depended on that trade would persist for more than two centuries; and many citizens of the United States can trace their descent to victims of the European hunger for cheap labour. Of course, the English colonies were not alone in exploiting black people in this way (see Chapter 14, pp. 67f.).

The religious conflicts in early seventeenth-century England which we have already examined inspired a different group of colonies from that in Virginia. Already in the reign of James I, as Laud and his supporters gained increasing influence in the Church of England, many Puritans grew to despair of the way things were going in the church. A group of Separatists had already fled to Holland in 1608 to carry on their worship without harassment from the English authorities, but the New World seemed to offer them more promise; in 1620, they joined with a group of mainstream Puritans – the famous Pilgrim Fathers – to start a new life in Virginia. It seems to have been something of an accident that they actually landed and settled hundreds of miles north up the American coast

(185)

Farewell to England

The position of the Massachusetts colonists about church establishments was made quite clear by one of their pastors, Francis Higginson:

We will not say, as the separatists who were wont to say at their leaving of England, 'Farewell, Babylon!' 'Farewell, Rome!' but we will say, 'Farewell, dear England! Farewell, the Church of God in England, and the Christian friends there!' We do not go to New England as separatists from the Church of England; though we cannot but separate from the corruptions in it: but we go to practice the positive part of church reformation, and propagate the gospel in America.

The Mayflower.

from Virginia; but despite many hardships they persisted in their colony of Massachusetts. Together with neighbouring settlements, this area of colonization came to be known as New England.

The reign of Charles I brought further power in England to Laud's party, and a corresponding interest in New England from Puritans. Thousands of people went out; and the proportion of ministers among them was remarkably high. The value which the settler leadership placed on godly learning can be gauged from the fact that as early as 1636 they founded the beginnings of a university with Harvard College at Cambridge, Massachusetts. The states which they set up, rather paradoxically at first sight, gave monopoly status to an established church which was Congregationalist in character; they were no more interested in religious freedom for all than was the English government of Charles I. For some Separatists this was intolerable. Roger Williams (*c.*1604–83) faced banishment by Massachusetts leadership for opposing their church establishment, and so founded a new colony eventually named Rhode Island (1636); it soon became a haven for Protestant refugees from Congregationalist constraints. Here was one small beginning for a new spirit in the English

(185)

Toleration in Maryland

Part of the 'Act concerning Religion' of the Maryland Assembly, 1649. The 'Lord Proprietory' mentioned was the second Lord Baltimore.

No person or persons whatsoever within this Province, or the Islands, Ports, Harbours, Creeks, or havens thereunto belŏnging professing to believe in Jesus Christ, shall from henceforth be any ways troubled, molested or discountenanced for or in respect of his or her religion nor in the free exercise thereof within this province or the islands thereunto belonging nor any way compelled to the belief or exercise of any other religion against his or her consent, so as they be not unfaithful to the Lord Proprietory, or molest or conspire against the civil government established or to be established in this province under him or his heirs.

religious tradition: toleration for religious diversity.

English Roman Catholics also came to have a stake in the new colonial adventures, despite the Puritan colonists' detesting Catholicism even more than they did Charles I's Anglicanism. This was thanks to the enterprise of a convert to Roman Catholicism, George Calvert (1580?–1632); Calvert enjoyed the favour of James I to such an extent that the king made him an Irish peer, with the title of Lord Baltimore, when he was forced to resign his government office on his conversion. Baltimore determined to find a New World refuge for English Catholics, still suffering persecution for their loyalty to Rome, and the colony which he inspired was named Maryland after Charles I's Roman Catholic Queen Henrietta Maria (1632). Naturally the new colony faced bitter hostility from other colonies, who were given opportunity to interfere by the confusion of the British Civil Wars; in order to maintain freedom of manoeuvre for Catholics, Baltimore's son persuaded the Maryland Assembly to pass an 'Act concerning Religion' (1649) which  offered religious freedom to all Trinitarian Christians. So Roger Williams and Baltimore had arrived at rather similar situations by very different religious routes: they had built states which had no religious establishments. Yet Maryland went one step further than Rhode Island, for it showed the world, however cautiously and despite many setbacks, that Roman Catholics could live in peaceful equality with Protestants in a state where neither had the advantage.

The extent of intolerance in the Congregationalist New England colonies was revealed when Quakers arrived from England during the Interregnum; the Massachusetts authorities found their religious antics as terrifying and infuriating as did Puritans back home. A series of laws were passed against them, and these were used to back a vicious persecution; between 1659 and 1661 four Quakers were hanged. Charles II's Anglican government in England would have no part in such extremes, and the criticism which the persecution aroused demonstrated the problems of the Congregationalist monopoly. Things were made worse by the very fact that the colonies were now prospering and growing; not all the increased population wanted to be part of the existing religious establishment. The well-known tragedy of the Salem Witch Trials (1692) further discredited the Congregationalist leadership, which allowed the hysteria to mount and executions of convicted witches to take place. The founding fathers of New England had had a vision of a regulated commonwealth which would be a perfect Christian society, but although Congregationalist established churches persisted in New England through the eighteenth century, the original monopoly system was hopelessly compromised: the first American Dream to be shattered.

Having so disturbed the life of New England, the Quakers were to make a different contribution to the new colonies through a remarkable member of their community called William Penn (1644–1718). Unusually well-placed socially for a Quaker, Penn used his friendship with Charles II's Catholic brother, the future James II, to secure the foundation of two new enterprises: Pennsylvania and Delaware (1681). In both colonies there was to be complete religious freedom, and indeed, the religious mix in Pennsylvania was soon very wide, including many Continental refugees such as persecuted Lutherans and Mennonites. Once more, as in Rhode Island and the first years of Maryland, the pattern which would later become characteristic of the United States was emerging: a Christian commonwealth in which the state had no active role, and where Christian churches of very various character found themselves on an equal footing.

In all this religious and colonizing activity, there was little concern to carry the work of Christian mission to the native population, whom the incomers christened 'Indians'. The settlers' main concern was to protect the salvation of their own communities, which were generally seeking refuge from the home country to practise religion in their own way; this concentration meant that few were inclined to make much effort to reach out to the tribes beyond their settlements. There were noble exceptions throughout the century among all religious groups, outstanding among whom was the Massachusetts Congregationalist John Eliot (1604–90), and pressure from those sympathetic to the Indian plight ensured that some reservations of land were made for them on a permanent basis. However, again and again a depressing pattern emerged in relations between settlers and Indians; initial tolerance and co-operation gave way to enmity and violence, with the colonists inevitably in the long run defeating the natives because of their technological superiority. This was eventually even the pattern in Pennsylvania, where William Penn made strenuous efforts to make his settlers respect Indian rights and to keep good relations with them. As we will see in the next chapter, this was not merely a North American tragedy; the aggressive and destructive character of Western European civilization would emerge wherever Europeans had effective power.

Power in North America was to pass to the increasingly mixed European population of the thirteen colonies which had emerged from the English settlements by the early eighteenth century. British armies would confirm an English-speaking dominance in North America by their victories over the French and Spanish during the eighteenth century; this would be decisive for the future of the United States and indeed of the world English language community. The patterns of American religion which have been so influential for Catholic and Protestant alike were thus already laid by the English initiatives of the seventeenth century.

Towards toleration

The tangled story of the British Reformations and their seventeenth-century consequences have shown us how toleration emerged both in the mother-country and in its American offshoots. The Church of England's seventeenth-century splits have never been fully healed to the present day; but the triumph of the Anglicans over their opponents was not complete enough to allow them to ignore Dissent.

The 1689 Toleration Act was there to stay. In America, idealistic leaders had shown that the toleration which in England was largely a reluctant concession to political circumstances could be made the basis of life within society. The Civil Wars of the mid-seventeenth century had in any case left most English people with a profound distaste for war in the name of religion. The new mood was to emphasize *The Reasonableness of Christianity*, which was the title of a highly influential book by the English philosopher John Locke (1632–1704); reasonable people should not indulge in violence over a reasonable faith. We will examine the wider long-term consequences of this mood in Chapter 15; but first we must consider the world mission spearheaded by the Catholic powers of the sixteenth century.

For further reading

J. C. Brauer, *Protestantism in America*, SCM Press and Westminster Press 1966

H. Brogan, *The Longman History of the United States of America*, Longmans 1985

C. Cross, *Church and People 1450–1660*, Fontana Books 1976

A. G. Dickens, *The English Reformation*, Fontana Books 1964

G. R. Elton, *Reform and Reformation in England 1509–1558*, Edward Arnold 1977

G. R. Cragg, *The Church and the Age of Reason 1684–1789*, Penguin Books 1966

P. Hughes, *The Reformation in England* (three volumes), Hollis 1953

Keith R. Thomas, *Religion and the Decline of Magic*, Penguin Books 1973

14
The Evangelization of the World
Fifteenth to Eighteenth Centuries

**A caravel
(illustration from the 'Letter of Christopher Columbus').**

The great discoveries of the fifteenth and sixteenth centuries were the signal for the beginning of world-wide evangelization. The church really became 'Catholic'. Inextricably bound up with trade, colonization, political fortunes and world wars, evangelization was affected by the consequences and thereby often lost its purity. Nevertheless a remarkable group of people achieved a good deal over the course of three centuries. In the eighteenth century, the church's internal crises rose to the surface again over foreign missions, and the wars of the French Revolution for the time being interrupted the relationship between the church and the countries overseas.

I · The Great Missionary Enterprises of Modern Times

1. Conditions and motivation

Conditions

Tied to the great discoveries, world-wide evangelization depended largely on the material, commercial and political conditions of distant expeditions. The humanists had rediscovered the fact that the world was round, something which had been taught in antiquity. The stern-post rudder, the compass, the multiplication of masts and sails enabled a discovery ship to be built on the Iberian peninsula, the caravel, which was to brave the oceans. Sailing had not become any the less slow and dangerous, and the consequences of this were important for missionary activity. A journey from Lisbon to Goa (in India) and back took from eighteen months to two years; it often took five years to make the return voyage between Seville and Manila, and half the company could perish on the way. One can thus understand the heavy loss of missionaries and the long period over which sees remained vacant, since the appointments were made in Europe; and one can also understand the protracted arguments, such as the disagreements over rites.

Gold, pepper and souls

It was a whole society, a product of Christianity, which did the voyaging. It is necessary to take note of the overall motivation of the discoveries, in which everything is hopelessly muddled.

At the end of the fifteenth century economic conditions forced the Mediterranean countries to go in search of the gold that was needed for trade with the East, and to head towards the West to obtain cheaper spices, found on the plantations and produced by slave labour.

While accounts of voyages (like those of St Brendan and Marco Polo) excited the imagination, the idea of crusading remained alive. The capture of Ceuta in 1415 from the Moslems by Portugal, and the capture of Granada (1492) by the Spanish, were the starting points for major expeditions. Could not Islam be taken from behind with the mysterious Prester John who was now located in Ethiopia? Had not the point been reached when the kingdom of God was to be established once for all upon the earth with the conjunction of the new world and the restoration of Jerusalem, as Joachim of Fiore announced?

Many people also hoped to be able to avoid the damnation of millions of souls. Towards the end of the sixteenth century the idea sprang up amongst Catholics of being compensated for the losses which Protestantism had brought about in the Roman Church. The future of the church lay abroad. During the seventeenth century, many people made a connection between inner mission and foreign mission.

All the motivations were inextricably mixed: 'gold, pepper and souls'. The discoverers, the conquerors and the missionaries too behaved in a way which would seem contradictory and scandalous to us. They set up crosses and massacred the Indians. In Mexico, Cortez had the Indian woman Marina baptized before he took her as his concubine. In Peru, Pizzaro demanded an enormous ransom from the Inca Atahualpa, baptized him and then had him strangled (1533).

187 Gold, Pepper and Souls

These texts from Christopher Columbus are a good indication of the mixed motives of the discoverer of America: crusade, millennarian dreams, the struggle against the Jews, the quest for gold, spices and slaves, and the conversion of peoples to the Christian faith.

Extracts from the logs and letters of Christopher Columbus

In this present year 1492, your Highnesses [Isabella and Ferdinand of Spain] *put an end to the war against the Moors who dominated Europe and brought it to a conclusion in the most noble city of Granada.*

Your Highnesses, as Catholic princes, loyal to the holy Christian faith and propagators of it, enemies of the sect of Mohammed and of all idolatries and heresies, resolved to send me, Christopher Columbus, towards the so-called regions of the Indies, to survey princes and peoples, to see the disposition of lands and all the rest, and to advise on the way in which one could convert these peoples to our holy faith. And you ordained that I should not go towards the east by the accustomed route, but by the western way – a way of which we know only that no one so far has ever taken it. So, having driven from your realms all the Jews who might be found there, your Highnesses resolved to send me to these countries with a sufficient armada.

December 1492 at Hispaniola (Haiti)

In his goodness, may our Lord Jesus Christ see to it that I find this gold mine . . . I hope that when I return my men will have procured a barrelful of gold and that the gold mine will have been discovered. There must also be spices in quantity there. Within three years, your Highnesses could be undertaking the reconquest of Jerusalem.

1498, third voyage

From here one could send, in the name of the Holy Trinity, as many slaves as one could sell, as well as brazil wood (wood for painting) . . . There is a need for many slaves, in Castille, in Portugal and in Aragon. I do not think that one can get them from Guinea any longer; and even if they came, a slave from here is worth three from there . . . So here there are slaves and brazil wood. There is even gold if He who showed it to us allows, and if He deigns to give it us in due time.

1502–1504, third voyage

What an excellent product is gold! It is from gold that riches come. The one who has gold can do whatever he wills in this world. With gold one can even bring souls into paradise.

2. Missionary organization

Patronage

During the fifteenth century, in a series of Crusade Bulls, the Holy Office granted the Portuguese sovereign temporal and spiritual jurisdiction over the lands that had been conquered and those that were still to be discovered. The discovery of the West Indies (America) by Christopher Columbus in 1492 set up a tension between the two powers on the Iberian peninsula. In 1493 Pope Alexander VI intervened as arbiter. He marked out the territory discovered: the West to the Spaniards, the East to the Portuguese. The pope left the responsibility for organizing the church to the two kings in their respective domains: the demarcation of dioceses, the appointment of bishops, and so on. To some degree the sovereigns became the heads of new churches. The pope contented himself with ratifying the appointments rather than intervening directly. All these concessions made up the right of patronage: Portuguese *padroado* and Spanish *patronato*. This patronage caused serious inconveniences. Evangelization was subject to all the hatreds of colonization and politics. The two countries proved to be jealous of their rights, even though it would have been impossible for them to fulfil their duties. Portugal, a country with one and a half million inhabitants, could not supply the needs of the church in half the world. It demanded that all foreign missionaries should go through Lisbon. The kings of Spain were more conscientious, but many other nations like France also threw themselves into the conquest of the world and Francis I said ironically: 'I would very much like to read the clause in the testament of Adam which excludes me from the parcelling out of the world.'

The Congregation of Propaganda

These difficulties prompted the Holy See to take a firm grip on evangelization by setting up in 1622 the Congregation of Propaganda (for the Propagation of the Faith) which was also responsible for the conversion of heretics and schismatics in Europe and the Middle East. However, there could be no possibility of going back on the rights of patronage. The arguments over jurisdiction grew in number. The Propaganda (today the Congregation for the Evangelization of the Peoples) was a kind of ministry of missions. Spurred on by its first secretary, Ingoli, it launched a massive inquiry into missionary activity in the world. It supplied the missionaries with resources: a polyglot printing house, seminaries and universities. It created vicars apostolic, missionary bishops who were responsible directly to the pope.

Missionaries

Secular priests would accompany the conquerors. They were often people who had doubts, or were in difficulty in Europe, or adventurers who wanted to make their fortune, and they had only a limited role in evangelization. The first missionaries to the new worlds were primarily members of the old religious orders: Minims, Augustinians, Carmelites, Mercedarians and above all Franciscans and Dominicans. With Francis Xavier, in 1540 the Jesuits began to take part in missions. They became the main missionaries of modern times, concerned with apostolic spirituality and method. The seventeenth-century societies of priests – Lazarists, Sulpicians, and so on – sent some of their members overseas. The Paris Society of Foreign Missions, founded in 1663, put its priests exclusively at the service of the Propaganda missions.

3. The Christian conscience and colonization

Dependent on the conquerors and on the merchants on whose ships they had travelled, the missionaries were soon confronted with serious problems relating to conquest and colonization.

The abuses of colonial exploitation

The conquerors left Europe to make their fortunes overseas, in search of gold, spices, and later on sugar and coffee. It was not only the conquest of the West Indies (America) which caused the death of the Indians through war, but also diseases brought over from Europe (e.g. measles, smallpox), as well as the hard labour in the mines forced on the Indians. The result was a rapid decrease in, if not the extermination of, the native population. By the middle of the sixteenth century the original population of the Antilles had completely disappeared. The Spaniards divided up the lands and the people (under a system called *encomienda*), and the result was a disguised form of slavery for the Indians. In

1511, the Dominican Montesinos preached a sermon denouncing the exploitation of the Indians which provoked the anger of the settlers, who took the affair to the Spanish court. The laws of Burgos (1512) upheld the *encomienda*, but insisted that the Indians be treated as free men and that their masters should remember their Christian principles.

Bartolomé de Las Casas

Things did not change much, but the struggle for justice towards the Indians was taken up by a settler priest, Bartolomé de Las Casas (1474–1566). He, too, had exploited the Indians, and had been 'converted' in 1514. After setbacks to peaceful colonization he became a Dominican

The fight for justice in the Spanish colonies

Bartolomé de Las Casas made himself the champion of the Indians in the Western Indies (America) from 1514 until his death in 1566. He describes how a Dominican, Anton Montesinos, had begun the fight for justice in a sermon to the colonists of Hispaniola (St Dominica) in 1511.

Codex Vindobonensis. Aztec, around the sixteenth century. Pictographic writing.

Montesinos' sermon

You are all in a state of mortal sin. You live in this state and you will die in it, by reason of the cruelty and the tyranny that you show to these innocent peoples. What right do you have to keep these Indians in such cruel and horrible slavery? Who could have authorized you to wage all these detestable wars on people who lived quietly and peaceably in their country, and to exterminate them in such unimaginable numbers, by murder and unprecedented carnage? How can you oppress them and exhaust them in this way, without giving them food or tending to the diseases to which they are fatally exposed by the excessive labour that you demand from them? Would it not be more just to say that you are killing them in order to extract and amass your daily gold? What care do you take to see that they are converted? Are not these people human beings? Do they not have a soul? Do they not have reason? Are you not obliged to love them as yourselves?

(189) One does not abolish idols in a day

To erect crosses and to invite the Indians to show signs of respect towards them is a good thing, provided that one can make them understand the significance of these acts. But if one does not have enough time, or cannot speak their language, it is useless and superfluous, because the Indians can suppose that one is offering them a new idol which represents the God of the Christians. In this way one may be encouraging them to revere a piece of wood as a god, which is idolatry.

The safest way to proceed, the only rule which Christians should observe when they are in pagan countries, is to give a good example by virtuous works, in such a way that, according to the words of our redeemer, 'seeing your works, they may praise and glorify your Father' and may think that a God who has such worshippers can only be good and true.

Las Casas, *History of the Indians.*

and devoted his whole life to getting the king to put an end to the *encomienda* and making experiments in peaceful evangelization (*la vera paz*). It appears that it was thanks to him that Pope Paul 189 III, in his Bull *Sublimis Deus* (1537), affirmed that the Indians were free men and must not be converted by force. In 1540, Las Casas depicted the horrors of the conquest in his *Very Brief Narrative of the Destruction of the Indians*. He was the indirect inspiration of the *New Laws* (1542) by which Charles V did away with the *encomienda*. When in 1545 Las Casas became Bishop of Chiapa in Guatemala, he came up against the hostility of the settlers, and returned to Spain for good in 1547. At the same time in Spain the theologian Francesco de Vitoria questioned Spain's right to colonize in his *Lessons on the Indians and the Rights of Law*, published in 1539 by the University of Salamanca. He protested vehemently against the behaviour of the conquerors. Las Casas was inclined to think that an end should be put to all conquest, but those for and against engaged in verbal sparring and the results were indecisive.

The battles of both Las Casas and his friends respected the Christian conscience. It was one stage in the awareness of the rights of man. However, despite some improvements, the exploitation went on because the times were contradictory. The king laid down humanitarian rules but was well aware that the colonies brought in revenue and that the settlers had not braved the seas just to carry on the same mediocre existence that they had had in Spain. The Indians had to produce the gold by working in the mines which decimated them. They went on dying.

Slavery

Replacing Indians who had been killed meant new expansion for the slave trade, which had long disappeared in the Christian West. Undoubtedly, in the Middle Ages Christians captured by Turks had been enslaved and in revenge Turkish prisoners had been sold. Hence the idea that prisoners taken during a holy war could be enslaved. The Iberian peninsula had a small permanent core of these slaves. The discovery of America resulted in an enormous demand for labour and gave rise to the trade in Blacks who could be obtained on the African coast. This trade lasted until the beginning of the nineteenth century. Between fourteen and twenty million Blacks were transported in this way. In order to justify the slavery and the trade, the arguments of Aristotle, who spoke of classes of men who were slaves by nature, were brought out again. The curse on the sons of Ham (see Gen. 9.5, which was supposed to refer to the Africans) was recalled. In short, there was a good deal of hypocrisy. Slavery was a necessary evil for the good of the economy. Besides, it was said, slavery allowed the Blacks to come into contact with the Christian faith! Missionaries took part in the trade and had their own slaves. The Blacks did not have de Las Casas to defend them, but only charitable individuals such as the Jesuit Pierre Claver, who made an attempt to improve their lot in Colombia during the seventeenth century.

The meeting of cultures

Conquerors and missionaries were brutally confronted with civilizations and cultures about which they knew absolutely nothing at all. After the initial euphoria some of the practices they met with, like the human sacrifices of the Aztecs, shocked them deeply. Moreover, the missionaries were offering a Christianity which was the fruit of fifteen centuries of development in European culture. They were unable to separate the message from its cultural wrapping. This gave rise to a double attitude. The 'clean sweep' method involved the destruction of native religions, which were seen as manifestations of the devil. But the destruction of the old religions also meant the destruction of cultures and societies. The converts had more or less to adopt the

European culture tied to Christianity: clothing, the sense of private property, and so on.

However, there was a willingness to understand these cultures which were so strange. Las Casas asked for respect for Indian cultures, which he had learned to appreciate. Missionaries such as the Franciscan Sahagun (1500–1590) in Mexico did remarkable work as ethnologists. In India and in China the Jesuits became familiar with the grandeur of the old civilizations and wondered whether they could not be adapted to European Christianity. These problems were never fully resolved and were to become one of the factors in the missionary crisis of the eighteenth century.

II · Across the Continents

1. Africa

A continuation of the crusades, Portuguese expansion along the coast of Africa from Ceuta (1415) to the Cape of Good Hope (1486) and Mozambique (1498) was the start of the first evangelization of Africa. For several years the kingdom of the Congo (south of the lower course of the river Zaire or Congo) gave rise to the greatest hopes. Portuguese missionaries baptized the king in 1491 and a Congolese church blossomed under Alfonso I (1506–1545), 'a very Christian king'. The ruler organized his kingdom on the model of Portugal and his son was the first black man to become a bishop (1521). In 1596 the capital Salvador became the seat of a bishop. The kings of the Congo wanted to preserve their political and economic independence. A Congolese ambassador was sent to Rome in 1612. But the Portuguese took up arms against King Antonio I, who refused them the right to prospect for mines. He was conquered and beheaded in 1665. The Portuguese were less interested in this country than in Angola. Evangelization continued to make progress. The Congregation of Propaganda sent Capucins, many of whom have left reports. Under the inspiration of a Congolese woman, Beatrice, one of the first African-Christian syncretisms, Antonionism, appeared and was harshly suppressed. Beatrice was burned in 1706. Collusion between colonial enterprise in its most odious form, the slave trade, and mission, gave a completely false picture of evangelization.

(190)

(191)

During the seventeenth century it was the turn of French missionaries to come. A son of the king of Assinia on the Ivory Coast was baptized in Paris in 1691. The Lazarists did not succeed in making a permanent settlement in Madagascar (1648–1674). The Spirit Fathers began a mission in Senegal in 1776. On Reunion and Mauritius various priests worked among those who had been transplanted, colonists and slaves.

2. The Americas

Latin America

The Spanish government took seriously its task of organizing the church. It created thirty-four bishops between 1511 and 1620. The bishops, who were usually chosen from the religious orders in the capital, were conscientious, and some of them were quite remarkable, like Zumarraga, a Franciscan who was Bishop of Mexico from 1528–1547, and Toribio of Mogrevejo, Bishop of Lima from 1581 to 1606, who was canonized. These bishops summoned numerous provincial councils and diocesan synods to organize their churches, the most

Slavery, commerce and evangelization in Africa

Commerce, and particularly the trade in black slaves countenanced by the missionaries, completely perverted the proclamation of the gospel in Africa. The King of the Congo was aware of this, the Capucin missionary was not.

(190) Complaints of Alfonso I, King of the Congo (1506–1543), to the King of Portugal

We ask your Highness not to believe the evil said of us by those whose only concern is their commerce, to sell those whom they have acquired unjustly, who by their trade are ruining our kingdom and the Christianity which has been established there for so many years and which cost your predecessors so much sacrifice. We are concerned to preserve this great gift of faith for those who have acquired it. But that can be difficult here when European goods exercise such fascination on the simple and the ignorant that they abandon God in order to secure them. The remedy is the suppression of this merchandise which is a snare laid by the devil for those who sell and those who buy. The lure of gain and cupidity lead the people of the country to steal their compatriots, including members of their own kin and ours, regardless of whether or not they are Christians. They capture them, sell them and barter them. This abuse is so great that we cannot remedy it without striking hard, very hard.

(191) Mission journal of Fra Luca Caltanisetta, Capucin, in the Congo

On 14 July 1695, during the mission to Damma, a merchant wanted to buy a female slave and the small child whom she was still breast-feeding. Seeing her master talking with the merchant, this woman rightly suspected that she was going to be sold. She took her child and, full of rage, threw him on a stone. Then she took several arrows from a man's hand and furiously thrust them into her belly; and in this way, in her despair, she died without baptism. In the course of this mission I had much to do and say against the fetishists.

(1696) I destroyed an altar made by the priests (or fetishists) of the pagans of Nzonzo. This altar was a place surrounded by stakes with animal skulls set on top of them: one large and four small. Some women complained at my destroying these objects; they said to me: 'Does not the father have his practices when he says the mass? We have ours, too.'

(1697) In the course of my first septennial I have administered a total of 20,981 baptisms and blessed 110 marriages.

Luca da Caltanisetta, *Diaire congolais (1690–1701)*.

important of which were held in Mexico and in Lima. But the civil authorities sometimes refused to confirm them.

Pastoral missionary work

The first evangelization was often a show of faith and strength: crosses were set up, idols were destroyed and there were spectacular ceremonies. In order to discredit the Inca tradition, the Viceroy Francisco of Toledo had a descendant of the royal Inca line, Tupac-Amaru, put to death in 1572. Even in the seventeenth century the aim of the Visitation of Idolatry was the systematic tracking down of the remains of the old religion. It was really sweeping the table clean. However, the missionaries made a serious

Teotihuacan, Mexico.

effort to learn the local languages (Nahuatl in Mexico and Quechua in Peru). They composed catechisms, sermons and drama in the local language and themselves became historians of the ancient civilizations. The king of Spain ordered some of their ethnological work to be destroyed.

If baptism was given quickly, the missionaries proved more parsimonious when it came to the eucharist. The Indians were not usually ordained priests. A catechism based on those of Spain was combined with original audio-visual effects: drawings, music, symbolic actions. Some sermons in the native language were evidence of considerable understanding of the peoples, but at the same time they developed a providentialist apologetic in favour of Christianity and the Spaniards, inviting the Indians to resignation and appealing to fear.

192

The Christian communist republic of the Guaranis

In the region of the three rivers Parana, Paraguay and Uruguay the Jesuits set about evangelizing and pacifying the nomadic tribes. They settled them in *reductions*, Christian villages protected from colonialist exploitation. The first settlement dates from 1610. There were to be about thirty of them, comprising 500,000 inhabitants.

Communal living was organized entirely on Christian foundations. Each *reduction* was under the control of two or three Jesuits, and the superior in Paraguay was the link between them. There was no such thing as private property which could be handed on. Everything was owned in common. Paraguay seemed to be the realization of Utopia.

With the treaty of Limites in 1750 the *reductions*

The Good Shepherd: a sermon preached in Quechua to the Indians of Peru (1646)

Francisco Davila (1573–1647), a Spanish priest who was born and died in Peru, was very sensitive to the drama of the Indians of Peru, to the way in which they were ravaged, to the miseries caused by colonial conquest, and to the destruction of their traditional society. In this sermon given in Quechua, an Indian language, he shows both a great understanding of his flock, but also a readiness to justify the misfortune of the Indians in terms of providence, something that a modern reader finds painful.

I am the good shepherd of the llamas, the shepherd with a great heart. For his llamas he has no fear of death. The shepherd who receives wages, and whose animals, his llamas, do not belong to him, when he sees a puma leaping, flees and runs away as fast as he can. The puma seizes a llama and scatters the others. And that is because the shepherd receives wages, because the animals are not his. I am the good shepherd who knows his animals, and the animals also know me.

But if he is the shepherd, who and what are his llamas, his animals? We are, and we alone. All human beings, men and women, are the llamas of Jesus Christ.

Perhaps one of you may now say in your heart: 'Father, we others, we Indians, are not as the whites; we have a different origin, a different form, and so we are not the llamas of God, and the God of the whites is not the God of the Indians. Since the time of our ancestors we have had our huacca*, our idols, and our* umu*, our priests.*

Moreover, before the whites came here the runas *(the Indians) multiplied prodigiously in the wild sierra, on the heathland. The maize, the sweet potato, the quinua, the occa, the llama, the animals which provide wool, all this food was limitless.*

At that time there were no thieves . . . But since the white men have come, all the runas *have become thieves. If that is the case, then we Indians are different from the whites, we are not the same thing. Consequently, we cannot see how we can be the llamas, the animals of Jesus Christ. Because of that, we others, we Indians, are only Christians outwardly, in appearance; we feign the mass, the sermon, the confession, because we are afraid of the padre, the* corregidor*.*

Our hearts think only of our huacca*, because with them things went well with us. And now, see that we have suffering and the villages which once became Christian have disappeared. Even their names have gone and we do not know them. The whites have taken all our fields. And spinning, weaving, making rugs, is something reserved for the* corregidor*.'*

My son, I am glad that you have said all that, and glad to have heard it. Glad in one part of my mind, but in another I am pained and saddened. Why am I glad? Because I know your heart, what you think, and that I can care for you as though you were sick. And why am I saddened? It is because up to now the Indians have not believed, have not accepted the word of God, though they have heard so many sermons, so much teaching . . .

Hear me and take heed. All that happens, life and death, multiplication and disappearance, health and disease, everything in this world and the other is solely in accordance with the will of God. Consequently, when it is his will, the people of one nation conquer another nation and dominate it; and another day, the conquerors become the conquered. But many times, if he annihilates a province with many towns and many people, we can see that it is because they had sinned.

It is because of their prior faults that God has begun to chastize the Incas, making them die and the runas *along with them. And God has not done that simply by chance; he has done it with his very great, insurpassable knowledge. The whites have been the* alguazils *of God. They have come for that purpose . . .*

Otherwise, for not having worshipped the true God, and also for other faults, the souls of all the Indians would go to hell . . .

We are all created by God; we are the animals of Jesus Christ. He is our true shepherd, who has given us his word to eat so that we might be saved thanks to it and he might lead us on high, into the golden enclosure, the country in which one does not have to die. Whereas in the life that you lead it is the accursed devil, the liar, who is your shepherd, to lead you with his lies to the torments of hell . . . Spit on the devil, the sorcerer, the witch, and follow God alone, Jesus Christ . . .

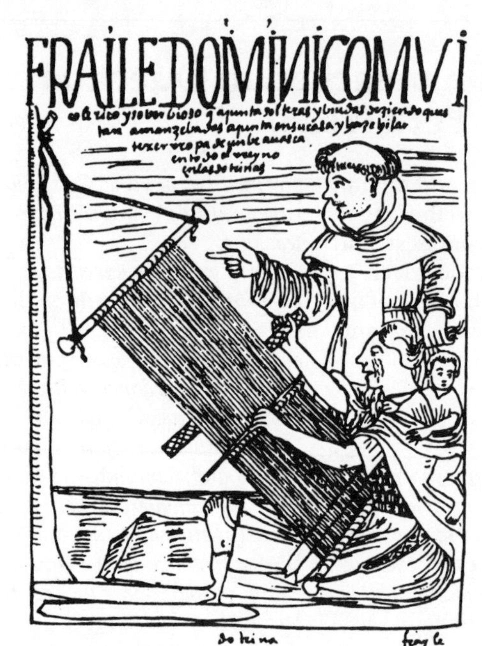

The Dominican brother.

The Franciscan brother.

passed from Spanish into Portuguese control. The Guaranis resisted for some time, but the suppression of the Jesuits in 1768 dealt the death blow to the *reductions*. There was little left: the Jesuits had been too paternalistic and had not trained people to be really responsible.

French America

The evangelization of Canada began with the foundation of Quebec in 1608 by Champlain, which resulted in the coming of the Recollects in 1615. In 1632 the Canadian mission was entrusted to the Jesuits, who followed the nomads as they wandered from place to place and forced them to settle. They had some success with the Hurons, but met with opposition from the Iroquois, who were supported by the English. In 1639 the first missionary nuns, the Ursulines, settled in Quebec. The best known of them was Marie of the Incarnation (1599–1672), who was also a remarkable mystical writer. The Sulpicians settled in Montreal in 1642. Several missionaries suffered martyrdom. The reports of the Jesuits published in France each year between 1632 and 1673 gave great prominence to their missionary activity in Canada. By the valley of the Mississippi, Canada was the starting point for the missions to Louisiana. In spite of remarkable men like Mgr Montmorency-Laval, Bishop of Quebec, who died in 1708, the results of the missions to the Indians were disappointing. There were only two thousand Christian Indians by the end of the eighteenth century.

The Antilles, where France had founded colonies on Spanish territory (Guadeloupe, Haiti), remained an area where the spiritual climate was low. For fear of separatism, the royal government would not allow dioceses and schools to be set up. Many of the priests were of an inferior calibre. The Jesuits who learned Creole in order to catechize the slaves encountered opposition from the colonists.

The conquest: Do you eat this gold? We eat this gold.

The bad confession.

Parochial life in Peru at the beginning of the seventeenth century: forced marriage.

Children punished at catechism.

At the beginning of the seventeenth century a Spanish-Inca half-caste, Felipe Guaman Poma de Ayala, described the injustices of the Spanish conquest and parish life in Peru in words and pictures (*Nueva crónica y buen gobierno*, Institut d'ethnologie de Paris, 1936 and 1968).

3. Francis Xavier, India and Japan

The two methods of Francis Xavier

Francis Xavier, born in Navarre in 1506, met Ignatius of Loyola in Paris and was one of his seven companions who took the vow of Montmartre in 1534. Appointed by Ignatius to be a missionary to the Indies, he arrived at Goa, the centre of the Portuguese East Indies, in 1542. Without having had time either to learn the languages or get to know the way of life, he baptized several thousand people along the Fishing Coasts in the south-east of India after the most cursory of catechisms. In 1545 he was in Malacca, in 1546 in Indonesia.

In 1549, with a few companions, he reached Japan, landing at Kagoshima on the island of Kyushu. The Japanese scene appeared to him to be a complex one, and he had to reconsider his missionary methods. He understood the necessity of learning the language carefully, of getting to know Japanese philosophy and of observing the country's customs, for example by wearing a silken robe. He had to bide his time in

Francis Xavier in India

In this letter of January 1545 Francis describes his missionary method in the villages of Travancore (South India). It seems very summary, and hardly concerned with a knowledge of the culture of the people he meets. Later, in Japan, Francis was to be much less expeditious. He required of the missionaries a solid intellectual training to enable them to cope with educated Japanese.

In one month I baptized more than ten thousand people. This was my method: when I arrived in the villages of the infidels who called on me to convert them to Christianity, I gathered together all the men and the children of the village in one place and, beginning with the proclamation of the Father, the Son and the Holy Spirit, I had them make the sign of the cross three times, and invoke the three persons, confessing the one God. Then I recited 'I confess to God', followed by the Creed, the Commandments, the Lord's Prayer, the Ave Maria and the Salve Regina. I translated all these prayers into their own language two years ago and I know them by heart. Gradually they all repeated them, both great and small.

When the prayers were over, I gave them in their own language an explanation of the articles of faith and the commandments of the law. Then I made all of them ask forgiveness publicly from God our Lord for their past life . . . After the sermon, I asked them all, men and children, if they really believed the articles of faith. They all told me that they did, so I recited each of the articles in a loud voice. After each article I asked them whether they believed, and crossing their arms in front of them they told me that they did. Then I baptized them, writing down the names of each one for them. The men then returned home and sent their wives and families for me to baptize in the same way as I had baptized them. When I had finished the baptizing, I sent them to tear down the buildings in which they kept their idols, and once they were Christians I made them break the statues of the idols into little pieces.

Portrait of St Francis Xavier in Goa.

order to win a convert. Such was the 'second method' of Francis Xavier. He decided to go on to China, fount of Japanese wisdom, but died on 3 December 1552 on an island facing Canton.

The impassioned letters that Xavier wrote to Europe, which were very quickly published and sometimes altered, made him into a kind of modern-day missionary. Legend attributes millions of conversions and numerous miracles to him.

Japan's Christian century

The Japanese penchant for the novelties of European civilization and the divisions of the feudal system were the cause of many conversions. The local chiefs, called daïmios, demonstrated their independence by choosing Christianity. The number of Christians grew to 300,000. They were to be found particularly in the south, on the island of Kyushu and in the regions of Kyoto and Edo (Tokyo). The prime instigator of this first church was the Jesuit Valignano, who was visitor from 1579 to 1606. He chose adaption.

Rivalries between Europeans, both sailors and missionaries, the concern of the new shoguns (prime ministers), the Tokugawa, to restore Japanese unity against the daïmios and the opposition between Buddhists and Shintoists all resulted in the persecution of Christians. In 1597, twenty-six missionaries and faithful were executed at Nagasaki. In 1614 Christianity was outlawed throughout Japan. The executions grew in number, accompanied by the most frightful tortures. After the revolt of Shimbara in 1636, 35,000 Christians were massacred. Japan was closed to missionaries until the nineteenth century.

The missionaries, who were few in number – never more than a hundred – did their best to understand the Japanese language and civilization: they even printed translations. They also passed on elements of European culture. Cautiously, some Japanese priests were ordained (fourteen in 1614). A bishop resided in Nagasaki between 1598 and 1614. Communities were formed consisting of *doyukus* (religious who were not priests), catechists, heads of villages and their associates, and this enabled them to keep going in the absence of a priest. The mission stations depended for their existence on gifts from Europe and above all on taking part in trade between Europe and Japan, which sometimes rebounded against evangelization.

Crucifixion of the martyrs at Nagasaki, 1597. Etching by Callot dating from 1622, the year in which a great many more Christians were burned and decapitated.

India

The evangelization of India by the apostle Thomas may be hypothetical, but the presence of Christians in the south may go back to the fifth century. These Christians spoke Syriac and were attached to the Nestorian church of Mesopotamia. When the Portuguese settled in Goa they wanted to impose the Latin church on the

Christian Expansion Between

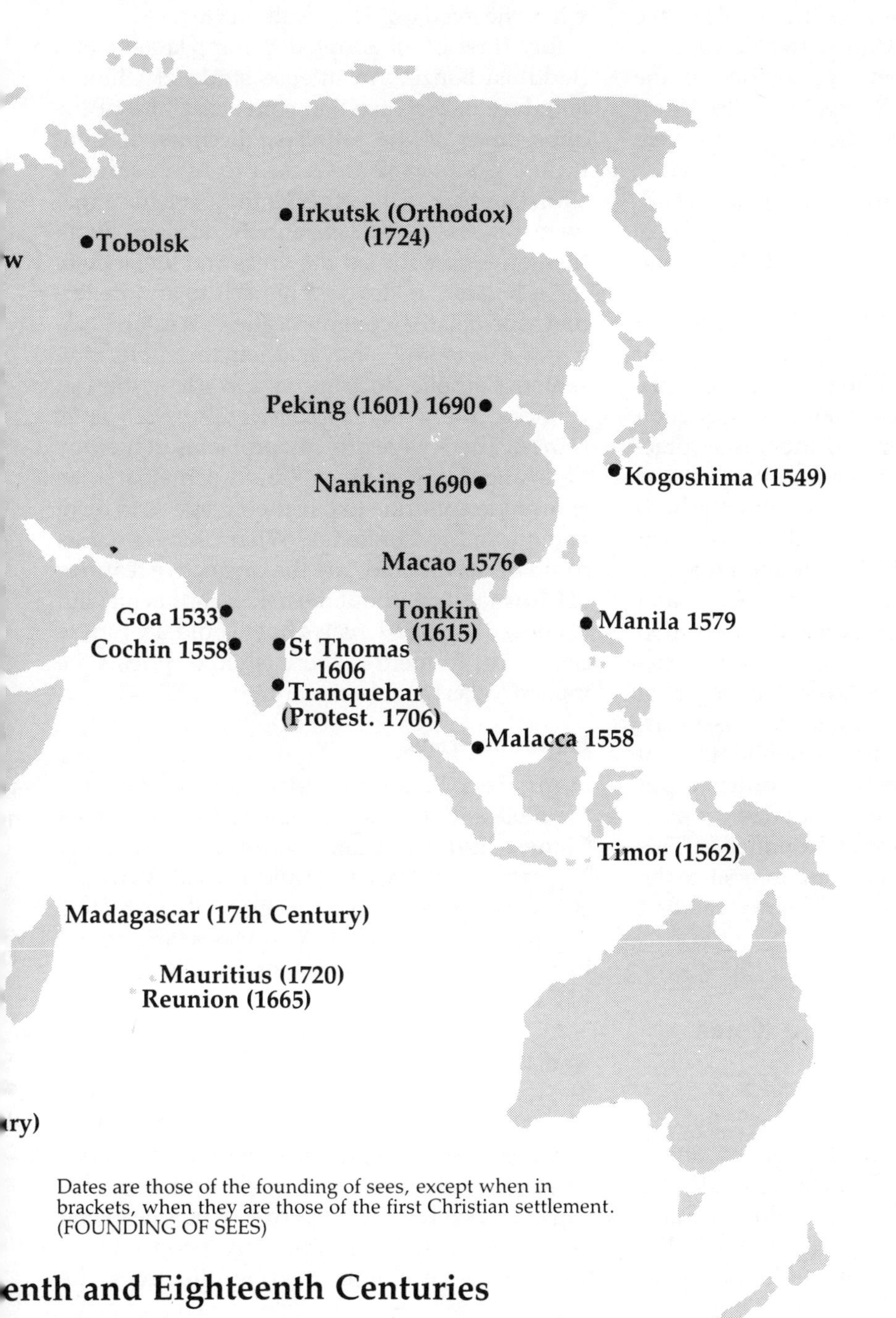

Dates are those of the founding of sees, except when in brackets, when they are those of the first Christian settlement. (FOUNDING OF SEES)

›enth and Eighteenth Centuries

Christians, and this led to conflicts and schism. Starting from Goa, which was at first a bishopric and then the episcopal see for the whole of the East from the Cape to China, the Portuguese attempted a summary evangelization on the 'clean sweep' principle. Francis Xavier took part in it on several occasions. Many baptisms were performed without a real church being formed.

Robert de Nobili (1577–1656), an Italian Jesuit, arrived in India in 1605. He lived for fifty years in Madura, in the south. He learned Tamil and Sanskrit, refused to be assimilated into a Portuguese colony and wanted to be thought of as a Christian *sannyasi* on the model of penitent Hindus. He adopted the life-style of the Brahmans, the superior caste. Making a distinction between social behaviour and idolatrous practices, he allowed converts to retain the customs of their caste such as *kudumi* (not cutting the hair) and wearing a girdle. He allowed the omission of those rites of baptism which were repugnant to Indians, like breathing on the candidate and spittle. Nobili's methods aroused opposition from several missionaries and led to denunciations to Rome. The pope accepted some of Nobili's modifications in 1623. Some missionaries adopted the life-style of the penitents from the lowest castes, the *pandaras,* in order to put themselves at the service of the poorest people.

In 1706 Lutherans settled at Tranquebar. This was one of the first Protestant missions since the beginning of the Reformation. In 1733, the first Indian pastor was ordained.

4. China, Indochina and Korea

From Macao to Pekin

The Portuguese settled at Macao in 1557. By 1565 there was a Jesuit house in the colony, and a bishop shortly afterwards. The Chinese converts were made to cut their hair and adopt a European life-style. In 1578 the Jesuit visitor Valignano sent two priests into the interior of China, Ruggieri and Mateo Ricci. The latter, in five stages, between 1582 and 1601, reached Peking, where he lived until his death in 1610.

Ricci first of all adopted the appearance of a Buddhist bonze. An intense study of Chinese language and civilization convinced him of the importance of the scholars, disciples of Confucius. Confucianism seemed to him nearer to Christianity than the other Chinese religions that were practised, Taoism and Buddhism. From then on Ricci adopted the dress and life-style of the scholars. He devoted himself to an intellectual apostolate, communicating Western science, astronomy and mathematics. He presented Catholic doctrine in a work written in Chinese, the *True Exposition of the Doctrine of Heaven*. There were difficult problems in the way of evangelizing China. Could Christians be allowed to continue to pay their respects to dead parents and to Confucius? What Chinese words could be used to indicate the distinctive features of Christianity without the risk of confusion with Chinese religion? Finally, how could a Chinese clergy be formed? Where should priests be trained? Was Latin necessary?

Hope and crisis

In 1615 Pope Paul V authorized the translation of the Bible and liturgical texts into Chinese, but a Chinese liturgy did not in fact come into being. The services of learned Jesuits (Schall, Verbiest, etc.) were appreciated at the imperial court. They organized a calendar, drew up laws, and so on. In 1688 Jesuit mathematicians from King Louis XIV arrived in Peking.

At the end of the seventeenth century things were looking very hopeful for Chinese Christianity. There were two or three hundred thousand Christians, and 120 missionaries. But the quarrel over rites (see below) and the conflict of authority between Portuguese patronage and the Propaganda angered the emperors, who set several persecutions in train. The only people to be tolerated were the learned Jesuits from the

194

The Evangelization of China

A new style of missionary, Mateo Ricci (1552–1610)

Fr Matteo Ricci (1552–1610), Jesuit missionary in China.

Father Mateo wore the dress of the men of letters, chiefly that of those who call themselves preachers of the law. This dress is truly modest; the hat is little different from our own, and is even fashioned in the form of a cross. Nor did he set out to be the preacher of the divine law in dress alone, but much more so by his speeches. For he gave himself over entirely to refuting one or another sect of idols (Buddhism and Taoism). When it came to the men of letters, however, not only did he not censure them; on the contrary, he praised them greatly, and even commended Confucius, the prince of them, because he had preferred keeping silent about what he did not know of the other life to making up fables, and had shaped the precepts of his law to give a good form to the life of the individual and good government to his family and to the kingdom, in law and equity. This way of dressing and going about in public seemed quite new, but it was greatly approved of by the men of letters. Father Mateo had composed a summary of Christian doctrine in Chinese, in such a way as to suit it mainly to pagans.

Extract from Nicolas Trigault, *Histoire de l'Expedition chrétienne au royaume de la Chine* (1617).

195 The baptism of moribund infants in China

One particular theology, disturbed over the fate of infants who died unbaptized, led the missionaries to baptize as many moribund infants as possible, outside any family or community context. A Jesuit Father in Peking gives an account of this apostolate for a benefactress in Europe.

In most years our churches in Peking alone can reckon on five or six thousand of these children being purified by the waters of baptism. This harvest is more or less abundant, in proportion to the number of catechists than we can support. If we had a sufficient number, their care would go beyond the moribund infants who are exposed to die; they would have yet other occasions to exercise their zeal, above all at certain times of the year, when smallpox or other epidemics kill off an unbelievable number of small children . . . One could win over infidel midwives, who would allow Christian girls to follow them. It often happens that the Chinese, finding it impossible to feed a large family, order the midwives to drown girls in a bowl of water as soon as they are born. These sad victims of the need of their parents would also find eternal life in the very waters which removed them from a short and perishable life.

Letter of Fr d'Entrecolles, Peking, 19 October 1720, in *Lettres édifiantes et curieuses de Chine par des missionnaires jésuites* (1979).

Peking Court. The suppression of the Jesuits (from 1762 onwards) worsened a situation which was finally put in jeopardy by the French revolution.

Indochina

After suffering persecution in their own country, the Japanese Christians settled in Cochin China, in Cambodia and Siam. The Jesuits concerned

196

Instruction from the Congregation of Propaganda on the practice of the Vicars Apostolic (1659)

By creating vicars apostolic (bishops directly under Rome), the Propaganda sought to engage in missionary action free of political implications. It also gave good advice, even if this was not always easy to interpret on the ground. We can see this in the dispute over rites.

Do not employ any zeal, do not advance any argument to convince these people to change their rites, their habits and their customs, unless they are manifestly contrary to religion and morality. What is more absurd than to transport France, Spain, Italy or any other country of Europe to the Chinese? Do not introduce our countries to them but the faith, this faith which neither rejects nor blesses the rites and customs of any people, provided that they are not detestable, but on the contrary seeks to guard them and protect them. It is so to speak inscribed in the nature of all men to esteem, to love, to put above all the world the traditions of their country and that country itself. Nor is there any more powerful cause of alienation and hatred than to make changes in the distinctive customs of a nation, particularly those which have been practised for as long as anyone can remember.

themselves with these regions from 1615 onwards. They transcribed the Vietnamese language in Latin characters. For twenty years (from 1625 to 1645) Vietnam was the primary concern of the Jesuit Alexander de Rhodes, though he was never able to live there permanently. For Rhodes, the basis of evangelization was a good knowledge of the language, the training of catechists to ensure a permanent Christian presence, the utilization of Vietnamese culture and an understanding of its customs. He wanted to form a local clergy.

Vicars apostolic

Rhodes' approaches to Europe resulted in the appointment of vicars apostolic for the Far East (1658). These were bishops who did not occupy a see but were directly under the pope (the Propaganda) in the mission field. Pierre de La Mothe and François Pallu, the vicars apostolic, arrived in Siam in 1641: they ordained the first Vietnamese priests and founded a seminary in Siam for the whole of the Far East. They dissociated themselves from the methods of the Jesuits. Arguments over jurisdiction grew.

Wheel from the chariot of the sun (the sun god Suriya) at Konarak, in Orissa, India.

Buvaneguar in Orissa, temple of Rajanari (twelfth to thirteenth century).

Dancing Shiva (twelfth century).

A lay church in Korea

In the seventeenth and eighteenth centuries Korean scholars discovered Christianity through books which had come from China. In 1784 Yi Seung-hun, a young scholar on a voyage to Peking, was baptized there. On his return to Korea, in the company of another scholar, Yi Piek, who worked out a Christian theology from the Confucian tradition, he himself founded a Christian community with baptism, confession and mass. Seized with doubt, he asked Peking for a priest. But this first community was destroyed by persecution.

Russian Asia

In its eagerness to expand towards the East and embark on a progressive conquest of Siberia, the Russian church became a missionary church. In the sixteenth century the archbishops of Kazan converted the Tartars around the town. Philaret, the Metropolitan of Tobolsk, sent missionaries to Kamchatka in 1705 and Iakutsk in 1724. Some Russian prisoners had formed an Orthodox community in Peking in 1689. At the end of the eighteenth century some monks from Lake Ladoga settled in Alaska and founded an Aleutian-speaking community there.

(197) The beginnings of Christianity in Korea

The distinguishing feature of the first church of Korea is that it was established by converted lay Koreans. That caused difficulties subsequently.

In a letter of 1789 Yi Seung-hun (Peter Li) describes the religious situation in Korea to French missionaries in Peking. He is disturbed because he has been told that he acted against the rules of the church.

When I was baptized (by the fathers in Peking) I had only a superficial knowledge of what I should know . . . When I arrived in my own country I had nothing more urgent to do than to study my religion in the books which I had brought and to preach to kinsfolk and friends. In my career, I met a wise man who had found a book of our religion which he had studied for several years . . . He it was who instructed me; we helped one another to serve God, and helped others to serve him. In the number of a thousand, they submitted to the faith and ardently asked to be baptized. At this general request, I baptized several of them with the ceremonies observed at the baptism which I received in Peking. At this juncture persecution broke out: my family suffered more than any other and this forced me to leave the company of my brothers in Jesus Christ. But so that the baptisms should not stop, I appointed two others in my place. One was the wise man whom I mentioned earlier, and the other was a man who had suffered a good deal from the persecution: he died in 1785 in the autumn of the year after he had been taken.

Towards the spring of 1786 the Christians met together to discuss how they should confess to one another. It was decided that Kia should confess to Y and to Pin, but that Kia and Y, and Y or Pin, could not make mutual confessions. The Christians again met the same autumn; it was decided that I should say the holy mass and that I should administer confirmation. Not only did I accede to their wishes, but I gave the same power to say mass to ten others. As to the ceremonies, I observed them as they are recorded in different books and hours of prayer, omitting some and adding others.

A high official. Korean painting from the end of the eighteenth century.

III · Missions from the European Perspective and the Crisis of the Eighteenth Century

1. Missions and European opinion

Missionary literature

From the sixteenth to the eighteenth centuries missionary literature enjoyed a great success among other travel literature. From 1549 to 1619 ninety-eight works in French were published in Japan. There were numerous publications on China. Two regular series of publications of the Jesuits reached a wide public: the *Reports of the New France* (an annual volume from 1632 to 1673) and *Informative and Curious Letters* (in thirty-four volumes from 1702 to 1776, often re-issued immediately afterwards). Some of these writings, especially those of the Chinese Jesuits, had great scientific value and made a significant contribution towards the growth of geographical knowledge amongst Europeans. They demonstrated the existence of very old civilizations, and some very advanced ones, which were different from those of Europe. The philosopher Leibniz was filled with enthusiasm to see Europe and China reaching out towards each other to perfect all that lay between them.

A new picture of non-Christians

Familiarity with missions encouraged European Christians hesitantly towards a new understanding of non-Christians. Some Jesuits thought that the Chinese had retained elements of the primitive revelation. Was it not possible to look upon some pagan religions as forerunners, 'figures' of Christianity? This optimistic view disturbed theologians like Bossuet and the Jansenists.

Amongst some 'philosophers' – Bayle, Voltaire, Diderot and the Encyclopaedists – missionary literature became a weapon against Christianity. The tolerance of the Chinese was contrasted with the intolerance of Louis XIV. The morality of the Chinese proved that it was not necessary to have a revelation. Chinese chronology went back well beyond that of the Bible. Moreover, during the eighteenth century some people who had become aware of the inhumanity of slavery regarded the pseudo-justifications which Christians gave for it with irony.

2. The great mission crisis

In the Far East, conflicts of jurisdiction increased between the bishops appointed by Lisbon through patronage and the vicars apostolic of the Propaganda. Each side would annul the decisions of the other.

The dispute over rites

More serious was the dispute over rites, because it called into question the methods of the missionaries and the attitude of Christianity when faced with other cultures. In India and China missionaries disagreed over certain subjects: language – what name to give to God in native tongues? liturgy – should the Christian rites be adapted? traditional customs – should Christians be allowed to honour their dead or retain the caste system? and so on. Jesuits in China and

China seen from Europe

Many European thinkers became interested in what the missionaries said about China, often drawing very different conclusions.

The philosopher Leibniz showed great enthusiasm for this encounter between China and Europe. He thought that it should bring together the different Christian confessions.

I think that a singular concern of destiny has as it were joined together the most civilized and the most ordered extremities of our continent, Europe and China . . . Perhaps these two most cultivated nations, by stretching out their arms to one another, will gradually perfect all that is to be found. I fear that soon, under all the similarities, we shall be inferior to the Chinese; it will be almost necessary to receive missionaries from them in order to learn from the use and practice of natural theology, just as we send them missionaries to teach them revealed theology . . . The plan to bring the light of Jesus Christ to distant countries is so fine that I do not see what differentiates us . . . I think that mission is the greatest concern of our times, as much for the glory of God as for the general good of humankind.

Leibniz, texts from 1697.

Pascal is disturbed at certain claims that Chinese chronology antedates that of the Bible.

History of China – I believe only the histories, whose witnesses got themselves killed.

Which is the more credible of the two, Moses or China?

It is not a question of seeing this summarily. I tell you there is in it something to blind, and something to enlighten.

By this one word I destroy all your reasoning. 'But China obscures,' say you; and I answer, 'China obscures, but there is clearness to be found; seek it.'

Pascal, *Pensees*, 592.

India had more or less accepted these adaptations. Missionaries from the other orders (Dominicans, Franciscans, the Paris Foreign Mission) regarded them as concessions to idolatry. This conflict often stirred up the conflict between patronage and propaganda. The argument going on in Europe came to be increasingly allied with the theological conflicts of the old church: Jesuits against Jansenists, liberals against conservatives, and so on.

Condemnation of Chinese rites by Pope Clement XI in 1704

3. One cannot in any way or for any reason allow Christians to preside, serve as ministers or take part in the solemn sacrifices or oblations which are customarily made at the time of each equinox to Confucius and to departed ancestors, since these are ceremonies which are steeped in superstition.

7. Christians cannot be allowed to keep in their own homes in honour of their ancestors, as is the custom of the Chinese, tablets on which is written 'the Throne' or 'the Seat of the Spirit' or 'the Soul' of such a person, by which is signified that the soul or spirit of such a dead person sometimes comes to stop or to rest there.

The condemnation of Chinese and Malabar rites

The dispute which had begun in the mid-seventeenth century took a sharper turn in 1693. Mgr Maigrot, the vicar apostolic in China, forbade the use of the Jesuit vocabulary to denote God in Chinese, and the performance by Christians of traditional Chinese rites (such as veneration of ancestors and of Confucius). Although the Jesuits solicited a different interpretation from the Emperor Kang-Hi (that the rites were civil acts), in 1704 the Holy Office upheld Maigrot's basic position. The pope sent a legate, Charles de Maillard de Tournon, to sort out the problem on the spot. He forbade accommodations in India (Malabar rites) and in China. He died in Macao under house arrest in 1710. In 1715 the pope made a solemn condemnation of Chinese and Malabar rites. In the face of the uproar let loose by the mission, a new legate, Mezzabarba, who succeeded in returning to Europe alive, granted some concessions (1721), but these did not affect anything. Finally, the Chinese and Malabar rites were condemned afresh in 1742 and 1744. The difficulties continued until 1939. (200)

The missions victims of international politics

The waning of the Catholic powers in the colonial expansion at the same time led to a weakening in missionary activity. The treaty of Utrecht in 1713 left the mastery of the seas to Spain and France. The Treaty of Paris in 1763 marked English dominance in America and in India.

The banning of the Society of Jesus in all Catholic states, followed by its suppression by the pope in 1773, put an end to the activity of 3000 missionaries throughout the world. The numbers provided by the other orders or by the secular clergy were much less. A great many Christians were left to their own devices.

The French Revolution led to the drying up of resources and numbers. It became difficult for French Catholic missionaries to travel by sea because of the maritime power of England. Therefore Protestant missionary societies sprang up in Great Britain to fill the place that they had left.

The final results of the Propaganda in the eighteenth century were disillusioning. A certain feeling of powerlessness developed. 'The West has had to give up its intention of converting the East as such.' However, we should remember that the church had now become fully universal. While no good solution had been found, the problem of the encounter between Christianity and other civilizations had been put in a way which was often more judicious than it was to be in the nineteenth century.

For further reading

Stephen Neill, *A History of Christian Missions*, rev. ed. Penguin Books 1986

G. H. Dunne, *Generation of Giants, the Jesuits in China*, University of Notre Dame Press 1969

J. Gernet, *China and the Christian Impact*, Cambridge University Press 1984

C. P. Groves, *The Planting of Christianity in Africa*, four volumes, Lutterworth Press 1938–58

J. Laures, *The Catholic Church in Japan*, Greenwood Press 1970

S. Neill, *A History of Christianity in India*, Cambridge University Press 1984–1985

R. Ricard, *The Spiritual Conquest of Mexico*, University of California Press 1966

15

New Worlds: Britain and North America

Eighteenth Century

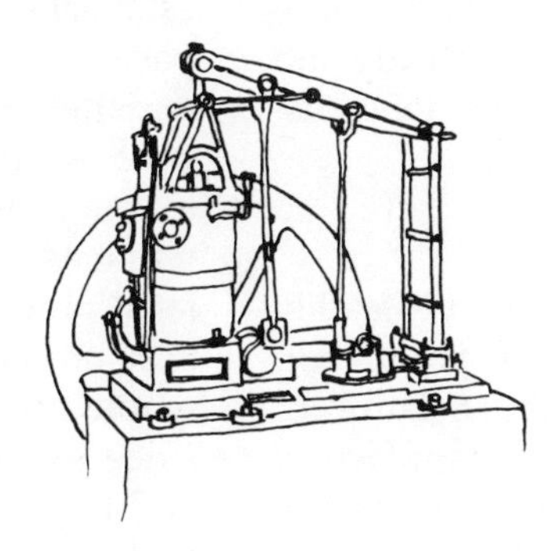

I · The Industrial Revolution

It was during the eighteenth century that Britain emerged for the first time as a world power, which, despite the permanent loss of its thirteen colonies in North America (1776–83), would by the early nineteenth century prove capable of taking the lead in destroying Napoleon's attempt to establish French dominance in Europe. Part of the reason for this remarkable change of status for what had been a second-rank power on the edge of the European world was that Britain was the first country to experience an Industrial Revolution and the consequent immense changes in society. Now no part of the world remains unaffected by the coming of this new force, and the churches have had to do their best to cope with a wholly different way of life.

Economic growth

This Revolution did not happen overnight. Massive growth in the British economy began about 1750, accompanied by a steady rise in the population: by the 1780s the new situation was becoming apparent to all well-informed observers. In 1700, there were few great towns in England apart from London, and they were nearly all the towns which had been great ports and market centres for centuries; the centuries-old pattern of a concentration of wealth and population in the south-east of the country also persisted. In 1800, there had been a dramatic shift to the north; small urban centres like Manchester and Leeds had become great towns sustained by the concentration of workshops and factories producing manufactured goods, particularly textiles. Gradually, within this new proliferation of manufacturing centres, a new source of power became increasingly important: steam. Used to power engines especially for the spinning of thread for textiles, steam made possible a whole variety of processes and a previously undreamt-of speed in production; yet the ancient energy source of water power also remained important, both harnessed from the fast-running streams of northern England and Scotland for industrial mills, and tamed into canals to make possible the slow but steady and cheap transport of bulky items over long distances.

Changes in society

Through this Revolution, British society steadily changed, both in distribution of population through the country and in the balance of occupation between farming and manufacture (although it is important to remember that even in the 1830s, a majority of British people still lived in the country and had some connection with farming). The British as a whole were also much wealthier, and even poorer people had expectations of spending money on consumer goods which would simply not have been available to their ancestors. All these facts presented problems for the churches. Probably most serious in the long term were the first stirrings of a consumer society, interested in new ways of using leisure time and enjoying a new range of luxuries small and great: but the more immediate problem was posed by the shift in population to large towns concentrated in the North. The established Church of England's strength in pastoral care lay in its intricate patchwork of parishes; yet this structure was at its weakest precisely in those areas which were giving birth to the new population centres. Creating new parishes involved cumbersome and expensive legal procedures. Moreover, the parish worked best at coping with the spiritual needs of its whole population in settled rural communities; since the early Middle Ages, the more mobile and less easily-supervised people of the towns had presented problems to pastors.

II · English Churches in the Eighteenth Century

There were further problems for the Church of England in coping with a complex new situation. The struggles of the seventeenth century had

meant that the church had lost groups of devoted lay-people and clergy in two directions, both Catholic and Evangelical: on the one hand, Non-Jurors, and on the other, Dissenters. There were still High Churchmen among the clergy, particularly influential during the reign of the devout Queen Anne (1702–14), and always sternly resisting any further concessions to Dissenters; but when the Hanoverian George I came to the British throne in 1714, the High Church group were suspected of hankering after the restoration of the exiled Stuart dynasty (the son and grandchildren of James II), and the new government favoured more reliable clergy. These tended to be Latitudinarian in their theology; in other words, they deplored the sort of extremes in doctrine which had led to so much conflict during the seventeenth century, and they regarded Christianity as a reasonable faith, which should play down the mysterious and the awe-inspiring.

Eighteenth-century English society

The Anglican Church had an essential role in society, according to the essayist Joseph Addison (1672–1719):

It is certain that country-people would soon degenerate into a land of savages and barbarians were there not such frequent returns of a stated time, in which the whole village meet together in church with their best faces, and in their cleanest habits, to converse with one another upon indifferent subjects, hear their duties explained to them, and join together in adoration of the Supreme Being.

The great eighteenth-century English pottery manufacturer Josiah Wedgwood (1730–95) had no doubts of the benefits which industrialists like himself conferred on their country: his description of the change in his native Staffordshire is redolent of the exuberant self-confidence and optimism which would characterize English society in the Industrial Revolution:

. . . ask your parents for a description of the country we inhabited when they first knew it; and they will tell you that the inhabitants bore all the marks of poverty to a much greater degree than they do now. Their houses were miserable huts, the land poorly cultivated and yielded little of value for the food of man or beast, and these disadvantages, with roads almost impassable, might be said to have cut off our part of the country from the rest of the world, besides rendering it not very comfortable to ourselves. Compare this picture, which I know to be a true one, with the present state of the same country, the workmen earning near double their former wages, their houses mostly new and comfortable, and the lands, roads and every other circumstance bearing evident marks of the most pleasing and rapid improvements . . . Industry has been the parent of this happy change.

Industrial society might breed radical views which seemed to threaten church and state, as this worried report to the Secretary of War in 1792 makes clear. 'Paine' is the Radical activist Tom Paine (1737–1809); although he was a celebrated free-thinker, the Associations for political reform mentioned here gained their main support in Sheffield not from the religiously unorthodox, but from mainstream Protestant Dissenters.

. . . At Sheffield . . . I found that the seditious doctrines of Paine and the factious people who are endeavouring to disturb the peace of the country had extended to a degree very much beyond my conception; and indeed they seem with great judgment to have chosen this as the centre of all their seditious machinations, for the manufactures of this town are of a nature to require so little capital to carry them on that a man with a very small sum of money can employ two, three or four men; and this being generally the case there are not in this, as in other great towns, any number of persons of sufficient weight who could by their influence, or the number of their dependents, act with any effect in case of a disturbance. As the wages given to the journeymen are very high, it is pretty generally the practice for them to work for three days, in which they earn sufficient to enable them to drink and riot for the rest of the week, consequently there can be no place more fit for seditious purposes.

The mode they have adopted for spreading their licentious principles has been by forming Associations on terms suited to the circumstances of the lowest mechanics, of whom about 2500 are enrolled in the principal Society, and that it may not be confined, they allow any man to be present who will pay 6d for admission . . .

The Latitudinarians

The Latitudinarians included many devout and conscientious pastors, modelling themselves on the learned and talented preacher and Latitudinarian divine John Tillotson (1630–94), who replaced the Non-Juror William Sancroft as Archbishop of Canterbury, but theirs was a 'low-temperature' religion; and too many of them were prepared to profit from the Hanoverian government's wish to keep a tight control over the church's affairs. Governments were aware that bishops' votes in the House of Lords could be useful to get their business through; and potential bishops were keenly aware that there were huge differentials between the most wealthy and the most poorly endowed bishoprics. If a clergyman wanted to mount the ladder to the top financial prizes in the church, it would probably mean paying court to the politicians. This close identification with the government's wishes was bad for the church's morale, and matters were made worse because increasingly, senior positions in the church became the preserve of the nobility and gentry who supported the Hanoverian succession. Many clergy lived on meagre incomes which bore no comparison with the wealth of this clerical élite.

The Dissenters

Protestant Dissent, after its seventeenth-century defeats and disappointments, may have only commanded the allegiance of a quarter of a million of England's six and a half million people by 1760; moreover, it had lost virtually all support among the nobility and gentry who mattered in politics. The more prosperous Dissenters tended to be Presbyterians and Congregationalists rather than Baptists, although the Quakers were settling down now to include many who did well out of commerce and industry. Theologically, Dissent was losing its enthusiasm for the Calvinism which had been such an inspiration to it during the previous century; like the Church of England, it grew to distrust religious fervour, and without the restraints which established status placed on Anglican theology, many Dissenting congregations drifted into Unitarianism, a common theological fashion of the time.

Nevertheless the Dissenters hung on to their identity and also made a substantial contribution to the nation's education by maintaining Dissenting Academies; supplying both school and further education because Dissenters were excluded from Oxford and Cambridge, these were often more advanced and varied in what they provided than the ancient universities. Dissent could also pride itself on its literary heritage; apart from the poetry of John Milton (1608–74), it could boast in the craftsman Independent preacher John Bunyan (1628–88) the author of one of the best-known religious works in the English language, *Pilgrim's Progress*. The ministers Isaac Watts (1674–1748) and Philip Doddridge (1702–51) both wrote hymns which put them among the leaders of sacred song in the Western church; indeed, it was Dissent which kept the most lively tradition of singing hymns in eighteenth-century Britain.

Roman Catholicism in England

The life of Roman Catholicism in eighteenth-century England has some curious similarities to that of Protestant Dissent; in effect, it was treated as a rather peculiar Dissenting sect. The days of heroism in the face of persecution were largely over, although popular anti-Catholicism continued to simmer beneath the surface, and as late as 1780, exploded into an orgy of hatred, random loss of life and destruction of property in the Gordon Riots in London. However, particularly as any prospect of restoration of the Catholic Stuart dynasty faded in the mid-eighteenth century, Catholics were accepted as an eccentric minority who could practise their religion if they were discreet. Many of the gentry families who had sustained the Catholic Church through the

English Dissent

A Dissenter's testimony

Edmund Calamy (1671–1732) achieved fame as the first historian of those who had suffered from the Anglican reaction in 1662. Here he reflects on the trials and privileges of being a Dissenter.

Nor can it be thought unreasonable for us to prize our liberty yet the more, because it comes to us as the fruit of the prayers and tears, the sufferings and hardships, the conflicts and vows of our fathers before us. Some of us, I doubt not, may well remember that in the course of our education, in the midst of their most sorrowful complaints of their own hard usage, they to prevent our being disheartened would freely entertain us with the hopes they had for better things reserved for us. These better things through the great mercy of God we have in good part lived to reach. And therefore we should take heart, cheerfully following them as far as they followed Christ: adhering firmly to the cause of truth and purity, liberty and charity in conjunction and trusting God with the sequel.

Edmund Calamy, *A Continuation of the Account . . . of the Ministers . . . ejected* (1727).

Isaac Watts reflects on time

Isaac Watts here writes not a hymn, but a poetic reflection on the transitoriness of human life; it is a very eighteenth-century touch that a machine, a pocket-watch, should be the subject of his meditation.

My watch, the solitary kind companion
Of my imprisonment, my faithful watch
Hangs by, and with a short repeated sound
Beats like the pulse of time, and numbers off
My woes, a long succession, while the finger
Slow moving points out the slow moving minutes,
The slower hand the hours. O thou dear engine!
Thou little brass accountant of my life.
Would but the mighty wheels of heav'n and nature
Once imitate thy movements and whirl away
These clouded wintry suns, these tedious moons
These midnights!

difficult times were now dying out or being absorbed into the Anglican establishment, but a broader base for Catholicism was emerging in their place among the professional classes of the towns. Leadership of the community through these largely unspectacular years was appropriately in the hands of Bishop Richard Challoner (1691–1781), a shrewd and moderate rather than a colourful pastor; Challoner was the author of a devotional work entitled *The Garden of the Soul* which was a great success among Catholics and, suitably doctored, achieved wide esteem among English Protestants as well.

III · Catholicism in Ireland

Catholic resistance

In Ireland, too, Catholics were enjoying a period of relative calm after a century and a half of misfortune and persecution. Their troubles had begun in the sixteenth century, when the English Crown began taking a more consistent interest in the territories of the Lordship of Ireland which it had held since the twelfth century; part of the new Tudor attempt to turn Ireland into a well-regulated English dominion was the imposition of a church settlement on the subservient Irish Parliament in Dublin. Elizabeth I intended this church to be on the lines of the Church of England, but she faced a very different situation in Ireland: neither the Gaelic-speaking Celtic population nor the descendants of mediaeval English settlers showed much enthusiasm for the government's plans, and there was too much else for the colonial administration to do to give the new church settlement the support which it needed. At the same time, an energetic missionary effort inspired by Counter-Reformation Catholicism and led particularly by the orders of friars, brought the bulk of the Irish, both Gaelic and 'Old English', to associate loyalty to Rome with resistance against the new English colonial pressure. The result was that by 1600 Ireland had two church structures side by side: a Protestant Church recognized by the government and endowed with what remained of the ancient church lands, and a hierarchy recognized by Rome, commanding the allegiance of most of the Gaelic and Old English population.

'Ulster plantations'

The cultural divide which has disfigured Irish life into modern times became acute in the seventeenth century. The government of King James VI and I encouraged Protestants, especially from Scotland, to settle in Ulster, the most strongly Gaelic part of Ireland, as a means of curbing its resistance to the colonial régime. By 1641 the trauma of these 'Ulster Plantations' and the general English assault on traditional Irish patterns of life brought about an explosion of Irish discontent: a full-scale rebellion designed to bring about a Catholic and predominantly Gaelic régime in Ireland. This became part of the wider wars which disrupted the whole British Isles for two decades; in the course of it, both Catholic and Protestant committed atrocities which would have a long life in the folk-memory of the other side. The Catholic cause was thoroughly crushed by Oliver Cromwell's armies and fared little better under the restored Charles II; Irish attempts to uphold the cause of the Catholic James II after he had fled England for Ireland were brought to eventual defeat by William III at the Battle of the Boyne (1690).

The defeat of James II meant that Catholics would now be regarded as second-class citizens, potential traitors to the Protestant regime, and during the early eighteenth century they became victims of a harsh series of Penal Laws, designed (in the words of the Victorian historian W. E. H. Lecky) 'to make them poor and to keep them poor . . . to degrade them into a servile caste'. The Anglican Church of Ireland retained established status, although it represented mainly the small Protestant landowner class which now ruled the country. The bulk of the population remained Catholic despite all hardships, with Presbyterianism strong among the descendants of the Scots settlers in Ulster.

Two churches

The wide support which Catholicism continued to enjoy combined with government lethargy to bring a gradual end to active persecution by the 1730s; the Catholic Church was able to build up a clandestine structure of dioceses and parishes, and even openly maintain houses of the religious Orders. As Rome gradually dropped its support for the exiled Stuart royal family, Catholicism began to seem less of a political threat to the government; and from 1763, Great Britain found itself with a large colonial Catholic population in what had been French Canada. This was bound to soften official attitudes to Irish Catholics; a number of government measures eased the church's position, although there was still harsh legislation against popular unrest among poverty-stricken tenant farmers. Paradoxically, this unrest often united hard-pressed Protestants and Catholics against the exactions of their landlords; yet by the end of the eighteenth century, Catholic political activity was once again alarming rich and poor alike among the Protestant population. In 1797, the first Orange Lodge was founded in Dublin to defend Protestantism, and in the following year, the ruthless suppression of a Catholic insurrection influenced by French revolutionary ideas revived old bitternesses and strengthened the sectarian division in Irish society.

(204)

Why are papists aggrieved?

Josiah Hort (?1674–1751) was the Anglican archbishop of the Irish see of Tuam when in 1745, against the background of Jacobite and Catholic-supported rebellion in Scotland, he issued this pastoral charge to his diocesan clergy. Hort had many Protestant Dissenting friends, including the great Isaac Watts, and here we see his fair-mindedness struggling with his disdain for Catholics.

You will notice that I am not for inciting your people to act offensively towards the Roman Catholics, for they have made ample profession and declarations of remaining quiet and amenable to the government at this time; and I would in charity hope that they are in good earnest; but however, it is the part of wisdom to guard against the worst, while we hope for the best; and I am sure they are best to be trusted when they see us prepare for our defence . . . Your only course must be to visit them at their houses, and to show them by friendly reasonings where their true interest lies . . . You may fairly ask them, if their persons and properties have not been in safety ever since they remained quiet and peaceable . . . Do not their Protestant landlords and masters treat them as kindly as their popish ones? And, do not their poor receive more charity from Protestants than from those of their own religion? Penal laws have indeed been made against them, but chiefly against their priests, for the defence of the government against their dangerous principles and practices; but what do the bulk of the papists feel from these laws? . . . Now, if these are all undeniable facts, what can any modest and reasonable papist desire more, and how can he be aggrieved?

IV · The Evangelical Revival

New religious groups

If English religion in the early eighteenth century was generally characterized by its 'low-temperature' spirituality, the different impulses which made up the Evangelical Revival can be seen as a reaction to this cast of mind. The Evangelical spirit was hungry to save souls, and impatient at what it saw as the obstacles which the existing churches presented to this goal. Some Evangelicals found that they could use the structures of the Church of England to achieve their ends, but some were drawn to found new organizations outside it, particularly in the great outburst of energy which became Methodism, and which had nowhere near ended its growth by 1800; the same impulse also brought new life to the fairly static world of Protestant Dissent. Evangelicalism recalled the enthusiastic partisans of the Protestant Reformation who had grown dissatisfied with the compromise of Elizabeth I's church, and who had fuelled Puritanism; so the Puritans, apparently so resoundingly defeated in the Anglican revival of Charles II's restoration, may be seen as the spiritual forebears of eighteenth-century Evangelicals.

It is difficult to trace the beginnings of the new spirit, but one source must be the voluntary religious societies which were springing up in the Church of England from the 1680s, rather like the *collegia pietatis* of the contemporary German Pietist movement (see Chapter 16 below). Certainly one aspect of Pietism had a direct link with the beginnings of Evangelicalism: the remarkable world-wide missionary activity of Count Zinzendorf's Moravian Brethren, who first made contact with the English religious societies during the 1720s and who, as we shall see, were to have a particular effect on the ministry of John Wesley. Alongside their contribution was the work of a wayward genius, George Whitefield (1714–70), whose sermons were to electrify congregations in Britain and America alike; in increasingly uneasy colleagueship with him were the two brothers John and Charles Wesley (1703–91 and 1707–88 respectively). All three would become and remain priests of the Church of England, but Whitefield and John Wesley were both destined to found institutions beyond its confines.

The Wesley brothers

The Wesleys came from a clerical family which included ministers driven out of the church by the Anglican triumph of 1660–2, but their father and mother were devout High Church Anglicans, Mrs Susanna Wesley indeed becoming a Non-Juror for much of her life. From the close-knit, perhaps rather claustrophobic family life of their father's country rectory, the brothers went to Oxford university, where they became involved in a group of religiously earnest young men who gained the nickname of 'the Holy Club' – the group which from the regularity of its life was also to gain a second rather contemptuous nickname with a very distinguished future career: the 'Methodists'. It was in Oxford in 1732 that they were to meet Whitefield, then a poverty-stricken student from Gloucester. Inspired by the devotional fervour of the High Church party (by now rather beleaguered in the church), the Wesleys were ordained and volunteered as missionaries to the new English American colony of Georgia; on the stormy Atlantic voyage out to America, John first met the Moravians, who much impressed him by their piety and calmness in the face of danger. In other ways the Georgia expedition was a disaster, mainly thanks to John's clumsiness in dealing with the complexities of pastoral problems in the turbulent life of the new colony. Back in England, much chastened, John was to find a new sense of direction through a fresh contact with the Moravians: the experience of 1738 which he was to term 'conversion'.

The 'Aldersgate experience' was to transform John Wesley's ministry; now the German evangelical tradition was to bring a new element to his rooting in Anglican Catholic spirituality and, combined with the chances of the British situation, this powerful mixture was to lead him in a radically new path. Wesley was determined to bring his message of salvation to as many as possible; given the ramshackle organization of the Church of England, he was bound to strike out on his own to achieve this. From 1739 rather diffidently following the lead of George Whitefield in preaching in the open air, he was astonished to find the explosion of feeling which such public proclamation could produce; evidently he was answering a deep yearning for salvation which the established religious institutions could not satisfy.

Methodist organization

Soon Wesley was having to organize thousands of fervent believers into religious societies, and in the process, he revealed himself as having a genius for organization. To finance a movement of such proportions, complete with travelling preachers assisting him, and to provide permanent spiritual fellowship for his people, he improvised a system of classes, each with a leader, and a pattern of circuits for preaching the gospel which would unite these groups: all responsible to a central conference of preachers. This carefully-structured and centralized religious organization made Methodism rather reminiscent of the great religious movements within the Counter-Reformation Catholic Church: and Methodism's appeal to religious emotion, particularly through the inspired hymns of Charles Wesley, also represented a rediscovery of a part of the Catholic Christian heritage which the Reformation had obscured in English religious life.

Anglican reaction

Some Anglican parish clergy were also swept up in evangelical enthusiasm, and gladly co-operated with Wesley; a formidable character like William Grimshaw of Haworth, Yorkshire (1708–63) had the force of personality to turn his whole parish into something like a Methodist circuit. However, more clergy were puzzled by and hostile to this unconventional initiative, which for all Wesley's fierce loyalty to Anglicanism, drifted ever further away from the structures of the church. Such were the provisions of English law on building places of worship that Wesley was forced to register his growing number of chapels as Dissenting meeting-houses, while he himself was responsible for a decisive break with Anglican church order when he began ordinations on his own initiative. The need was desperate, for the occasion was the plight of his Methodist people in North America after the colonists had successfully fought the British government for their independence (1776–83). Wesley, a firm believer in the central value of the eucharist for Christian life, saw that the former colonies had lost most Anglican clergy in the aftermath of the British defeat (there had never been an Anglican bishop in North America, thanks to government obstruction), and determined to make provision of his own; in 1784 he first ordained Dr Thomas Coke (1747–1814) as 'superintendent' for America.

Methodism in America

Wesley was none too happy when Coke and his colleague Francis Asbury (1745–1816) imitated him in taking their own initiative and assumed the title 'bishop' instead of superintendent; the

John Wesley

Wesley's conversion

24 May 1738 has always been given a special place of honour in Methodism as the date of John Wesley's experience of conversion, although modern historians are more inclined to see this as one stage only of a gradual spiritual journey. Characteristically, the experience seems to have begun for Wesley amid the solemnity of Anglican liturgy, and continued through the hearing of a central text of the German Reformation. The Society in Aldersgate had Moravian connections.

In the afternoon I was asked to go to St Paul's [Cathedral, for Evensong]. The anthem was, 'Out of the deep have I called unto Thee, O Lord: Lord, hear my voice . . .' In the evening I went very unwillingly to a society in Aldersgate Street, where one was reading Luther's preface to the Epistle to the Romans. *About a quarter before nine, while he was describing the change which God works in the heart through faith in Christ, I felt my heart strangely warmed. I felt I did trust in Christ, Christ alone for salvation; and an assurance was given me that He had taken away* my *sins, even* mine, *and saved* me *from the law of sin and death.*

Wesley's preaching

Thursday 26 April 1739 – While I was preaching at Newgate on these words, 'He that believeth hath everlasting life', I was insensibly led, without any previous design, to declare strongly and explicitly that God willeth 'all men to be' thus 'saved'; and to pray that, 'if this were not the truth of God, He would not suffer the blind to go out of the way; but, if it were, He would bear witness to His word'. Immediately one, and another, and another sunk to the earth; they dropped on every side as thunderstruck. One of them cried aloud. We besought God in her behalf, and He turned her heaviness into joy. A second being in the same agony, we called upon God for her also; and He spoke peace unto her soul. In the evening I was again pressed in spirit to declare that 'Christ gave Himself a ransom for all'. And almost before we called upon Him to set His seal, He answered. One was so wounded by the sword of the Spirit that you would have imagined she could not live a moment. But immediately His abundant kindness was showed, and she loudly sang of His righteousness.

result was that unlike Methodism in the British tradition, American Methodism has always been episcopal in organization, although it has no doctrine of an episcopal apostolic succession. However, his misgivings did not stop him proceeding with further ordinations for difficult pastoral needs within the British Isles, despite the protests of his more cautious brother Charles. Wesley avoided facing up to the break with the Established Church which his actions had brought nearer, and it was only after his death in 1791 that the Wesleyan Conference was forced into a breach (for long showing its unhappiness at the situation by calling itself a 'Connexion' rather than a separate church). As the Methodist work in Britain continued to expand, the tensions within such an exuberant movement caused many splits and the founding

Wesley and a bishop

Joseph Butler, Bishop of Bristol (1692–1752), was a conscientious clergyman and a very distinguished philosopher, but his encounters with John Wesley were not a success, as this fragment of an interview (18 August 1739) reveals. However, it is worth noting that this comes from Wesley's own memory of what took place!

(Butler) Mr Wesley, I will deal plainly with you. I once thought you and Mr Whitefield well-meaning men; but I cannot think so now. For I have heard more of you: matters of fact, sir. And Mr Whitefield says in his Journal: 'There are promises still to be fulfilled in me.' Sir, the pretending to extraordinary revelations and gifts of the Holy Ghost is a horrid thing – a very horrid thing!
(Wesley) My lord, for what Mr Whitefield says Mr Whitefield, and not I, is accountable. I pretend to no extraordinary revelations, or gifts of the Holy Ghost: none but what every Christian may receive and ought to expect and pray for . . . But pray, my lord, what are those facts you have heard?
(B) I hear you administer the sacrament in your societies.
(W) My lord, I never did yet, and I believe never shall.
(B) I hear, too, that many people fall into fits in your societies, and that you pray over them.
(W) I do so, my lord, when any show by strong cries and tears that their soul is in deep anguish. I frequently pray to God to deliver them from it, and our prayer is often heard in that hour.
(B) Very extraordinary, indeed! Well, sir, since you ask my advice, I will give it to you very freely. You have no business here, you are not commissioned to preach in this diocese. Therefore I advise you to go hence.
(W) My lord, my business on earth is to do what good I can. Wherever, therefore, I think I can do most good, there must I stay, so long as I think so. At present I think I can do most good here; therefore, here I stay. As to my preaching here, a dispensation of the gospel is committed to me, and woe is me if I preach not the gospel wherever I am in the habitable world! Your lordship knows, being ordained a priest, by the commission I then received I am a priest of the Church Universal. And being ordained as Fellow of a College [Lincoln College, Oxford], *I was not limited to any particular cure, but have an indeterminate commission to preach the word of God in any part of the Church of England. I do not therefore conceive that, in preaching here by this commission, I break any human law. When I am convinced I do, then it will be time to ask, 'shall I obey God or man?' But if I should be convinced, in the meanwhile, that I could advance the glory of God and the salvation of souls in any other place more than in Bristol, in that hour, by God's help, I will go hence, which till then I may not do.*

Passages taken from the *Journal* of John Wesley, London 1909, Vol.I, 472–3; II, 184, 256–7.

of new denominations, most of which were at last reunited in 1932.

The Countess of Huntingdon's Connexion

George Whitefield did not found any such large-scale organization, although through his co-operation with the pious English noblewoman Selina, Countess of Huntingdon (1707–91), he was associated with the foundation of the small church known as the Countess of Huntingdon's Connexion. This offshoot, separate from Anglicanism for much the same reasons as John Wesley's Methodists, followed Whitefield in its staunch Calvinism: in this Whitefield grew steadily to be at odds with the Wesleys who, true to their Anglican Catholic background, remained firm believers in the offer of universal salvation (Arminians).

V · The 'Awakenings' in America

Quarrels and controversy

Whitefield belongs as much to the story of American Evangelicalism as to Britain, for his great preaching gifts were to have a marked effect there. The 'Awakenings' in the thirteen British American colonies were intimately connected both with what was going on in British Evangelicalism and, through the presence of Continental Lutheran congregations in North America, also with the older movement of German Pietism. However, there was also a distinctive American dimension: the colonies' roots in Puritan dreams of a new godly Commonwealth which would remedy the corruption of Old England. By the end of the seventeenth century these dreams had come to seem very threadbare, and many felt that the Calvinist Congregationalist establishments of New England had lost their way. Nevertheless, from the 1720s the same Calvinist impulse which had so inspired the early colonists was beginning to produce fresh energy: and frequently fresh quarrels! A group of Presbyterian ministers in the Middle Colonies led by Gilbert Tennent (1703–64) caused controversy by insisting on the importance of individual conversion in church life, in reaction to what they saw as the formalism of much contemporary religion; they found a powerful if unlooked-for ally in George Whitefield when he began a series of spectacular preaching tours in 1739, often reaching great crowds by speaking to them in the open air.

The scenes of wild enthusiasm which Whitefield's sermons generated (although he did not encourage such outbursts) set a tone of emotionalism which was to remain characteristic of 'Revivalism' in American Protestant religion: and even during the eighteenth century, the gulf between this religious style and a more restrained, reflective strain in American Protestantism became obvious. Nevertheless, the character of leadership in the New England Awakenings, to the north of the Middle Colonies, shows that no caricature can be made of the movement as mere simple-minded emotionalism. Here the outstanding figure was Jonathan Edwards (1703–58), firmly in the New England Congregationalist tradition, eventually President of what would become Princeton University and an exponent of Calvinism in rigorous philosophical terms; he was happy to co-operate with Whitefield.

Baptist influence

Not all strands of the Awakenings shared the Calvinism of Tennent, Whitefield and Edwards. In the Southern Colonies, the main growth through revivals came among the Baptists, who largely shared the Arminian theological outlook of the Wesleys; indeed, with the founding of the Sandy Creek Association (1758), the Awakenings was responsible for the founding of a new denomination, the Separate Baptists, which was to have a major influence on the religious life of the South in the United States. In the next decade came the beginnings of Methodist work in the Thirteen Colonies; once Wesley had provided for its leadership, Methodist Episcopal evangelistic work would use the pattern of the revival to become one of the leading forces within American Protestantism.

Varieties of American Protestantism

It is difficult to overestimate the influence of the Awakenings in shaping the American Protestant tradition, and hence the dominant strand of

Whitefield in America

Thursday, Nov. 22 1739. Set out for Neshaminy (twenty miles distant from Trent Town), where old Mr [William] *Tennent lives, and keeps an academy, and where I was to preach to-day, according to appointment. We came thither about twelve, and found above three thousand people gathered together in the meeting-house yard, and Mr William Tennent* [Junior] *preaching to them, because we were beyond the appointed time. When I came up, he soon stopped, and sang a psalm, and then I began to speak. At first the people seemed unaffected, but, in the midst of my discourse, the hearers began to be melted down, and cried much. After I had finished Mr Gilbert Tennent gave a word of exhortation . . .*

After our exercises were over, we went to old Mr Tennent, who entertained us like one of the ancient patriarchs. His wife seemed to me like Elizabeth, and he like Zacharias; both, as far as I can find, walk in all the ordinances and commandments of the Lord blameless . . . It happens very providentially, that Mr Tennent and his brethren are appointed to be a Presbytery by the Synod, so that they intend breeding up gracious youths, and sending them out into our Lord's vineyard. The place wherein the young men study now is, in contempt, called the College. It is a long-house, about twenty feet long, and nearly as many broad; and, to me, it seemed to resemble the school of the old prophets . . . From this despised place, seven or eight worthy ministers of Jesus have lately been sent forth; more are almost ready to be sent; and a foundation is now being laid for the instruction of many others. The devil will certainly rage against them; but the work, I am persuaded, is of God, and will not come to naught. Carnal ministers oppose them strongly; and, because people, when awakened by Mr Tennent, or his brethren, see through them, and therefore leave their ministry, the poor gentlemen [Tennent's ministers] *are loaded with contempt, and looked upon as persons who turn the world upside-down.*

Friday, Nov. 23. Parted with dear Mr Tennent and his worthy fellow-labourers; but promised to remember each other publicly *in our prayers. Rode to Abingdon, about ten miles from Neshaminy, and preached to above two thousand people from a porch-window belonging to the meeting-house. It is surprising how such bodies of people, so scattered abroad, can be gathered at so short a warning. At Neshaminy, I believe there were nearly a thousand horses. The people, however, did not sit upon them to hear the sermon, as in England, but tied them to the hedges; and thereby much disorder was prevented. As soon as I had done, I had fresh invitations to go to several places, should time and business permit. Though it was cold, the people stood very patiently in the open air, and seemed in no hurry to return home after the discourses were ended.*

George Whitefield's Journals, Banner of Truth 1960, 354–5.

English-speaking Protestantism in the world today. The immediate effect was to increase still further the varied character of American Protestantism, and to make it unrealistic for any one Protestant church to seek dominance and privileges from the civil government; this was another factor in encouraging the separation of church and state which has become such a feature of American life. In addition, this variety helped each Protestant church to see itself as part of a greater whole; it was thus in the American Protestant mix that the idea of a denomination, renouncing a claim to represent the entire identity of Christianity, came to maturity. Particularly in the South, the evangelistic concern of the Awakenings prompted a greater interest in bringing Christian faith to the black slave population, who in return would reward undeserving white Christianity with the gift of their own rich spiritual life. Moreover, the Christianity of the Awakenings was filled with a sense of expectancy, self-confidence and excitement which was to become characteristic of American life in general, quite apart from religion; and so the Awakenings contributed powerfully to the ethos of what is now one of the world's two super-powers.

For further reading

S. F. Ahlstrom, *A Religious History of the American People*, Yale University Press 1972

J. C. Brauer, *Protestantism in America*, SCM Press and Westminster Press 1966

H. Brogan, *The Longman History of the United States of America*, Longmans 1985

Rupert Davies, A. Raymond George and Gordon Rupp (eds.), *A History of the Methodist Church in Great Britain*, Volume 1, Epworth Press 1965

A. D. Gilbert, *Religion and Society in Industrial England. Church, Chapel and Social Change, 1740–1914*, Longmans 1976

C. S. C. McAvoy, *A History of the Catholic Church in the United States of America*, University of Notre Dame Press 1970

N. Sykes, *Church and State in England in the Eighteenth Century*, Cambridge University Press 1934

M. R. Watts, *The Dissenters*, Volume 1, *From the Reformation to the French Revolution*, Oxford University Press 1976

16

The Church in the Age of Enlightenment and Revolution

Europe in the Eighteenth Century

St Verny in the vineyards at Orcot (Limagne).

From the end of the seventeenth century, new attitudes to religion became evident. At the same time, religious elements from the seventeenth century were strongly carried over into the eighteenth. However, from the middle of this century signs of flexibility began to appear in the church. This can be explained by the philosophy of the Enlightenment, some representatives of which militated against Christianity. Signs of life were, however, evident in Catholicism and in Protestantism, which experienced revivals in several ways. The French Revolution appeared as the triumph of the Enlightenment and the enemies of the church. But the persistence of a faith purified by trial forced the political powers to restore to the church its place in society.

I · Changes in the Eighteenth Century

1. A traditional church gathers speed

The fruits of the previous century

It was at the beginning of the eighteenth century that the renewal efforts of the century before bore full fruit: the training of the clergy, the purification of religious devotions, the development of missions, regular forms of worship and so on. Most of Europe remained Christian with regional variations. On the eve of 1789, ninety-five per cent of the population of rural areas, almost the whole of France, were still Easter communicants. This helps us to understand the religious restoration in the nineteenth century.

The Jansenist quarrel was also part of the heritage from the preceding century. It continued throughout the eighteenth century. For the most part, the French bishops had accepted the condemnations of the bull *Unigenitus* (1713). Some of them, however, led by the Archbishop of Paris, rejected the Bull and appealed to a General Council. This group of 'appellants' proved to be extremely active, in spite of their relatively small numbers. It was notable as much for its Gallicanism, i.e. its support of France, as for its doctrinal Jansenism. In this context the priests of Utrecht, unhappy about the Roman orientation of their church, elected an archbishop who had himself consecrated by an 'appellant' French bishop. That is the origin of the schism of Utrecht (the Jansenist church or the Old Catholic Church of Holland).

In France, the government tried to quash this opposition by imprisonments, by condemning Soanen, Bishop of Senez, at the Council of Embrun in 1727, and by various repressive measures. In 1728 the appellants created a clandestine journal, the *Ecclesiastical News*, which managed to keep going until the end of the century. In 1730 they saw miraculous cures performed at the tomb of one of their number, the deacon Paris, in the cemetery of St Médard, as a sign of divine approval. Soon, pathological phenomena occurred: convulsions and cures (of blows and wounds received by the penitents). The movement descended into the ridiculous.

The eighteenth century also had its forms of sanctity with figures as different as Alfonsus Liguori (1696–1787) and Benedict Labre (1748–1783). The former, a doctor of the church, freed the church from Jansenist influence through his moral writing, and gave a new vigour to popular mission by founding the Redemptorists. The latter commended a contemplative saintliness to be achieved by travelling on pilgrimage after pilgrimage, in poverty and squalor.

Signs of flexibility

From 1750 onwards, areas of lukewarm feeling became evident on the French religious scene. Religious practice declined dramatically in some towns but also in some parts of the countryside. The decline in religious legacies (for the celebration of masses, gifts for good works), the decline in the number of brotherhoods, a slackening off in morality and fear inspired by the church (in the matter of birth control, the increase of illegitimate children), a falling off in vocations, a decline in religious reading, the taking over of charitable works by the state, and so on were regarded as a set-back. However, we have to be careful how we interpret these things. Certainly the signs indicate a lessening in conformity and routine. But would it not be better to speak of the slow disappearance of one type of Christianity in favour of another, rather than of de-Christianization? According to some people, two curves crossed each other, a quantitive descending one and a qualitative rising one.

Mediocre training and clergy

We know of many priests and bishops who were first-rate. However, absenteeism was still common among the bishops. The more the century progressed, the more the episcopate became the preserve of the nobility, both in France and Germany. The monasteries fell to wrack and ruin. In France, from 1766 onwards, the Commission of Regulars suppressed 426 houses. In 1783 Joseph II suppressed all the contemplative houses in Austria and the Low Countries.

Popes without prestige

The popes were nonentities. They were almost all old men chosen at the end of conclaves made interminable by the intrigues of Catholic powers. They entangled themselves in the government of the Papal States, which were said to be worse administered than those of the Grand Turk. The only one to stand out was Benedict XIV (1740–1750), who was interested in the sciences and was comparatively open to the problems of his time.

2. The Enlightenment attack on Christianity

The triumph of reason

At the end of the seventeenth century a 'crisis of the European conscience' arose. One of its main witnesses was Pierre Bayle (*Thoughts on the Comet*, 1682; *Historical and Critical Dictionary*,

A society of atheists can be perfectly moral

Pierre Bayle (1647–1706), born a Calvinist, became a Catholic for a few years and then returned to being a Calvinist. He taught philosophy and history at Sedan and then at Rotterdam. Bayle was critical of all religious confessions, including Calvinism, preaching tolerance all his life.

A society of atheists would practise civil and moral actions just as well as other societies, provided that it saw that crimes were severely punished and that it attached honour and infamy to certain things. As ignorance of the first Creator Being and Conserver of the world would not prevent the members of this society from being sensitive to glory and scorn, to recompense and punishment, and to all the passions we can see in other men, and would not quench all the light of reason, one would see among them people who kept good faith in trading, who helped the poor, who were opposed to injustice, who were loyal to their friends . . . Anyone who wants to be fully convinced that a people lacking in the knowledge of God would make itself rules of honour and be very careful to observe them has only to see that among Christians there is a certain worldly honour which is directly contrary to the spirit of the gospel . . .

Compare the manners of some nations who profess Christianity; compare them, I say, one with another, and you will see that what goes for dishonesty in one country is not so deemed in another. Therefore it must be that the ideas of honesty which prevail among Christians do not come from the religion which they profess.

Pierre Bayle, *Thoughts on the Comet*, 1682.

1695–7). In the eighteenth century a group of writers came into prominence: Voltaire, Diderot, d'Alembert. Brought up as Christians, often by the Jesuits, these 'philosophers' wanted to judge everything according to the 'light' of reason, which they set against the obscurities of Christian revelation. What should be remembered about this Enlightenment philosophy is its aspect as an anti-Christian war machine. Without denying it, it has to be said that this ideal of reason also corresponds to a distinction of spheres. Science takes on a language of its own and dissociates itself from metaphysics. Sincere Christians shared this passion for reason. The Freemasons, whose first lodge was founded in London in 1717 and who propagated this Enlightenment ideology, thought of themselves as Christians. The reference work of the Enlightenment, the *Encyclopaedia* or *Rational Dictionary of Science, Art and Crafts* (1751–1772), included the future Pius VII among its subscribers, and at least to begin with, theologians were involved in producing it.

Reason against revelation

Explicit atheism was rare. It would have been dangerous to express it openly. Many were able to pride themselves on it secretly: the priest Meslier (who died in 1729), d'Holbach, Helvetius, Sade. The majority of 'philosophers' thought that there was need for a religion for the people. God was a guarantor of order. Most of them were inclined towards deism, a natural religion which did not go against reason and which excluded all revelation: God became Voltaire's 'Great Watchmaker', 'a pensioner flung on the scrap heap'. Dogma was contrasted with reason and nature. The church stood out by reason of its intolerance and its support of tyranny. Voltaire campaigned for the rehabilitation of several victims of religious intolerance. In refusing to follow nature, Christianity was a

Christianity is opposed to nature

In their private writings, authors could express their thought freely; in their publications, they had to be somewhat prudent.

Revealed morality is not compatible with natural morality

Every devotee is hard, pitiless, implacable, a poor husband, a poor citizen, a bad brother, and so on. These duties are too subordinated to others.

One of the worst effects of religious duties is the degradation of natural duties; it is a ladder of chimeric duties raised up above real duties. Ask a priest whether it is worse to piss in a chalice than to slander an honourable woman. 'Piss in a chalice – sacrilege!', he will tell you. There is no public punishment for calumny, but there is the fire for sacrilege. The result is to reverse any real distinction of crimes in a society.

There are two moralities in the gospel, the book to which we must refer, or be completely ignorant on this point. There is a general morality common to all people. And there is a morality which is truly Christian morality. Now the latter is the most anti-social morality that I know. Take the trouble to re-read the Sermon on the Mount. Re-read the whole gospel and select the distinctive precepts of Christianity; then tell me whether there is anything more capable of unloosing human ties, of whatever nature.

Diderot, Unpublished commentary on the *Letter on Man.*

I believe in God, though I get on very well with atheists. It is very important not to mistake hemlock for parsley; but it does not matter whether one does or does not believe in God.

Diderot to Voltaire, 11 June 1749.

The Religion of Rousseau

In the face of the rationalism of Enlightenment philosophy, Jean-Jacques Rousseau rehabilitated religious sentiment in a sense which is not that of Catholic orthodoxy, but prepared for Romantic religion.

The profession of faith of a pastor in the Savoy

I also confess that the majesty of the Scriptures astounds me, and that the holiness of the gospel speaks to my heart. Consider the books of the philosophers with all their pomp; how petty they are alongside Scripture! Can it be that a book both so sublime and so simple can be the work of human hands? Can it be that he whose history it tells was only a human being himself? . . .

The death of Socrates, in philosophical tranquillity with his friends, is the sweetest that one could desire; that of Jesus, expiring in torment, injured, mocked, cursed by all people, is the most horrible that one could fear. On taking the cup of poison Socrates blesses those who offer it to him, weeping; Jesus, in the midst of frightful torture, prays for his relentless executioners. If the life and death of Socrates are those of a wise man, the life and death of Jesus are those of a God . . .

For all that, this same gospel is full of incredible things, of things which are repugnant to reason, and which are impossible for any sane man either to conceive of or admit. What does one do in the midst of these contradictions? My child, one must always be modest and circumspect, respect in silence what one can neither reject nor understand, and humble oneself before the great Being who alone knows the truth.

Jean-Jacques Rousseau, *Emile.*

hindrance to the good nature of humanity. So it was necessary to struggle for the overthrow of the church and Christianity: 'let us obliterate the infamy', proclaimed Voltaire. The primacy of reason did not prevent the end of the eighteenth century from rediscovering a taste for esoteric things and a new irrationality. Dissatisfied with the dry rationalism of Voltaire, Jean-Jacques Rousseau (1712–1778) wanted to restore sentiment to its right place in a natural religion. He thus enabled religion to get over the hurdles of the Revolution and prepare for Romanticism.

3. The church stamped by Enlightenment philosophy

Catholic enlightenment

The church tried to defend itself against attacks by the traditional methods: the censorship of pernicious books; a demand for the state powers to intervene; apologetic works, none of which was very striking. However, the rational ideal was not looked upon by the churches only in a negative way. It inspired achievements and reforms at the heart of Catholicism. In France, some titles took account of the spirit of the time: *An Easy Way of Being Happy in this Life and Ensuring Eternal Happiness; A Philosophical Catechism; A Catechism of the Harmony between Reason and Religion*. In Germany the Catholic Enlightenment suggested a return to the sources, a purification of worship, a renewal of tolerance and a rapprochement with the Protestants. Catechisms were developed which could be used by Protestants and Catholics alike. One of the most striking representatives of this movement was J.M. Sailer (1731–1832), a Bavarian priest and professor of pastoral theology, who took various initiatives in spirituality and practised an ecumenism before that was invented (an interconfessional Bible circle).

Anti-Romanism and enlightenment despotism

It happened that these innovative movements coincided with the anti-Roman movements aimed at increasing the standing of the local churches and their clergy over against the pope: Gallicanism and so on. Von Hontheim (1701–1790), known as Febronius, the coadjutor Bishop of Trier, gave his name to a doctrine which reduced the power of the pope in the church as far as possible: Febronianism (1763). The Synod of Pistoia, held in Tuscany in 1786 and convened by a Jansenist bishop at the instigation of Grand Duke Leopold, brother of the Emperor Joseph II, upheld the tenets of Febronianism and suggested a wide programme of church reform in the spirit of the Enlightenment. Joseph II gave his name to a finicky type of interference in the life of the church: Josephism. Non-Catholics benefited from the Edicts of Tolerance in 1781. Joseph II ruled that religious orders were not to be dependent on a foreign leader. He suppressed contemplative convents in order to make use of their wealth to found new parishes. He completely reformed the seminaries, to the dissatisfaction of the seminarians, who wrecked the premises. A sacristan king, he laid down rules governing the liturgy, burial, the use of bells and so on.

The martyrdom of the Jesuits

Faced with a very weak papacy, the 'enlightened' despots sought to become masters of the church. They associated the principles of the Enlightenment and the Catholic Enlightenment with old claims (Gallicanism), so the suppression of the Society of Jesus by the different Catholic states and then by Pope Clement XIV in 1773 was the result of the combined efforts of philosophers, Gallicans, Jansenists and other religious orders. The Jesuits suffered the consequences of the decadence of the European monarchies and the papacy, formerly their firmest support, but also of their relentless determination in theological conflicts. Over this, the popes showed themselves to be completely subservient to the ruling powers, and remained insensible to the sufferings of the Jesuits. Their repatriation from the missions took place in terrible conditions. Clement caused the last General of the Jesuits to be imprisoned, and in prison he died. In Portugal, the Marquis of Pombal had more than eighty Jesuits executed.

II · The Revivals in Protestantism and in the Eastern Churches

In the churches of the Reformation, the spirit of the Enlightenment often pointed theology along the path of rationalism and cultural secularization. At the same time, on many occasions revivalist movements tried to stir the churches out of the torpor of being state institutions.

1. German pietism

Pietism was a reaction against the worldly tendencies of Protestantism at the end of the seventeenth and beginning of the eighteenth centuries. The Protestant churches were official state

(210)

Mystical nostalgia in a Lutheran

Johannes Scheffler (Angelus Silesius) (1624–1677), who came from Breslau, went to several European universities before returning to his native Silesia. A Lutheran, he expressed his mystical experience through little two-line poems in the *Cherubic Pilgrim*, which he published after being converted to Catholicism.

Though Christ were born a thousand times in Bethlehem and not in you,
You would remain lost eternally.

Alas, we humans are like little birds in the forest;
we utter our cries together, each singing our note with you.

There is no reason for a rose; it blossoms because it blossoms.
It does not call attention to itself, does not ask whether anyone can see it.

Unless paradise is first within you,
believe me, you will never enter it.

O noble spirit, tear off your bonds, and do not let yourself be chained in this way;
You can find God more magnificently than all the saints.

Blossom, frozen Christian, the month of May is at your door.
You will be dead for eternity unless you blossom here and now.

institutions. Personal experience like that of Luther had given way to doctrinal orthodoxy. Many Protestants would have liked to restore first place to the personal element in faith. Protestantism was always distrustful of mysticism, which it regarded as the unclean side of religion compared to faith alone. However, some nostalgic people continued to read *The Imitation of Christ* and mediaeval authors. Jakob Boehme (1575–1624), the shoemaker from Gorlitz, worked out a kind of pantheism and mystical syncretism which was suspect to Lutheran orthodoxy. (210) Angelus Silesius (Johannes Scheffler, 1642–1677), influenced by Boehme, expressed a deep spiritual experience by means of original poetry in his *Cherubic Pilgrimage*. The opposition he encountered led him to become a convert to Catholicism and later a priest.

Philip Spener and the development of pietism

Pietism was a way of giving voice to these aspirations at the heart of Protestantism. Philip Spener (1635–1705), a Lutheran pastor from Alsace, was its instigator. He travelled much around Europe and gathered around him small groups to read the Bible and pray. These we know as the *collegia pietatis* (prayer or study groups). (211) From this came the term pietism, which originally was a form of mockery. Spener laid the foundation for his work in his *Pia Desideria* (Pious Wishes, 1675), of which the essential points were: the setting up of small groups to study the Bible, the recognition of a universal priesthood, the importance of experience over theology, charity in theological polemics, an integration with mediaeval spirituality and a reform of preaching in a catechetical direction. The experience of conversion was all-important, and was acquired by undergoing a deep crisis. Children of God go through an initial period of despair and then, through inner struggle, they come out of their confusion and find peace. Through this experience they gain inexpressible happiness, and have to give public expression to it. Pietism endorsed an affective and sentimental piety and restored good works to an important place.

Pietism, the main influence of which came

Pietism

Philip Spener (1635–1705), a Lutheran pastor who came from Alsace, wanted to reintroduce emotion to religion without departing from Protestantism.

The Christian religion does not consist in abstract knowledge of it, in subtleties relating to idle questions, of the kind which people are inclined to engage in beyond measure in our day; it consists in coming to know our Saviour Jesus Christ, the true God, as he must be known, by means of his Word, in fearing him from our innermost depths, loving him and calling on him, moved by a true faith, in obeying him on the cross and in his life, in loving others from the bottom of our heart, in helping them by taking pity on them. And for ourselves, in our lives, in the presence of danger and death, it consists in abandoning ourselves with an unquenchable confidence to the grace that Christ gives us, looking to eternal life with God.

Philip Spener, *Pia Desideria, or Aspirations from the bottom of the heart for the betterment of the true evangelical churches which may be agreeable to God.*

from the University of Halle in Saxony, gave birth to numerous charitable institutions such as schools and colleges, prompted missions to foreign countries, and inspired musicians such as Handel (died 1759). In spite of some opposition from Lutheran orthodoxy to the rather exalted 'assemblies of the saints', a large part of eighteenth-century Germany was pietistic. It was Count Zinzendorf who was to give pietism an international dimension.

2. Zinzendorf (1700–1760), the enlightened despot

Nicholas Ludwig, Count Zinzendorf, the godson of Spener, was born in Dresden. Raised in an atmosphere of very feminine piety, and deprived of male friends, he always looked on Jesus as a brother. From his childhood, he realized that religion is a matter of the heart and not of reason. At Halle, he underwent a deep experience at the time of his first communion, but rejected the regulated conversion of the pietists. While he was travelling through Europe, meetings with Christians of all persuasions made him see in them simple specializations of the truth. In 1727 he welcomed to his estates refugees from the Moravian brotherhood, heirs of the Hussites, and reorganized them into a kind of theocracy marked by his authoritarianism. Zinzendorf had himself ordained pastor, and then Moravian bishop. He stayed in the Lutheran church, but accepted that all shades of Protestantism should exist side by side and gave his group a pietist stamp. The community was structured and divided into grades according to spiritual advancement and stations in life: groups of married couples, young girls, widows, children, and so on. Prayer, interspersed with singing, went on day and night.

Worldwide expansion

Banned from Saxony in 1738 because of these innovations, Zinzendorf became a missionary. He sent Moravian brothers to America, and stayed there himself for a few years. There were groups affiliated to the brothers throughout the whole of Europe. After his return to Saxony, Zinzendorf narrowed down his interests. To the mode of inspiration in Lutheranism and pietism, which gave an important place to sentiment and the passion in the Christian life, together with the joy of being saved, he added a certain childlike attitude towards Jesus and developed the festive side of worship. Shortly after the death of Zinzendorf the Moravians became a new Christian denomination: The Church of the Unity of Brethren. The Moravians by then had 226 missionaries throughout the world.

The increased importance attached to sentiment sometimes led to a hostility to dogmatism which was in tune with the rationalism of the Enlightenment. But Pietism gave Protestantism a new impetus. The Moravian brothers were a direct inspiration to the Methodism of John Wesley.

Nicolas-Ludwig von Zinzendorf (1700–1760)

Count Zinzendorf, brought up in Pietism, revived the Moravian Brothers, the heirs of the Hussites. In an authoritarian way he made them into a community in which emotionalism and missionary zeal had pride of place. The Count's piety had a very special place for Jesus. Here he is talking to children.

It was always my good fortune to feel my Saviour constantly in my heart . . . I have lived for many years after the fashion of a child with him; I have spoken with him for hours, like a friend with his friend . . . In my conversations with him I was very happy and I expressed my gratitude for all the good that he had done through his incarnation . . . I did what I could to be happy until that extraordinary day on which I was so deeply moved by what my Creator had suffered for me that I began by shedding a thousand tears and attached myself to him even more firmly and was united with him in tenderness. I continued to talk to him when I was alone, and I believed with all my heart that he was very close to me . . . So it is that I have lived for more than fifty years with my saviour and I find myself happier every day.

3. The Eastern Churches

Peter the Great

Tsar Peter the Great (1694–1725) showed a readiness for an authoritarian modernism of Russia in the spirit of the Enlightenment. Having forbidden for a period of twenty years the election of a patriarch of Moscow, in 1721 he suppressed the patriarchy and imposed a spiritual rule on the Russian church. From then on there would be a college, the Holy Synod, made up of bishops and priests, at the head of the church. This Synod was presided over by a lay procurator appointed by the Tsar. The procurator became the real chief administrator of the church, which lost all independence over against the ruling powers. Catherine II (1762–1796) continued this secularization of the church.

A living spiritual tradition

Quite independently of political upsets, the Orthodox spiritual tradition remained alive in the Greek world as well as the Russian. Mount Athos continued to be the great religious heart of all Orthodoxy. In 1782 a monk of Athos, Nicodemus the Hagiorite, and Macarius, Bishop of Corinth, published in Venice the *Philokalia* (love of beauty), which brought together all the patristic texts on prayer from the earliest times, and in particular what was called the Jesus prayer (see Vol.1, p.189). Translated into Russian by another monk of Athos, Paissy Velichkovsky, in 1793, the *Philokalia* enjoyed a great success in the Slavonic countries, a success which was boosted still more in the nineteenth century by the use which was made of it in *Tales of a Russian Pilgrim*. The monastic spiritual tradition was illustrated, too, by other figures like St Tikhon, who was Bishop of Voronezh before becoming a monk of Zadonsk.

Saint Tikhon of Zadonsk (1724–1783)

The life of Tikhon was written by one of his fellow-monks, Tcheboratev.

He never set out on foot or in a carriage without taking his psalter which he always carried under his gown, since it was a small book. He ended up knowing the whole psalter off by heart. He also blessed me with this book. On his journey wherever he was going, he would always read his psalter aloud; sometimes he would sing the verses very loudly. He went to mass every day and sang himself in a choir stall; he rarely sang without bursting into tears. At the monastery of T, towards midnight, he went round the church and prayed in front of every door, genuflecting; at the same time he burst into floods of tears. I witnessed this. Sometimes I listened and heard him say 'Glory to God in the highest' and read the sacred psalms. He prayed in front of the west door for more than half an hour; then he returned to his cell with rapid steps. There he worked hard; sometimes he cut his own wood . . . One day he had gone for a walk behind the monastery; when he got back he said to me: 'In the forest I saw a tree stump from which one could make two cart loads of firewood or even more. Bring the axe to chop it up.' We went into the forest and began to swing the axe; he took off his gown and began to work in his shirt. He used to say to us: 'He who lives at ease does not cease to sin.' He never took his ease. In the morning, before mass, he would write edifying books which are still around today; they are read by many people who aspire to the salvation of their souls.

He would feed the orphans and the needy; he was charitable towards all poverty and all distress. He gave away all that he had . . . Nobles and rich merchants would give him large sums of money. But not content to distribute all his money to the poor, he also gave away his linen and kept only what he wore.

The Maronite church

Among the churches of the Middle East, the Lebanese Maronite church was physically attached to the Roman church. That is to say, it received close attention not only from the papacy but also from French ambassadors and missionaries. Unfortunately these attentions took the form of a desire to Latinize this church. The Synod of Mount Lebanon, held in 1736 under the presidency of a Roman envoy, bears witness to this.

III · The Shock of the Revolution

With the French Revolution, some of the spirit of the Enlightenment became reality: the triumph of reason in politics and the war with Christianity. Carried by the conquering armies, revolutionary ideas took over the whole of Europe. If the French clearly distinguished the Revolution from the Napoleonic era, Europeans considered the two periods a single whole. Napoleon, 'Robespierre on horseback', spread a revolutionary ideology as far as the steppes of Russia.

1. A new church organization

The clergy and the beginnings of the Revolution

In an attempt to resolve a financial and political crisis, the royal government convened the States-General, and there was a gathering of representatives of the three orders which made up the country: the clergy, the nobility and the Third Estate. The lists of grievances expressed desires for reform in the church as much as in other areas of national life. It was not possible, however, to detect any particular animosity against religion. All the delegates, including Robespierre, took part in a candlelight procession on 5 May 1789 which marked the opening of the assembly. The clergy were represented by a majority of priests who agreed to join up with the delegates of the Third Estate to form the National Constituent Assembly.

In view of the claims and the troubles in the countryside, on the night of 4 August the clergy and the nobility renounced all their privileges. On 26 August the Assembly voted the *Declaration of the Rights of Man and of the Citizen*, the fundamental principles of the new régime. The

Declaration took its inspiration from the doctrines of the Enlightenment philosophers and the American Bill of Rights proclaimed at the moment of United States independence in 1776. Freedom, equality and the right of ownership were the inalienable rights. On 2 November 1789, at the suggestion of Talleyrand, Bishop of Autun, the wealth of the clergy was put at the disposal of the nation, thus becoming national property. The state took over the support of the clergy and the services which they provided (aid, teaching, etc.). As the church owned a sixth of all the land in the country, the sale of church goods involved an unprecedented transfer of property. Since it was acquired by the bourgeoisie and the rich farmers, the national wealth swung these two classes in favour of the revolution. Unfortunately, this was also the origin of a devastation of many artistic riches: churches and monasteries were demolished or transformed for new uses. On 13 February 1790 the Constituent Assembly forbade the taking of religious vows. Those who wanted to carry on with a regular religious life could do so in houses, where they re-formed their groups. For the male monasteries, it was a real haemorrhage: at Cluny thirty-eight monks out of forty hung up their habits. In the women's convents the loyalty was much greater. However, the measure scarcely disturbed Catholic opinion.

The oath to the Civil Constitution.
A caricature: 'How to get the oath from bishops and aristocrats' (Bibliothèque nationale).

The Civil Constitution of the Clergy

The Constituent Assembly, which had completely reorganized the government and administration of France, wanted to harmonize the organization of the church with it. Those who were behind the *Civil Constitution of the Clergy* were not anti-religious, but greatly influenced by the spirit of the Enlightenment, by Gallicanism, and by the guiding principles of Josephism or the Synod of Pistoia. The geography of the church was completely reshaped. The dioceses were reduced from 135 to 85, one per department, of which ten were archdioceses. There was to be one parish for every 6000 inhabitants. Bishops and priests would be elected by the same electors, including non-Catholics, who elected the various officials of the department or district. In this way the legislators thought to return to the origins of the church. A bishop would require his metropolitan (archbishop) to install him; he would write to the pope only to inform him of his appointment and to assure him that he was in communion with him. This constitution was voted in on 12 July 1790 and reluctantly proclaimed by the king on 24 August.

The constitutional oath

However, the objections raised at the time of the discussion were taken up again by thirty out of thirty-two bishops deputed to the Constituent Assembly. They did this in a document in which they protested against the fact that the modification of the status of the church had been carried out without the pope's agreement (October 1790). The pope did not reply immediately. On 27 November 1790 the assembly directed that all practising members of the clergy should take an

(214)

Pope Pius VI condemns the principles of the French Revolution

In the letter *Quod aliquantum* of 10 March 1791 the pope condemned

. . . this absolute liberty which not only assures people of the right not to be disturbed about their religious opinions but also gives them this licence to think, write and even have printed with impunity all that the most unruly imagination can suggest about religion. It is a monstrous right, but it would seem to the Assembly to derive from the equality and the freedom natural to all men. But what could be more senseless than to establish among men equality and this unbridled freedom which seems to quench reason . . . What is more contrary to the rights of the creator God who limited human freedom by prohibiting evil, than 'this liberty of thought and action which the National Assembly accords to man in society as an inalienable right of nature'?

oath of allegiance to the nation and the king and swear to uphold the constitution, which included the new church organization. Only 7 bishops out of 160 took the oath; as for the priests, the proportions varied depending on the area: over the whole of France it was about half. True, some had their reservations, since they did not know the pope's position. Those who had not taken the oath were not allowed to exercise their ministry, and were replaced towards the end of 1790: constitutional bishops were elected and priests ordained.

Papal condemnation

In March-April 1791 Pope Pius VI condemned the *Civil Constitution of the Clergy* and those principles which prompted the legislators in Paris. The Rights of Man were contrary to revelation: they ignored the rights of God and truth by extolling freedom to the exclusion of all else. The pope demanded that all those who had taken the oath should retract, and prohibited the newly-elected bishops from exercising their functions. It was schism. On the one hand there

The abbey of Cluny, sold as a national possession in 1798, demolished under the Directory, the Empire and the Restoration. On the left are the wings of monastic buildings reconstructed in the middle of the eighteenth century.

A Revolutionary Christ

In 1790 and 1791 some priests and pamphleteers attempted to portray Jesus as the first of the revolutionaries. They did not bring about a real change of thought. In subsequent years the Revolution was violently anti-religious.

Jesus was a true sans-culotte, *a full-blooded republican. He developed all the principles of moral equality and the purest patriotism. He faced every danger; he rebelled against the great who in all periods have abused their powers. He castigated the harshness of the rich; he attacked the pride of kings and priests.*

The Son of God rebelled against the aristocrats of the nation. Meditate on this important truth, my brothers. He did not cease to be indignant in public about the tyrants of the people, those who exacted unjust taxes, the despots of thought, all the oppressors. The unworthy aristocrats deceived the multitudes who grovelled before their pride: they instilled into the vile soul of their slaves the rage which drove them against the liberator of humanity. My brothers, having said this I would die happy: 'It was the aristocracy which crucified the Son of God.'

was the constitutional church, the only one recognized by the state, which had taken over the places of worship; on the other there was a resisting church which remained faithful to Rome. We must not simplify things too much. Not every priest who took the oath (the jurors) was necessarily bad or corrupt, nor were those who refused (the non-jurors) necessarily heroes. There were many different motives. Some priests took the oath so that they could stay in their parishes. Many of the constitutional bishops were very worthy pastors, such as Abbot Gregory, Bishop of Loir and Cher. However, the haste to elect new bishops and then to ordain priests meant that some dubious choices were made.

2. A way of the cross for the Church of France

For about a decade, religious life was deeply troubled in France, even without the violence that continued. Until the spring of 1792 the non-juring church was tolerated. Deprived of

An example of an anti-religious masquerade. In the background is the banner of St Roch; on the right is a figure disguised as a bishop; a chalice is being desecrated (Bibliothèque nationale).

places of worship, priests who had refused the oath celebrated elsewhere. Sometimes burials, baptisms and weddings were causes for dispute. After the Legislative Council had declared war on Austria in April 1792 and French defeats were mounting, resisting priests were seen as enemies within and were deported (expelled). The bishops had already emigrated. It was the turn of the priests, of whom 30,000 to 40,000 left for countries throughout the whole of the rest of Europe. Those who stayed were liable to be arrested.

War on religion

Internal and external problems led to a toughening up of the measures against the non-jurors, and soon against all forms of religious life. About 300 church people who had been imprisoned as non-jurors perished in the course of the massacres of September 1792, being numbered among a thousand victims. In the same month the civil register (of births, marriages and deaths) was taken away from the clergy and entrusted to the civil authorities. Divorce became legal. The constitutional church lost what little prestige it had, because no one any longer had need to consult it officially. The execution of the King, Louis XVI, on 21 January 1793 had more than a political significance. For a Christian it was an unforgivable sin to lay hands on the Lord's anointed. This, together with a refusal to be conscripted, was the origin of uprisings in Western France, the Vendée and Britanny, cruel wars which claimed hundreds of thousands of victims.

The Reign of Terror

The hatred of Christianity and the wish to destroy it reached its peak during the Terror, which lasted from September 1793 to July 1794. A

Revolutionary de-Christianization

One of the forms of the de-Christianization campaign in 1793–1795 was to ask priests to renounce their priesthood by sending back their letters of priesthood.

Letter from Bevalet, former Episcopal Vicar at Strasbourg, to the President of the National Convention

25 Brumaire, the year 1793, second year of the one and indivisible French Republic

Citizen President,

I am sending you my letters of priesthood. I ask you to pay my respects to the Convention. The sole title of honour that I am keeping is a civic certificate, earned by the zeal which I have not ceased to show, since the revolution, for the rights of humanity and the glory of the republic; it is a certificate to which I attach some value.

First priest of the former province of Alsace to be decorated with the national cockade; first to take the oath; first to give away his silver buckles and to make his patriotic gift; creator of the Popular Society of Belfort; the first in Strasbourg to tear away the veil of hypocrisy with which superstition and fanaticism were covered in this city . . . and lastly the first to be wherever the voice of my country called me and where there was need to avenge the calumnies of the malicious, fanatics and aristocrats, I would want to continue to be the first in taking the step which I take today . . .

I completely lack any fortune; but I am also without care or ambition: the justice of the Convention keeps me at peace. However, if I may dare to ask it for anything, it is not to leave me idle, but to let me be of use to the Republic.

Taken from *Documents d'Histoire, 1776–1850*, 1, 1944, 72.

216

Republican calendar was instituted, religious buildings were destroyed, masquerades were held in churches, there was a cult of reason, a campaign for the abdication and marriage of priests, and numerous priests, religious and laity were executed as traitors and fanatics. Even if political reasons were often given by the revolutionary tribunals, it could be said that there were many real martyrs. Robespierre sought to curb these excesses by having a vote on the Cult of the Supreme Being (May 1794). However, by the middle of 1794 all external forms of worship had almost disappeared. The constitutional church no longer functioned. The fall of Robespierre (on 9 Thermidor/27 July 1794) marked the end of the Reign of Terror and the beginning of a respite for religion.

Revolution exported

The victories of the revolutionary armies brought about a certain number of annexations to the Republic or the creation of satellite states such as the Batavian Republic, the Cisalpine Republic, the Ligurian Republic, the Roman Republic, and so on. The decrees on religion were applied in different ways. Different oaths were extracted from the priests of these countries. Convents were suppressed in Belgium, which had been annexed, and their goods sold. Priests and bishops who had refused to take an oath of perpetual hatred of royalty had to emigrate. In October 1797 the University of Louvain was closed. Six hundred Belgian priests were condemned to deportation. These measures, together with conscription, provoked a Peasants' War in September 1798. On the other hand, in the old United Provinces, the Republic of Batavia, the French presence resulted in freedom for the Catholics who had formerly only been tolerated. Having opted for revolutionary ideas in the face of the old powers, Catholics obtained complete freedom of worship and all civil rights.

In February 1797 the Directory imposed on the pope the treaty of Tolentino which, besides resulting in the loss of territories, called for a considerable sum of money and works of art. After this an incident occurred which allowed the authorities to chase the pope out of Rome and establish the Roman Republic there at the beginning of 1798. A shameless pillage ensued. Forced to retreat, the French abducted Pius VI as their prisoner as far as Valence on the Rhone, where he died on 24 August 1799. Many people thought they had seen the last of popes.

The *coup d'état* on 18 Brumaire (9 November 1799) did not change anything in the early weeks. But lassitude here and there moved people to think that a compromise was called for.

3. The Napoleonic era

The Concordat

On 14 March 1800 the cardinals met at Venice and elected a new pope, Cardinal Chiaramonti, who took the name of Pius VII. When Bishop of Imola, he had affirmed that the democratic form of government was not incompatible with the gospel. Bonaparte, who became First Consul, thought that he could not govern without bringing about a religious reconciliation amongst the

Pius VII.

Proposal on religion by Napoleon Bonaparte at the time of the negotiations on the Concordat

My policy is to govern in accordance with the wishes of the majority. That, I believe, is the way of recognizing the will of the people. I finished the Vendée war by making myself a Catholic; I established myself in Egypt by making myself a Moslem, and I won people over in Italy by becoming Ultramontane. If I governed a people of Jews I would rebuild Solomon's temple (16 August 1800, to the Council of State).

I do not see religion as the mystery of the incarnation but as the mystery of the social order: it associates with heaven an idea of equality which prevents the rich being massacred by the poor.

Religion is a kind of inoculation or vaccination which, by satisfying our love of the miraculous, guarantees us charlatans and sorcerers: the priests are worth more than all the Kants and the dreamers of Germany. How can one have order in a state without religion?

Society cannot exist without inequality of fortunes, and inequality of fortunes cannot subsist without religion. When a man dies of hunger alongside one who has eaten to bursting point, it is impossible for him to accept the difference unless there is an authority which says to him: 'This is how God wills it; there must be poor and rich in the world; but then, during eternity, the sharing will be different' (1801).

French, but his religious vision was entirely political. He entered into extremely arduous negotiations with the Holy See, represented by Cardinal Consalvi. These ended up with the Concordat of 15 July 1801. The essential points of this can be seen in Box 218. After he had extracted resignations from all the bishops of the old order, the pope exercised a power which was unprecedented since the beginning of the church. Those who owned national property were not disturbed. The government guaranteed the clergy's salary. There was no question of religious

The 1801 Concordat

Convention between His Holiness Pius VII and the French Government

The Government of the Republic recognizes that the Catholic, Apostolic and Roman religion is the religion of the great majority of citizens.

His Holiness similarly recognizes that this same religion has gained and at this moment still expects the greatest good and the greatest renown from the establishment of Catholic worship in France and from the particular profession made of it by the Consuls of the French Republic.

As a consequence, after this mutual recognition, both for the good of religion and for the maintenance of internal tranquillity, they are agreed on what follows:

Article 1. The Catholic, Apostolic and Roman religion shall be freely practised in France; its worship shall be public, in conformity to the police regulations which the government shall judge necessary for public tranquillity.

Article 2. A new demarcation of French dioceses shall be made by the Holy See, in concert with the government.

Article 3. His Holiness shall declare to the bishops of France that he expects of them, with a firm confidence, for the sake of peace and unity, every kind of sacrifice, even that of their sees . . .

219

The Organic Articles

The police rules contained in Article 1 of the Concordat were much more developed than the Concordat itself. The pope was not consulted about them. Here are some of these seventy-seven Organic Articles.

1. No bull, letter, rescript, decree, mandate, provision, signature serving as provision or other missive from the court of Rome, even if only relating to specific matters, can be received, published, printed or otherwise executed without the authorization of the government.

2. No individual calling himself nuncio, legate, vicar or apostolic commissioner, or priding himself in any other denomination, can exercise any function on French soil or elsewhere in matters relating to the Gallican church without the same authorization.

24. Those who are chosen to teach in the seminaries will subscribe to the declaration made by the clergy of France in 1682 . . . They will submit to teaching there the doctrine contained in that declaration.

orders. Finally, the Concordat revoked many of the provisions of the *Civil Constitution* and the Concordat of 1516; like the king, the First Consul appointed archbishops to whom the pope gave canonical status. The important thing was that the Concordat restored religious peace by re-establishing links with Rome.

When Bonaparte submitted the concordat to the vote of the assemblies he added to it 77  *Organic Articles*, detailed regulations concerning church life in the spirit of old Gallicanism or Josephism. The pope protested about this in vain. The position for Protestants was equally regulated. Also on 18 April 1802, Easter Day, the re-establishment of Catholic worship in France was celebrated in Notre Dame, Paris. There was great rejoicing throughout the country. In the same month of April Chateaubriand published *The Genius of Christianity*, an intellectual and sentimental restatement of traditional religion.

Reorganization according to the Concordat

The French dioceses were reduced in number to sixty, of which ten were archdioceses. It was not difficult to bring about the resignation of the constitutional bishops. As for the survivors of the old episcopate, more than thirty refused to resign. Some, a small number, involved the faithful in their resistance. This was the origin of the Petite Église, which has managed to keep going until now in the West and in the area around Lyons. In his nomination of new bishops, Bonaparte planned a mixture in order to make reconciliation easier: he chose sixteen bishops from before the Revolution, twelve old constitutional bishops and thirty-six priests. Bonaparte's uncle, Joseph Fesch, who was included among the latter, became Archbishop of Lyons and a cardinal.

In the territories annexed by France and the satellite countries, Bonaparte reorganized the church on more or less the same lines as he had done in France: he reduced the number of dioceses and introduced the equivalents of the Organic Articles. It was Germany which underwent the greatest changes. For one thing the left bank of the Rhine, annexed to France, became the seat of legislation. The old ecclesiastical principalities disappeared for ever, their territories annexed by France or given to the princes

(Cession of Ratisbon, 1803). The wealth of the convents passed to the governments. The Germans called this secularization.

A short honeymoon

In France the honeymoon period lasted for several years. The church gradually pulled itself together, although the numbers of clergy were reduced in comparison with the old order because of resignations, deaths and the infrequency of ordinations during the previous ten years. The seminaries had to be reopened and the places of worship restored. And so began the renewal which was to reach its height under the Restoration (see Chapter 17). Bonaparte reached the height of his popularity among Catholics when he persuaded the pope to come and crown him emperor in Notre-Dame, Paris, on 2 December 1804. On his progress through France Pius VII received a triumphant welcome everywhere. Church officials in France did not cease to sing the praises of Napoleon, the Lord's Anointed, the New David, Cyrus, Constantine, Charlemagne, and to emphasize the duty owed to the emperor in the imperial catechism (1806).

The new struggle between the priesthood and the empire

In 1806 there was tension between the pope and the emperor. It lasted until the fall of Napoleon. As part of his war with England, Napoleon wanted the pope to submit to the obligations of the continental blockade: the ban on trade with England and her allies. The pope refused, and the situation deteriorated. In 1808 Rome was occupied by French troops. In May 1809 the Papal States were reunited with the French empire. The pope excommunicated the usurpers. On 6 July the pope was put under house arrest at Savona (near Genoa) until March 1812. The bull of excommunication was published in France despite the police. Pius VII then refused to consecrate the bishops nominated by Napoleon and there were soon seventeen dioceses without a bishop. So that he could marry Maria Theresa of Austria, Napoleon obtained an annulment of his marriage with Josephine from the religious authorities in Paris, who were cooperative. The Roman cardinals who were in Paris refused to attend the wedding, which took place in 1810.

In order to get out of the impasse caused by having dioceses without bishops, Napoleon summoned a national council in Paris in 1811. The bishops affirmed their loyalty to the pope but did not want to incur the emperor's displeasure, and undertook to go to win over Pius VII. However, he would not give way. Napoleon had him taken to Fontainebleau in June 1812. When subjected to force the pope made some concessions (the Concordat of Fontainebleau) which he very quickly went back on. Military disasters led the emperor to send the pope to Rome, where he made a triumphal entrance on 24 May 1814.

4. The legacy of the Revolution

Irreversible changes

French and European Catholicism came out of the Revolution greatly changed. For the most part, the wealth of the church had passed into the hands of the laity. There was to be no going back on the first great secularization of French society. Of the ecclesiastical princes, the pope alone still retained temporal powers. Freedom of worship was built into the legislation. The people of France were able to declare themselves either non-Catholic or non-Christian. By the creation of a civil state, the stages of human life escaped from the control of the church, which also lost control of teaching.

Undoubtedly the time was not ripe to uphold the most extreme decisions of the Revolution, but they would be taken up again in the fairly near future: the separation of church and state, divorce. At some time, much later on, the

Napoleon crowning himself.

anticlericalism or atheism of the state would claim a basis in the Revolution.

A purified church

The faith of Christians emerged purified by what they had been through. The church had to go back to its essential mission. The Concordat gave it features which were to last for a century. It had a clergy which was worthy and strongly structured, and which depended closely on the administration. The bishops, called 'purple prefects', were absolute masters in their dioceses. They moved their priests as they pleased. A priest tended to become a dedicated and serious petty official, who had been recruited from a modest background in a way which gave him social promotion. It was difficult for him to be prophetic.

The misfortunes of the popes had moved good Christian people who saw the return of the Holy See as the only way of defending the church against the pretensions of public power. This loyalty to the pope, which came to be called 'ultramontanism', lasted throughout the nineteenth century.

Two Frances

The legacy of the Revolution has divided France until quite recent times. While the 'liberals' went back to revolutionary principles of freedom and equality, Catholics, who were in the majority, saw the revolution as the work of Satan. That is why in the nineteenth century Catholics who wanted a religious and social restoration along the lines of the old order ranged themselves against liberals who wanted to hold on to what had been gained by the Revolution. The conflict moved away from the heart of the church when some of the Catholics realized that the principles of 1789 were incompatible with the gospel, and that it was useless to seek to resurrect a bygone age.

For further reading

W. J. Callahan and D. Higgs (eds.), *Church and Society in Catholic Europe of the Eighteenth Century*, Cambridge University Press 1979

G. R. Cragg, *The Church and the Age of Reason 1648–1789*, Penguin Books 1960

L. Cognet, *Post-Reformation Spirituality*, Burns and Oates 1959

E. E. Y. Hales, *Revolution and Papacy 1769–1846*, Eyre and Spottiswoode 1960

N. Hampson, *The Enlightenment*, Pelican History of European Thought Volume 4, Penguin Books 1968

R. A. Knox, *Enthusiasm*, Oxford University Press 1950, reissued Collins Flame 1987

J. McManners, *French Ecclesiastical Society under the Ancien Regime*, Manchester University Press 1960

J. McManners, *The French Revolution and the Church*, SPCK 1969

R. R. Palmer, *Catholics and Unbelievers in Eighteenth-Century France*, Burns and Oates 1939

17

Restoration and Liberalism

1815–1870

Rheims Cathedral.

After Napoleon had disappeared from the political scene, the preceding quarter-century seemed for many people to be an episode that was best forgotten. Europe and the church had to be restored to the time before 1789. In fact the nineteenth century did see a definite religious revival, traces of which have remained down to our own times. However, those who refused to implement the principles of 1789 became increasingly numerous. Freedom could not be hampered by authoritarianism on the part of princes nor by the orthodoxy of a church. In order to defend its identity the Catholic Church often felt obliged to fight against this threatening liberalism which worked its way even among Catholics themselves. To find a solution to these problems, Pope Pius IX called a Vatican Council in 1869.

I · Restoration

1. The principles

After the upheavals of the Revolution and the Empire, the Congress of Vienna (1814–1815) undertook a reorganization of Europe according to the principle of legitimacy. The pope got his states back; Tsar Alexander I, who was in a mystical phase, signed the treaty of the Holy Alliance on 26 September 1815 with the Emperor of Austria and the King of Prussia. 'In the name of the Most Holy and Undivided Trinity' the three sovereigns, who represented three Christian confessions, took it upon themselves to rule according to Christian principles and to offer aid and assistance to one another.

Eternal values

An ideological literature rejected revolutionary principles and exalted the eternal values of the past: religion, morality, hierarchy. Mankind did not have rights but duties. The most influential thinkers were two who wrote in French. For Louis de Bonald (1754–1840) the monarchy and Catholicism were indissolubly connected: one could not exist without the other. Joseph de  Maistre (1753–1821) from the Savoy saw the revolution as a divine punishment. Divine right had to be restored to the monarchy and the pope recognized as the guarantor of universal order.

However, twenty-five years of history cannot be wiped out with the stroke of a pen. Those who had benefited from the revolution wanted to hold on to what they had gained. There were considerable inconveniences in associating religious and political restoration, because attacks on political régimes at the same time challenged a church which was held to be in solidarity with them.

2. Political restoration and religious reconstruction in France

The throne and the altar

The throne and the altar were mutually supportive. If King Louis XVIII (1814–1824) was not particularly pious, his brother Charles X (1824–1830) had himself crowned at Rheims and succumbed to bigotry. Members of the government, such as the nobles returning from exile, went to mass and joined in the processions. Catholicism once again became the religion of the state. The bishops were almost always chosen from amongst the nobility; the money spent on worship was increased. The Concordat of 1801 remained, but around twenty extra dioceses were created in 1822. Freedom of worship was continued, but divorce was suppressed. Property taken away from the church was not restored. Public opinion did not always accept these measures in favour of religion. Behind this sometimes hypocritical façade, the work of religious restoration was under way.

Religious reconstruction

The intention of the Restoration church was to re-Christianize the masses, whose practice of Christianity had become weaker during the years of the Revolution. Great attention was paid to the recruitment of clergy by reorganizing the major seminaries and multiplying the minor ones which had escaped state supervision. The annual number of ordinations to the priesthood, which had not been more than 500 under the Empire, reached the record number of 2357 in 1829. And so the number of parishes could be greatly increased, particularly in the countryside. In half a century 5000 new parishes were

Ultramontanism at the beginning of the nineteenth century

Joseph de Maistre and Lamennais saw the power of the pope as the foundation of all society. In this they were opposed to the Gallicanism of the officials and bishops, but stood close to Christian people, who had an increasing veneration for the pope.

Joseph de Maistre

Without the pope Christianity is no longer, and as an inevitable consequence, the social order is smitten in the heart. The church must be governed like any other organization; otherwise there would no longer be aggregation, cohesion, unity. This government is therefore by nature infallible, that is to say absolute; otherwise the pope would not govern . . . There is nothing shocking about the idea of all Christian rulers united by religious brotherhood in a kind of universal republic under the measured supremacy of the supreme spiritual power.

On the Pope (1819).

Lamennais

There is no church without the pope; there is no Christianity without the church; there is no religion and no society without Christianity. Consequently, as I have said, the life of the European nations has its source, its unique source, in the papal power. Had not the Catholic religion, by the influence which it exercises even in countries in which it has ceased to be dominant, been opposed to the progress of Protestant unbelief, there would long since have ceased to be a single trace of Christianity, and if these countries were still inhabited, it would be by a race of barbarians more ferocious and more hideous than the world has ever seen. Such would be the fate of the whole of Europe, had it been possible for Catholicism to have been completely abolished there. Now every attack on the power of the Sovereign Pontiff tends in that direction: it is a crime of lèse-religion *for the Christian of good faith capable of putting two ideas together; and for the man of the state it is a crime of* lèse-civilization, *of* lèse-society.

De la Religion considérée dans ses rapports avec l'ordre social (1825).

added to the 27000 which existed in 1825. Jean-Marie Vianney (1786–1859), the Curé of Ars, brought to the humble position of country priest an influence which it had never had before.

Hundreds of congregations

The congregations provided the church with extremely effective personnel. Gradually the old orders were revived. In 1814 Pius VII reformed the Jesuits, who were reluctantly let back into France. Numerous new congregations of men and women, in France and elsewhere, came into being between 1815 and 1870. Many small religious groups which had formed spontaneously under the Revolution turned into congregations under the Restoration. Fr de Clorivière (1735–1820) and Adelaide de Cicé had renewed the form of religious life by founding the Society of the Daughters of the Heart of Mary, which did not require any distinctive outward sign of its members so that they could adapt in times of persecution. But on the whole all nineteenth century foundations were alike. The intention was often to respond to local needs: teaching, looking after the sick and the poor. Foreign missions were a new dimension for some of them. Their spirituality was in accordance with traditional trends – Ignatian, Dominican, Franciscan, with devotion to the Sacred Heart and to the Virgin (700 congregations had a dedication to Mary), with the concerns of the age, such as that of reparation. Some were marked by the perspective of the preceding years.

3. Across Europe

Italy

The Papal States made a great effort to wipe away the traces of the French presence, like vaccination and street lighting. The main posts remained in the hands of churchmen. Anticlericalism grew, fanned by secret societies like the *carbonari*. Across the whole of Italy a strong movement in support of a united Italy grew up, which presupposed the removal of the old states. This was unacceptable to the papacy. While the south of Italy remained under the influence of the old order, the north showed itself to be much more active by the foundation of new congregations and charitable works (Joseph-Benedict Cotolengo, Don Bosco) and by the intellectual activity of such priest-philosophers as Rosmini (who died in 1855) and Gioberti (died 1852).

Germany and Austria

In Germany the reorganization of territories meant the end of the old principle of *cuius regio, eius religio* (of whom the region, of him the religion). Catholics were now put under the jurisdiction of Protestant princes. Acceptable solutions had to be found. These were the object of long negotiations and often tensions. Catholics of the Rhineland learned to reorganize themselves in the face of the awesome power of the kings of Prussia. The king of Bavaria, Ludwig I (1825–1848), made Munich into the great centre of German Catholicism.

Joseph Görres (1776–1848), national hero and professor of history at the University of Munich, formed a circle of Catholic thinkers. In 1826 the young Döllinger began a brilliant career as a church historian at the same university. It was also at Munich that Johann-Adam Möhler (1796–1838) gave up his teaching post as a church historian and theologian. In his book *Unity in the*

Jean-Adam Möhler (1796–1838)

J.-A. Möhler was not able to come to full flower in his short career as theologian at Tübingen and then at Munich. In his theology of the church, his life's work, he wanted to indicate the importance of history and spiritual experience.

Christianity cannot be reduced to expressions, formulae and locutions. It is spiritual life, inner life, a holy power. All the forms of teaching and all dogmas are without value unless they express this inner life which they presuppose to have been realized to some extent. One can even say that since such an expression is always limited, it does not exhaust life, which is inexpressible; it is always beyond reality. But life cannot be communicated (in the sense of being expressed) and cannot be fixed, since the communication, this expression, can only be achieved through words, concepts, conventions . . . The words are not a matter of indifference; on the contrary they are very important . . .

Since Christianity is considered as a new divine life given to men and not as a simple abstract, inanimate concept, it follows that like all life it is capable of development and growth . . . The essential principle of the identity of the Christian conscience of the church at different periods of its history does not require a static state.

J.-A. Möhler, *Die Einheit der Kirche* (1825).

Church he tried to get away from a legal and hierarchical view of the church in order to understand it on the basis of its internal principle, the Holy Spirit, expressed in a life of communion. In Vienna, the holy Redemptorist Clement Hofbauer (died 1820) made himself the guiding force of a group of intellectual Catholics which included Clement Brentano, who transcribed the visions of Catherine Emmerich, the theologian Günther, and so on.

The Protestant world

In Prussia, King Friedrich-Wilhelm III forced the fusion of the Lutheran Church and the Calvinist Church into a United Evangelical Church (1817). Several German states followed his example.

Two themes stand out from the many Protestant groups that sprang up, those of revival and liberalism. The revivalist movement, the heirs of Pietism and Methodism, put the accent on piety, feeling and outward actions. Some of them saw the Christian life as a series of periodic revivals. Sometimes tinged with millenarianism, they were particularly numerous in the Anglo-Saxon world of Europe and North America.

Protestant liberalism sought to make Christianity acceptable in a scientific world which was very different from that of the Reformers. Rationalism was introduced into theology. Frederick Schleiermacher (1768–1834), who was strongly influenced by the Moravians, is thought of as the father of liberalism. In his *Speeches on Religion for its Cultured Admirers* (1799), Schleiermacher began from conscience: 'Religion is neither thought nor action but intuitive contemplation and feeling.' Religion is the feeling of dependence on the absolute. From that starting point dogmas were relativized and subjectivity became the norm.

22

Reacting against dependence on power, some individuals founded free churches. In Denmark, two very different individuals illustrate the religious revival. Grundtvig (1783–1872) preached a popular Christianity in which the most important place was given to the sacraments and the canticles. The philosopher Sören Kierkegaard

Friedrich Daniel Ernst Schleiermacher (1768–1834)

Schleiermacher, a product of Moravian piety, wanted to safeguard religion and inward Christianity even from the philosophical thought of his time. This new reading of religion has led him to be regarded as the father of Liberal Protestantism.

To make clear to you what is the original and characteristic possession of religion, it resigns at once all claims on anything that belongs either to science or morality. Whether it has been borrowed or bestowed it is not returned. Religion does not seek to determine and explain the universe in accordance with its nature, as metaphysics does; it does not seek to perfect it and complete it by the development of the freedom and the divine free judgment of man, as morality does. In essence it is neither thought nor action but intuitive contemplation and sentiment. It seeks to contemplate the universe intuitively; it seeks to observe it piously in its manifestations and its distinctive actions; it seeks, as passively as a child, to be grasped by it and to be swept away by its direct influences. Thus in essence and effect it is totally opposed to metaphysics and morality . . . It seeks to see in man, no less than in any other particular and finite being, the infinite, the copy and representation of the Infinite.

F. D. E. Schleiermacher, *Speeches on Religion to its Cultured Despisers* (1799), Second Speech.

The starets

In traditional monastic Russian life, the starets (plural startsy) is the spiritual master who initiates the young novice. In the course of the eighteenth and nineteenth centuries the startsy, often venerable old men, became the spiritual directors of the Russian spiritual élite. The most famous were those of the monastery of Optino in the province of Kaluga. In *The Brothers Karamazov* Dostoievsky gives a portrait of the starets Zossima. The writer seems to have borrowed features from several famous startsy.

What, then, is a starets? A starets is a man who takes your soul and your will into his soul and will. Having chosen your starets, you renounce your will and yield it to him in complete submission and complete self-abnegation.

Ordinary people as well as great aristocrats flocked to the startsy of our monastery, so that, prostrating themselves before them, they could confess their doubts, their sins and their sufferings, and ask for counsel and admonition.

It was said by many people about the Elder Zossima that, by permitting everyone for so many years to come and bare their hearts and beg his advice and healing words, he had absorbed so many secrets, sorrows and avowals into his soul that in the end he acquired so fine a perception that he could tell at the first glance from the face of a stranger what he came for, what he wanted, and what kind of torment racked his conscience. Indeed he sometimes astounded, confounded and almost frightened his visitor by this knowledge of his secret before he even had time to utter a word . . .

Many, almost all, who went for the first time to have a private talk with the elder, entered his cell in fear and trepidation, but almost always came out looking bright and happy, and even the gloomiest face was transformed into a happy one.

Dostoievsky, *The Brothers Karamazov*, Penguin edn, 28–30.

(1813–1855) called for a Christianity which broke with the world; this was a forerunner of the existentialism of the following century.

The Orthodox world

Throughout the nineteenth century, in the Ottoman empire, which was in steady decline, the conquered nations fought for their independence. As a result of the uprising in Greece in 1821 Patriarch Gregory of Constantinople, after celebrating the liturgy on Easter Day, was hung by the Turks from the great gate of the patriarch's house. In 1832 Greece finally achieved independence, and the Greek church, refusing to be dependent on a patriarch who was under the yoke of the Turks, proclaimed itself autocephalous in 1833.

In Russia the Raskolniki persisted in their opposition to the official church and divided into several sects. The church's submission to the ruling power did not prevent it from maintaining the spiritual tradition of past centuries. Seraphim of Sarov (1759–1833) began the tradition of startsy (the plural of starets) in the nineteenth century. Thinkers tried to revive Russian religious awareness of the sources of Orthodoxy. The Slavophiles set themselves up against those who were Westernized and inspired by democracy and socialism. The novelist Dostoievsky (1821–1881) explored the depths of madness, sin and atheism.

II · God and Freedom

1. The revolutions of 1830

The Catholic restoration sparked off strong opposition from the liberal bourgeoisie, especially in France. Editions of Voltaire's books multiplied. In his songs, Béranger ridiculed the over-pious king and attacked the Jesuits. The Ordinances of Charles X which suppressed the freedom of the press provoked an uprising of the people of Paris (27–29 July 1830). The resentment against the régime took a violently anti-clerical turn, in the form of the sacking of the archbishop's residence in Paris, attacks on priests in soutanes, and the destruction of mission crosses. Things gradually calmed down, and the new king Louis Philippe was accepted for better or worse by the Catholics.

Across Europe

Revolution was contagious. Unhappy at their absorption into the kingdom of the Low Countries, the Belgians rebelled. The Catholics did not hesitate to ally themselves with the liberal anti-clericalists against the Dutch sovereign. In 1830 the Belgians established the independent kingdom of Belgium on liberal lines: a quasi-separation of church and state, freedom of worship, of teaching, of the press. Catholics had made use of liberal ideas and the embarrassed papacy had to accept them.

The death of Pius VIII on 30 November 1830 occasioned an uprising in the Papal States. It took fifty days to elect Pope Gregory XVI, a monk little versed in politics. In order to put an end to the uprising, the pope appealed to Austria, which was held in contempt by liberal Italians. On 25 March 1831 order was restored, but Gregory XVI was unreservedly numbered among the enemies of freedom.

In November 1830 Poland, under the rule of the Tsar of Russia, rebelled and proclaimed its independence. The Russians crushed the Poles and recaptured Warsaw on 8 September 1832. The repression was terrible. Large numbers of Poles left their country and found sympathetic liberal and Catholic surroundings in the West. The Poles asked the pope to intervene, as did Gagarin, the Tsar's representative. Could Gregory XVI support the insurrection in Poland and fight it in his own states? In a letter of 9 June 1832 he advised the Poles to submit. 'Submit to your powerful emperor who has your good at heart.' This caused indignation and amazement in Poland and in Europe.

Ought not the church to take notice of the people's aspirations towards freedom? Was it not the moment to reconcile God and freedom? That is what Lamennais and his friends thought.

2. Lamennais and *L'Avenir*

From ultra-royalism to liberalism

Felicité de La Mennais (1782–1854) was born at St Malo and grew up under the Revolution. He was self-taught, educating himself through a vast amount of reading. He was not very interested in religion, and had his first communion at the age of twenty-two. He soon caught the zeal of his brother Jean-Marie, a priest, for rebuilding the church of France under the Empire and the Restoration. In 1816 Felicité became a priest himself and took up the pen – journalism – as the means of his ministry. In 1817 his *Essay on Indifference* made him one of the most celebrated writers in the land. His aim was to prevent his contemporaries from being led placidly towards atheism: without religion, everything would crumble. In political matters Felicité was at that time an ultra-royalist. He counted on the steadfastness of the government to give the church back its rights and its social role. He even found that the king was not doing enough. Lamennais was somewhat excessive in his polemics against the impious university, and the Archbishop of Paris chastized him. In retaliation, faced with the Gallicanism of the bishops and officials, he was resolutely ultramontane. For him, as for Joseph de Maistre, the infallible pope was the pinnacle of the political-religious edifice.

By founding various orders, Jean-Marie and Felicité worked for a religious revival. Jean-Marie founded the Daughters of Providence and the Brothers of Christian Teaching for primary education. With the Congregation of St Peter the two brothers wanted to train a clergy which was both nourished by tradition and open to the times. In his house of La Chênaie, Felicité devoted himself to his disciples, many of whom played an important role in the church. Welcoming him warmly to Rome in 1824, Pope Leo XII acknowledged that 'he is a man who must be led with hand on heart'.

Some of the government measures like the ordinances of 1828 which restricted the freedom of the church caused Lamennais to break completely with the restored monarchy: by its subsidies, it was making a slave of the church. The separation of church and state would be preferable. Poverty would give the church back its freedom. Rather than relying on the king and the pope, would it not be better to rely on the pope and the people?

L'Avenir

To Lamennais, the July 1830 revolution was providential; the world was to be given a new lease of life through freedom and freedom was to be given a new lease of life through God. With his friends Lacordaire, Montalembert, de Coux and Gerbet, on 15 October 1830 Lamennais founded a journal with the title *L'Avenir* (The Future), which carried at its masthead 'God and Freedom'. The journal was of interest to those who were fighting for independence: the Poles, the Irish. It proposed a renewal of the church and society based on freedom: freedom of conscience and worship without distinction, the separation of church and state, the freedom of the press and of association, decentralization, and so on. De Coux aroused his readers to the social question. The tone of the journal was sometimes over the top. The bishops, who thought that the idea of the separation of church and state was unthinkable, showed their disapproval by applying indirect sanctions against the subscribers. *L'Avenir* ceased publication on 15 November 1831. Frowned on by the French bishops, Lamennais, Lacordaire and Montalembert decided to take their case to the pope, whom they had always supported. 'Pilgrims for God and Freedom', they arrived in Rome at the end of December 1831 at a rather inopportune time. The pilgrims waited three months before having a disappointing meeting with Gregory XVI, at which neither the question of *L'Avenir* nor future preoccupations were raised. The publication of the letter from the Pope to the Polish bishops in June 1832

Lamennais by P. Guérin.

L'Avenir

The journal founded by Lamennais and his friends appeared from 15 October 1830 to 15 November 1831. His programme, which has been taken over by all modern democracies, made him a scandal to the bishops and Catholic nobility of the time.

Appeal to priests to give up their stipends (18 October 1830):

Ministers of the one who was born in a manger and died on a cross, return to your origins; of your own will steep yourselves again in poverty, in suffering, and the word of the suffering God, the poor God, will be as effective on your lips as it was in the beginning. With no other support than this divine word, go down like the twelve fishermen into the midst of the peoples and begin the conquest of the world again. A new era of triumph and glory is in preparation for Christianity. See on the horizon the signs which foretell the rising of the star and, as messengers of hope, burst into the song of life over the ruins of empires, the débris of all that comes to pass.

Legislative programme (7 December 1830):

We call, first, for freedom of conscience or freedom of religion, full, universal, without distinction and without privilege, and therefore, as far as it affects us who are Catholics, for total separation of church and state. This necessary separation, without which there would be no religious freedom for Catholics, involves on the one hand the suppression of the church budget and on the other the absolute independence of the clergy in the spiritual order. The priest will still be subject to the laws of the country, similarly to and to the same degree as other citizens.

Secondly, we call for freedom of teaching, because it is a natural right and as it were the first freedom of the family; because without it there is neither religious freedom or freedom of opinion.

In third place we call for freedom of the press . . .

In fourth place we call for freedom of association . . .

In fifth place we call for an extension of the principle of election, so that it penetrates right to the heart of the masses . . .

In sixth place we call for the abolition of the baneful system of centralization, which is a deplorable and shameful relic of imperial despotism. According to our principles all interested parties have the right to self-administration.

infuriated Lamennais, who left Rome, which he called 'this gigantic tomb where there are only bones to be found'. A few weeks later, on 15 August 1832, the encyclical *Mirari vos* appeared which, without naming Lamennais, condemned all his ideas and those of *L'Avenir*. Within a short time the editors of *L'Avenir* submitted. But Lamennais was not left in peace. His enemies were busy, and episcopal commands rained down. In the end, in April 1834, Lamennais published *Words of a Believer*, in which he expressed all that was in his heart: his hatred of all tyranny, his trust in the people. His language was suffused with the Bible and with the romanticism of the period. The typesetters cried as they composed the work. Its success was enormous. In June 1834 the encyclical *Singulari nos* condemned the work and its author.

A lonely struggle

Lamennais' system was crushed. The papacy was incapable of being the basis for a renewed church and humanity. Lamennais wanted to remain true to the people, but he was alone. For twenty years, as an indefatigable journalist and writer he defended the poor and oppressed, beginning with the rebel silk workers of Lyons. He was preparing a religion of the future, a religion of the people and of humanity. A supporter of universal suffrage, an enemy of the death penalty, he thought that one day the feeling of brotherhood would put an end to all war. In 1848 his dreams seemed to have been realized; he became a deputy and founded the journal *Le Peuple Constituant* (The People Decide). Disappointment came quickly after the June revolution. He died on 27 February 1854; in accordance with his last wishes he was buried in a communal grave.

All Lamennais' desires have now become fact: the separation of the church from the state in France, freedom of teaching and of the press. Beyond question after 1830 French Catholics waged a campaign for freedom of teaching, but in isolation from other freedoms. Ultramontanism continued to make progress, but in an anti-liberal direction. A Catholic liberalism made itself felt gradually, but without Lamennais' breadth of vision.

3. 1848: Euphoria of short duration

Economic and social transformation

Although much advanced in England, industrialization was far less so on the continent, where France until the middle of the nineteenth century was still seventy-five per cent rural. All the same, mines and textile industries had given rise to urban sprawls in which the most wretched poverty was rife. Economic liberalism was not governed by any rules so far as salary and hygiene were concerned. Catholics who were  often politically conservative regretted the disappearance of the guilds of the old order, which imposed a certain amount of control. As a temporary measure they founded charitable institutions which relieved the immediate poverty and encouraged the workers to higher moral and religious standards. As a longer-term measure, Lamennais and de Coux in *L'Avenir* denounced the exploitation of workers and proposed a new economic and social organization based on political democracy. Frederick Ozanam worked towards the reconciliation of

Man reduced to the level of a machine

With considerable verve Cardinal de Bonald, Archbishop of Lyons, complains that the worker is exploited like a machine, but because he restricts himself to the moral level, he does not draw very precise consequences for economic structures.

How does greed see a man? As nothing but a functional machine, a wheel which speeds up movement, a lever which lifts, a hammer which breaks the rock, an anvil which shapes iron. And what is the young child? Greed sees it as nothing but as a cogwheel which has not yet gained all its power. In the eyes of greed, that is the whole of human nature. And if you ask it where the salvation of society lies, it will point out to you the continual motion of machines, the uninterrupted activity of the productive worker, the steam which annihilates distances . . .

Pastoral instruction and mandate of Mgr Cardinal de Bonald on the sanctification of Sunday, issued in Lent 1842.

All Republicans in February 1848

In a general euphoria, the proclamation of the Republic on 25 February 1848 seemed to rally all the French including the clergy. The clergy delivered magnificent sermons when blessing the banners of liberty.

Show the faithful the example of obedience and submission to the Republic. Frequently make a vow to yourselves to enjoy this freedom which makes our brothers in the United States so happy; you will have this freedom. If the authorities wish to deck religious buildings with the national flag, attentively heed the desires of the magistrates. The flag of the Republic will always be a flag which protects religion . . . Agree to all measures which may improve the lot of the workers. It must be hoped that at last a sincere and effective interest will be shown in the working class.

Cardinal de Bonald to his priests.

Citizens, Jesus Christ was the first, from up on his cross, to make the magnificent words 'Freedom, equality, brotherhood' resound throughout the world.

The Christ who died for you on the tree of liberty is the holy, the sublime Republican, of all times and all countries. Indeed, freedom is derived from Calvary.

Sermons by parish priests preached in 1848.

the social classes: 'Let's become barbarians'; i.e., let's have the same attitude to the workers as the church had at the time of the great invasions. These first social Catholics were contemporaries of the first socialists, many of whom were inspired by Christian principles: St-Simon, Fourrier, Cabet, Buchez, and the editors of the journal *Atelier*. These latter refused charity. It was a matter of procuring justice and transforming the economy and society.

The people's spring

The discontents of many – Republicans, Catholics clinging to the old dynasty, the unemployed – converged and led to the revolution of February 1848. The Republic was proclaimed on 25 February and welcomed favourably by all. The provisional government called for prayers. The priests blessed the pillars of freedom. The whole world seemed to be reconciled. Lacordaire, who had become a Dominican, Ozanam and Abbé Maret founded the journal *L'Ère nouvelle* (The New Age), a kind of replica of *L'Avenir*.

The revolution swept over the whole of Europe: Austria, Germany and Italy. The latter two countries thought that the moment had come for national unity. Abbé Gioberti thought that the pope ought to head an Italian confederation. Pius IX, at the peak of his popularity, refused to undertake a crusade against Austria, which controlled part of Italy. The disappointments began.

The days of June 1848

In France, elections were held in a wave of enthusiasm on Easter Day, 23 April 1848. Fifteen ecclesiastics were elected, including Lacordaire. The electors, for the most part inexperienced country people, had responded to the orders of the nobility (lords of the manor and priests) and appointed a conservative assembly which was ignorant of the social problems of the capital. The unemployed poured into Paris to be taken on in the national workshops. When these were deemed to be too costly and were suppressed, the workmen put up barricades in Paris and civil

Lacordaire by Chassériau (Louvre museum).

Louis Veuillot.

Resignation, a prime Christian virtue

The bloody days of June 1848 in Paris spread panic among those with property and especially among the Catholic nobility. Euphoria collapsed. The poor were called on to show resignation in the name of religion, which was used as a means of social defence.

The church has said to the poor: you shall not steal the goods of others, and not only shall you not steal them, you shall not covet them. In other words, you shall not listen to this treacherous teaching which ceaselessly fans in your soul the fire of covetousness and envy. Resign yourself to poverty and you will be eternally rewarded and compensated. That is what the church has been saying to the poor for a thousand years, and the poor have believed it until the day when faith was snatched from their hearts.

Montalembert, Speech to the Chamber of Deputies, 20 September 1848.

We bring to you, the poor, the hopes of religion, as a magnificent compensation for what fortune has refused you and as a powerful reason for resignation and patience.

Mgr Sibour, Archbishop of Paris.

war raged from 23–26 June. The archbishop, Mgr Affre, was killed while preaching on reconciliation. The numbers of the dead could be counted in thousands. Eleven thousand prisoners were sentenced. 'Look, it's the barbarian invasion with which they've threatened us,' exclaimed Montalembert. The fine unity had disappeared. (227) Catholic nobility like Louis Veuillot and his journal *L'Univers* campaigned for order. The anti-clerical bourgeoisie moved closer to the church because they were waiting for it to preach submission and resignation to the people. It was because of this that the prince Louis Napoleon could be elected President of the republic with a landslide majority (December 1848). The legislative assembly which met in May 1849 consisted mostly of conservative Catholics and royalists.

The revolution in Rome

Pius XI, who had disappointed the Italians, tried out reforms in his states, but his minister Rossi was assassinated. Terrified, the pope left Rome and the Romans proclaimed a republic in February 1849. The French assembly exploded in riot. The government of Louis-Napoleon sent an army which took Rome in June 1849 and reinstated the pope. Absolutism took back all its rights.

III · The First Vatican Council

1. The political and religious context

The question of Rome

Military aid from Napoleon III allowed the king of Piedmont, Victor Emmanuel, to bring together most of the Italian territories and proclaim himself king of Italy in Florence in March 1861. The pope lost the major part of his territories. Taking French Catholic opinion into consideration, Napoleon III kept troops in Rome so that the pope could stay in command of Rome and its surrounding areas. Everyone was waiting for the death of Pius IX. Although it was a matter of lands, the Roman question poisoned the life of the church until 1929.

The pope could not be other than appalled at this exaltation of freedom, which seemed to him to be the cause of the evils in the church.

Catholic division over liberalism

Catholics were unanimous in wanting to defend the temporal power of the pope and to put up a united front against socialist doctrines. But they were divided on their attitude to the society of their times, which was marked by liberalism. The intransigent Catholics, represented in France by Louis Veuillot and his journal *L'Univers*; by Mgr Pie, Bishop of Poitiers; and by Dom Guéranger, Abbot of Solesmes, wanted to see the church recover its former influence and privileges. Battle lines had to be drawn up against all that threatened the church, such as the freedom to publish anything whatsoever. These intransigents had the liberal Catholics as their targets. With their more realistic attitude, the latter took note of social evolution and decline in religion. They only asked that the state should maintain a favourable neutrality and that Catholics should be content with the same freedoms as others. The principles of 1789 had to be sorted out. There had to be a Christian dimension to freedom. But from a social point of view these liberal Catholics remained to all intents and purposes conservative, if not reactionary. Their main spokesmen were Mgr Dupanloup, Bishop of Orleans, and Montalembert, upon whom Rome put the blame for having stressed the advantages of freedom to Catholics at a congress

The Syllabus (1864)

Taking up certain passages from his former writings, Pope Pius IX condemned eighty contemporary errors. This catalogue constitutes the *Syllabus Errorum*. However, the condemnation of an error does not necessarily indicate what is the positively correct doctrine. This allowed Mgr Dupanloup to put forward a moderate interpretation of these condemnations.

The following affirmations are condemned.

55. The church must be separate from the state and the state separate from the church.

63. It is permissible to refuse obedience to legitimate princes and even to revolt against them.

77. In our age, it is no longer useful for the Catholic religion to be considered the only state religion, to the exclusion of all other forms of worship.

78. In some Catholic countries the law has rightly provided that foreigners who come to settle there shall enjoy the right to the public practice of their particular forms of worship.

79. It is false that civil liberty for all forms of worship and the full power allowed to all to manifest all their thoughts and all their opinions openly and publicly leads people more easily to spiritual and moral corruption and to an extension of the plague of indifferentism.

80. The Roman Pontiff can and must reconcile himself to and take account of progress, liberalism and modern civilization.

held in Malines in 1863. They used the journal *Le Correspondant* as a means of expression.

Reason and faith

Christianity and more especially Catholicism were also called into question by philosophy and science during the nineteenth century. The philosophy of Kant affirmed that the existence of God could not be proved by reason; the positivism of Auguste Comte denied anything supernatural. In his *Life of Jesus* (1863) Renan reduced Jesus to a human being. What relationship could be established between reason and faith?

The pope's place in the church

The question of Rome and the personality of Pius IX favoured the progress of ultramontanism. Catholics were indignant at seeing the pope deprived of his states because they thought that temporal powers guaranteed spiritual independence for the pope. Many Catholics wanted to see papal infallibility defined more clearly. By proclaiming the Dogma of the Immaculate Conception of Mary in 1854, the pope indirectly affirmed his infallibility. But devotion to the pope sometimes verged on the ridiculous when he was called the 'deputy God of humanity' or 'the continuation of the incarnate word'. Clarifications had to be made.

Partial responses

Yielding to pressure from several bishops, Pius IX took a stand against the evils of the time in two documents dated 8 December 1864. In the encyclical *Quanta cura* he condemned rationalism, Gallicanism, socialism, liberalism and so on after the fashion of Gregory XVI. To the encyclical he attached a catalogue (*Syllabus*) of twenty-four propositions which were condemned. The last proposition seemed to imply the rejection of the whole of modern society. The hard-line Catholics were overjoyed. The anti-clerics sniggered: the pope was going to pull up the railway lines to Rome. The liberal Catholics, who felt themselves

The First Vatican Council (1869–1870)

The relationship between reason and faith.

Some definitions from the constitution *Dei Filius* of 24 April 1870:

If anyone says that the substance or essence of God and of all things is one and identical, let him be anathema.

If anyone says that the one true God, our Creator and Lord, cannot be known with certainty through his works in the natural light of human reason, let him be anathema.

If anyone says that it is possible that the dogmas propounded by the church can, as a result of the progress of science, be given a meaning different from that which the church has understood and continues to understand, let him be anathema.

Papal primacy and infallibility

Some extracts from the constitution *Pastor Aeternus* of 18 July 1870:

We, adhering faithfully to the tradition received from the beginning of the Christian faith – with a view to the glory of our Divine Saviour, the exaltation of the Catholic religion, and the safety of Christian people (the sacred Council approving), teach and define as a dogma divinely revealed: That the Roman Pontiff, when he speaks ex cathedra *(that is, when – fulfilling the office of Pastor and Teacher of all Christians – on his supreme Apostolical authority, he defines a doctrine concerning faith or morals to be held by the Universal Church), through the divine assistance promised him in blessed Peter, is endowed with that infallibility, with which the Divine Redeemer has willed that His Church – in defining doctrine concerning faith or morals – should be equipped: and therefore, that such definitions of the Roman Pontiff of themselves – and not by virtue of the consent of the Church – are irreformable. If anyone shall presume (which God forbid!) to contradict this our definition: let him be anathema.*

Bettenson, *Documents of the Christian Church*, 273f.

disapproved of, were dismayed. As a way out of the impasse, Mgr Dupanloup, in a document in which in other respects he affirmed his belief in the temporal power of the pope, tried to give an acceptable meaning to the papal texts. The pope accepted the interpretation and tempers cooled down a little.

In the context of the church's difficult relations with the modern world and of the controversies within the church itself, Pius IX decided to call the Vatican Council.

2. The meeting of the Council

Setting up

The Council assembled on 8 December 1869. The proposed aims were vague and general, but everyone thought that the main subject would be the definition of infallibility. Out of a thousand functioning bishops, a little more than 700 took part in the Council. The whole world was represented, but only by European bishops. Commissions had prepared a large number of dossiers on many different subjects; political and military circumstances limited the work to two spheres.

Work

(29) The constitution *Dei Filius*, voted for on 24 April 1870, was the outcome of the discussions on the relationship between reason and faith. Faced with the errors of rationalism, pantheism and fideism, the council defined the existence of a personal God who could be attained by reason, while at the same time affirming the necessity of revelation. There could be no conflict between reason and faith.

Papal infallibility had not been officially included in the work to be done in respect of the church. A majority of bishops called for the introduction of the discussion on infallibility while a minority opposed it, thinking that the time was not opportune for a definition. Among the latter were several German and French bishops, including Dupanloup; these left the council so as not to scandalize the Catholics. The (30) Fathers voted on the constitution *Pastor Aeternus* on 18 July 1870 in the midst of acclamations and a formidable storm. Essentially, the document was an affirmation of papal primacy and infallibility. After so much verbal exaggeration, infallibility was reduced to reasonable proportions.

The adjournment of the Council

On 19 July 1870 war was declared between France and Germany. Napoleon III withdrew from Rome the troops which were protecting the pope. On 4 September Napoleon fell from power. On 20 September Italian troops occupied Rome, which became the capital of the kingdom of Italy. The council was adjourned and never reconvened.

3. The results of the Council

The decisions of the council were generally accepted. The only people to reject them were a few German university staff around Döllinger in Munich. Some of them formed an Old Catholic Church with well-defined limits. They soon joined up with the Jansenist church of Utrecht.

Vatican I left a feeling of imbalance. Through lack of time, the council had discussed the pope but not the bishops, though doubtless the time was not ripe for a theology of the episcopate. This lack of time was perhaps providential. In the end the definition of infallibility had fewer consequences than those of primacy. Strictly speaking, the pope exercised infallibility only in the definition of the Assumption in 1950. On the other hand, in affirming his primacy the council accorded the pope 'ordinary, immediate and episcopal jurisdiction over the whole church'. The primacy favoured the centralization on Rome and increased the prestige and strength of the papacy at a time when it had lost its temporal power. It still remained to reconcile this primacy with the power of the bishops. The affirmation of collegiality would have to wait until Vatican II. The definitions of Vatican I sometimes increased the tension between political society and the church. This was the excuse for anti-clerical measures in various countries.

For further reading

C. Butler, *The Vatican Council*, Fontana Books 1962

H. McLeod, *Religion and the People of Western Europe 1789–1970*, Oxford University Press 1981

A. R. Vidler, *Prophecy and Papacy: A Study of Lamennais, the Church and the Revolution*, SCM Press 1954

18

The British Experience

Nineteenth Century

In sustaining the struggle against Revolutionary France which culminated in the defeat of Napoleon in 1815, Great Britain emerged as the foremost European power on a world-wide scale, and retained that position well into the middle of the century: possessing the largest navy and (even after the loss of the thirteen North American colonies) the most extensive overseas empire, she was also the first great power to undergo the transformation of the Industrial Revolution and enjoy the wealth which sprang from it. Although other nations would challenge her world power and develop their own industrial might, Britain built up a still larger colonial empire which in fact reached its greatest extent only after the First World War. It is not surprising, therefore, that the various strands of British religion exercised a world-wide influence during the nineteenth century.

I · The Fortunes of Church Establishments

The century began with the Anglican Church still established in England, Ireland and Wales, and the established Presbyterian Church overwhelmingly dominant in Scotland; it ended with Anglicanism disestablished in Ireland, on the eve of disestablishment in Wales, and with the Church of Scotland split into two. Unlike Continental disestablishments and church schisms, these changes had little to do with the impact of liberalism or secularism (see Chapter 19), but rather resulted from a vigour of competition within British religious life which had few parallels in continental Europe. In Ireland, the Roman Catholic majority, and to a lesser extent Presbyterianism, successfully challenged the Anglican monopoly; in England and Wales, Protestant Dissent (now increasingly called 'the Free Churches') asserted its growing share of the nation's religious life. In Scotland, bitter disputes about the purity of the Presbyterian system divided the Established Church from within.

1. The Church of England faces change

The Anglican Church at the beginning of the century was still affected by the haemorrhage in its structure represented by the growth and gradual separation of Methodism. This disaster had left many church leaders on the defensive and determined to resist any further encroachment on the church's position; yet such defence was hampered by the long-standing deficiencies in organization which made the church ill-equipped to meet the pastoral challenge posed by the Industrial Revolution. The governments of England in the troubled decade after the French Wars (1792–1815) saw Anglicanism as a bulwark against any growth of popular revolutionary fervour on the continental model, and in 1818 granted a million pounds for new churches in urban and industrial areas. This was the first time for a century that the English state had given financial help to the church, and it would be the last. By contrast, within a few years, many churchmen would come to see the state as a threat rather than as a support.

State measures

The first sign of change came with the passing of an Act of Parliament in 1828 removing nearly all civil disabilities on Protestant Dissenters by repealing the seventeenth-century Test and Corporation Acts; now Dissenters were more or less on an equal footing in political life with Anglicans. Even more momentous was the Act emancipating Roman Catholics in 1829; although this had one eye on the political troubles of Ireland, it applied to the rest of the United Kingdom as well. By these measures, the British state had admitted the principle that Dissenters and Catholics could be fully citizens of the realm, and that meant that henceforward, it would be impossible to sustain the old view beloved of staunch Anglicans that there was an inseparable common identity between the state and the established church. However, more drastic measures were to follow. In 1832 an Act was passed reforming and standardizing the chaotic British electoral system, and the ensuing elections produced an administration drawn from the 'Whig' party determined on wide measures of reform in the nation's life. Part of this reforming activity must be to remove some of the gross inequalities in the church's structure: not to confiscate its very considerable wealth, but to force its use in more efficient ways. There were also further measures of relief for Protestant Dissenters in 1836.

The aristocratic Whig leaders who promoted these reforms were rather unlikely candidates to be cast in the role of revolutionaries, but their policies seemed to conservative churchmen to signal the end of everything they cherished. More moderate Anglicans saw the need for structural reform, and in 1835, in a brief change of government, they secured the establishment of an Ecclesiastical Commission to oversee the church's wealth. In the long term, this would prove one of the Anglican Church's best protections against destructive criticism. Nevertheless, reforming activity and Dissenting pressure to continue the assault on Anglican privilege created an atmosphere of crisis in the church, which made many oppose the most reasonable changes; and it was from this bitter opposition that one of the most important movements of the nineteenth century took an unexpected beginning: the Oxford Movement.

2. Evangelicalism and the birth of the Oxford Movement

Evangelical activity

Probably the most vital force in church life at the beginning of the century was that part of the Evangelical Movement which had stayed within the eighteenth-century church structure, carrying on its activity through individual parishes and through voluntary societies for mission work at home and abroad (notably the Church Missionary Society, founded 1799). One Evangelical clergyman, Charles Simeon (1759–1836), was particularly influential because he was based in Cambridge; virtually all graduates among the clergy had gone to Oxford and Cambridge universities, at a time when there were no alternative sources of Anglican clerical training, and so Simeon's powerful evangelical zeal working on successive generations of Cambridge undergraduates could be a major factor in moulding the future outlook of the men in the parishes. In 1815 the Evangelical party, often the object of suspicion and hostility from church leaders in the eighteenth century, gained its first place on the episcopal bench with the appointment of Henry Ryder (1777–1836) as Bishop of Gloucester; this signalled that Evangelical clergy were now part of the Anglican establishment. At the same time, Evangelical activity in social reform secured its greatest triumph with the passage through parliament first of the abolition of the slave trade (1807) and then the abolition of slavery itself throughout the British empire (1833): this through long years of campaigning spearheaded by the MP William Wilberforce (1759–1833), who lived just long enough to see his work complete.

Keble's 'Assize Sermon'

By comparison, the successors of the old High Church group in church life, so influential under Charles I and the later Stuarts, had lost their leading role, and their attitudes were to be found more generally in the Anglican Church in Ireland than in England. They were characterized more by the practice of careful scholarship and quiet pastoral work than by much zeal for promoting their views; and the reforms of the 1830s seemed to challenge everything that they stood for. Yet it was a protest against these reforms by one of their number, John Keble (1792–1866), which was to send the High Church cause into a new phase of dynamism; the occasion was an eminently sensible proposal to reform the Anglican Church in Ireland, principally by suppressing ten bishoprics. Keble, an Oxford academic (or 'don'), saw this as a symbol of the abandonment by the British state of any pretence of support for Christian authority, and the idea of suppression by government order deeply offended his High Church belief in the church's right to order its own affairs. He embodied his unhappiness in a sermon to the Oxford Assize Judges on 14 July 1833.

This 'Assize Sermon' was to become famous as the beginning of the Oxford Movement, so called because so many of its important figures were

Evangelicals and the poor

The lay leadership of the Evangelicals consisted mostly of wealthy and influential men – hence their nickname 'the Clapham Sect', from the fact that so many of them lived in the then fashionable south London suburb of Clapham. Here William Wilberforce reflects, honestly if a little patronizingly, on the gap between rich and poor, and defends Evangelical theology from the charge of élitism:

It may perhaps be not unnecessary . . . to add a few words in order to obviate a charge which may be urged against us, that we are insisting on nice and abstruse distinctions in what is a matter of general concern; and this too in a system which on its original promulgation was declared to be peculiarly intended for the simple and poor. It will be abundantly evident, however, on a little reflection, and experience fully proves the position, that what has been required is not the perception of a subtle distinction, but a state and condition of heart. To the former, the poor and the ignorant must be indeed confessed unequal; but they are far less indisposed than the great and the learned, to bow down to that 'preaching of the cross, which is to them that perish foolishness, but unto them that are saved the power of God, and the wisdom of God'. The poor are not liable to be puffed up by the intoxicating fumes of ambition and worldly grandeur. They are less likely to be kept from entering into the straight and narrow way, and, when they have entered, to be drawn back again, or to be retarded in their progress, by the cares and pleasures of life. They may express themselves ill: but their views may be simple, and their hearts humble, penitent, and sincere. It is, as in other cases; the vulgar are the subjects of phenomena, the learned explain them: the former know nothing of the theory of vision or of sentiment; but this ignorance hinders them not from seeing and thinking; and though unable to discourse elaborately on the passions, they can feel warmly for their children, their friends, their country.

Practical View of the Prevailing Religious Conceptions of Professed Christians in the Higher and Middle Classes in this Country contrasted with Real Christianity (1797).

Oxford dons. Like Charles Simeon in the Cambridge of a generation before them, these men could have a wide influence on Anglican church life because they were based in one of the two main training-grounds for the church's clergy. The effect of Keble's protest and the moves which he and his friends then made to publicize their cause showed that they had tapped a source of deep unease among Anglicans. The centre of their appeal was their concentration on the corporate life of the church: a Catholic emphasis which the eighteenth-century Anglican Church had almost lost in its flight from High Church theology.

Tracts for the Times

For all the achievements of the Evangelicals, they had concentrated on individual conversion and had rarely projected a vision of the church as a living body, with a link to the church of all ages through its constituted hierarchy of bishop, priest and deacon. Now the enthusiasm which many former Evangelicals showed for the Oxford Movement's ideas indicated that the new group was supplying a real need; it was giving fresh meaning for the ramshackle structures of the Established Church. Keble and his friends produced a pamphlet series significantly entitled

Tractarian thought

An extract from Keble's Assize Sermon

One of the most alarming [omens of an apostate mind in a nation] *is the growing indifference, in which men indulge themselves, to other men's religious sentiments. Under the guise of charity and toleration we are come almost to this pass: that no difference, in matters of faith, is to disqualify for our approbation and confidence, whether in public or domestic life. Can we conceal it from ourselves, that every year the practice is becoming more and more common, of trusting men unreservedly in the most delicate and important matters, without one serious inquiry, whether they do not hold principles which make it impossible for them to be loyal to their Creator, Redeemer and Sanctifier? Are not offices conferred, partnerships formed, intimacies entered upon – nay, (what is almost too painful to think of) do not parents commit their children to be educated, do they not encourage them to intermarry, in houses on which Apostolical Authority would rather teach them to set a mark, as unfit to be entered by a faithful servant of Christ?*

I do not now speak of public measures only or chiefly; many things of that kind may be thought, whether wisely or no, to become from time to time necessary, which are in reality as little desired by those who lend them a seeming concurrence, as they are, in themselves, undesirable. But I speak of the spirit which leads men to exult in every step of that kind, to congratulate one another on the supposed decay of what they call an exclusive system.

Newman's Tract 90

This was the Tract which caused such public outcry against the Tractarians for apparently reversing the plain Protestant meaning of the Anglican Thirty-Nine Articles of faith. The reference to 'subscriptions' shows, ironically, that Newman was trying to gain a wider basis of support for retaining the requirement for subscriptions of assent to these Articles from Catholic-minded Anglicans who were unhappy about them.

. . . *That there are real difficulties to a Catholic Christian in the Ecclesiastical position of our Church at this day, no one can deny; but the statements of the Articles are not in this number: and it may be right at the present moment to insist upon this. If in any question it is supposed that persons who profess to be disciples of the early Church will silently concur with those of very opposite sentiments in furthering a relaxation of subscriptions which, it is imagined, are galling to both parties, though for different reasons, and that they will do this against the wish of the great body of the Church, the writer of the following pages would raise one voice, at least, in protest against any such anticipation* . . .

[Conclusion:] . . . *the Articles are evidently framed on the principle of leaving open large questions on which the controversy hinges. They state broad extreme truths, and are silent upon their adjustment.*

Lastly, their framers constructed them in such a way as best to comprehend those who did not go so far in Protestantism as themselves. Anglo-Catholics then are but the successors and representatives of those moderate reformers; and their case has been directly anticipated in the wording of the Articles. It follows that they are not perverting, they are using them, for an express purpose for which among others their authors framed them . . .

Cardinal Newman.

Texts taken from H. Bettenson, *Documents of the Christian Church*, OUP ²1963, 316–7, 318, 321.

Tracts for the Times against Popery and Dissent (it was from these *Tracts* that the party gained the alternative nickname of 'Tractarians'): they felt that they were defending the true Catholic Church against attacks on two fronts within Christianity, let alone against the liberal rationalism of post-Revolutionary Europe. Their heroes were the High Church divines of the seventeenth-century Church of England; essentially they were a backward-looking, highly conservative group.

3. The Oxford Movement: crisis and growth

Newman's conversion

The Movement was destined to suffer what seemed at the time a fatal blow to its aims, the loss of several of its leaders to Roman Catholicism. The most prominent of these was John Henry Newman (1801–90), one of the former Evangelicals who found a wider appreciation of the Church in the Oxford Movement, and who advocated a view of Anglicanism as a middle way (*via media*) between Rome and Protestantism. However, Newman provoked a widespread outcry after writing Tract 90 of the *Tracts for the Times*, in which he had tried to interpret the doctrinal formularies of the Church of England as in basic agreement with the doctrines of the Council of Trent (see above, Chapter 12); his shock at this hostile reaction fuelled his growing conviction that real authority lay in the Church of Rome, and in 1845, despite deep regret for his beloved Anglicanism, he became a Roman Catholic.

233

Influence on Anglican worship

The departure of such figures as Newman lent weight to the views of Dissenters and Protestant-minded Anglicans who bitterly opposed Tractarianism as Roman Catholicism in disguise; yet this was not the end of the Movement. Some of its leaders held firm, notably the saintly Oxford scholar E. B. Pusey (1800–82), and it gained a new character from the initiative of a group of Cambridge undergraduates, who expressed their fascination with the past by founding the Cambridge Camden Society (1842) to study mediaeval church architecture and the worship which had inspired it. The Tractarians had drawn on the Catholic past for theological inspiration, but they had not taken much interest in that same past to change the day-to-day worship of the church. Generally Anglican worship up to the 1840s was a rather dull recitation of the Prayer Book services plus a long sermon, to which those of Evangelical persuasion might add hymns, in imitation of successful Dissenting and Methodist practice. Now those whom the Camdenians inspired made bold experiments in taking up mediaeval liturgy to bring colour and high-quality music to worship in parish churches; they sustained a craze for restoring mediaeval churches to their Gothic state and for building new churches in the same style, and by rediscovering the sacramental life of the mediaeval church, they came to lay great stress on the eucharist as the centre of Christian life. Their followers preferred the label 'Anglo-Catholics' rather than the Oxford nickname of 'Tractarians'; opponents of the movement more abusively termed them 'Ritualists'. Anglo-Catholics' influence on Anglican worship was eventually much wider than their own circle; it was the first stirring of a rediscovery of beauty and dignity in worship which is still spreading through the whole Protestant world.

Revival of monastic orders

The Catholic revival in Anglicanism as much as the Evangelical movement concerned itself with winning over the increasing proportion of industrial and urban English people who had no real contact with organized religion. The Anglo-Catholics often caused misunderstanding and puzzlement among those whom they sought to reach, but the energy, devotion and enthusiasm shown by parish priests with Tractarian or Anglo-Catholic views won them much affection and success in their work. They also inspired efforts to restore monastic life to the Anglican Church, taking advantage of the fact that monasticism had never been condemned outright by the authorities of the English Reformation; first communities of women were established, notably by Priscilla Sellon (*c.*1821–76), and more hesitantly and never in such numbers, male communities as well. Gradually, despite grave suspicions and much public hostility, the church hierarchy recognized the value of what monasticism represented. Anglican monastic orders have not become as numerous or as influential as in the Roman and Orthodox worlds, but as with Anglo-Catholic liturgical experiment, they have had a wide impact on the spirituality of Western Protestantism in general; they have helped to restore an awareness of the value of community life and contemplation to those parts of the Western Church which rejected such forms as popish superstition at the Reformation.

Conflict

Nevertheless, the Oxford Movement also brought Anglicanism acute conflict. Evangelicals furiously opposed Anglo-Catholicism, and the long-drawn-out battles between the two parties took up a great deal of unnecessary energy in the church's life, a battle moreover which the Evangelicals had clearly lost by 1900. The Evangelicals' defeat was to drive them into the sidelines of Anglican church life in England until as late as the 1960s, although they gained an

Ritualism, popery and the opposition

One expression of the extreme Protestant reaction to Anglo-Catholicism was a work by Walter Walsh entitled *The Secret History of the Oxford Movement*, which sold well and ran into many editions. Here Walsh gives good British reasons for opposing both Ritualism and Popery:

Popery is an enemy to National Prosperity . . . Looking abroad throughout the whole world, we find that Popery degrades the nations, instead of raising them to a higher level. The Ritualists cannot point to a single Roman Catholic country which is even on a level with, much less superior to, Protestant countries. On the contrary, Popery has dragged down Spain from her proud eminence, to be the most degraded and poverty-stricken nation in Europe, excepting Turkey. It has kept the South American republics and nations in a state of degradation, immorality and ignorance deplorable to behold. Would any Englishman wish this Protestant country to become what the Papal States were under the temporal rule of Pope Pius IX? Would English working men wish to exchange wages with their brethren in any Roman Catholic country in the world? . . . Before we listen with pleasure to the Reunion with Rome plans of the Ritualists, let us calmly consider the facts, not only of history, but of the everyday life around us. When we contrast Popish countries with Protestant lands, can we doubt any longer which religion most promotes National Prosperity? . . . Common sense can answer these questions in only one way. Protestantism and National Prosperity go together, like Siamese twins . . . And let it not be said that this is an argument which Christians should ignore, for has not the Word of God taught us that true 'Godliness is profitable unto all things, having promise of the life that now is, and of that which is to come' (1 Timothy iv.8)?

Walsh, 1899 edn, 362–3.

increasing influence in the Church of Ireland after its disestablishment in 1869, in reaction to the strength of Roman Catholicism in Irish life.

If both the Tractarians and the Camdenians were primarily backward-looking in their ideals, reflecting the mediaevalizing romanticism which was so common in nineteenth-century Europe, the Anglo-Catholic movement was to broaden its interests and diversify from its conservative roots. Its original impetus had come from its anger that the State should interfere with the church, and many Anglo-Catholics continued to build on this insight that the church had an independent voice of its own; in particular, many priests ministering in slum parishes were appalled at the social injustice which these areas embodied. Some of them became champions of the oppressed through socialism, and their views would be influential in moulding the present-day stance of world-wide Anglicanism on social questions. By the 1870s, others were taking an interest in the new intellectual movements which were affecting theology and biblical criticism (see below), greatly shocking the older generation of more conservative Tractarian leaders, but again contributing much to the synthesis of twentieth-century Anglican scholarship.

4. The Church in Scotland

The established Presbyterian Church of Scotland had very different origins from the Church of England; whereas the Anglican Church took its shape from carefully-considered decisions of the Crown, the Scottish Church looked to four crucial events which in fact all represented revolts against that same Crown. The first was the overthrow of the mediaeval church and the defeat of Mary Queen of Scots in 1560, the second, the Solemn League and Covenant which the leading Scots politicians had made in 1638 as part of their revolt against the government of Charles I, and the third, the declaration of Presbyterian church order and Calvinist orthodoxy made at Westminster in 1646 during the British Civil Wars, in conjunction with English Presbyterians: the Westminster Confession. The fourth was the final overthrow of episcopacy and the establishment of Presbyterianism in 1690 following the national rejection of James II (on the context of all these events, see Chapter 13 above).

Founding of the Free Church of Scotland

The consequence was that there was a fierce spirit of independence in the Scottish Church, and an obsessive determination to remain faithful to the course of events which had shaped its distinctive character. The splits within the church which began in the eighteenth century and which became acute in the nineteenth all centred on this determination. The issue which focussed disputes was one which had far less significance in the Church of England: private patronage, or the right of private individuals to exercise choice in appointments to pastoral office in the church. Private patronage offended against the basic character of the Presbyterian system, and when in the early nineteenth century the state in the shape of the Scottish law courts began intervening with legal judgments against those who wished to abolish private patronage, this interference violated another basic assumption of Calvinist theology: the absolute right of the church to govern its own affairs. Such was the fury of many church members at the continuing survival of private patronage that in 1843 came the Great Disruption: more than a third of the church's ministers left to found the Free Church of Scotland, led by one of the most able and energetic ministers of the day, Thomas Chalmers (1780–1847). Their aim was nothing less than to create an entire alternative church without the shackle of private patronage, and to a great extent, they succeeded: church buildings, ministers' stipends and houses, foreign missions and a host of other enterprises representing a huge outburst of lay support, made financially

The Scottish disruption

The 1842 Claim of Right

At its customary annual meeting in Edinburgh, the 1842 General Assembly, the Church of Scotland's supreme governing body, issued a solemn protest about the interference of the Scottish civil courts (the Court of Session) which had upheld the right of private patrons. It ranks as one of the classic statements of the church's spiritual independence.

. . . the General Assembly, while recognizing the absolute jurisdiction of the Civil Courts in relation to all the temporalities conferred by the State upon the Church, claim as of right freely to possess and enjoy the liberties and rights and privileges bestowed on the Church according to law; declare that they cannot in conscience intrude ministers on reclaiming [objecting] *congregations or carry on the government of Christ's Church subject to the coercion attempted by the Court of Session; protest against sentences of the Civil Court in contravention of the Church's liberties, which rather than abandon they will relinquish the privileges of establishment; and call on all Christian people everywhere to note that it is for loyalty to Christ's Kingdom and Crown that the Church of Scotland is obliged to suffer hardship.*

The British government rejected the Claim of Right and the resolutions about patronage which accompanied it, and so in the following year, a dramatic walk-out at the meeting of the General Assembly, led by the previous year's Moderator (Chairman), heralded the formation of the Free Church. The Scottish judge Lord Cockburn recalled the scene:

As soon as Welsh, who wore his Moderator's dress, appeared in the street, and people saw that principle had really triumphed over interest, he and his followers were received with the loudest acclamations. They walked in procession down Hanover Street to Canonmills . . . through an unbroken mass of cheering people and beneath innumerable handkerchiefs waving from the windows. But amidst this exultation there was much sadness and many a tear, many a grave face and fearful thought, for no-one could doubt that it was with sore hearts that these ministers left the Church, and no thinking man could look on the unexampled scene and behold that the temple was rent, without pain and sad forebodings.

possible by the new industrial prosperity of midlands Scotland.

Reunion

The result was two parallel Presbyterian churches devoting much energy and money to duplicating each other's work, a situation made more absurd when private patronage was indeed abolished in the Established Church in 1874. After this, reunion was inevitable, although it took until 1929 to complete, and even then left small bodies representing the irreconcilable elements from the 1843 and earlier schisms. In the process, nearly all the aims of the leaders of the Disruption were achieved: the Church of Scotland remains established, and indeed represents the majority of the population both churchgoing and non-churchgoing, but is free of interference in its affairs from the secular power. Despite its continuing suspicion of the Anglican ethos, it has come to make its own rediscovery of the richness of liturgy, and even become host to a community following a version of the religious life at the ancient Celtic monastic centre on the island of Iona.

Catholic presence

Throughout the centuries from the Reformation, the Catholic Church has maintained a presence in Scotland, although this was mostly in the remotest parts, particularly certain Western Isles, following the abandonment of Catholicism by nearly all the Scottish nobility in the half-century after the Scottish Reformation. Survival was despite fierce Protestant repression, and was at first very tenuous indeed. The first signs of revival after the destruction of the Reformation came in the aftermath of the disestablishment of Protestant episcopacy in 1690; the new Presbyterian establishment was weak and the Episcopalians were in great disarray, so there was a chance for Roman missionaries to work in the Highlands. However, dramatic growth did not come until the nineteenth century, and was overwhelmingly caused by immigration of Irish Catholics seeking work in the sudden prosperity of industrial Scotland: one of the periodic exchanges of population between the two countries which have continued for at least fifteen hundred years. Suddenly there were Catholics everywhere in midlands Scotland, particularly Glasgow, much to the horror and anxiety of the established Presbyterian Church; in 1878, the Catholic Church recognized this new strength by providing bishops with territorial titles for Scotland. Until very recent years, the Catholic Church in Scotland has retained a distinctively Irish flavour, and the Protestant and Catholic communities have continued to live separate existences, although generally without the terrible violence which has afflicted their relations in Ireland.

Episcopalian revival

Episcopalianism also underwent a revival in the nineteenth century, although on a much more modest scale. The disestablishment of 1690 was a terrible blow, the effects of which were compounded by the Episcopalians' obstinate 'Jacobite' loyalty to the exiled Stuart dynasty, and their consequent association with catastrophic defeats for attempts at Stuart restoration in 1715 and 1745. The resulting paradox was a continuing suspicion and hostility to these struggling champions of episcopacy from the episcopal Church of England south of the border, and it was not until the Scottish Episcopalians mostly recognized Stuart restoration as a lost cause, with the death of the Pretender Charles Edward in 1788, that relations with English Anglicans began to improve. However, in the meantime, the Scottish Episcopalians had performed an unexpected service for the Episcopal Church in North America. After the American War of Independence (1776–83) it was very difficult for Anglicans in the former thirteen colonies to organize themselves; they had no bishops, and it was very difficult to get any consecrated by English or Irish bishops who owed loyalty to the defeated colonial power. The solution was to go to the tiny and harassed Scottish Episcopalian Church, which was still refusing to swear loyalty to the Hanovarian dynasty on the British throne, and get the Scottish bishops to consecrate bishops for North America. Consequently, the American Episcopal Church has its bishops in succession from Scotland; ironically, these consecrations took place in 1784, the same year in which John Wesley solved the same problem for his North American followers in a different way (see above, Chapter 15).

The eventual recognition of Scottish Episcopalianism by and development of links with the Church of England was a two-edged asset, because although it meant some assistance in rebuilding the church's worship life and structures of government, it also meant that Episcopalianism seemed as English to many Scots as Scottish Roman Catholicism seemed Irish. A similar association with England may account for the fact that Baptists, Congregationalists, Quakers and Methodists have remained a small minority among Scottish churchgoers; in the case of Methodism, it may have been the continuing importance of Calvinism within the dominant Presbyterian Church which meant that the Arminian message of Methodism had comparatively little effect.

II · English Churches beyond the Establishment

1. The Free Churches

The nineteenth-century use in England and Wales of the term 'Free Churches' for the various Methodist connexions and the groups formerly known as Dissenters or Nonconformists was on the analogy of the Free Church of Scotland, the church produced by the Scottish Disruption of 1843; however, a new name for these denominations reflects their changed and improved status in the nation. The Evangelical Movement of the eighteenth century had not just affected the Church of England and brought about the various new bodies centring on Methodism, but it had strongly influenced the older Dissenting Churches and reversed the steady decline which had seemed their likely fate after their seventeenth-century defeats.

Freedom for Dissenters

During the nineteenth century, this growth was encouraged by the wholesale removal of the various disabilities which had made Dissenters second-class citizens; by the end of the century, all English universities, formerly Anglican preserves, were open to them, and they could take their full part in national political life. This generally meant support for the Liberal party, despite the fact that for long its leader was a devout High Church Anglican, W. E. Gladstone (1809–98); in return for political activism, Free Churchmen pressed for Liberal support on such issues as the complete abolition of the special status of the established churches, particularly in education. As in Continental Europe, control of education became one of the fiercest battlegrounds of politics, yet here it was as much a contest between rival religious bodies rather than clericalism versus secularism (contrast the struggle, for instance, in France, Chapter 19). Other causes also engaged the political energies of Free Churchmen, such as the regulation and restriction of the alcohol trade: politicians needed to take note of 'the Nonconformist conscience', even if tangible political results of this Free Church pressure were perhaps not very great.

Confidence and energy

The Free Churches' aggression in these struggles was fuelled by a new self-confidence born of their greatly increased share of national religious life. It came as a great shock to the Church of England when the only official religious census in the nation's history, in 1851, revealed the Established Church as having a minority share of the churchgoing population: five and a quarter million as opposed to five and a half for the Free Churches and Roman Catholicism. Free Church confidence was expressed in grand new buildings which housed large congregations listening to sermons from great preachers like the Baptist Charles Haddon Spurgeon (1834–92), and singing an ever more luxuriant variety of devotional hymns. Free Churches also showed much energy in overseas missionary work, and developed new organizations through which they could work at home. A drive to greater pastoral effectiveness encouraged even those denominations which had been traditionally suspicious about central organizations to develop such central structures, notably the first Baptist Union in 1813; most surprising was the cautious move of the Independents, always determined to preserve the freedom of the individual congregation, to form a Congregational Union, beginning in 1832.

Growth in Wales

The greatest Free Church growth in strength was in Wales, where the religious energy of the eighteenth century had been channelled largely into Calvinistic Methodism; this formed itself into a separate denomination (now known as Welsh Presbyterianism) by 1811. The established Anglican Church was hampered in Wales by an organization which found it difficult to adapt to the sudden growth of industrial society in south Wales, and it was also identified with English-speaking Wales against Welsh culture. This meant that a confrontation between Nonconformity and Anglicanism in Wales took on a cultural and linguistic dimension which gave it added bitterness: the Free Churches felt that they reflected the true Wales, and that the disestablishment of the Anglican church would be part of the assertion of Welsh nationhood. Disestablishment eventually came in 1920, having been taken up as a cause by the Welsh Liberal politician David Lloyd George; ironically, by that stage, Free Church strength was beginning to decline and the Anglican Church becoming more representative of the Welsh religious constituency than it had been for a century.

Methodist schisms

In the Methodist movement, disagreements mostly about the way in which church government should be conducted helped to produce a bewildering number of new bodies separate from the main Wesleyan body, the largest of which was the Primitive Methodist Connexion (founded 1811). At the same time, the Wesleyans drifted further from their Anglican roots, shocked by what seemed to them to be the Romanist excesses of the Oxford Movement, and by the success of Anglo-Catholicism in gaining a respected place in the Established Church. Methodism took its place among the Free Churches, despite lingering Wesleyan regrets. Gradually the violent emotions of the various Methodist schisms cooled, resulting, as in the Church of Scotland, in a series of reunion schemes which culminated in a general union of most British Methodist churches in 1932. One offshoot which stayed out of this union was perhaps the most unexpected product of Methodist energy: the Salvation Army, founded by William Booth (1829–1912), a Methodist local (lay) preacher, in 1865; more than any other British denomination, it was the Salvation Army which used the techniques of revivalism which had been pioneered in the Evangelical Protestantism of the United States, combining this concern to save souls with a practical outreach to the very poor and homeless. The Army also became distinctive among non-Quaker Christian churches in having no form of sacramental life, despite its very strictly disciplined hierarchy of 'officers' and activists.

2. The Catholic Church: a new role in England

Emancipation

The nineteenth century was an age of remarkable change for the Roman Catholic Church in England, in terms both of numbers and of status. The first event of great significance was Catholic emancipation in 1829, which was accompanied by an increasingly frank recognition by the British government that Roman Catholicism was overwhelmingly the dominant church in Ireland; as part of English attempts to conciliate the Irish Catholic majority, the privileged status of the

Catholic emancipation

Part of the opening of the 1829 Act of Parliament. The 'various Acts' mentioned were all of the late seventeenth or early eighteenth century:

WHEREAS by various Acts of Parliament certain restraints and disabilities are imposed on the Roman Catholic subjects of His Majesty, to which other subjects of His Majesty are not liable: and whereas it is expedient that such restraints and disabilities shall be from henceforth discontinued; and whereas by various Acts certain Oaths and certain Declarations, commonly called the Declaration against Transubstantiation, and the Declaration against Transubstantiation and the Invocation of Saints and the Sacrifice of the Mass, as practised in the Church of Rome are or may be required to be taken, made, and subscribed by the Subjects of His Majesty, as qualifications for sitting and voting in Parliament, and for the enjoyment of certain offices, franchises, and civil rights: Be it enacted by the King's most excellent Majesty, by and with the advice and consent of the Lords Spiritual and Temporal, and Commons, in this present Parliament assembled, and by the authority of the same, that from and after the commencement of this Act all such parts of the said Acts as require the said Declarations, or either of them, to be made or subscribed by any of His Majesty's Subjects, as a qualification for sitting and voting in Parliament or for the exercise or enjoyment of any office, franchise or civil right, be and the same are (save as hereinafter provided and excepted) hereby repealed.

The 'papal aggression'

The Durham Letter

The establishment of Catholic territorial bishoprics stirred up a deep-seated reaction which even swept away the British Prime Minister, Lord John Russell, who issued a public reply in *The Times* newspaper to an open letter to him from the Bishop of Durham. It is notable how Russell makes the link-up common in the popular mind between Roman Catholicism and the Anglican clergy of the Oxford Movement.

My dear Lord, – I agree with you in considering 'the late aggression of the Pope upon our Protestantism' as 'insolent and insidious', and I therefore feel as indignant as you can do upon the subject.

I not only promoted to the utmost of my power the claims of the Roman Catholics to all civil rights, but I thought it right and even desirable that the ecclesiastical system of the Roman Catholics should be the means of giving instruction to the numerous Irish immigrants in London and elsewhere, who without such help would have been left in heathen ignorance. This might have been done, however, without any such innovation as that which we have now seen.

. . . I confess, however, that my alarm is not equal to my indignation. Even if it shall appear that the ministers and servants of the Pope in this country have not transgressed the law, I feel persuaded that we are strong enough to repel any outward attacks . . . There is a danger, however, which alarms me much more than any aggression of a foreign sovereign.

Clergymen of our own Church, who have subscribed the Thirty-Nine Articles and acknowledged in explicit terms the Queen's supremacy, have been most forward in leading their flocks 'step by step to the very verge of the precipice' . . . I have little hope that the propounders and framers of these innovations will desist from their insidious course. But I rely with confidence on the people of England; and I will not bate a jot of heart or hope, so long as the glorious principles and the immortal martyrs of the Reformation shall be held in reverence by the great mass of a nation which looks with contempt on the mummeries of superstition, and with scorn at the laborious endeavours which are now making to confine the intellect and enslave the soul . . .

Anglican Church of Ireland was ended in 1869. The fortunes of English and Irish Catholicism were further linked by a great wave of Irish immigration to England, particularly encouraged by the terrible economic conditions which prevailed in Ireland during the 1840s; the same impulse to flee Ireland would benefit the Catholic Church in Scotland and the United States.

Catholic reorganization

The greatly increased number of Catholics in England which resulted from this great population shift encouraged the papacy to make proper provision for pastoral oversight; in 1850 there was set up a system of bishoprics with territorial titles (nevertheless carefully avoiding the historic territorial titles enjoyed by Anglican bishops). This move created a furious outcry among British Protestant opinion – it was labelled 'the Papal Aggression' – but most unexpectedly, this was the last great explosion of anti-Catholic feeling in England, the end of a consistent theme in mainstream English politics since the sixteenth-century Reformation.

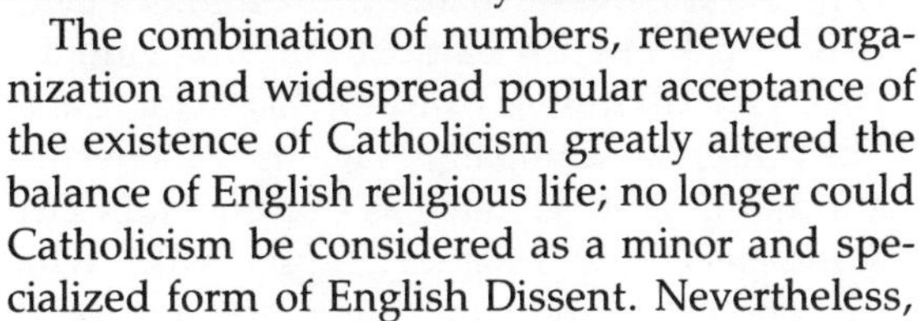

The combination of numbers, renewed organization and widespread popular acceptance of the existence of Catholicism greatly altered the balance of English religious life; no longer could Catholicism be considered as a minor and specialized form of English Dissent. Nevertheless,

Cardinal Wiseman looks to the future

Russell was not the only one who could appeal to the English people. In a pamphlet of 1850, Nicholas Wiseman (1802–65), newly appointed Cardinal Archbishop of Westminster, made his own appeal, this time to English moderation. For the moment this probably reflected pious or diplomatic hope more than reality, but in the long run Wiseman proved to be prophetic. His pamphlet blamed the uproar on the fears of a threatened Anglican establishment, and he also sought to comfort his own Catholic flock:

Thanks to you, brave and generous, and noble-hearted people of England! who would not be stirred up by those whose duty it is to teach you gentleness, meekness, and forbearance, to support what they call a religious cause, by irreligious means; and would not hunt down, when bidden, your unoffending fellow-citizens, to the hollow cry of No Popery, *and on the pretence of a fabled aggression.*

Thanks to you, docile and obedient children of the Catholic faith, many of you I know by nature fervid, but by religion mildened, who have felt indeed – who could help it? the indignities that have been cast upon your religion, your pastors, and your highest chief, but have borne them in the spirit of the great Head of your church, in silence and unretorting forbearance. But whatever has been said in ignorance, or in malice, against us, or against what is most dear to us, commend with me to the forgiveness of a merciful God; to the retributions of His kindness not to the award of his justice . . . The storm is fast passing away; an hònest and upright people will soon see through the arts that have been employed to deceive it, and the reaction of generosity will soon set in. Inquiry is awakened, the respective merits of Churches will be tried by fair tests, and not by worldly considerations; and Truth, for which we contend, will calmly triumph. Let your loyalty be unimpeachable, and your faithfulness to social duties above reproach. Shut thus the mouths of adversaries, and gain the higher good-will of your fellow-countrymen, who will defend in you, as for themselves, your constitutional rights, including full religious liberty.

there was a delay in full acceptance. In organization, the church was virtually a new structure, far more dominated by the clergy than in the days when lay trustees were the main force in sustaining Catholic congregations; it partook of the general authoritarianism which came to characterize Catholicism during the nineteenth century, a new attitude confirmed by the total denial of the ordained status of Anglican clergy issued with English Catholic encouragement by Pope Leo XIII in 1896 (the bull *Apostolicae Curae*). The internal campaign against modernism affected English as much as Continental Catholicism (see below, Chapter 21, pp. 195ff.), which contributed to the continuing isolation of the Catholic Church in English life; despite its continuing growth, it retained an exotic flavour which remained well into the twentieth century. Only after the Second World War has its religious constituency become part of the mainstream of English life, as the descendants of the original Irish immigrant community gained prosperity and acceptance; now, with a considerable numerical decline in the traditional English Free Churches, we can begin to see how great the realignment of forces in English religion has been. The foundations for the modern influence of Catholicism in English life were firmly laid in its nineteenth-century expansion.

III · A New Outlook to Face

1. Basic social change

To concentrate exclusively on institutional change in British religion would give a very misleading picture of what was happening to the churches during the nineteenth century; indeed, the very vigour (and frequently, alas, vigorous bitterness) of the church's institutional life often concealed from church people that they were living in an age of rapid change which would present Christianity with an entirely new set of problems requiring new answers. Britain was the society which had industrialized first, and it was therefore the society which first experienced these pressures. After the eighteenth-century technological revolution which increasingly concentrated on industrial mass production, the nineteenth century harnessed this technology to dramatic improvements in transport, first through the use of steam power based on coal, and then through the invention of the internal combustion engine fired on other fossil fuels (Gottlieb Daimler's engine was invented in 1885). The gradual stages of improvement leading to the widespread use of the bicycle would also prove of great significance. The improvements in sea, rail and road transport which resulted from these developments gave a potential for mobility in the population which had no precedent.

A Revolution in communications

In the short term, the revolution in communications which this represented seemed to benefit the work of the church. Evangelistic work at home and overseas could be carried out more easily, and great crowds could be gathered for the mass revivalist meetings which became such a feature in all Western Christian activity, particularly among Evangelical Protestants. However, on a longer time scale, the mobility of population brought by the new prosperity and heightened economic activity of industrial society undermined the settled communities which had been the basis of Christian life for so long. People became used to the strict separation of work and leisure which the factories and offices of Western society produced; and for many, the Christian religion became one possible activity among many for leisure time. Mass entertainment and sport might take the place of organized religion.

Secularism

The consequences were there for the perceptive to see in British society from as early as the 1880s: although the churches were still growing in numbers, the population was growing still faster, and consequently the proportion of churchgoers was beginning to fall. This movement accelerated during the twentieth century. In many Western societies, notably in Britain and Scandinavia, a vague indifference to Christianity, even if a benevolent indifference, became more common than the militant hostility first seen in the French Revolution, but it was just as fatal for traditional religious practice. The era of secularism, a word invented by the English rationalist writer George Jacob Holyoake (1817–1906), had arrived.

2. Intellectual revolutions: geology and biblical criticism

Far more obvious than these underlying social changes were the great revolutions in the way that the educated élite viewed the past: the overall history both of the created world and of the biblical documents which were the cornerstone of the Christian faith. The growth of geological study vastly extended the age of the earth and made it difficult to see the biblical record as the whole story or even the most important story; a revolution in historical research techniques demanded that the Bible be treated as a historical document subject to the same limitations and shortcomings as any other.

Darwin and evolution

Most of the important steps forward in geology came in Britain; from the end of the eighteenth century, geological observations were being made which indicated a much greater age for the earth and for humankind than had previously been considered. There was nothing destructive for faith in this. Many of the leading geologists were Anglican clergy who saw their work as further demonstrating the marvels of God's creation and illustrating the argument for divine design: an argument which received an influential exposition in the extremely popular book *View of the Evidences of Christianity* (1794) by the Anglican Archdeacon William Paley (1743–1805).

238

It was a young and conventionally pious admirer of Paley, Charles Darwin (1809–82), whose research was to transform the picture; in a series of books, most notably the *Origin of Species* (1859), Darwin presented a picture of evolutionary development which not only meant that humankind had evolved from apes and in origin from the simplest forms of life, but (probably more seriously for Christian faith) that instead of a benevolent divine providence lying behind this process, there was an impersonal struggle for survival which determined which species would be successful in evolution. Naturally this was a challenge to the biblical record, but although there were many bitter disputes as to whether Christians could accept Darwin's findings, and there are still Christian groups which resist his conclusions, large numbers of Anglicans and Free Church people were prepared to accept the truth of the Darwinian model of creation by 1900. The Modernist crisis meant that Catholics worldwide would take longer to assimilate the new ideas (see below, Chapter 21).

Historical-biblical criticism

At the same time, the whole biblical record was coming under careful scrutiny using historical method. The pioneering steps in historical work

Geology and faith

The faith of Charles Darwin

Darwin's later religious beliefs have been the subject of some controversy, yet this statement in a letter he wrote late in life seems to show his position:

[I feel] *the extreme difficulty or rather impossibility of conceiving this immense and wonderful universe, including man with his capacity of looking far backwards and far into futurity, as the result of blind chance or necessity. When thus reflecting, I feel compelled to look to a First Cause having an intelligent mind in some degree analogous to that of man; and I deserve to be called a Theist. This conclusion was strong in mind about the time, as far as I can remember, when I wrote the* Origin of Species, *and it is since that time that it has very gradually, and with many fluctuations, become weaker. But then arises the doubt – can the mind of man, which has, as I fully believe, been developed from a mind as low as that possessed by the lowest animals, be trusted when it draws such grand conclusions?*

I cannot pretend to throw the least light on such abstruse problems. The mystery of the beginning of all things is insoluble by us, and I for one must be content to remain an Agnostic.

Charles Darwin.

Anglicans and Evolution

Frederick Temple (1821–1902), ex-Headmaster of Rugby, Bishop of Exeter and a future Archbishop of Canterbury, shows in this extract from his Bamptom Lectures of 1884 that a liberal-minded Anglican could come to find little but profit in the theory of evolution:

In conclusion, we cannot find that science, in teaching evolution, has yet asserted anything that is inconsistent with revelation, unless we assume that revelation was intended not to teach spiritual truth only, but physical truth also. Here, as in all similar cases, we find that the writer of the Book of Genesis, like all the other writers in the Bible, took nature as he saw it, and expressed his teaching in language corresponding to what he saw. And the doctrine of evolution, in so far as it has been shown to be true, does but fill out in detail the declaration that we are 'fearfully and wonderfully made; marvellous are Thy works; and that my soul knoweth right well'. There is nothing in all that science has yet taught, or is on the way to teach, which conflicts with the doctrine that we are made in the Divine Image, rulers of the creation around us by a divine superiority, the recipients of a revelation from a Father in Heaven, and responsible to judgment by His law. We know not how the first human soul was made, just as we know not how any human soul has been made since; but we know that we are, in a sense in which no other creatures living with us are, the children of His special care.

had been taken by the scholarly monks of the French congregation of St Maur in the late seventeenth century, but after that, German scholars became most prominent in applying these rigorous historical techniques to biblical criticism. Protestant Germany remained supreme in the field throughout the nineteenth century, notably through Julius Wellhausen (1844–1918), whose work on the Pentateuch transformed what had seemed the single work of

Moses into a rainbow of documentary sources. Historical criticism was aided by the new European-wide enthusiasm for archaeology, which British and French enterprise in particular used to explore the lands of the Near East. Much of this work had been inspired by the aim of confirming the record of the Old and New Testaments, but the overall result was to demonstrate how much the contents of scripture reflected a much wider religious world. What did this do for the unique divine inspiration of scripture?

It was not surprising that the result was an intellectual ferment in Christianity, which drove many sensitive and thoughtful people out of conventional faith. Darwin himself ended his days in a gentle and regretful agnosticism, and many bade goodbye to the religious views of their youth through the agency of two great books entitled *The Life of Jesus*: the first (1835), by David Friedrich Strauss (1808–74), a German Lutheran academic eventually driven from the church; the second (1863) by Joseph Ernest Renan (1823–92), a Breton seminarian whose faith had collapsed. The message of both was that the New Testament picture of the Christ was a construct which distorted the reality of the man Jesus. The efforts of most European governments to extend education and create universal literacy meant that it would not simply be a small intellectual minority who would come to hear of such ideas: however imperfectly and gradually, they would affect the thinking of everyone in the new industrial society. Could the various branches of the Western church make an effective and positive response?

For further reading

Owen Chadwick, *The Victorian Church*, two volumes, A. & C. Black 1966, 1970, reissued SCM Press 1987

G. Faber, *Oxford Apostles. A Character Study of the Oxford Movement*, second edition, Faber 1974

K. J. Heasman, *Evangelicals in Action*, Geoffrey Bles 1962

J. D. Holmes, *More Roman than Rome: English Catholicism in the Nineteenth Century*, Burns and Oates 1981

H. McLeod, *Religion and the Working Class in Nineteenth-Century Britain*, Oxford University Press 1984

E. Norman, *The English Catholic Church in the Nineteenth Century*, Oxford University Press 1984

A. R. Vidler, *A Century of Social Catholicism 1820–1920*, SPCK 1964

–, *The Church in an Age of Revolution*, Penguin Books 1961

19

Secularization, the Defence of Religion and Pluralism

The Churches in Politics and Society from 1870 to 1939

With varying degrees of speed, the phenomenon of secularization spread throughout Europe; daily life slipped gradually out of the sphere of the church. The governments came to control the institutions which are the cog-wheels of a country – civil service, teaching, welfare – and which had long been dependent on the church. In this atmosphere of conflict the church felt dispossessed and Catholics hurled themselves into a defence of religion: as they tried to reverse the unfavourable political current, and restore institutions parallel to those of the state, a Christian counter-society came up against a lay society. Time was needed to accept the distinction between the two spheres, for the state to recognize the limits of its own domain and Catholics to find a new place in this secularized society.

I · Across Europe up to 1914

1. The popes and Italy

Three popes

Pius IX reached the last years of his life, which according to Robert Aubert had the twofold character of an apotheosis and a melancholy decline. He died in 1878 after thirty-two years as pope, the longest pontificate in history. His successor Cardinal Pecci, aged 68, took the name of Leo XIII and reigned for twenty-five years. Firm in his principles, he was an accommodating man with a sense of what was possible and was concerned with all the important issues of his era. The conclave of 1903 saw the final intervention of politics in the election of a pope. The Austrian government opposed the election of Cardinal Rampolla, who was considered too favourable towards France, so the cardinals chose a pastor, Cardinal Sarto. The child of a poor family, Pius X had experience of all degrees of ministry: curate, parish priest, bishop. Pius X was primarily concerned with pastoral care: children's communion, music and liturgy, the reorganization of seminaries. He was repelled by politics but had to cope with delicate situations – separation in France, modernism, and so on, in which he stuck very rigidly to his principles. A likeable person because of his goodness and simplicity, he appeared to everyone as a man of faith. He was canonized in 1954.

Neither electorate nor elected

In Italy the Roman question called forth all the energy of Catholics. The papacy had refused to come to terms with the kingdom of Italy. The pope considered himself to be a prisoner in the Vatican. Catholics were forbidden to take part in political life; they could neither elect nor be elected. This attitude left the field free for anticlerical governments which increased the irritations suffered by the church: there was a ban on processions and pilgrimages; monasteries were stripped of their possessions. However, all this did not hinder the rapid rise of a new congregation, the Salesians of Don Bosco.

Catholics felt themselves unhappily torn between their attachment to the pope and patriotism. They devoted their energies to the furtherment of religious and social action which was centralized in the Opera dei Congressi (1875). This movement contributed to a deepening of religious awareness and the training of the laity. But very strict supervision by the religious authorities gave rise to unease at the time of Pius X. Both laity and priests (like Romolo Murri) called for autonomy for Christians in temporal matters and the possibility of taking part in political life.

2. Germany

The Kulturkampf

In January 1871 the proclamation of the German Empire set the seal on the unity of Germany around Prussia and its sovereign, Kaiser Wilhelm I. Catholics were ill at ease in this predominantly Protestant state under the control of Chancellor Bismarck. They organized themselves to defend their traditions and religious freedom. In their annual assemblies (Katholikentage), in which the laity played a predominant part, they touched on the major current problems. They also formed a political party, the Centre Party, to respond to the attacks from the National Liberal Party. Moreover they put forward an advanced social programme, inspired by Mgr Ketteler, Bishop of Mainz.

The definition of papal infallibility had caused ripples in Protestant circles. Bismarck was irritated at the lack of enthusiasm among Catholics for a united Germany, which they would have liked to have been based on Austria. The Catholics were opposed to the Germanization of Poland under Prussian domination. And so the Prussian government attacked the Catholic Church for political reasons. Falk, the Kultusminister (a post which covered both religion and education), gave his anti-clerical legislation the name 'battle for culture' (Kulturkampf), i.e. a struggle against Catholic obscurantism. Favours were granted to the Old Catholics in universities. Jesuits and members of religious orders were expelled. The clergy were obliged to pursue their studies in Germany. Preachers who criticized the government were persecuted. In spite of fines and imprisonments, the Catholics put up resistance. Episcopal sees were left vacant, parishes were without priests. Bismarck found himself in an impasse. The Centre Party made progress in the elections.

Appeasement

Bismarck was disturbed at the progress of Socialism, which he thought ultimately more dangerous than Catholicism. The election of Leo XIII favoured détente. Gradually the rules of the Kulturkampf were relaxed or dropped. By 1887 the whole thing was to all intents and purposes at an end. All that remained was the ban on the Jesuits and the obligation of civil marriage. From this time on, relations between the German power and the Catholics were to be good. The Centre Party even showed itself to be too docile to the ruling power. Thus the Catholics became quite conformist and even nationalist. In their opposition to Bismarck they had been clear on the Polish question or militarism. Once they were reconciled they no longer had any reason to oppose the established order.

3. The other countries of Europe

Austria and Switzerland experienced struggles similar to the Kulturkampf: schools and the marriage ceremony were secularized, and monasteries suppressed. Tensions eased off in Austria in 1879. In Switzerland Mgr Mermillod, known everywhere for the interest which he showed in social problems, was hounded from his post as Vicar Apostolic of Geneva. After ten years of very active exile in France he was able to return in 1883 as Bishop of Fribourg, Lausanne and Geneva.

In Belgium and the Netherlands, the principal struggles were over schools. But with well-disposed governments (a Catholic party in Belgium) the Catholics succeeded in obtaining a ruling on schools which satisfied them.

The Iberian peninsula

In Spain and Portugal the religious conflicts flared into violence many times. In Spain, periods of being well-disposed towards the church alternated with crises of anti-clericalism, as at the time of the short-lived Republic (1873–1875) and during the years 1909–1912. The execution of the anarchist Francisco Ferrer in Barcelona in 1909 resulted in the sacking of churches and monasteries and the assassination of priests. Measures against religious orders were taken in the years following. In Portugal, the assassination of the king in 1908 was soon followed by the proclamation of an extremely anti-clerical republic which attacked the religious orders and declared the separation of church and state.

England

The second part of the nineteenth century witnessed a real renaissance of Catholicism in England, particularly in the towns, evidenced both by the numbers of the faithful and by the personalities of the leaders. Pope Leo XIII recognized the intellectual work done by Newman by making him a cardinal in 1879. Cardinal Manning, also a convert, and Archbishop of Westminster from 1865 to 1892, was particularly concerned with the problems of industry, and several times acted as arbitrator in social conflicts. The Catholic Church in Ireland, already grappling with poverty and emigration, was solidly behind its people in their struggle for independence, in spite of silence from Rome.

II · French Catholics and the Third Republic

1. The Republicans and the beginnings of laicization

At the end of 1875, France was endowed with a Republican constitution by a conservative assembly with Monarchist sympathies. But in the years which followed, all the affairs of state passed into the hands of the Republicans: the Chamber of Deputies, the Senate, the Presidency of the Republic (1879). This was the result of universal suffrage.

Republicans and Catholics

'Republicans' were at that time defined by their admiration for the Revolution which had rescued them from the slavery in which they had been kept by the nobility and priests. Heirs of the Enlightenment, often positivists and Freemasons, they believed in the untrammelled progress of science. To them, Catholics seemed to be political opponents who wanted to restore the monarchy and survivors of an obscurantist religion which was doomed to disappear.

Without questioning the freedom of worship, the Republicans wanted to restrict religion to the realm of private life and build up an education system away from the clutches of the church, and that called for a battle against the congregations. 'Clericalism is the enemy,' said Gambetta. The Republicans encouraged anti-clericalism in various forms, and created institutions parallel to those of the church: patronages, gymnastic societies, and so on. The term Republican became a synonym for 'enemy of religion'. It appeared impossible for a Catholic to be a Republican.

Rallying

Without having any particular sympathy with the Republic, Leo XIII wanted Catholics to side with the existing régime so that they could safeguard the spiritual interests of the Church of France. This policy was known as *ralliement*, rallying. Acting on instructions from the pope, in the toast of Algiers on 18 November 1890, Cardinal Lavigerie affirmed that everyone should accept the institutions of the country. The message was not well received. Leo XIII intervened personally by means of the encyclical *Au milieu des sollicitudes* ('In the midst of cares', February 1892): the Catholics were to accept the Republic and, if necessary, fight legislation by honest means. The reception of the encyclical was lukewarm. Many paid lip service to it. Those who 'rallied' were looked upon with disfavour by both Monarchist Catholics and Republicans, who saw this only as a treacherous tactic.

2. Towards the separation of church and state

The Dreyfus affair and the revival of anti-clericalism

The arrest and trial of the Jewish Captain Alfred Dreyfus for treason in 1894 was not a religious matter to begin with, but when Dreyfus' conviction was reviewed in 1898 because the evidence demanded a retrial, the Catholics, because of antisemitism and nationalist feelings, mostly chose the side of the anti-Dreyfusards. According to Catholic opinion as presented by Catholic newspapers, the evils of the church sprang from a Jewish-Masonic and Protestant conspiracy. Without much critical sense, Catholics welcomed accusations and pseudo-revelations about the Jews and the Freemasons. So they were against the Jew Dreyfus, all the more since the honour of the army, in which there were many Catholics, was at stake.

The Catholics were then assimilated into the nationalist leagues of extreme right-wing Dreyfusards who seemed to be endangering the Republic. 1898 saw the birth of the Monarchist nationalist movement, Action Française, which seduced many Catholics. It represented a setback to the rallying movement. Dreyfus was eventually pardoned after long and bitter controversy; so having won a political victory, the Dreyfusards decided to take up arms against those who threatened the Republic. The church was going to have to foot the bill.

The struggle against the congregations

Waldeck-Rousseau, head of government, took steps against those members of religious orders who had become involved in politics, the Assumptionists, and then worked out legislation against the congregations which had grown up without definite legal status. They were upbraided for their political action, their riches, their rejection of human rights, and their influence on some of the youth group whom they made an opposition to Republican youth.

The law of 9 July 1901, which on the whole was very liberal towards the associations, made an exception of the congregations: they had to obtain special authorization from the Chamber of Deputies or the Senate.

In 1902 the new head of government, Emile Combes, a one-time seminarian who had become fiercely anti-clerical, turned the law on associations into a militant law. He closed 3000 educational establishments which had not been authorized. In 1903 he caused all requests for authorization to be refused *en bloc* with the exception of a few missionary congregations. Finally in 1904 he forbade even authorized congregations to do any teaching. The dispersion of the congregations gave rise to some painful scenes, such as the expulsion of the Carthusians. Men and women belonging to religious orders had to shut their schools and return to the lay state, or else go into exile. It was a traumatic experience for them to live in the secular world when they were old and had no resources.

Anti-clericalism broke out to an unprecedented degree. Outcasts in the administration, teaching and the army, practising Catholics had files opened on them and were kept under surveillance. Processions were attacked, sometimes with loss of life. Saints which had given their names to streets had to make way for heroes of the Republic and of science.

The separation of church and state

The Concordat existed, but what did it mean in such a context? A great many small things led to the breaking off of diplomatic relations between France and the Vatican in July 1904. Everything was pointing towards separation. Catholics observed the Concordat for doctrinal and financial reasons. Some supporters of separation wanted to make de-Christianization a machine. Others, in particular the law reporter Aristide Briand, wanted a moderate separation which

The separation of church and state in France (1905)

The militant laicism of the socialist deputy Maurice Allard (10 April 1905)

It has to be said very loudly that the Church, Catholicism or even Christianity is incompatible with any republican régime. Christianity is an outrage to reason, an outrage to nature. I also declare very clearly that I wish to pursue the idea of the Convention and to complete the work of de-Christianizing France which was taking place in utter calm and as happily as could be imagined until the day when Napoleon concluded his Concordat . . .

And why do we Republicans and above all we socialists want to de-Christianize this country? Why are we fighting against religion? We are fighting against religion because we believe – and I say this again – that it is a permanent obstacle to progress and civilization.

The separation law (9 December 1905)

Article 1. The Republic safeguards freedom of conscience. It guarantees the free practice of worship, restricted solely by the restrictions decreed below in the interest of public order.

Article 2. The Republic does not recognize, pay wages for or subsidize any form of religion. As a result, from the 1 January following the promulgation of the present law, all expenses relating to the practices of religion will be removed from the budgets of the state, the departments and the communes.

241 The encyclical *Vehementer* (11 February 1906) of Pius X

This theory of separation is the clearest negation of the supernatural order. In fact it limits the action of the state to the pursuit of public prosperity in this life, though that is only a secondary matter for political societies; and as though such a thing were alien to it, it is in no way concerned with the ultimate reason for their existence, which is eternal bliss.

The dispositions of the new law are contrary to the constitution according to which the church has been founded by Jesus Christ . . . As a result this church is in essence an unequal society, that is to say a society comprising two categories of person, the shepherds and the flock . . . These categories are so distinct that the right and authority necessary for promoting and guiding all the members towards the goal of society reside only in the pastoral body; as to the multitude, its sole duty is that of allowing itself to be led and of following its pastors as a docile flock.

would burst the abscess of anti-clericalism. The Law of Separation was promulgated on 9 December 1905. It recognized freedom of conscience and abolished the budget for worship. The churches' possessions were handed over to administrative religious associations formed by the faithful of the various denominations.

The Concordat of 1801 was abolished in a unilateral manner because the other signatory, the pope, had not been consulted. Pius X condemned the law for a first time in principle in the encyclical *Vehementer* (February 1906), and for a second time (August 1906) when forbidding the formation of administrative religious organizations which took no account of the hierarchical organization of the church. Meanwhile, the survey of the churches' possessions had led to violent incidents in some places. Because of its

associations with them, the church had to abandon seminaries, presbyteries, bishoprics, which were handed over to the community. However, in order not to inflame the situation, the churches and many of the presbyteries were allowed to use the buildings as before and the community was responsible for their upkeep.

The advantage of a crisis

This period remained a painful memory for Catholics. The wound healed slowly. The Church of France was left materially impoverished. Between 1905 and 1914 ordinations fell by a half. Lacking money of its own, the church appealed to the generosity of the faithful to maintain the clergy. Some priests contemplated manual labour, and in 1906 founded an association of Worker Priests. The clergy often found themselves obliged to depend on the better-off among the faithful. Many Catholics turned towards the extreme right, in this case to Action Française.

However, in the long term the separation had beneficial aspects. It took the heat out of anticlericalism, but above all the Church of France had recovered her freedom, which had formerly been continuously hampered by the Organic Articles. The bishops were able to meet together and make a united effort in pastoral care. The church was able to build new places of worship without interference, and to create parishes. The separation also contributed to the reconciliation of the bishops and pope, who now elected them directly.

III · From the First World War to the 1930s

1. Christians in the Great War

During the 1914–1918 war, Catholics identified themselves completely with the objectives of their nation states. It was demonstrated on all sides that being a Catholic did not make a person less patriotic. Catholics even bid higher by putting the resources of their religion at the service of their Fatherland and of victory. All over the place bishops offered up prayers 'for the success of our armies'. How was God to be found in all this? It has also to be said that national feelings were much stronger than international socialism. In France the war allowed Catholics to rediscover their place in the nation as a community. The members of religious orders who had been sent into exile came back to take up arms. The solidarity of the trenches enabled the two Frances to come together again. On both sides Catholics mobilized to serve right and their fatherland. In France, Mgr Baudrillard, Rector of the Catholic Institute in Paris, in more than one polemical work sponsored a Committee of French Propaganda Abroad; the German Catholic universities responded with a work that was just as polemical.

Pope Benedict XV's peace proposals

Although it was not quite the first time in history that such a thing had happened, the Holy See had some difficulty in assessing its position in a war in which there were Christians on both sides who to some degree or another expected the pope's support. The Holy See attempted some humanitarian actions; exchanges of the wounded, the organization of army chaplaincies. From the beginning of his pontificate Benedict XV made many pleas for peace. He would have liked to have prevented Italy from entering the war in 1915. On 1 August 1917,

24

The church in the 1914–1918 war

The pope seriously offended French public opinion as a whole by proposing the abandonment of war reparations and being vague about the return of Alsace and Lorraine to France. Among Catholics, including the clergy, national feeling was stronger than traditional submission to the sovereign pontiff.

The peace proposals of Pope Benedict XV (1 August 1917)

First of all, the basic point must be that the material force of arms is replaced by the moral force of law; hence a just accord on all sides for the simultaneous and reciprocal reduction of armaments, according to rules and guarantees to be established, to the degree necessary and sufficient to maintain public order in every state. This is to be followed by the replacement of armies, the institution of arbitration with its supreme function of peacemaking, according to norms which are to be agreed and sanctions to be taken against the state which refuses either to submit international questions to arbitration or to accept its decisions.

As for reparations and the costs of war, we see no other means of resolving the question than by laying down as a general principle a complete and reciprocal waiver, which moreover would be justified by the immense benefits to be gained from disarmament.

As to territorial questions, like those discussed for example between Italy and Austria and between Germany and France, there is room for hoping that considering the immense advantages of a lasting peace with disarmament, the parties in conflict would want to examine them in conference.

Address by the Dominican Fr Sertillanges on French peace on 10 December 1917 in the church of La Madeleine in Paris

Most Holy Father, we cannot for a moment accept your calls for peace. We confess that to prolong this war for even an hour would be a crime if it were possible to bring it to an end by a reassuring treaty. (As that is not possible) our peace would in that case only be a conciliatory peace. It would not be the peace of diplomats, nor the peace of Stockholm, nor the peace of the Soviets, nor the illusory but sincere peace of our socialists; it would not even be – and this we regret with all our heart – peace achieved by a fatherhood which put itself between the two camps. It would be peace by bitter war to the end, the peace of power employing violent means, the peace of the soldier. We are sons who sometimes say 'No, no', like the rebellious son in the gospel.

during a general lull, Benedict XV launched a peace appeal to all the parties in the war, putting forward specific proposals and even offering himself as mediator. This was certainly a compromise peace. The pope's appeal was on the whole badly received. The French would have preferred the pope to condemn Germany. Catholics themselves refused to respond to the appeal, as Fr Sertillanges, a Dominican, made quite clear. The German Catholics were more favourably disposed. In the end, only the socialists gave it any favourable consideration. The pope had undoubtedly underestimated the difficulties. Such a conflict could not be ended by a compromise but called for the complete defeat of the enemy.

2. Post-war attempts at reconciliation

A new Europe

Italy had arranged for the Vatican to be excluded from discussions over peace treaties, for fear lest the Roman question be raked up again. The Vatican was not able to become a member of the League of Nations. The peace treaties disappointed the Holy See, which thought that they were motivated more by a desire for revenge on Germany than by justice. There was much talk at the time of a Protestant peace, because the great Catholic state, Austria, had been carved into pieces. It ought to be noted, however, that the Catholic states, Poland and the Baltic countries, regained their independence. In another context, Catholic Ireland at last attained its independence in 1921.

Reconciliation

The ten years which followed the war were marked by the resolution of numerous conflicts between the church and states. The popes Benedict XV (1914–1922) and Pius XI (1922–1939) proved to be reconcilers. There was even a short-lived attempt at reconciliation with Soviet Russia during the Geneva conference of 1922. The Russian Revolution of 1917 had allowed the calling of a council and the election of a Patriarch of Moscow, Tikhon, in 1918. The Holy See hoped to obtain complete religious freedom in Russia, in particular for the Uniate Churches attached to Rome. A papal mission left for Russia bearing aid to the victims of the civil war and famine. All these efforts did not prevent persecution from breaking out on all the religious groups in Russia, and priests and bishops were eliminated in their thousands.

In France the war had put paid to the old quarrels. The 'Blue Horizon' Chamber of 1919 did not go back on the lay laws, but wanted religious peace. Alsace-Lorraine came back to France and continued to be included under the terms of the Concordat. On 16 May 1920 Joan of Arc was at last canonized: a special representative of France was sent to Rome. In 1921 diplomatic relations were re-established between France and the Vatican. Finally, in 1924, the church recovered legal support with the Diocesan Associations.

The Lateran Accords (1929)

Under Pius XI, fifteen concordats with states were signed, in mutual recognition of the rights of the church and the states. This policy of appeasement reached its peak with the Lateran Accords of 1929, which provided a solution to the Roman question. There were two aspects to this agreement, which was signed with Mussolini, who hoped for prestige from it for his régime. In one treaty Pius XI recognized the kingdom of Italy, with Rome as its capital, and Italy recognized the sovereignty of the pope over the Vatican City, a tiny state of 44 hectares. In addition, a Concordat governed relationships between Italy and the church. A new period in this history of the papacy began. The Lateran Accords were renewed in 1945, and a revised Concordat was signed in 1984.

Catholic Action and Action Française

In France, the left-wing coalition government under Edouard Herriot elected in 1924 again led to anti-clerical actions; this time they prompted a strong Catholic response. Following this, in 1926 first Cardinal Andrieu, Archbishop of Bordeaux, and then Pius XI condemned Action Française: Catholics might no longer belong to it and those who did not obey were subject to strict disciplinary measures by the church.

The next decade saw a more positive step in the formation of Catholic Action, not only in France but elsewhere in Europe. In Belgium in 1925, Abbe Cardijn launched Jeunesse Ouvrière Chrétienne, which began in France under Abbé Guerin the next year. This youth movement led to further specialized youth movements: for those working in agriculture, students and so on, each movement for young men was paralleled by one for young women. As a consequence the 1930s became a 'golden age of French Catholicism': Christian trade unions developed and writers like Claudel, Mauriac, Maritain and Bernanos made a deep impression. However, that did not prevent divisions among Catholics, in particular over what attitude to take to growing totalitarianism.

3. Christians against totalitarianism

Italian Fascism

After the war, Italian Catholics were able to take part in political life. In 1919 the priest Don Sturzo (1871–1959) founded the Italian Popular Party, the first form of Christian democracy. The party scarcely had time to establish itself, because in October 1922 Mussolini and the Fascists took power. Fascism (from the word *fascio*, meaning a group of old warriors) was born out of a wounded nationalism (the war had not brought Italy all that it hoped for), economic difficulties and upsets caused by strikes and fear of Bolsheviks. Formed from a minority group of anticlericalists, the Fascists were close in outlook to the conservative Catholics who were afraid of Communism and mistrusted an unstable democracy. Catholic opinion therefore was favourable to Mussolini, who intended to settle the Roman question. Don Sturzo, receiving little support from Pius XI, had to go into exile in 1924. The Catholics were not particularly upset at the dissolution of all political parties in 1926. The Lateran accords of 1929 reinforced Mussolini's position.

However, Fascism became increasingly totalitarian. Its aim was to integrate the citizen into all the organizations of the party from birth to death. 'I take a man at birth,' said Mussolini, 'and do not let him go until the moment of his death, a moment when it is the pope's job to look after him.' The church's movements seemed to be in competition with the Fascist organizations. In 1931, religious buildings were sacked and Catholic youth groups disbanded. Pius XI reacted fiercely in the encyclical *Non abbiamo bisogno* ('We have no need', June 1931), in which he protested against the totalitarianism of the state. The church had to have the means of carrying out its educational work, which was indispensable. However, the pope compromised to some degree by ordering Catholic Action not to get involved with any political, trade-union or sporting activity.

(244)

At the time of the Ethopian War (1935–1936), Pius XI did not dare to oppose the conquering nationalism of Fascism in which the majority of Catholics shared. The Vatican journal *Osservatore Romano* had spoken truthfully, if guardedly, when it said that the need for living space did not justify an unjust war of conquest. But bishops blessed flags and regiments were sent to Africa. The pope contented himself with expressing his pleasure when peace returned, and Italian missionaries were swallowed up in Ethopia. French Catholics expressed a degree of unease about it and said so. They were indirectly censured by the suspension of the journal *Sept*.

German Nazism

Nazism (the National Socialist Party) was born in the context of Germany's defeat, in which the right wing saw the work of foreign agents: Jews, socialists and Bolsheviks. Hitler reorganized these dissatisfied people into a political group and set out his ideology in his work *Mein Kampf* (My Struggle). It was made up of racism, antisemitism and hostility to Christianity. From 1922 to 1929 largely a minority movement, Nazism was generally condemned by the bishops: a Christian could not be a Nazi.

In the context of an economic crisis, Hitler

came to power in January 1933 in the guise of a 'saviour'. Catholics did not want to appear bad Germans by setting themselves up against him. Conservative Catholics (such as von Papen) joined up with him. They feared Communism as the alternative. Hitler, who did not have an absolute majority, obtained full power with the votes of the Catholic Centre Party, which agreed to disband several weeks later when all the trade union organizations and political parties were supressed. The bishops protested against the Nazi Party.

To reconcile the Catholics Hitler signed a general Concordat between Germany and the Vatican on 20 July 1933. Cardinal Pacelli, Secretary of State to Pius XI, had been the chief negotiator. Very favourable to Catholics on the surface, this Concordat was deeply ambiguous. The church thought that it had a legal basis for resistance. But the Concordat helped the consciences of Catholics to doze. Some of them were to say later: 'The Concordat took the reins out of our hands.' Very soon came a build-up of slanders against the clergy, racial measures and the dissolution of Catholic movements. It is true to say that for the most part German Catholics were antisemitic.

Catholics and other Christians at first remained passive. There was even a movement of 'German Christians' which was openly pro-Nazi. However, from 1934 onwards, under the leadership of the theologian Karl Barth and the Pastor Martin Niemöller, German Protestants came together under the name of the 'Confessing Church' at a clandestine synod at Barmen in Wuppertal and published a declaration of faith which resisted Nazism. Few in numbers, several members of this church became victims of Nazism. Dietrich Bonhoeffer, one of the best known, was hanged in 1945. He exercised a very great influence by the writings which were published after his death.

In 1937 the pope rebelled and reacted by means of the encyclical *Mit brennender Sorge*, published at the same time as the encyclical about Communism.

Atheistic Communism

Since October 1917, Socialism had a fatherland, Russia. The Communist revolution had its agents, the Third International, the Comintern and the national Communist parties. Western Christians knew little about the events in Russia. But Communism really disturbed them when it became a political force in the West. In 1931, the proclamation of a Republic in Spain had resulted in the first violent anti-clerical demonstrations: the church remained powerful and rich. After a few more years of peace, the victory of the Popular Front (a consortium of the parties on the left) in February 1936 was accompanied by vandalism against churches and convents. On 18 July 1936, General Franco rebelled against the Republic at the start of a civil war which was to last three years: more than a million were killed. The Republicans, of whom the Communists formed only a small part, made a fierce attack on the church: 2000 churches were burned and 7000 priests massacred. Franco's war seemed to be an anti-Communist crusade. Almost all the bishops allied themselves with Franco's nationalists in a collective letter of 1937. But if the majority of Spanish Catholics went over to Franco, it was the resistant minorities who remained faithful to the Republic, like the Basques, whose priests were shot by Franco's men. The crusade concealed the defence of a number of interests other than religious ones and the conduct of Franco's army was no different from that of the Republican army. Outside Spain, Catholics were divided on the subject of Franco. Bernanos, in Spain, at the beginning of the conflict, denounced the trickeries that were hidden behind religion. The Vatican granted recognition to the nationalist government from September 1937. Nazi Germany and Fascist Italy gave aid to Franco, and the international brigades to the Spanish Republic.

In the Face of Totalitarianism

Italian Fascism

We are in the presence here of a whole series of authentic affirmations and no less authentic facts which beyond doubt aim at – and to such a considerable degree have already been successful in – monopolizing the young, from earliest childhood to adulthood, for the full and exclusive use of a party and a régime. This is on the basis of an ideology which is explicitly resolved on pagan statolatry (worship of the state), real and proper, as much in conflict with the natural rights of the family as with the supernatural rights of the state.

For a Catholic, to claim that the Church and the Pope must limit themselves to the external practices of religion – the mass and the sacraments – and that the rest of education belongs totally to the state, cannot be reconciled with Catholic doctrine.

Pius XI, Encyclical *Non abbiamo bisogno*, 29 June 1931.

German National Socialism

Anyone who takes race or people or the state or the form of the state or the seats of power or any other basic value of human community – all things which have a necessary and honourable place in the earthly order – anyone who takes these ideas and removes them from this scale of values, even religious values, divinizing them in an idolatrous cult, reverses and falsifies the order of things created and ordained by God.

As persons, human beings possess the rights that they hold from God; these must be maintained over against the collective society, safeguarded from any attack which would tend to deny, abolish or neglect them.

Pius XI, Encyclical *Mit brennender Sorge*, 14 March 1937.

Atheistic Communism

The struggle between good and evil, the sorry legacy of original sin, continues to rage in the world. Whole peoples run the risk of lapsing into a barbarism more fearful than that in which the greater part of the world was still entrapped at the coming of the redeemer. You will have understood that this menacing peril is Bolshevik and atheistic Communism.

Communism is intrinsically perverse, and one cannot accept collaboration with it in any area on the part of anyone who wants to save Christian civilization. If some were to cooperate with the victory of Communism in their country, led astray by error, they would be the first to fall, victims of their aberration; and the more the regions Communism manages to penetrate are distinguished by the antiquity and greatness of their Christian civilization, the more devastating will prove the hatred of the 'godless'.

Pius XI, Encyclical *Divini Redemptoris*, 19 March 1937.

The Popular Front in France

In a less dramatic manner, French Catholics were also confronted by the Popular Front, which was victorious in the legislative elections of May 1936. Catholics were caught in the rise of extremes: on the right wing leagues like the Croix de Feu; on the left, the Christian revolutionaries of Terre Nouvelle, who superimposed the hammer and sickle on the cross. Maurice Thorez, secretary of the Communist Party, without much success proposed a policy of the 'outstretched hand' to Christians. The Popular Front did not have the sympathy of the majority of Catholics, but it did not offer any chance to a return of anti-clericalism. Catholics were encouraged to make distinctions between Communist doctrine and individual Communists. They asked themselves whether Christianity and Communism were compatible. In an interview

The Spanish Civil War

For the majority of Catholics and for the Holy See, Franco's uprising was a crusade against Communism. Georges Bernanos had thought this initially, but having witnessed the summary executions perpetrated by Franco's men in Majorca, he attacked the pseudo-crusade and the reciprocal violence.

I think that the Spanish Crusade is a farce. It sets against one another two partisan masses which were already in confrontation at an electoral level, and will always confront one another in vain because they do not know what they want, exploiting force instead of knowing how to make use of it.

The Spanish War is a charnel house. It is the charnel house of principles, true and false; of intentions, good and bad. When they have cooked together in blood and mud, you will see what they become, you will see the soup into which you have plunged. If there is a sight deserving of compassion it is that of these unfortunates who have squatted for months around the witches' cauldron, stabbing at it with a fork and each one boasting of the piece that he has got – Republicans, Democrats, Fascists or anti-Fascists; clerical and anti-clerical, poor people, poor devils.

I have seen with my own eyes, I tell you, I have seen a small Christian people, peaceful by tradition, sociable in the extreme and almost to excess, suddenly becoming hard; I have seen these faces, even children's faces, growing hard . . .

Georges Bernanos, *Les Grands Cimitières sous la lune* (1938).

given to the Catholic weekly *Sept*, Leon Blum, the head of government, affirmed the possibility of a collaboration between the Catholics and the Popular Front. The year 1936 saw the acceptance of political pluralism amongst Catholics in France.

Pius XI against totalitarianism

We have already mentioned Pius XI's protest at all the abuses of Fascism in the 1931 encyclical  *Non abbiamo bisogno*. Pius XI took a stand against Nazism and Communism in two encyclicals published within a few days of each other. The  encyclical against Nazism, *Mit brennender Sorge*, dated 14 March 1937, was smuggled into Germany and read from pulpits on the following 21 March. The encyclical, in part drafted by the German Cardinal Faulhaber and Cardinal Pacelli, categorically condemned the racism, antisemitism and idolatry of the state, and denounced the many violations of the Concordat. The encyclical *Divini Redemptoris* of 19 March 1937 condemned atheistic Communism as 'intrinsically perverse' and forbade all collaboration with it. The pope invited his hearers to refer to the social doctrine of the church to find an answer to social problems.

Prevailing opinion was more inclined towards the condemnation of Communism, a universal danger, than to that of Nazism, which appeared to be a local affair. Pius XI was preparing for a renewed attack on Fascism in the face of the Italian bishops in February 1939 when he died. In his unfinished speech he recalled the persecutions of Nero, slandered of Christians. A few months later, the totalitarian states caused the outbreak of the Second World War.

For further reading see the books listed at the end of Chapter 21.

20

A Worldwide Christianity

1800–1940

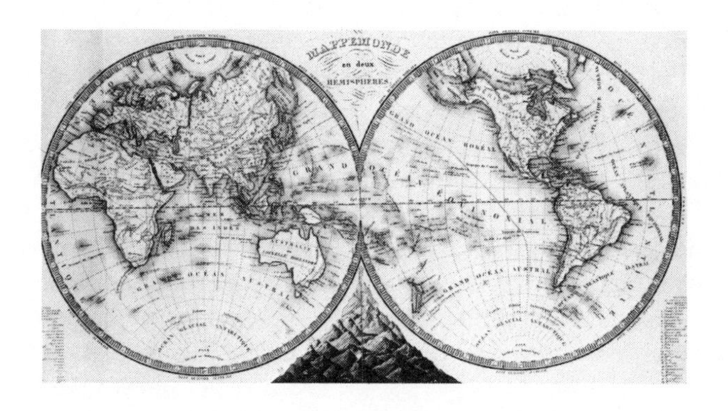

With the religious restoration at the beginning of the nineteenth century, the overseas missions which had been dormant since the Revolution also revived. Throughout the century there was a great upsurge of founding mission support schemes and numerous orders of men and women to carry the gospel to distant places. Right up to the 1870s, the missionaries left for unknown countries without always having the support of their governments. At the end of the century, European imperialists divided up the world among themselves and introduced their own national missionaries into the colonies they had conquered. Evangelization was profitable, but not without numerous ambiguities which disturbed the papacy at the time of the First World War. At that time a concern arose to form local churches which had their own clergy and forms of religious expression drawn from their own cultures.

I · The Beginning of the Missionary Revival in the Nineteenth Century

1. New political and religious circumstances

The English victory at Trafalgar in 1805 had given England the mastery of the seas and prevented Catholic missionaries from going overseas. At that time the Protestant missionary societies began their preaching in foreign fields. The treaties of 1814–15 restored freedom to travel on the seas. Spain and Portugal had begun to decline. Their American colonies had proclaimed their independence. From this time on England and France were the two great competing powers in the maritime field, that is to say in commercial, colonial and missionary matters. To simplify things somewhat, England as the protector of Protestant missions was often contrasted with France as the protector of Catholic missions.

Voyages and explorations

Throughout the century sail was gradually giving way to steam. With the opening of the Suez Canal in 1869, which almost halved the duration of the voyage from London to Bombay, the Far East came nearer. The explorers penetrated the interior of the continents of which only the edges had been known. These were scholars, adventurers and emigrants in search of territories. There were also missionaries. *The Journey to Tibet* (1843–1846) by the Lazarist fathers Huc and Gabet was a best-seller. Livingstone (1813–1873), who explored the course of the Zambezi, was a doctor and a priest.

Missions and romanticism

In their eagerness to restore religion and to go back to the tradition of the old order, Christians rediscovered foreign missions at the same time as home missions (cf. Chapter 17). In 1802, in *The Genius of Christianity*, along with the values of the Christian past, Chateaubriand praised missions and missionaries. This was the beginning of that missionary romanticism which has inspired numerous works and journals right up to the present day: mission as an exotic adventure and at the same time as an element of French influence. The eighteenth-century Jesuits' *Edifying and Curious Letters* were constantly reissued during the nineteenth century.

As in the past, Christians were concerned for the eternal salvation of all 'those seated in the darkness of the shadow of death'. The same spirit inspired the missionaries who travelled through France and those who undertook to take the gospel to the 'savages'. The Catholics wanted to outdo the Protestants and vice versa.

Some people wanted to found new Christianities freed from the obstacles which had been encountered in Europe. A missionary was in the same position as the apostles of the earliest church when they took the gospel to those who were hearing about Christianity for the first time. The utopian socialists also wanted to establish their socialist ideals beyond the seas!

At the same time Christians, like many of their contemporaries, were concerned to put right many tragic human situations. Evangelization was always accompanied by an attempt to civilize and introduce humanity. The missionaries were teachers, doctors, nurses, sometimes scholars. They felt sorry for 'the unhappy children of Ham' (the African Blacks) sold into slavery by Arabian merchants when the European treaty was broken. In a perspective centred on Europe, Christians, as Europeans, were hit by the slow progress of civilization in certain countries. In the nineteenth century, all Europeans thought

The birth of missionary romanticism

The Genius of Christianity influenced the whole of missionary literature during the nineteenth century and sometimes even beyond:

The cults of idols have known nothing of the divine enthusiasm which animates the apostle of the gospel. The ancient philosophers themselves never left the avenues of Academe and the delights of Athens to go on a sublime impulse to humanize the savage, instruct the ignorant, heal the sick, clothe the poor and sow concord and peace among enemy nations. That is what Christian religious have always done and still continue to do. Neither seas, nor storms, nor polar ice, nor tropical heat stop them: they live with the Eskimo in his seal-skin; they feed on whale-oil with the Greenlanders; they traverse the solitary wastes with the Tartar or the Iroquois; they mount the Arab's dromedary or follow the Kaffir into the burning deserts; the Chinese, Japanese and Indians have become their neophytes. There is no island or reef in the Ocean which has managed to escape their zeal. And just as in former times there were not enough empires to satisfy the ambition of Alexander, so the earth is not enough for their charity.

Chateaubriand, *Le Génie du christianisme* (1802), Part Four, Book 4, Chapter 1.

that the world was moving towards a universal civilization. Christianity would, of course, be the religion of this civilization.

2. The organization of missions

The originality of the nineteenth century showed itself in the huge effort that went into organizing missions, finding funds, personnel, building up structures and, to a lesser degree, working out a doctrine. Missions occupied an important place in the Christian conscience, so the church learned to be concerned with the evangelistic enterprise.

The roots of missions among the people

The example was set in Protestant circles, often among Baptists. In 1792 the cobbler William Carey preached at Nottingham in favour of missions. He founded the Baptist Missionary Society. 1795 saw the birth of the London Missionary Society. Several Bible societies founded during the same period began to publish Bibles in the various languages of the world. They were to serve as a basis for evangelization. These societies appealed to poor as well as rich to give a contribution each week. Collection boxes were placed in public areas. French priests who had gone abroad during the Revolution made this example known on their return to France.

This Protestant competition was a challenge to Catholics, often at the expense of Christian charity. Polemic multiplied. Each of the confessions accused the other of bad faith and dishonest methods in converting the heathen. In France, after 1815, the Paris Foreign Mission got going again in a small way. It appealed for funds and in 1817 launched an association aimed at spreading the faith. In Lyons, Pauline Jaricot took responsibility. She perfected the Protestant practice of making a weekly contribution by organizing donors by the dozens, hundreds and thousands. In addition, the French priests who worked in America also begged from their compatriots. Organizations published magazines to publicize their missionary activities. The *Annals of the Propagation of the Faith*, founded in 1823, was the first of its kind. The *Annals* published 'letters from bishops and missionaries of the two worlds' and invited intelligent follow-up letters. The monthly circulation about 1830 was 15,000 and 178,000 in 1846, and it was published in several languages. Within a century, between 1823 and 1919, 380 missionary journals had been founded.

The missionary personnel

At the beginning of the century many priests left Europe individually, at the request of, among others, bishops in the United States. The old missionary congregations gradually revived: the Paris Foreign Mission, the Lazarists, the Fathers of the Holy Spirit. Then there were the great versatile orders: the Jesuits, Franciscans, Dominicans. Old congregations, like the Daughters of Charity, added mission work to their main activities. A nineteenth-century novelty was the foundation of congregations which were specifically missionary: 53 male foundations and 200 female foundations. From this time on, the Congregations of the Propaganda had a significant staff.

As for Protestant missionaries, they came from many different missionary societies founded during the century. In 1900 there were more than 300 societies; some of them were attached to official churches, but many were autonomous and contained Christians of different denominations. England provided the greatest number, followed closely by the USA. There were German, Dutch and Swiss societies. In France, the Society of Protestant Missions of Paris was founded in 1822. In due course native Christians became pastors, from 1863 in Lesotho (Southern Africa), and local autonomous churches were formed.

Missionary methods

The main concerns of the missionaries and the methods they used depended partly on their place of origin. At the beginning of the nineteenth century the Protestant missionaries usually came from the towns. Recruited directly from among the artisans – blacksmiths, weavers, carpenters – they had an essentially biblical training. Later they were to be recruited more from the middle classes. Going out in pairs, they laid emphasis on the value of example in a missionary household, which they contrasted with the behaviour of the European colonists. The Protestant missionaries wanted to form an indigenous middle class. The Catholic missionaries came mainly from the most Christian country areas of France, Ireland and Poland. They adapted themselves more easily to the farming communities of the countries they were evangelizing.

The missionaries took with them the ways of life they were used to in Europe: to begin with, if possible, a chapel. The Protestants urged the reading of the Bible. Catholics put the main stress on worship, trying to give it a solemnity which would be impressive. The missionaries made a great effort systematically to learn the local language. In many places they established linguistics. The civilization to which they belonged was one of the written word. School was the privileged means of acquiring both faith and civilization. This preoccupation with schools led to their being responsible for the destructuration of local cultures. Certainly it took time for the missionaries to take note of oral traditions and customs, which they often suspected of being idolatrous. To all this they added humanitarian service to the people. Building materials and plumbing were provided, financed with gifts brought from Europe. Catholics were more orientated towards charitable aid; Protestants, more stamped with the capitalist mentality, emphasized the advantage of economic activity: the reorganization of the plantations and work as a means of sanctification.

Papal directives

The papacy had very quickly taken its responsibility for the direction of missions to heart. The

The missionary thought of Pope Gregory XVI

Gregory XVI, who might seem profoundly reactionary in his political thought, proved to be a pioneer in the sphere of mission. Before becoming pope he had been prefect of the Congregation of Propaganda entrusted with mission. Written some months before his death, the Propaganda instruction *Neminem profecto* of 23 November 1845 is Gregory XVI's missionary testament. One can only regret that his directives about local clergy were not followed.

In truth, each and every head of a mission, no matter what title they may hold, must, as the bishops have always desired, present to the episcopate as many candidates as possible, in order to promote and consolidate Catholicism. They must augment the number of bishops and one day at last establish the hierarchy of the church.

Similarly, they must do everything possible, as one of their most important duties, to see that the Christians of the country are promoted to clergy status and to the priesthood . . . This is very urgent, and seminaries must be opened in which all young men with a priestly vocation may be well trained over the necessary period by studying the sacred disciplines . . .

In this way the long-standing wishes of the Holy See will be fulfilled, to have priests worthy to perform an ecclesiastical function and also worthy of promotion to the episcopate. We reject the custom which would make the clergy of the country auxiliary clergy; it must be abolished. All workers of the gospel are equal, whether they come from the country or are European.

Missionaries associated with people of different political opinions must not themselves be involved in political and secular affairs. They must not join any party or be a factor of division in the nation.

Care must be taken to see that missionaries make an effort to understand the social life of these peoples. In presenting the teaching of the gospel they must not fail to attach due value to the work and art of these faithful.

Collectanea S.C. De Propaganda Fidei I, 541–5.

Gregory XVI after a portrait by Paul Delaroche (Versailles museum).

Propaganda was reorganized in 1817. Cardinal Bartolomeo Capellari was its Prefect from 1826 to 1831, at which time he became pope under the name of Gregory XVI (1831–1846). There was therefore a long continuity in missionary policy. Gregory XVI condemned the slavery of the Blacks in 1829. The instruction *Neminem profecto* of 1845 put forward very firm directives: in particular the pope called for the formation of local churches with an indigenous clergy at all levels. The First Vatican Council had prepared texts on missions, but they could not be discussed. These still stressed an indigenous clergy. The promises made by Rome in this respect were scarcely followed in the nineteenth century. The training of clergy on the spot presented several problems, and there was no shortage of missionary vocations from Europe. Besides, the more the century advanced, the more Europeans felt their technical, economic and intellectual superiority over the rest of the world. Christians thought that the defects of certain races prevented them from attaining the priesthood.

Throughout the century, the Roman authorities developed the administrative supervision of missions, multiplying their territories: vicariats and apostolic prefectures.

3. Missions and colonization

It is not scandalous to say that at the beginning of the twentieth century the missionary worked in the same breath for Christ and for his country. The missions were involved in the relationship between Europe and the rest of the world. The relationships were unequal ones, in one direction: Europe reached out to Africa and Asia with all its might. The missionary thrust was often the precursor of colonization.

The missionary revival as a forerunner of European imperialism

When missionaries again began to leave Europe in the years from 1815 to 1820, European public opinion was not very interested in colonies in distant lands. The missionaries had few means at their disposal and put themselves on the level of travellers and explorers. Sometimes rivalries between Protestants and Catholics or the persecution of Christians involved the intervention of European governments pushed by religious groups (as in Oceania and Indo-China).

The era of imperialism

After 1870, the European powers rivalled one another in the conquest of new territories: in 1885 the Treaty of Berlin divided Africa into areas of influence. Article 6 recognized the freedom of preaching under the protection of the colonial powers. Colonization opened up an immense field to evangelization and mission could favour colonization. Colonial powers and missions joined together in a common task: building schools, hospitals, and so on. The colonizers wanted the missionaries to be of their own nationality. When the territory changed hands, the old missionaries were replaced by those of the new owner.

However, there was not always perfect agreement between the missionary, the administrator, the soldier and the colonist. While loyal to the occupying power, the missionaries did not pay any less attention to the abuses of colonization, and the administrators thought of the missionaries as a rival power. The latter were closer to the people by their presence among them and by their knowledge of the language. They protested against the forced labour and an industrialization which destroyed traditional structures. Although French anti-clericalism was not exported to the colonies, the missionaries accused the administrators of favouring Islam at the expense of Christianity.

II · Across the Continents

1. World-wide European emigration

If European emigration had already begun in the preceding centuries, it expanded considerably in the nineteenth. All the Christian confessions established themselves overseas and there acquired their own characteristics.

Canada

The high birth-rate among the French Canadians and the supply of Irish immigrants resulted in the rapid growth of the Canadian Catholic community. Tensions with the English government did not last. The action of Mgr Plessis, Bishop of

Quebec from 1806 to 1825, was the beginning of the organization of the Canadian church. A large number of sees was created, together with Catholic universities (Laval in 1851, Ottawa, and so on). The Catholics had been given their own schools under the supervision of the parishes. Canadian Catholics pursued their missionary activities in their own country towards the Indians and then the Eskimos.

The United States

All the religious confessions made generous use of the freedom which the United States constitution allowed them. The Baptists and Methodists became the largest denominations in the country. The United States was the country where dream after dream was played out. Preachers accompanied the pioneers in their march to the West and brought people together in camp meetings. There were moral exhortations, prayers, songs, sudden conversions and extraordinary phenomena involving a greater or lesser degree of hysteria.

At the time of Independence, the Catholics numbered only about 30,000. The first see, that of Baltimore, was founded in 1789. Several Frenchmen played a part in the organization of Catholicism in its early days, for example the Sulpicians in Baltimore, the bishops in Louisiana. Catholicism was enriched by European immigration. It was first and foremost the Irish who occupied the key positions in the American church, and they have kept them to the present day. Then, in the second half of the century, came the Italians, the Germans, the Poles . . . American Catholics were originally the poor and the working classes who lived in the towns. Some of them tried to organize themselves into national churches. The Irish opposed this and advocated integration into the American nation.

The national councils of Baltimore (of which the first was held in 1852) organized a church in which institutions multiplied. Fearful of Protestant contamination, it developed a scholarly Catholic network. All the European congregations settled in and grew in numbers. Local congregations also sprang up, such as the Sisters of Charity of St Joseph, founded by Elizabeth Seton in 1809, or the Fathers of St Paul (Paulists), founded by Isaac Hecker in 1858. At the beginning of the century there were several attempts to evangelize the Indians, who were continually being pushed towards the West and progressively eliminated. With regard to the colour problem, the Catholics shared the mentality of their compatriots. With very few exceptions, they made little effort at thought or evangelism. The number of Black Catholics remained very small. It was the beginning of the twentieth century before American Catholics showed any interest in missionary work. In 1911 the Catholic Missionary Society of America (the Maryknoll Fathers and Sisters) was founded.

In the face of certain centrifugal tendencies, two bishops strove to integrate the Catholic Church into American society and defend its originality over against the churches of Europe. Cardinal Gibbons (1834–1921), Archbishop of Baltimore, prevented Rome's condemnation of the Knights of Labour, an organization of workers which had the attraction of being a secret society (1887). This condemnation would have rebounded to the discredit of the church in the working-class milieux which formed the foundations of American Catholicism. Mgr Ireland (1838–1918), Bishop of St Paul, would have liked to integrate the Catholic schools into the state system, but public opinion was against him. He persuaded Catholic officials to take part in the Parliament of Religions in Chicago in 1893, thereby showing that the American church was not opposed to liberalism. With Cardinal Gibbons, Mgr Ireland attempted to limit the effects of the condemnation of 'Americanism' by Leo XIII in 1899. Under this name, disappointed Roman theologians noted a propensity in American Catholicism towards pragmatism, towards the exaltation of natural virtues and a low estimation of the religious life. The two bishops complained to Leo XIII of the harm done to their church by this term 'Americanism', which was seen as a new heresy.

Latin America

Napoleon's grip on Spain and Portugal provoked an uprising of the Spanish and Portuguese colonies in America; their independence was finally achieved during the years 1817–1823. The church, thrown into deep disarray by the flight of some bishops who remained faithful to the Spanish sovereign, regained some order when Gregory XVI decided to recognize the new republics.

The governments were only representatives of the old colonists who owned the land. The situation of the Indians remained pitiful. As power changed hands, often violently, between liberals and conservatives, the church generally sided with the latter, since the liberals pursued an anti-clerical policy. The church's influence declined during the course of the nineteenth century. The positivism of August Comte became widespread among the ruling classes. The plenary council of the Latin American Bishops in Rome in 1899 began a degree of Catholic renewal. From a complicated history, we should note the Mexican revolution of 1910 which resulted in the constitution of 1917. The legislators wanted to extol the indigenous past, eliminate the traces of colonization and thus reduce the church's influence by forbidding church officials to be heads of schools, putting a limit to the number of priests, etc. Catholics rebelled in the name of Christ the King (the *Cristeros*); civil war raged from 1926 to 1929. Persecution did not die down until 1937.

Australia

Australia, at first a penal colony, became an immigrants' country at the beginning of the nineteenth century. Amongst the immigrants, the Irish formed a strong Catholic nucleus with its own hierarchy – an archbishop in Sydney and two bishops in 1842. The long episcopacy of Cardinal Moran, Archbishop of Sydney from 1884 to 1911, marked the blossoming of Australian Catholicism. A national seminary was founded, plenary councils and congresses were held and Catholics played a part in trade unions and in the Workers' Party.

2. Oceania

Oceania turned into a race-track between Protestants and Catholics. The Protestants of the London Society of Missions arrived in Tahiti in 1797. In 1817 John Williams, at the age of twenty-one, disembarked on the Society Islands. He sailed from island to island in his boat *The Messenger of Peace*, building houses, churches and schools, noting down customs. While he was evangelizing the New Hebrides he died, being eaten by cannibals. The Catholics reached Oceania in 1827. Two congregations shared the islands: the Fathers of Sacré-Coeur de Picpus had the eastern part and the Marist Fathers of Lyons had the west. There were often minor skirmishes with the Protestants, like the Pritchard affair in Tahiti in 1836. All the islands were quickly evangelized during the century. The Protestants were in New Caledonia in 1840; the Catholics celebrated their first mass there in 1843. In New Guinea, Christian progress was later and slower. Amongst a great number of missionaries, mention should be made of the Marist saint Pierre Chanel, who was killed at Futuna in 1841; Françoise Perroton (1796–1873) at Wallis, the founder of a women's congregation for Oceania; and Fr Damien, a Picpus Father, who devoted himself to the lepers on the island of Molokai (Hawaii) and himself died of leprosy in 1889. Oceania had the advantage of being a place where cultures met. The Protestant missionary Maurice Leenhardt (1878–1954) at the same time completed a major work on ethnology in New Caledonia. Christian preaching some-

A kind of syncretism: The cargo myth in New Guinea

The cargo myth has developed from the end of the nineteenth century to our day. The text which follows reflects the way in which it was expressed in the 1930s.

In the beginning Anut (God) created the heaven and the earth. On the earth he gave birth to all the flora and fauna and then to Adam and Eve. He gave these power over all things on earth and established a paradise for them to live in. He completed his beneficial work by creating and giving them cargo: canned meat, steel utensils, sacks of rice, tins of tobacco, matches, but not cotton clothing. For a time they were content with that, but finally they offended God by having sexual relations. In anger God chased them out of paradise and condemned them to wander in the bush. He took the cargo away from them and decreed that they were to spend the rest of their existence being content with the minimum needed to live.

God showed Noah how to build the ark – which was a steamship like those one sees at the port of Madang. He gave him a peaked cap, a white shirt, shorts, socks and shoes . . . When the flood ended, God gave Noah and his family cargo as a proof of his renewed goodness towards the human race . . . Shem and Japheth continued to respect God and Noah and as a result continued also to benefit from the resources of cargo. They became the ancestors of the white races who have profited from their good sense. But Ham was stupid. He uncovered his father's nakedness . . . God took the cargo away from him and sent him to New Guinea, where he became the ancestor of the natives.

God had said to the missionaries: 'Your brothers in New Guinea are plunged into utter darkness. They have no cargo because of the folly of Ham. But now I have pity on them and want to help them. That is why you missionaries must go to New Guinea and remedy the error of Ham. You must put his descendants on the right way. When they again follow me, I will send them cargo, just as today I send it to you white people . . .'

times gave rise to syncretisms like the cargo cult; it was a kind of re-activation of old myths through the reading of the Bible. In being converted to Christianity, some Melanesians expected a paradise which would have the advantage of European comforts. They were deceived more often than not.

3. Asia

India

The renewal of missionary activities meant the reappearance of the old problems: quarrels over jurisdiction and quarrels over worship. The British Raj favoured freedom of movement and freedom of preaching. The caste system encouraged a tendency to ghettos by the formation of Christian villages, and got in the way of setting up local clergy. Protestants and Catholics were brought together through their schools, which accepted people of all religions. The Jesuits opened a novitiate for Indians in 1847. At the same time a seminary for training local clergy from the whole of India was founded at Candy in Ceylon.

China

At the beginning of the century Chinese Christians – priests, laity and missionaries – were constantly persecuted. The Chinese government did not want to allow entry to traders and missionaries. After several conflicts, the Western countries, by the 'unfair treaties' of 1842 and after, succeeded in opening up the Chinese

251

Unfair treaties in China and xenophobia

From 1842, the European powers imposed their political and economic will on China, in what are called the 'unfair treaties', which almost always contain religious clauses. The result was a Chinese xenophobia towards the Europeans, which periodically broke out in violence.

Treaty of Whampoa (1844)

Article 22. All French who arrive at one of the five ports, no matter how long their stay, will be able to rent houses and stores in which to keep their goods, or to prepare land and build houses and stores on it themselves. Similarly, the French can establish churches, hospitals, hospices, schools and cemeteries.

Treaty of Tien-Tsin (1858)

Article 3. Official communications of French diplomatic and consular agents with the Chinese authorities shall be written in French, but to facilitate dealing with them they shall be accompanied by as exact a Chinese translation as possible . . . In case of divergence the French text is to be preferred.

Article 13. Since the essential object of the Christian religion is to bring men to virtue, members of all the Christian communities shall enjoy entire security for their persons, their properties and the free exercise of their religious practices; and effective protection shall be given to missionaries travelling peacefully into the interior of the country.

Documents de l'histoire 1776–1963 (1964), Vols 1 and 2.

252 Anti-Christian tract of a Chinese secret society around 1875

Accursed be these Europeans, these missionary dogs or these governors of dogs who come to preach a barbarous religion and destroy the holy wisdom, who profane and defame the holy Confucius, although they have not studied the first page of a book. Heaven can no longer tolerate them and the earth refuses to bear them; let us strike them, and send them to meditate eternally in the depths of hell. May their tongues be cut out because they seduce the masses by their lies and their hypocrisy has a thousand means of tearing out the heart . . . Let us throw their bodies in the desert to be food for dogs.

In *Les Missions catholiques*, 22 October 1875.

ports, and in creating the possibility of founding religious establishments. France thought of itself as the protector of missions to China. Catholic missionaries had French passports. The Holy See would have liked to have had direct relations with China, but in 1885 France objected to a delegation being sent from Leo XIII to the Chinese government.

The apparent success of Christian missions was not without its dark side. The missionaries were foreigners loyal to the European powers who went on to carry out what amounted to an economic carving-up of China. Bursts of xenophobia engineered by secret societies multiplied. The most serious occurred in Peking in 1900: the fifty-five days of Peking. Dozens of missionaries, members of religious orders and bishops, and thousands of the faithful, were massacred along with other Europeans. European troops took the town and demanded enormous compensation from China. However, in 1901, Fr Lebbe, a Belgian Lazarist, had been extremely shocked by the nationalism of some European missionaries and had become aware of the humiliation of the Chinese.

The Catholics could chalk up an impressive number of ecclesiastical areas and faithful. But if one estimates the total number of Christians,

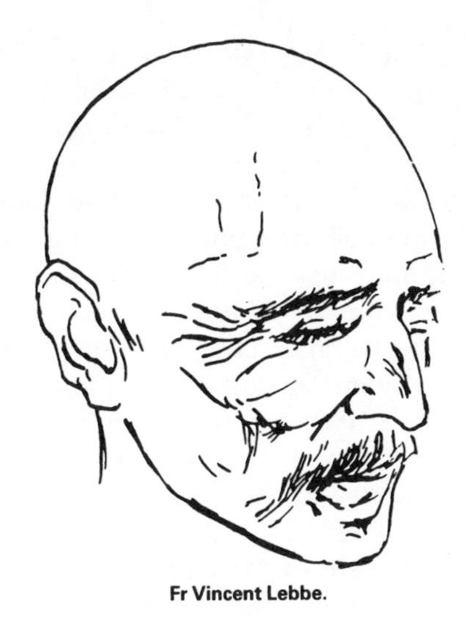

Fr Vincent Lebbe.

Catholic and Protestant, at five million in 1949, that represents only one per cent of the Chinese population. Although there were some specialists, the missionaries were less interested in traditional Chinese culture than they had been in the seventeenth and eighteenth centuries. The many schools and universities, such as the Aurora University run by the Jesuits at Shanghai, first of all offered an education with a Western stamp, concentrating on sciences and languages. The training of the Chinese clergy remained very Latin and tended to detach them somewhat from their family and cultural roots.

The discovery of Old Japanese Christians at Nagasaki in 1865

The establishment of a chapel at Nagasaki in 1865 allowed Christians who had lived a clandestine existence since the seventeenth century to come into the open. For them the criteria of Catholicity were the Virgin Mary, the Sovereign Pontiff and the celibacy of priests. A missionary, M. Petijean, takes up the story.

On Friday 17 March around 12.30 p.m. about fifteen people were standing at the door of the church . . . Three women said to me, hands crossed in front of them and in a low voice: 'Our hearts, the hearts of all of us who are here, are no different from yours.'

The woman asked: 'Where is the image of St Mary?' The sight of the statue of Our Lady with the child Jesus reminded them of Christmas, which they told me they celebrated in the eleventh month.

Only a very small number of people know the words of baptism. They keep Sunday and feast-days holy. Now they are fasting. Peter the Baptizer gave us the most important information. First of all let me say that his baptism formula would seem valid . . . He also told me about the rosary, which Christians are accustomed to recite as we do . . . Finally he asked us about the Great Head of the Kingdom of Rome, whose name he wanted to know. When we told him that the august vicar of Jesus Christ, the holy pontiff Pius IX, would be very happy to learn the comforting news that he and his Christian compatriots had just given us, Peter exploded with joy. Nevertheless, before leaving us he wanted to reassure himself further that we really were the successors of their old missionaries.

'You don't have any children?' he asked us timidly.

'You and your Christian and pagan brothers in Japan are the children that the good God has given us. We cannot have other children. Like your first missionaries, the priest must observe celibacy all his life.

On hearing this, Peter and his companion prostrated themselves on the ground and exclaimed, 'They are virgins, thank God, thank God.'

Almost all the Christians had an identical organization. There are two main leaders in most villages: the first is called the prayer leader and the second the baptizer . . .

In F. Marnas, *La Religion de Jesus resuscitée au Japon* I, 1896.

Japan and Korea

As in China, Western pressure was to force open the Japanese ports which had been closed to Europe since the seventeenth century. From 1853 onwards the United States and then the Europeans succeeded in gaining entry to the Japanese ports and obtained the right to build churches for their nationals. In 1865 at Nagasaki a missionary discovered the descendants of seventeenth-century Christians who had retained their faith and worship without clergy. With the Meiji (progress) era, Japan opened itself up to Western civilization. Universal religious freedom was granted in 1873. Missionaries and members of religious orders settled in large numbers, above all founding schools, because the Japanese were anxious for Western learning. In 1891, Leo XIII established an ordinary hierarchy. But the miracle of the seventeenth century was not repeated. In the nineteenth century the Japanese were interested in science and the techniques of Europe, but not in connection with Christianity. On the other hand, the development of nationalism and Japanese imperialism (victories over China, over Russia in 1905 and over Korea) made Christians who had ties with a Western religion suspect.

In 1831 a vicar apostolic was appointed for Korea, where Christianity had always been outlawed. In spite of intermittent persecution, which lasted until 1885, the number of Christians increased.

Indo-China

The help which Mgr Pigneau de Behaine (died 1799) had brought to the Vietnamese king Gialong to help him regain his throne was worth several years of peace to Christians. The persecutions began again in 1825 and went on for half a century. Missionary activity was carried on nevertheless. In the reign of Tu-Duc (1847–1882) there were many martyrs, and a French bishop asked Napoleon III to intervene to defend the Christians and the missionaries. A Franco-Spanish expedition – a Spanish bishop had been executed at Tonkin – occupied Saigon in 1859. Tu-Duc ceded the south of Vietnam, Cochin-China, to France. The protection of missionaries resulted in colonization, and the church developed in the occupied regions. In 1885, Vietnam fell completely under French rule and, with Cambodia and Laos, made up French Indo-China. Vietnam was one of the rare countries of the Far East where Christians formed a significant section of the population (nearly ten per cent). Early on, there was an important Vietnamese clergy. In Vietnam one institution carried the weight of the church: the House of God. It grouped together all those who were at the service of the community – seminarians, catechists – as a kind of large family where all things were held in common. The catechists had been the ones who had kept the Christian community together during the persecutions. However, the cult of ancestors always remained an obstacle to evangelization.

Orthodox missions

The evangelization of Russian Asia went ahead with the systematic colonization of Siberia. The Russians had retained the Byzantine tradition of translating the Bible and liturgy into the different languages spoken by the peoples whom they met. This helped greatly in missionary work. Archimandrite Makary, a Jewish convert who had translated the Bible into Russian, established a mission in Western Siberia in the Altai and then translated scripture and the liturgy into the dialects of the region. John Veniaminov, as priest and then as bishop, from 1824–1868, was the spirit behind the Western Siberian mission, to the Yakuts of Siberia and the Eskimos and Indians of Alaska. Made Metropolitan of Moscow in 1868, he founded an Orthodox Missionary Society, which centralized Russian evangelism. With Nicholas Ilminsky, a lay linguist, the

Orthodox Mission in Siberia

Archimandrite Spiridon evangelized a number of people beyond Lake Baikal between 1896 and 1906. He published his missionary recollections in a journal in Kiev in 1917.

At the beginning of my life as a missionary I wanted above all to baptize as many people as possible, and I was very peeved if there was no one in a village to baptize. But as time went on, a great change came over me. This is how it happened.

I had once gone to visit a Mongolian to lie down in his hut. Among a number of idols hung an image of the Blessed Virgin with the child Jesus in her arms. 'Are you baptized?' I asked him. 'Yes,' he replied. 'Toui nyre khyma?' I asked him again. 'John,' the Mongolian replied. 'Then why do you have idols in your hut? You should only have Christian images, and you should pray to the true God, Jesus Christ.'

'My father, that is what I used to do, and I prayed only to your Russian god. But then my wife died, and then my son. I lost a lot of horses. I was told that our old Mongolian god was very angry with me, and that he had made my wife and son die and driven away my horses. So now I address my prayers to him and to your Russian god. You know, father, that is now very painful and sad to me, to have changed my god for yours, a new god.'

And as he said this, the Mongolian began to cry. I was very sorry for him, to the point of suffering myself and at the same time for all those who were like him. Then I suddenly understood what it is like to steal someone's soul, to rob him of his most precious possession, to snatch from him and deprive him of his holy of holies, his natural philosophy and religion, giving him nothing in return but a new name and a cross on his chest. The Mongolian of whom I speak seemed to me to be the most wretched and unhappy man in the world, deprived of his old religion and abandoned to the chances of destiny. From then on I promised myself that I would never baptize the native population, but only preach Christ and the gospel to them.

Archimandrite Spiridion, *Mes missions en Sibérie*, 1950.

Academy of Kazan became a centre for missionary study, in the middle of the nineteenth century. Ilminsky and his group sponsored a large number of translations of the Bible and a real Orthodox library in about twenty Siberian languages. A local clergy was established. The Russian church also evangelized abroad, the mission to Japan being the most notable example. Father Ivan Kasatkin, who took the name Nikolai when he became a monk, translated the New Testament and the liturgical books into Japanese shortly after 1860. The first two Orthodox Japanese priests were ordained in 1872. Nikolai became Bishop of Tokyo in 1880, and an Orthodox cathedral was built in 1891.

4. Africa

The era of the explorers

At the beginning of the nineteenth century Africa was still scarred by the slave trade. European governments had forbidden it, but it did not die out completely until slavery was abolished in the various colonies and territories of America. The trade was continued in East Africa by the Arab merchants. The concern for mission quickly revived. In 1833 the Paris Protestant Missionary Society sent missionaries to Lesotho in Southern Africa. The sisters of St Joseph of Cluny, founded by Anne Javouhey, settled in

Senegal in 1819. In 1841, Libermann founded the Congregation of the Sacred Heart of Mary to convert the natives, which soon amalgamated with the old Congregation of the Holy Spirit. In 1850 Mgr de Mazenod's oblates of Mary settled in Southern Africa.

An apostolic vicariate of the Two Guineas was created in 1842. This first evangelization set out from the European trading posts. The missionaries had to progress into the interior by making treaties with the local rulers. Africa proved to be the graveyard of missionaries. Many died a few months after their arrival, from illnesses such as yellow fever.

The personality and work of Cardinal Lavigerie

An internationally important figure who played a large part in the history of the French church, Lavigerie devoted himself completely to the evangelization of Africa when he was appointed Archbishop of Algiers in 1876. In 1868 he founded the African missionaries, the White Fathers; in 1869 the Farming Brothers and Farming Sisters, who became the White Sisters; and in 1879 the armed Brothers of the Sahara, new Knights Templar, who were supposed to protect the missionaries. Lavigerie thought that the mission should start in Algeria, the country which had rediscovered the Christianity of St Augustine. But he came up against the French government, who did not want the Moslems to be converted. Lavigerie tried to establish Christian villages by marrying off the male and female orphans who had been educated by the Brothers and Sisters. His activities even spread into Northern Africa, when he became Archbishop of Carthage in 1884.

Lavigerie, who had obtained the apostolic delegation of the Sahara and Sudan from the Holy See, worked out a general programme of evangelization. The missionaries had to adapt themselves to external customs: clothing, housing, food and language. But the only way in which Africa was going to become part of the church was through Africans. A continuing pastorate was based on a restored catechumenate.

On many occasions the White Fathers were massacred while crossing the Sahara. They succeeded in settling in the area of the Great Lakes. In 1886 young Christians of Uganda suffered martyrdom for their faith. In addition, Lavigerie was closely involved in the campaign against slavery, in which connection he made a European tour.

The division of Africa

In 1885 the Congress of Berlin marked out the areas controlled by the European powers in Africa: France, Britain, Belgium, Portugal and Germany. In 1902, the division of Africa was complete. The Europeans had set up their system of administration; they had stamped out slavery, which they had replaced by forced labour and portage. Evangelization was organized within each of the colonies. It was the great dawn of the church in Africa. The missionaries played an important role in matters of teaching and hygiene. They provided the first structures in Africa.

An alternative presence: Charles de Foucauld

After an active life as soldier and explorer, Charles de Foucauld (1858–1916) chose to become a contemplative. From his various hermitages in the Sahara (Béni-Abbès and Tamanrasset) he set out to evangelize, not by the word but by the presence of the most holy sacrament, by offering the divine sacrifice, by prayer, penitence, the practice of evangelical virtues, by love – both brotherly and universal – sharing the last crust of bread with all the poor, all creatures, everyone unknown, and trusting all humankind as beloved brothers. This discreet presence of a universal brother prepared the way for a direct

Instructions from Cardinal Lavigerie to the White Fathers of Equatorial Africa (1879)

Without denying that missionary preaching sometimes led to a deculturation of which those engaged in it were not aware, it is worth noting that the missionaries were often very reluctant to Europeanize the people they evangelized.

When a priest voluntarily leaves for equatorial Africa, he must resign himself in advance to enduring the evils which are inseparable from mission and not make all his letters supplements to the lamentations of Jeremiah.

The first condition of succeeding in the transformation of Africa is to train the Africans we choose in conditions which, materially speaking, leave them truly African. So far that has not generally been done, and I have to say that in Algeria we have fallen into the common error. That has led me to touch on this point.

Young black men, even those whom one wants to make teachers and catechists, must be left in a state which allows them an African life at their expense, and if possible, a state which honours them, which gives them influence and is accepted by all without question. This is so that they can give powerful help to the missionaries without working for them . . .

In speaking of the material education of our young Blacks I said that it had to be African. By contrast, their religious education must be essentially apostolic. There are two ways of making men like us. The first is to make them like us externally. That is the human way, that of the philanthropic civilizers, of those who say (as was said at the Brussels conference) that to change the Africans it is enough to teach them the arts and crafts of Europe. It is to believe that when they are housed, clothed and fed as we are, they will have changed their nature. But they will only have changed their dress. Their hearts will be just as savage, and perhaps even more so, for they will also have been corrupted, and what they have learned of our luxury and our softness will have contributed to that corruption.

The divine way is quite different. St Paul defines it by saying: 'I make myself everything to all men to win all to Jesus Christ' (I Cor. 9.22). The apostolate addresses itself to the soul; it is the soul which changes, knowing that the rest will come in addition . . . It makes itself a Barbar with the Barbars as it is Greek with the Greeks. That is what the Apostles did, and we cannot see that any of them sought first to change the material habits of the peoples. They sought to change their hearts, and once their hearts had been changed, they renewed the world.

Cardinal Lavigerie, *Ecrits d'Afrique*.

Cardinal Lavigerie after Bonnat (1888, Musée d'art moderne, Paris).

evangelization in the future when this should be possible.

Madagascar

English Protestant missionaries from the island of Mauritius settled in Madagascar in 1820. Made welcome by the king, Radama I, they brought the Bible, then writing and a simple alphabet. Their schools enjoyed a huge success. Writing afforded a certain power, and evangelization seemed to call into question the social structures of the kingdom. In addition the queen, Ranavalona I, from 1828 took it on herself to restore the tradition by attacking Christianity. The persecution lasted until 1861. The British missionaries had to leave the island. Possession of printed books was banned, and writing was reserved for

the court. 150 Christians were martyred. But Christianity endured and was passed on, although there were no foreign missionaries. The Bible was read in secret and hidden worship was arranged. In 1861 the Protestant missionaries were able to return. The Jesuits arrived, too, and there was competition between Protestants and Catholics. Queen Ranavalona II was converted to Protestantism in 1869. French intervention resulted in Madagascar becoming a French colony in 1896. Rivalry continued and increased; English Protestants had to give way to the French Protestants of the Paris Missionary Society.

African syncretism and messianism

Christian preaching quickly gave rise to syncretism. Contact between the cultures had often been too swift. The old religions, like the traditional structures, were weakened, but they held up and would not die. Too European to be accepted as it was, Christianity sometimes caused a feeling of frustration; to be a Christian did not mean that one shared the advantage of white people. And so there were those who worked out an African Christianity. This was perhaps both a political reaction against Europeans and a recovery of the symbolism of the old religions, by means of transformed Christian rites and imagery. In southern Africa, racial

The Malagasy martyrs of the nineteenth century

After describing the first efforts of Jesuit missionaries to preach the gospel in Madagascar, Fr Jouen, superior of the mission, speaks of Protestant Christians who are subjected to persecution within the island in the region of Teneriffe. This letter is dated Paris, 1 October 1860. Fr Jouen had paid a personal visit incognito to Teneriffe in 1856.

Finally, a word about the fate of our brothers the Christian ovas (Protestants). It is impossible to describe the degree to which they are persecuted by the stupid and barbarous superstition of the old queen (Ranavalona): torture by fire, torture by the pit and by boiling water, torture by the saw – there is nothing that she and her government do not invent to torture and exterminate them; and in spite of this they are in good spirit and nothing can dishearten them. The unfortunate person who is condemned to torture by boiling water is first bound with cords which sometimes cut into him so deeply that his flesh is broken; then he is thrown into the ditch dug in front of him and killed by having couldrons of boiling water poured on him. But there is a refinement of cruelty which can only have been suggested by hell; the victim's own family has to make the preparations for the torture.

Some years ago two unfortunate women had their bodies sawn in half to force them to denounce their Christian kinsfolk. These heroic women were stronger than the tortures, and nothing could extract a word from them. The two leaders of this little flock recently went to death by stoning singing hymns to the glory of Jesus Christ.

Résumé de quinze années de la Mission de Madagascar, an address given by R. P. Jouen, apostolic prefect, to members of the two councils of the Propagation of the Faith.

segregation drove the Blacks to found an Ethiopian church, which was connected with the Ethiopia of the Bible. It retained the worship of the dead and the cure of the sick by incantation. William Wade Harris, an Episcopal Christian from Liberia, following a vision of the Angel Gabriel in 1913, preached a religion based on the Decalogue which fought fetishes and accepted a moderate polygamy. In the Belgian Congo Simon Kimbangu, a Baptist catechist, had a vision in 1921. He announced the return of Christ and freedom from Belgian domination, which he saw as life imprisonment. It was the start of an important religious sect which was to expand after 1945.

III · Missions after the First World War

1. The results of the war

The 1914–1918 war dealt a blow to missions. The congregations lost part of their active forces. The young missionaries had been called up and did not return. Resources had dried up. More seriously, the German missionaries had been sent away or put under house arrest when the German colonies were taken by the French or English: Oceania, The Cameroons, Togo. The case of Dr Albert Schweitzer in Gaboon is famous. The fragmentation of the solidarity among Catholics tarnished the image of evangelization in the eyes of new Christians. The war had awakened a feeling of nationalism among the colonized peoples. The colonial troops taking part in the war had expressed some doubts about Christian civilization.

The encyclical *Maximum illud*

Unhappy at the turn events were taking, Pope Benedict XV reacted violently in the encyclical *Maximum illud* of 1919. In it he made a self-criticism of the church to which people were not accustomed. The pope admitted that he was afraid of the nationalism of the missionaries, which had destroyed both God's cause and that of their country, since they had looked on their field of action as a private hunting-ground. He said that he could not understand why, in countries that had been Christian for several centuries, there were no indigenous clergy and no real local churches.

2. The centralization of missions in Rome under Pius XI

Pope Pius XI implemented a certain number of the wishes of Benedict XV. He spelt out his teaching in the encyclical *Rerum Ecclesiae* (1926). To show that the church and her missionary work were above politics, the pope strengthened centralization in Rome and the role of the Propaganda by appointing Cardinal van Rossum as Prefect and Mgr Costantini as secretary. In order to affirm the church's independence from governments, Pius XI sent delegates and apostolic visitors who had no diplomatic function. In 1922 he transferred the headquarters of the Propagation of Faith from Lyons to Rome. In 1925, during the Holy Year, there was a grand

The need to appoint a local clergy

Apostolic letter of Pope Benedict XV, 30 November 1919, *Maximum illud*

The 1914–1918 war disturbed the missions. European missionaries had to leave those missions which did not have an indigenous clergy. Moreover the missionaries sometimes demonstrated an exaggerated nationalism contrary to the message of the gospel.

There is a point to which leaders of mission have the duty particularly to devote their attention, and that is the recruitment and training of an indigenous clergy. This stress by the popes could not prevent a regrettable situation. There are places where Catholicism was introduced some centuries ago and where there is only an indigenous clergy of an inferior kind. There is also more than one people which, though enlightened by the gospel at an early stage, able to raise itself up from barbarism to civilization and to find in its midst remarkable men in all the spheres of the arts and the sciences, has not succeeded over several centuries of beneficent action from the gospel and the church in producing bishops to govern it nor priests whose status made a mark on their fellow-citizens. We must recognize that there is something defective or wrong in the education given so far to mission clergy . . .

We are deeply pained to have seen in recent years the appearance of journals the editors of which show less eagerness for the interests of the kingdom of God than for those of their own nation. What amazes us is that there is no anxiety that such an attitude may deter the hearts of the infidels from religion. Since he is not the missionary of his country but the missionary of Christ, the Catholic missionary must behave himself in such a way that the first person he meets has no hesitation in seeing him as the minister of a religion which is not foreign in any nation because it embraces all men who 'worship God in Spirit and in truth' and because in it 'there is neither Greek nor Jew, circumcised or uncircumcised, barbarian or Scythian, bond or free, but all are one in Christ' (Col. 3.11).

exhibition in Rome which emphasized the intellectual and scientific work of the missions. In 1926 Mission Sunday was inaugurated (on the third Sunday in October). In 1927 St Thérèse of the Child Jesus became the second patron of missions. The agency *Fides* was set up to provide news of missions.

3. Towards the setting up of local churches

As Benedict XV had wished, Pius XI was deeply concerned to set up a complete clergy network in the missionary areas so that the churches could be self-sufficient when the Europeans were obliged to leave. He was influenced in this by Mgr Costantini, who was familiar with the Far East, and by Father Lebbe. In 1923, Pius XI appointed an Indian Jesuit as bishop. In 1926 the Pope himself consecrated the first six Chinese bishops in a solemn ceremony in Rome. 1927 saw the appointment of the first Japanese bishop at Nagasaki, 1933 the first Vietnamese bishop, and 1939 the first black bishop. By 1939, 48 mission territories had been entrusted to indigenous bishops.

At the same time, the pope insisted on training indigenous priests. He wanted a full training identical to that given to all other priests in the world. Regional seminaries directly responsible to the Holy See were set up. In Rome, the College of the Propagation of Faith was given a new stimulus. In order to escape from the too-nationalistic face of missions, Romanization was hammered home, but it did not solve all the problems.

Adaptation

People are fond of talking about the 'adaptation' of Catholicism between the two wars to native cultures, especially in the field of art. This was the object of Mgr Costantini's instructions on Christian art in missionary work (1937). They did not go very far. The corners of the roofs of Far Eastern churches were raised a little. The term 'adaptation' is a little over-scrupulous. The launching pad remained Europe. Moreover, many people understood that Christianity ought from the start to express the characteristics natural to each people. Although they were not the only ones, two priests tried to go some way towards this.

Father Vincent Lebbe (1877–1940), to whom reference has already been made, was very careful to respect the Chinese personality. He founded the first daily Chinese Catholic journal. His opinions made him several enemies among French missionary officials in China. In 1927 he founded the Auxiliary Missionary Society; this consisted of priests who put themselves at the disposal of native bishops. In China, he founded Chinese congregations of Brothers and Sisters.

Christianity and patriotism in China

Shocked by the French 'patriotism' of some European missionaries and by the control of Chinese missions by the French consul, Fr Lebbe remonstrated about this with his bishop. That brought disgrace upon him and forced him to return temporarily to Europe. However, the letter *Maximum illud* of Benedict XV (1919) and the ordination of the first Chinese bishops by Pius XI in 1926 confirmed that Fr Lebbe's views were well-founded.

Letter to Monsignor Reynaud, Ningpo, 18 September 1917

The Chinese Christians have the right, indeed the duty, to become patriots in the same way as the Christians of Europe and America. The impression that these seventeen years in the apostolate have given me, a very clear impression, is that the basic obstacle to the coming of the kingdom of God to these masses – I do not say that it is the only one – is the nationalist question. Humanly speaking, barring a miracle, the barrier which separates them from the church is impassable, and only we can tear it down. That is why if real patriotism is laudable and praised in European churches, it is necessary for the church of China. Patriotism is one of the indispensable human conditions for Catholicism taking root in the people and attracting the masses.

Monsignor, on my knees and with my forehead in the dust, I tell you that for thirty-three years as a bishop you have trained good priests; I have been told that some of them are well instructed and others indeed eminent. Has the thought never occurred to you that the best of all, for example Fr Sun, could bear comparison with Mgr Favreau or Fr Lepers? That Fr Zi could have been a district director? If you are afraid that your European colleagues cannot admit this, cannot submit to a superior of a race other than their own, are you not misjudging them? Are we priests not capable of doing for the love of Jesus Christ what so many European civilians do for love of money – on the railways, in the customs, in the schools? Moreover, our training of indigenous priests is dragging on for ever in preparation for auxilliary clergy . . .

The church one and pluriform

My stay of twelve years in India, my contact with Hindu friends, has only intensified in me this vision of total salvation by the Christ who is as universal as he is unique.

There are Christians who more or less identify the destiny of the world with the destiny of Christianity as it has been formulated in the first ten or fifteen centuries of history, seeing the accession of new people to Christianity as a numerical increase in the church and its wider diffusion in space. After St Thomas, after Trent, what further modifications does it have to learn? It has already achieved adult status, and anyone who enters it penetrates a temple in which no stone is missing.

On the level of revelation, the church has everything from the beginning, but on the level of the developments by which it enters the human sphere – or rather the human sphere is assumed and transformed – no century marks a definitive boundary . . . The church will never say only, as it said in the time of St Augustine, 'My tongue is Latin, Greek and also Syriac'; it will add Sanskrit, Tamil and Chinese along with all the ideas and sentiments which these languages convey and which have not penetrated the Mediterranean, Germanic and Slavonic world . . .

Spiritualities which have not yet burst forth, contemplative modes, new formulations of the mystery, types of adoration and consecrated life doubtless still await, and perhaps will await for centuries, the advent of civilizations like those of India and China into a church which is one and multiform. Yesterday's Christianity, which is that of today, will never be 'that which is to come'. In creation the eternal Spirit will always be that which is coming to pass.

J. Monchanin, *Théologie et Spiritualité missionaires*, 1985 (this passage was written in 1951).

He took Chinese nationality in 1933 and organized aid for the wounded during the Sino-Japanese war. Vincent Lebbe was always anxious that the church should not seem to be just a Western means of entry. Even before the term existed, he suggested a true 'inculturation' of Christianity in China.

Jules Monchanin (1895–1937), a priest from Lyons, very quickly showed a wide intellectual curiosity. Very interested in the encounter between Christianity and Hinduism, he left for India in 1938 as a member of the Auxiliary Missionary Society. He was soon able to found an ashram (monastery) with the Benedictine Henri le Saux. Both of them led a contemplative life which sought to relate the Christian monastic tradition to the eremitism of India.

For further reading

David B. Barrett (ed.), *World Christian Encyclopaedia*, Oxford University Press 1982

R. H. Glover and J. H. Kane, *The Progress of World-Wide Missions*, Harper and Row 1960

K. S. Latourette, *Christianity in a Revolutionary Age*, Volumes 3 and 5, Zondervan 1957–61

S. Neill, *A History of Christian Missions*, Penguin Books 1986

21

The Weight of Modernity

Christians Face to Face with Industrial Society, Contemporary Thought and Confessional Divisions 1848–1939

Fernand Léger, *The Builders* (1950, Biot, Musée national Fernand Legér, detail).

The church had given the impression, before 1789, of encompassing all aspects of human life. After the upsets of the Revolution, a world formed outside the church, embracing industrial and urban society, the new philosophies, and the sciences of nature and history. The fact was that this world, alien to the church, was opposed to the traditions which the church had handed down for centuries. At the same time Catholicism had to coexist with the other Christian confessions which up until then it had been able officially to ignore. For a long time religious leaders raised barriers against the threats from this outside world. However, the time came when Christians had to pay attention to the changes in the society in which they were living or else themselves become aliens who were no longer in a position to be able to spread the gospel.

I · Christians in Industrial Society

1. Questions for the church

The fear aroused by the June days of 1848 thrust the bishops and Catholic leaders back into the conservative group which approved the authoritarian regime of Napoleon III and displayed an intractable opposition to all forms of socialism. A saying attributed to Pius XI has often been quoted: 'The church lost the working class in the nineteenth century', and it is a commonplace to affirm that the church was solidly on the side of the wealthy classes. Much historical work requires us to qualify these statements.

The situation differed from country to country. In the Rhineland of Germany, for example, Catholicism remained firmly rooted in the working classes. In America and Australia the strongest centres of Catholicism were to be found among those who worked in the cities. In France the working class seemed to be born outside the church. The bishops, who were often drawn from the world of important landowners, did not entirely close their eyes to the blatant wretchedness of the first industrial suburbs. But they had a built-in inability to analyse the causes and find the remedies. The country people who were crammed into the industrial suburbs were without roots and were not welcomed into an appropriate structure. The old urban parishes had swollen disproportionately and there was no longer any possibility of a personal relationship with the priest. A priest in Paris complained about this in 1849. The clergy kept to the narrow sphere of individual morality. The industrialists were asked to be generous, the workers to be virtuous, not to slide into alcoholism and debauchery, to respect the commandments of the church like observing Sunday as a day of rest, etc.

The evolution of socialisms

The first socialisms referred to Christianity in their programme of economic reform. After 1848 they gradually abandoned their Christian inspiration, showing themselves to be irreligious and opposed to a church which thought of itself as on the side of political power and economic exploitation. For Proudhon (1809–1865), 'property is theft. God is the problem. The idea of religion must be replaced by the idea of justice.' With the publication of *The Communist Manifesto* of 1848 and then *Das Kapital* in 1867 Karl Marx worked out a scientific socialism: the class struggle was the mainspring of history; religion was the opium of the people. The International Association of Workers (1864) could appear as a counter-church. The religious leaders could only oppose this socialism which denied God and threatened completely to overturn the social organization which they thought was willed by God. They increased the calls for Christian resignation and the encouragements to set up charitable institutions.

2. Paternalism and Reformism

The trend represented by *L'Avenir* (Lamennais and de Coux) and *L'Ère nouvelle* (Ozanam) which combined democracy, freedom and reform faded away after 1848. It was not the liberal but the conservative Catholics who were interested in social problems. They thought, not without reason, that economic liberalism was responsible for the poverty because it had destroyed the structures of the old order, those of a patriarchal and corporate system. The need was therefore to go back to this past, to bring about a counter-revolution, to restore a hierarchical society

Why we are deserting you

Letter from the worker-senator Claude-Anthime Corbon to senator-bishop Dupanloup (1877)

Claude-Anthime Corbon (1808–1891), a wood carver, had been editor of the journal *L'Atelier*, which was of Christian inspiration. On several occasions he took part in French political life. In his letter to Mgr Dupanloup he explains why French workers are gradually being alienated from the church.

Sir, you have asked us this question: 'Who will tell me why these people are deserting us?' We are deserting you today because for centuries you have deserted us. When I say that you have deserted us I do not mean to say that you have refused us 'the help of religion'; no, your priestly interest bade you lavish it even on us. What I mean is that for centuries you have abandoned our temporal cause and your influence has been exercised in hindering rather than in helping us to be received in society. That is the first cause of the desertion of which you are the object . . . With infinite skill you have attached to yourself the material means of influence, what is called the nerve of war, i.e. riches. You have always confused your cause with that of a political party. But there was a time when, in contrast to what you are doing today, you generally confused your cause with ours – and I am glad to recognize that. This was during the first part of the Middle Ages.

Since the Renaissance, teaching has changed, above all that which is addressed to the downtrodden masses. It expressly turns them away from all thought of the redemption of this world. All that it commends to them is absolute submission to the established powers – though they are to be devoted to the church. It tells them that utter resignation to their wretched lot is agreeable to God. It does its utmost to lead them to believe that the more they are resigned to being humiliated, pressurized, obliterated in this world, the more they will enjoy a happy recompense in the next . . .

Although modern society is not religious in your style, it is more fundamentally, more broadly Christian than that inspired by Ultramontanism and Jesuitism. Without being concerned about what the other world might be, modern society does not postpone redemption to the day of the last judgment: it tries to realize it without delay as being unconditional; and that is why it is republican and democratic. Certainly it is not deserting the main liberators and those who show the compassion of the gospel.

whose leaders would be mindful of their responsibilities and incorporate the most deprived into a corporate system. These perspectives gave rise to numerous patterns of mutual aid, some of which were introduced into the factories of Christian industrialists. There were apprenticeship schemes, which covered about a fifth of Parisian apprentices in 1870: 'The members of the scheme are together like a large family. They have respect, affection and loyalty for their parents, their masters, their protectors.' There were also bodies with wider theoretical concerns, like the Charitable Economic Society founded in 1847 by Armand de Melun, one of the most active of socially-minded Catholics. This paternalism only irritated workers attracted by socialism. Armand de Melun himself acknowledged failure in 1871: 'The success of socialist ideas is not only because they gratify passions but because they appear as a solution, as a complete system; they are an answer to the difficulties of the social problem. We do not offer anything like it.'

In Germany

In Germany, industrial development came later, but Catholics understood better what was at stake. The social problem was not tackled through an aid organization but called for economic reorganization and state intervention. Mgr Ketteler (1811–1877), Bishop of Mainz, was the chief representative of German social Catholicism. Not very liberal, Ketteler was nostalgic for the mediaeval guilds, but he outlined structural reforms in his work *The Problem of Work and Christianity* (1864). 'The rich,' he said, 'steal what God has intended for all humankind.' Opposed to liberal capitalism and socialism, he dreamed of a corporate organization of society and called on the state to intervene to limit working hours, enforce Sunday as a rest day, allow workers to share in profits and help mothers at home.

Another German priest, Adolph Kolping (1814–1865), a former shoemaker, wanted to restore the trade guilds. Throughout Germany he formed groups of young workers, hoping that they would organize themselves regardless of patrons. Kolping was unable to convince the paternalistic French Catholics.

Reflections and realizations, 1870–1890

In Vienna, a disciple of Ketteler, Baron von Vogelsang, founded a review which became the organ by which Austrian Catholic socialists expressed themselves. Vogelsang violently criticized liberal capitalism to the point of his being regarded as a Christian socialist. He too called for state intervention. In Switzerland, from 1884 onwards Mgr Mermillod held a gathering each year of socially-minded Catholics of several nationalities who formed the Catholic Union of Social Studies in Fribourg. In Italy, within the Opera dei Congressi social reflection developed with Professor Giuseppe Toniolo. We should also recall here Cardinal Gibbons, who defended the Knights of Labour in the United States (1887); Cardinal Manning, as arbiter in the London dock strike of 1889; and Cardinal Moran of Sydney, who invited Catholics to join trade unions. The convergence of these reflections and actions resulted in the encyclical *Rerum novarum*.

3. The birth of a social doctrine of the church

Rerum novarum (15 May 1891)

From the beginning of his pontificate, Leo XII was uneasy at the rise of socialism and anarchy. The 1890s saw bloody strikes and anarchistic outrages. Was there not a risk that the whole working-class world would go over to socialism? The initiatives of socially conscious Catholics met with opposition from Catholics who supported economic freedom and were opposed to all working-class organization. Even the socially conscious Catholics did not agree among themselves. Some of them wanted the pope to intervene and support them by suggesting common thought and action. The encyclical *Rerum novarum* was both the fruit of all this social research and the product of the atmosphere of the 1890s.

The encyclical observed – albeit a little late! – that society had changed. The concentration of wealth had led to 'undeserved poverty' among the workers. Socialism was a false remedy, as it supported the suppression of private ownership, which was divinely willed. The true remedy was to be found in the Christian principles taught by the church: inequality was a law of nature. It was necessary for everyone to be united. The class war was unacceptable: 'no capital without work, no work without capital'. The state ought to intervene to establish fair distribution of goods, working hours, weekly rest, a living wage . . . In this way economic liberalism was condemned. Finally, professional associations were useful and necessary. The pope's preference was for corporations (bosses

Leo XIII: the encyclical *Rerum novarum* 'on the condition of the workers' (15 May 1891)

The language of Leo XIII is very dated, but the encyclical made a profound mark on Catholics at the time of its publication.

We are persuaded that it is necessary by prompt and effective measures to come to the aid of people of the lower classes, since for the most part they are in a situation of misfortune and undeserved misery.

The last century has destroyed the ancient corporations which were a protection for them without putting anything in their place. Every principle and every religious feeling has disappeared from the public institutions and so, little by little, isolated and defenceless workers have found themselves in time at the mercy of inhuman masters and victims of the cupidity of unbridled competition.

Rapacious usury has added to the evil. Condemned on many occasions by the judgment of the church, it has not ceased to be practised in another form by men greedy for gain, with insatiable cupidity.

To all this must be added the concentration of industry and commerce in the hands of a few, so that it has become the province of a small number of the rich and opulent, who in this way impose an almost servile yoke on the infinite multitude of the proletariat.

and workers) but he did not exclude trade unions (workers only).

The encyclical did not receive a very warm welcome in the working-class world and among socialists. Its importance lay within the church. The pope was not taking refuge in the past. He was asking Catholics to think about the world in which they were living and to imagine themselves within the framework of existing institutions: political régimes and trade unions.

The consequences of the encyclical

The encyclical freed socially-minded Catholics and gave them a new dynamism. They felt the pope's approval. In France, the impression given by *Rerum novarum* was reinforced by the 1892 encyclical on 'rallying', *Au milieu des sollicitudes* (see above, p.159). The two encyclicals gave rise to a number of social initiatives. However, paternalism remained.

In 1887 there had been isolated Christian trade unions which above all grouped employees together. In 1919 their progress allowed the foundation of the French Confederation of Christian trade unions. The journal *Le Sillon*, founded in 1894, which Marc Sangnier made the focal point of a movement, fitted into this democratic and social context of the encyclical. The *Social Chronicle of Lyons*, founded in 1892, was also one of its fruits. Started by Marius Gonin, a modest clerk, who had been involved in the Christian democratic movement, it took a detached attitude to politics and was more interested in social problems, with social secretariats in many areas, e.g. assurance, trade unions, co-operatives. The Social Week of 1904

Pius XI: The Encyclical *Quadragesimo anno*, 'on the restoration of the social order in full conformity with the precepts of the gospel' (15 May 1931)

When celebrating the fortieth anniversary of *Rerum novarum* in the context of the economic crisis, Pius XI widened the perspectives of Leo XIII.

There has been not merely an accumulation of wealth but a huge concentration of power and economic dictatorship in the hands of a few who are for the most part not the owners but merely the trustees and administrators of invested property, handling such funds at their arbitrary pleasure . . . This irresponsible power is the natural fruit of unlimited free competition which leaves surviving only the most powerful, which often means the most violent and unscrupulous fighters . . .

The new economic régime is coming into being at a time when rationalism has spread and become established. It is the result of an economics divorced from the moral law, and consequently its course has been left to human passions . . .

The experts in the social sciences are calling for a rationalization which will re-establish order in economic life. But this order must necessarily remain incomplete unless it realizes the admirable unity of the divine plan.

was the first of a long series. Each year in a different place this 'itinerant university' studied a social problem in the light of the gospel and papal teachings.

Very soon, difficulties arose between social Catholicism and the ecclesiastical hierarchy. Could the laity be independent of the clergy in a social sphere that was very close to politics? Pius X and the bishops, fearing collaboration with non-Catholics (inter-confessional trade unions in Germany), wanted to control and direct these democratic and social movements. The dream of one Christendom was still alive. Some people, like Marius Gonin and then Marc Sagnier, were willing to submit to church discipline, but in Italy Romolo Murri broke with the church in 1909.

The social doctrine of the church

This concentrated thought resulted in the formation of what is called the social doctrine or the social teaching of the church. The popes developed and enriched the thought of Leo XIII. In 1929, the Holy See defended the legitimacy of Christian trade unions, supported by the clergy and Mgr Liénart, Bishop of Lille, against the industrialists of the north of France. In 1931 the encyclical *Quadragesimo anno* of Pius XI (26 broadened the perspective of *Rerum novarum*. This was the period when Communism was becoming a threat and when the great economic crisis was at its worst. The pope continued to condemn socialism but went beyond the scope of the enterprise to take in the economy at a national level; he called for a complete reorganization of the economic and social order. The encyclicals on Nazism and Communism (1937) also referred to a Christian social doctrine over against the paganism of totalitarianism. However, this was more often a matter of theoretical affirmations than of specific solutions which tested them out.

II · The Difficult Confrontation between Catholic Tradition and Modern Science

1. The questioning of the Catholic tradition

The attack of philosophy and the sciences

In the seventeenth and eighteenth centuries the advances made by the sciences had seemed to call a certain number of revealed truths into question (cf. Chapters 12 and 16). As far as nineteenth-century philosophy was concerned (Kant), God could not be reached through reason. Moreover the idea of God was of no interest, if not alien. For Auguste Comte, the ages of religion and of metaphysics (mediaeval philosophy) were over. Humankind had arrived at the age of science, the age of positivism. Science believed in the unlimited advance of knowledge and a final retreat of religion, in a century in which the natural and historical sciences had made gigantic strides.

The research into prehistory by Boucher de Perthes (who died in 1868) pushed human origins back hundreds of thousands of years. The discovery of human fossils paved the way for an understanding of the evolution of human beings, a hypothesis which Darwin worked out systematically in his book *The Origin of Species* (1859). If human beings are descended from apes, if they have evolved, where does that leave the story of creation by God and original sin? And what about biblical chronology? Throughout the nineteenth century a large number of historical sources from antiquity and the Middle Ages were published. A science of religions was born. The writings of the Middle East, Egyptian hieroglyphs, Mesopotamian cuneiform were deciphered. The texts of the Old and New Testaments were studied and compared like those of any other religion, while Christians thought that the revealed texts were excluded from this kind of investigation. In his *Life of Jesus* (1835) David Friedrich Strauss saw Jesus as the product of the imagination of the first Christian communities. As we have seen (above pp. 135, 155), for Renan Jesus was no more than a man to be admired (*Life of Jesus*, 1863). Wellhausen's theories on the Pentateuch transformed Moses' work into a kaleidoscope of documentary sources. What had become of divine inspiration? Criticism discovered numerous legends in the history of Christian origins; science shook all acquired certainties.

The church's reaction

The first reaction was a defensive one. Sciences which attacked revelation were the work of the devil. We have seen how books thought pernicious were put on the Index and in 1864 the *Syllabus* condemned more solemnly a certain number of these doctrines (above, p. 135). The First Vatican Council made an attempt at a dogmatic clarification of the relationship between reason and faith (cf. Chapter 17). The religious authorities tried to obtain the support of public authorities. The course given by Renan at the Collège de France was suppressed after the publication of his *Life of Jesus*. With doubtful scholarship, polemicists and apologists defended the religious truths under attack.

Catholic exegesis in the middle of the nineteenth century

Jonah in his whale

The author, Abbé Glaire, was dean of the Faculty of Theology in Paris.

In the story of the whale we read that it swallowed up Jonah, kept him for three days and three nights in his belly, and then cast him out on the sea shore. The incredulous say that all these things are impossible, and that therefore they should not have a place in a work which one wants to claim as being true and divine.

We would remark, first, that the species of fish which swallowed up Jonah is not mentioned at all in scripture. Supposing that this fish was a shark, all the difficulties would disappear. The only point which presents a serious difficulty is the existence of Jonah shut up for three days and three nights in the belly of this fish. We have to show how this man could have lived in the belly of this fish – I do not say without a miracle, but without a contradiction. There is no doubt that by his power God can suspend for a time the penetration and the voracity of the acids which are in the most carnivorous and hottest stomach . . . just as on another occasion he suspended the heat of the flames for the three young men shut up in the furnace, and just as he made St Peter light enough to walk on the waters. There is nothing in all this which surpasses the power of the sovereign author of nature. Jonah was full of life and did not remain motionless in the belly of this fish. He was not affected by the digestive acid.

As to the impossibility of Jonah being able to breathe, almighty God could have made the blood of Jonah so still that he did not have to breathe so frequently, just as animals which remain underground for several months or at the bottom of the sea without breathing or as children in their mothers' womb where they do not breathe.

There is indeed nothing impossible in all that, nothing incompatible with the laws of nature, although in the circumstances all this is beyond the ordinary known laws and therefore miraculous.

J.-B. Glaire, *Les livres saints vengés ou la vérité historique et divine de l'Ancien et du Nouveau Testament défendue contre les principales attaques des incrédules modernes et surtout des mythologues et des critiques rationalistes* (1845).

The revival of the religious sciences among Catholics

In Germany the universities had very quickly resumed their activities after the revolutionary crisis, and the confrontation between Catholics and Protestants had been stimulating. Joseph-Ignatius Döllinger (1799–1890), 'the prince of German Catholic scholars', and his historical work have already been mentioned, as has John Henry Newman (1801–1890), who in a more isolated position in England shed historical light on the progressive formulation of dogma in his *Essay on Development*.

In France, the priority given to the recruitment of the clergy within the parochial framework and to political quarrels had rather dimmed intellectual activity among the clergy. There had of course been the gigantic effort of the Abbé Migne (1800–1875) to bring out a universal library for the clergy of a thousand volumes, the best-known of which are the Latin and Greek Patrologies, and the work of the Carmelite school created by Mgr Affre in 1845. But it was the freedom given to higher education (1875) which was the starting point of theological renewal in France. At the end of the nineteenth century the Rector of the Catholic Institute of Paris, Mgr d'Hulst, was very open. Abbé Louis Duchesne (1843–1922) studied Christian origins with critical discipline, demolishing a certain number of legends such as the apostolic origins of the French churches. A Dominican, Fr Lagrange, founded the École Biblique in Jerusalem in 1890. In Paris, Abbé Alfred Loisy, a specialist in oriental languages and conversant with German biblical studies, very quickly aroused anxiety by his teaching. In his thesis *L'Action* (1893), Maurice Blondel, a philosopher at the state university, thought that in order to reach his contemporaries he had to begin from a definition of humanity acceptable to all. Starting from action it was possible to discover that human beings aspire to a reality which transcends them. This was the immanent method. These thinkers and seekers had to defend themselves against some Catholics just as much as against unbelievers.

2. The modernist crisis

'Modernism' is a polemical term the content of which varies depending on who is using it. One historian, Poulat, saw the modernist crisis as 'all the fortunate or unfortunate efforts aimed at reconciling recent knowledge with the continuing demands of faith'. In this confrontation within the church, Catholics found themselves lined up on opposing sides. The die-hard conservatives rejected all use of modern science in their expression of faith. The 'progressives' wanted to put scientific disciplines at the service of religion, while at the same time safeguarding the unchanging requirements of faith. Those who most deserved the name 'modernists' thought that modern science demanded a profound revision of received ideas. Science had priority and Christianity had to adapt itself. This was its only chance of survival. The church had to be transformed from within. In the end, an extreme group came to the conclusion that Catholic beliefs could not hold up in the face of science. They became rationalists.

The modernist crisis affected a limited area, that of a small number of priests interested in intellectual problems and a few of the laity. The atmosphere was one of suspicion and of often ungrounded accusations. Writing was done under pseudonyms. Some people used a double language.

The church confronted modernity in all its spheres. That is why one speaks of political and social modernism in connection with Catholics who were involved in the democratic movement, Marc Sagnier and the Sillonist movement in France and Romolo Murri in Italy. The term modernism is also used of those who attempted the first steps at ecumenism, like Fernand Portal, a Lazarist who at the turn of the century envisaged a reunion between Anglicans and Catholics. However, the two major centres of the crisis were those of biblical studies and the significance of dogmas – and it was difficult clearly to separate the two.

The biblical question

In his courses at the Catholic Institute in Paris and in his journal *Enseignement biblique* (The Teaching of the Bible), Alfred Loisy, following German exegetical scholarship, put forward the theory that Moses could not be the author of the Pentateuch and that the first eleven chapters of Genesis could not be considered history. In 1893 he was called on to give up teaching. Very soon, his thought went beyond the Bible to concentrate on the relationship between religion and contemporary thinking. In 1902 a little red book by Loisy, *The Gospel and the Church*, made an enormous stir. Cardinal Richard, Archbishop of Paris, forbade people to read it; Loisy responded with another red book.

In his works Loisy outlined the first synthesis of his religious thought. In reply to the Protestant Adolf von Harnack, who reduced Christianity to a religion of God the Father and universal love,

The biblical question at the end of the nineteenth century

Alfred Loisy was barred from the Catholic Institute in Paris for a certain number of statements on the Bible which he thought to be the assured results of historical science. They no longer cause Catholics any difficulty today, even in Roman circles.

The Pentateuch, in the state in which it has come down to us, cannot be the work of Moses.

The first chapters of Genesis do not contain an exact and real history of the origins of humanity.

Not all the books of the Old Testament and the various parts of each book have the same historical character.

The history of religious doctrine contained in the Bible displays a real development of this doctrine in all the elements which comprise it: the idea of God, of human destiny and of moral law.

There is hardly any need to add that, for independent exegesis, as far as natural science is concerned the sacred books are not superior to the views generally held in antiquity.

The conflict of facts in the Gospels on a large number of secondary matters is indisputable, and instead of denying them one must look for satisfactory explanations: the author of the Fourth Gospel reported the discourses of the Lord quite freely, so that it is appropriate to study the way in which he edited them.

Closing lecture of a course given by Loisy in 1892/93, published in *Études bibliques*, 1894, 79f.

In 1900 Cardinal Richard was utterly flabbergasted to learn that the world had not been created in 4000 BC *as is written in his catechism.*

Cardinal Merry de Val would prefer to believe that Jonah had swallowed the whale than to have it said that the whale did not swallow Jonah.

Some day people will be surprised – I would like to hope, even in the Catholic Church – that a professor at a Catholic university has been judged dangerous for having said in the year of grace 1892 that the accounts in the first chapters of Genesis are not to be taken as strict history, and that the so-called agreement of the Bible with the natural sciences is a poor joke.

Alfred Loisy, *Choses passes* and *Memoires*.

Loisy affirmed: 'Jesus came to announce the kingdom, but what arrived was the church.' The kingdom was to be realized immediately. It was true that the church was its heir, but it had altered the facts so that it would last down the centuries. Loisy explained the historical evolution of the church and the formulation of its dogmas. For him, Catholicism really did come from the gospel and from Christ, but he was able to give the impression of making a distinction between the Jesus of history and the Christ of faith and of believing that doctrine evolved in line with knowledge. In December 1903 five books by Loisy were put on the Index. He submitted, while still maintaining that he could not destroy the results of his work in himself, which scarcely pleased the pope.

The significance of dogmas

In England George Tyrrell (who died in 1909) became a convert to Catholicism and a very successful Jesuit after his early studies. He sought to develop a doctrine of the supernatural and of faith compatible with the philosophy of the time, feeling himself to be inspired by Newman. The church is necessarily led to express its dogmas in new formulae. Revelation is a divine act by which the believer enters into mystical contact with God. There is no original representation, no communication of truth. However, this contact must be expressed. It is a prophetic knowledge in terms taken from contemporary culture, which theology interprets in its turn in terms of the culture of each period.

The Gospel and the Church

The publication of Loisy's little red book, *The Gospel and the Church* (1902), marks the beginning of the climax of the modernist crisis. Mgr Mignot, Archbishop of Albi, had approved its main outline. The affirmations which seemed shocking then are much less so when one reads them in the context of the work.

The message of Jesus consists in the proclamation of the nearness of the kingdom and an exhortation to repentance in order to be able to have a part in the kingdom.

All that has entered into the gospel of Jesus has entered into the Christian tradition. What is truly evangelical in the Christianity of today is not that which has never changed, for in a sense everything has changed, but that which, despite all external changes, arises out of the impulse given by Christ, is inspired by his Spirit, and serves the same ideal and the same hope.

Jesus proclaimed the kingdom, and what came was the church. It came by broadening the form of the gospel, which it was impossible to keep as it was, since the ministry of Jesus had been brought to an end by the passion.

It is natural that dogmatic symbols and definitions should relate to the general state of human knowledge in the time and place where they were formed. It follows that a considerable change in the state of science can necessitate a new interpretation of ancient formulae which, conceived as they were in another intellectual atmosphere, can no longer say all that they need to, or do not say it as they should. In that case a distinction is to be made between the material sense and the formula, the external image that it presents and which is in accord with the accepted ideas of antiquity, and its strictly religious and Christian significance, the basic idea, which can be reconciled with other views on the constitution of the world and the nature of things . . . Truth alone is immutable, but not its image in our spirit.

As a result of political and intellectual evolution, a great religious crisis has developed almost everywhere. The best means of remedying it does not seem to be to suppress all ecclesiastical organizations, all orthodoxy and all traditional worship, which would put Christianity outside life and humanity, but to make best use of what it is, with a view to what it must be; not to reject that which the Christian centuries have handed down to our own; to appreciate duly the need and usefulness of the immense development which has taken place in the church, to gather its fruits and to continue it, since the adaptation of the gospel to the changing conditions of humanity is more important today than it has ever been.

Alfred Loisy, *The Gospel and the Church* (fourth edition 1908).

Dogmas are the results of creations of religious experience. They have a moral value and are useful for the progress of humanity. Revelation is not external. Catholicism has to be evolved on the basis of a distinction between living faith and dead theology. These views meant that Tyrrell was expelled from the Society of Jesus. He was excommunicated in 1907.

The great melting pot

All these questions caused a great stir of ideas among theologians and philosophers throughout Europe: books and review articles were written and letters exchanged. In France Henri Bremond (1865–1933), who had left the Society of Jesus in 1904, at the same time as Tyrrell,

The condemnation of modernism by Pius X (1907)

The decree *Lamentabili* (3 July 1907). The propositions which follow are the propositions which are condemned, for the most part extracts from Loisy's books.

1. The ecclesiastical law which prescribes that books concerning the Holy Scriptures shall be submitted to prior censorship does not extend to writers involved in the scientific criticism or exegesis of the books of the Old and New Testament.
20. Revelation cannot be anything other than human acquired awareness of the relationships existing between God and man.
36. The resurrection of the Saviour is not strictly speaking a fact in the historical order but a fact in the purely supernatural order, neither demonstrated nor demonstrable, which Christian awareness has deduced little by little from other facts.
40. The sacraments were born out of an idea, an intention of Christ, interpreted by the apostles and their successors, under the inspiration and pressure of circumstances and events.
52. It was not in the mind of Christ to form a church as a society destined to endure for a long series of centuries on earth; on the contrary, in the mind of Christ the kingdom of God and the end of the world were equally imminent.
65. Catholicism today cannot be reconciled with true science unless it transforms itself into a kind of non-dogmatic Christianity, in other words a broad-minded and liberal Protestantism.

Pius X.

The encyclical *Pascendi* (8 September 1907) gives a kind of stereotyped portrait of the modernist. But no individual modernist ever had all these features.

Modernists combine and are a mixture of several personalities: the philosopher, the believer, the theologian, the historian, the critic, the apologist, the reformer. It is necessary to disentangle these figures if we want to gain a thorough knowledge of their system and take account of the principles and the consequences of their doctrines.

Taking in the whole system at a glance, who could fail to be amazed that we are defining the meeting point of all heresies? Modernists ruin not only the Catholic religion but, as we have already suggested, all religion.

corresponded with the principal modernists in France and abroad. Joseph Turmel, a priest from Rennes and a historian of dogma, said later that he wanted to undermine the basis of the faith. In Italy Ernesto Buonaiuti (1881–1946), a priest-philosopher and historian, wanted at all costs to adapt Christianity and infuse Christian values into a new ecumenical civilization. Friedrich von Hügel (1852–1925), by birth an Austrian but living in England, acted as a kind of liaison between the intellectuals of the time who have been mentioned above. A profoundly religious man, he was unable to lose his sense of faith and of the church. He always cherished the hope of a reconciliation between the church and science. At the same time, a host of people set themselves up as defenders of the faith by denouncing time and again anyone suspected of modernism.

3. The papal condemnations

Many books were put on the Index, journals were banned, priests removed from their teaching posts. They were not all modernists by any means, but rather 'progressives', like Marie-Josèphe Lagrange, Lucien Laberthonnière and Fernand Portal. The church seemed like a fortress under siege on all sides. It must be remembered that the modernist crisis occurred at the time when anti-clericalism and the separation issue were at their peak in France.

The general condemnations

Pope Pius X condemned modernism in two documents published in 1907. The decree *Lamentabili* brought together sixty-five propositions which were condemned. Four-fifths of them came from the writings of Loisy, though he was not named; these related to errors in sacred knowledge, the interpretation of scripture and the mystery of faith. The encyclical *Pascendi* offered a stereotype portrait of the modernist: it attributed to a single person the traits found in very different individuals who did not always have much in common with one another. Modernism, the encyclical concluded, is the meeting place of all heresies. The pope then went into its causes – ignorance, pride, modern philosophy – and sketched out the ways to fight against this pluriform heresy.

The condemnation of *Le Sillon* in 1910 was often regarded as the condemnation of social modernism. Religious leaders saw *Le Sillon* above all as a threat to the hierarchical organization of the church because of its championing of democracy.

The means of defence

The clergy were encouraged to return to the philosophy of St Thomas. The dioceses had to form watch committees which supervised the publications and teaching of priests and made frequent reports to Rome. Only obscure posts were entrusted to suspect priests. Without express permission clergy were not allowed to attend state universities, the most dangerous courses being those in philosophy and history. In 1909 a Biblical Institute was formed in Rome. In 1910 it was made compulsory for all candidates for major orders and for theological degrees, along with those who were to hold certain posts, to take an anti-modernist oath.

The consequences of the condemnations

Only a few priests refused to take the oath, about forty in all. Some of them concealed their deepest convictions in order to keep out of trouble. Loisy, who was excommunicated in 1908, pursued his career as exegete and historian at the Collège de France.

The pope seemed to have restored theological order. The whole affair really only concerned priests, and lay Christians were hardly affected by it. However, the problems caused by the encounter between the faith and the modern world remained. In new guises they are still being raised today. At the time the condemnations created an oppressive enough atmosphere. In some quarters there was a real mess. Many people who were open and faithful to the church were unable to express themselves and had to live in isolation. The condemnations reinforced the climate of intransigence and reaction and gave rise to what was to be called integralism. Many made a point of acting as informers to Rome. A secret society, the *Sodalitium Pianum*, referred to under the code name 'Sapinière', was organized under the leadership of a Roman prelate, Mgr Benigni, which created an international network to hunt down modernism.

Benedict XV kept his distance from these intrigues.

4. Towards reconciling the church and intellectual thought

The modernist current was swept along by an overvaluation of science and progress. But at the beginning of the twentieth century, and still more with the onset of the First World War, this omnipotence of science eased off somewhat. It did not answer all human problems. One cannot construct a morality on science. It was possible to detect a return to spirituality, sometimes even to Christian faith, at the end of the nineteenth century. A host of writers bore witness to this and by the period between wars Catholic writers had come to the forefront of literary life with authors like Claudel, Mauriac, Bernanos and Gabriel Marcel.

The condemnations of modernism for a while put paid to the research of Catholic exegetes. Many were prudent enough to confine themselves to scholarship and archaeology. It was not until 1943 and the encyclical *Divino afflante spiritu* of Pope Pius XII that it was possible to feel a lessening of pressure and find encouragement given to the work of exegetes.

In the spheres of history and dogmatic theology the atmosphere relaxed. It was no longer obligatory to assert that dogmas were not historical. Theologians like Chenu, Congar and de Lubac propounded a theology firmly rooted in the Fathers and in church history. Ecclesiology, like the relationship between the church and modernity, was no longer envisaged solely in legal terms or in terms of a conflict with society. Emile Mersch's *Theology of the Mystical Body* (1937) and Fr Henri de Lubac's *Catholicism* proved this.

III · The Hesitant Beginnings of Ecumenism

1. The Christian confessions at the end of the nineteenth and the beginning of the twentieth century

Population movements, waves of emigration and freedom of worship led those of different confessions to meet one another and live in the same place, and to ask questions about the break-up of Christianity in a world in which Christians were coming to be a minority.

The Eastern churches

Eastern Europe and the Balkans freed themselves from Turkish rule. Afterwards Greece, Bulgaria and Romania regained their independence. In each state, Orthodox Christians formed into autocephalous churches, i.e. each with its own patriarch. Orthodoxy very quickly embraced fifteen churches. The framework of the nation state helped the freedom of the church and of Christians. To the Orthodox churches have to be added the other Eastern churches, separated from Orthodoxy after the Council of Chalcedon – the Monophysites and Nestorians scattered through the Turkish and Arabian world; the Armenian, Jacobite, Coptic and Chaldaean churches.

The Russian church lived its last years under a Tsarist regime which did not allow it any evolution as an institution, but could not bury the freedom of thinkers. The philosopher Vladimir Soloviev (1853–1900) worked towards reconciliation with Catholicism. Leo Tolstoy (1828–1910)

His Holiness the Patriarch Tikhon.

advocated a non-violent, evangelical Christianity which earned him excommunication from the Holy Synod. John of Cronstadt (1829–1908), parish priest and profound mystic, combined an intensely spiritual life along the lines of the *Philokalia* with good works carried out to the point of self-deprivation. He founded charities reminiscent of those of Don Bosco. The 1917 revolution had allowed the Russian church to re-establish the patriarchy by electing Tikhon, but the new patriarch took charge of a church which was to suffer constant persecution under the Bolshevik régime.

Following the waves of emigration in the nineteenth and twentieth centuries, Eastern Christians settled in all parts of the world, in Western Europe, the United States, Australia. The genocide of Turkish Armenians in 1915 led to the dispersion of Armenians throughout the world. The Russian revolution also provoked an exodus.

The Protestant world

Protestantism has always been characterized by the increasing number of its denominations and by periodic revivals. We have seen how the Salvation Army, founded in London by William Booth in 1875, aimed at recapturing the inspiration of Wesley, evangelizing and seeking to fight against poverty, vice and sin among the working class. In 1876, in the United States a Holiness Movement sprang up, the result of a split from Methodism: its adherents waited upon the Holy Spirit for power to bear witness in a world won over by rationalism. An extension of this movement was Pentecostalism, which appeared in 1901 in Kansas and rapidly spread all over the place. Baptism by the Spirit experienced by believers renewed the marvels of Pentecost among the congregations: prophecy, ecstasy, the gift of tongues, healings. Pentecostalism was a church of the poor in which all could find a place and express themselves.

In Europe, one would have been forgiven for thinking for a time that Protestant theology was going to break up in the climate of modern philosophical and scientific opinion. In the early part of the twentieth century, several theologians made a profound contribution to the renewal of Protestant thought. Karl Barth (1886–1968), a Swiss pastor, broke away from current liberal opinion. He rediscovered and affirmed the transcendence of God, the Wholly Other over against culture, morality, history and feeling. God reveals himself in a living word: Jesus Christ. Theology is the assurance of faith in the Word of God. In his commentary on the *Epistle to the Romans* (1919) Barth, drawing on the intuition of the first Reformers, denounced the anthropocentrism of contemporary Protestant theology. God had to be listened to and obeyed. At the same time, from 1933 onwards Barth involved himself in the fight against Nazism. By reaffirming the absoluteness of the Word and of dogma (he wrote twenty volumes of dogmatics between

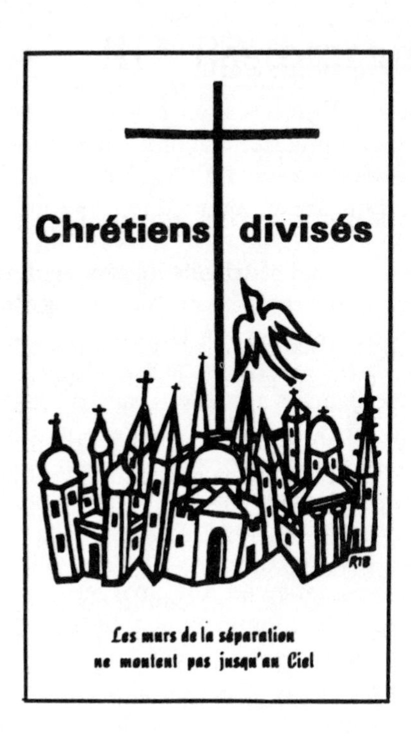

A poster circulated by the Centre for Christian Unity in Lyons to call Christians to prayer during the Week of Prayer for Christian Unity, which it has organized for a long time. Nowadays the Week of Prayer is supervised by the Roman Secretariat for Unity and the World Council of Churches.

1930 and 1967), Barth once again made Catholics take Protestantism seriously.

Rudolf Bultmann (1884–1976) is remembered as the founder of form criticism, which explored the basic material of which the Gospels were formed, and as the theoretical scholar who argued for demythologizing the New Testament. Paul Tillich (1886–1965), forced to leave Nazi Germany, settled in the United States. He sought to make a connection between theology and culture. He began from modern man and his questions, to move towards God. For him, religion was the substance of all culture. Culture was necessary as an expression of religion.

2. The birth of an ecumenism outside Catholicism

Christians did not wait until the twentieth century to realize that their divisions were an anomaly. The term ecumenism (*oikoumene* = the inhabited world) was used to denote this willingness on the part of different Christian groups to come together.

To begin with, Christians of the same confession were concerned to retain a degree of unity amongst members scattered world-wide. A universal Evangelical Alliance came into being in 1846 which brought together Protestants independently of their particular confessions. In 1867 the first Lambeth Conference gathered representatives of all the Anglican (Episcopalian) churches in the world. The conference meets every ten years. Later on came the World Alliance of Reformed Churches, the World Baptist Alliance, the World Lutheran Federation and the YMCA and YWCA (Young Men's/Women's Christian Association).

The scandal of division

In 1910, the Edinburgh Conference assembled representatives of the various Protestant missionary societies. Among the 1200 delegates there were some from Africa and Asia. These expressed the scandal they felt at the division of Christian missionaries, each of whom worked for his own missionary group or society. The final report underlined 'the need to seek to implant in each non-Christian country a church which is not divided . . . The time may come when the indigenous churches may themselves settle the problem of unity independently of the views and desires of Western missionaries.' No communion service could be held during the conference; but ecumenism had been born. It was agreed to have regular meetings. The Committee became the International Missionary Council.

The World Missionary Conference, Edinburgh 1910

This conference was considered to be the starting point for the ecumenism which ended in the formation of the World Council of Churches.

Here are the words of a delegate from a Far Eastern church, as reported by Pastor Boegner:

You have sent us missionaries who have made Jesus Christ known to us, and we are grateful to you for that. But you have also brought us your distinctions: some preach Methodism to us, others Lutheranism, Congregationalism or Episcopalianism. We ask that you should preach the gospel to us, and leave Jesus Christ himself to raise up from the midst of our peoples, by the action of his Spirit, a church in keeping with his demands, in keeping also with the genius of our church, which will be the church of Christ in China, the church of Christ in India, free from all the -isms which you bring in when preaching the gospel among us.

Unity of action and unity of doctrine

During the 1914–18 war Nathan Söderblom, Lutheran Archbishop of Uppsala, had launched appeals to Christians for world peace. After the war he founded the Life and Work movement, or Practical Christianity. 600 delegates from 27 nations met in Stockholm in 1925. They included Germans and their old enemies, representatives of Protestant confessions, but also some Orthodox. Delegates studied the relationship between the churches and society and problems of social justice. How could Christian principles be applied in daily life? A second meeting at Oxford in 1937, at which 124 churches and 44 countries were represented, affirmed the right to religious liberty in a totalitarian age.

In the wake of the Edinburgh Conference another movement, Faith and Order, was born. In it the leading lights were Anglicans (Charles Henry Brent and William Temple). The first important meeting took place at Lausanne in 1927: 400 delegates attended from 108 churches. The Orthodox were well represented. Discussions touched on a large number of questions of doctrine, such as ecclesiology and ministry. Although some people were impatient, the Assembly thought that it was necessary to take time to seek out the truth, and not to aim at union at any price. Another conference in Edinburgh in 1937, even better attended, called for an effort at mutual understanding from all believers, and recognized that unity had already arrived: 'We would not be able to seek for union among ourselves if we did not already possess that union. Those who have everything in common cannot bear to be separated' (William Temple).

Many people were members of both movements. From that fact came the idea of founding a joint organization, the World Council of Churches, which would combine Life and Work with Faith and Order. The decision, which was taken at Utrecht in 1938, could not be implemented until after the Second World War, in 1948.

The World Council of Churches

The Edinburgh Conference on Faith and Order in 1937 spoke of the unity which would be the basis of the later declarations of the WCC:

We are one in faith in our Lord Jesus Christ . . . We humbly acknowledge that our divisions are contrary to the will of Christ . . . We recognize in one another, across the barriers of our separation, a common Christian outlook and a common standard of values. We are therefore assured of a unity deeper than our divisions . . . We desire to declare to all men everywhere our assurance that Christ is the one hope of unity for the world in face of the distractions and dissensions of this present time. We know that our witness is weakened by our divisions. Yet we are one in Christ and in the fellowship of His Spirit.

The Report prepared at the inauguration of the WCC in 1948 made statements about the nature of the Council which included the following:

The World Council of Churches is composed of churches which acknowledge Jesus Christ as God and Saviour. They find their unity in Him. They have not to create their unity; it is the gift of God. But they know that it is their duty to make common cause in the search for the expression of that unity in work and life.

The Council desires to serve the churches . . . But the Council is far from desiring to usurp any of the functions which already belong to its constituent churches, or to control them, or to legislate for them . . . The Council disavows any thought of becoming a single unified church structure independent of the churches which have joined in constituting the Council.

3. The difficulties for ecumenism in the Catholic Church

Portal and Anglicanism

The Lazarist Fernand Portal had a chance meeting with the Anglican Lord Halifax in Madeira in 1890. The two men got on well together and Portal, who knew nothing of Anglicanism, first of all envisaged individual conversions of Anglicans to Catholicism. He very quickly came round to thinking that the two churches, Catholic and Anglican, could join together physically. In other words, the two hierarchies would come to an understanding. It seemed to Portal that the Anglicans had retained the essentials of the Catholic tradition, in particular apostolic succession through bishops. But in 1896 Rome declared that Anglican ordinations were null and void. That was the end of the dream of physical unity. Portal then thought that unity could come only from below, by an inner change of heart on the part of Christians. It was necessary to work slowly towards a meeting of minds and of intellectual reflection. To this end he launched a journal, the *Revue catholique des Églises*. He broadened his attitudes towards Orthodoxy and Protestantism. Despite his isolation in 1908, Portal continued his activity in a discreet way. From 1921 to 1925 conversations were resumed with Anglicans at Malines under the direction of Cardinal Mercier. However, the deaths of Portal and Mercier put an end to them.

The development of M. Portal

When he first met the Anglican Lord Halifax, Fernand Portal, a Lazarist, was thinking in terms of bringing back non-Catholics to the Church of Rome. He very soon arrived at a conception of ecumenism which was much more respectful of the personality of the members of other Christian confessions.

As a priest, of course I had to have the hope of converting this Anglican who came of his own accord to talk to me about religious questions. However, I soon observed that nothing allowed me to have any hope of such a result, and that if despite my opinions to the contrary I continued with a relationship which seemed pointless to others, it was because I believed that conversion was not the only goal to pursue. A meeting of minds, the discarding of prejudices are also substantial results worthy of being sought for their own sake. For his part I think that Lord Halifax felt equally soon the desire to instruct a priest who was still young about the Church of England.

Fr Fernand Portal.

Notes by F. Portal (1909) on the events of 1890–1896.

The means to be employed are not attempts at individual conversions, but work to break down the prejudices which still exist among Catholics and among separated Christians. Individual conversions get in the way, and only lead to the increase of mistrust.

There is an analogy between current conditions in the apostolate to the people and the apostolate as we see it in the separated churches.

The problem of church union can only be a distant goal which automatically appears as a conclusion of our studies. It is important to understand that there is a question of the church alongside the social question, the religious question and the philosophical question.

Proposal made to the Group for the Union of the Churches by F. Portal at its first meeting, 5 May 1911.

Papal opposition

Since the Catholic Church believed itself to be in sole possession of 'the truth', there was no question of the popes entering into dialogue with other Christians on an equal footing. Benedict XV politely refused to take any part in the embryonic movements towards unity. All he could do was to invite Christians to return to the true church. In the encyclical *Mortalium animos* of 1928, Pius XI forbade Catholics to involve themselves in the various ecumenical movements. As far as he was concerned, faith came before charity. In fact Catholics saw in Protestantism not much more than liberal tendencies which took little heed of dogmatic rigour.

Spiritual ecumenism

Catholics got out of this impasse by approaching ecumenism in another way, through prayer. In 1925, Dom Lambert Beauduin founded an abbey in Belgium at Amay-sur-Meuse, which was devoted to harmony with Eastern Christians. In it the liturgy was celebrated both in the Latin and the Byzantine rite. The monks of this united venture published a journal called *Irénikon*. In 1908 two Anglican priests had launched a week of prayer for Christian unity which ran from 18–25 January. But this week of prayer seemed rather like a crusade for the conversion of non-Catholics.

Abbé Paul Couturier, from Lyons, was to give 

Pius XI against growing ecumenism

The pope refused to take part in the first ecumenical movements (Life and Work, Faith and Order). He forbade Catholics to be involved in them, arguing that only the Catholic Church possessed the truth. He spoke as Gregory XVI and Pius IX had done in their day.

There are those who nurture the hope that it would be easy to lead people, despite their religious differences, to unite in the profession of certain doctrines accepted as a common basis of spiritual life. As a result they hold conferences and meetings . . . Such efforts have no right to the approval of Catholics, since they are based on this erroneous opinion that all religions are more or less good and laudable . . . By that very token, those who hold this opinion reject the true religion.

Thus the pan-Christians have founded associations which are usually directed by non-Catholics, despite their personal differences over the truths of faith . . . The enterprise has caught the good-will of a number of Catholics . . . Under the seduction of thought and the charm of words an undoubted error of the worst kind has slipped in, which is capable of ruining the foundations of the Catholic faith from top to bottom.

The Apostolic See cannot on any pretext take part in their conferences, and Catholics do not have at any price the right to support them by their vote or by their action. The Apostolic See has never allowed Catholics to attend meetings of non-Catholics; the union of Christians can only go forward by encouraging the dissidents to return to the one true Church of Jesus Christ, which they once had the misfortune to abandon.

Pius XI, Encyclical *Mortalium animos*, 6 January 1928.

The week of prayer for unity or the spiritual ecumenism of Abbé Couturier

It should be understood that this octave of prayer (18–25 January) is a spiritual work which each person offers up in the sincerity of his or her soul, the Orthodox remaining Orthodox, the Anglican remaining Anglican, the Catholic remaining Catholic.

Paul Couturier (1935).

The heart of the matter is to succeed in promoting ecumenical prayer among all Christian groups, a prayer which is an echo of our deep suffering over the horrible sin of disunity. We have all sinned. We must all humble ourselves, pray without ceasing and constantly ask for the miracle of total reunion. We certainly shall not see it, but our duty is to prepare for it, however distant it may be. Our universal Christ is waiting for the unanimous prayer of all Christian groups to reunite them when and as he wills . . . Neither Catholic prayer nor Orthodox prayer nor Anglican prayer nor Protestant prayer is enough. All are necessary, and all together.

Paul Couturier (1936).

considerable momentum to this week of unity by deeply rethinking its significance. In an article published in 1935, Abbé Couturier said that unity could not be the fruit of the proselytism of one church by another. Unity could come only from God, and ought to be prayed for by all Christians. They ought to ask for the unity which Christ wills, by the means that he would wish. Each person, in his own confessional group, should recognize the faults committed against unity over the course of the centuries. If each Christian church is faithful to its tradition and prayer, God cannot refuse Christians the unity for which Christ prayed. This language was accepted by non-Catholics. The Week of Prayer for Christian Unity became truly ecumenical. Abbé Couturier aimed equally at furthering mutual knowledge by founding in 1937 the Dombes Group, pastors and priests who met each year at the Trappist monastery of Dombes in the French department of l'Ain in a kind of ecumenical retreat at which they got to know one another. Later the group went on to study the comparative theology of the various Christian confessions.

For further reading

The nineteenth century

K. O. von Aretin, *The Papacy and the Modern World*, Weidenfeld and Nicolson 1970

O. Chadwick, *The Secularization of the European Mind in the Nineteenth Century*, Cambridge University Press 1978

A. Dru, *The Church in the Nineteenth Century: Germany 1800–1918*, Burns and Oates 1963

E. E. Y. Hales, *The Catholic Church in the Modern World*, Eyre and Spottiswoode/ Burns and Oates 1958

John T. Ellis, *American Catholicism*, University of Chicago Press 1969

A. C. Jemolo, *Church and State in Italy 1850–1950*, Blackwell 1960

M. Larkin, *Church and State after the Dreyfus Affair*, Macmillan 1974

J. McManners, *Church and State in France 1870–1914*, SPCK 1972

B. M. G. Reardon, *Liberalism and Tradition: Aspects of Catholic Thought in Nineteenth-Century France*, Cambridge University Press 1975

The twentieth century

C. Falconi, *The Popes in the Twentieth Century*, Weidenfeld and Nicolson 1968

Derek Holmes, *The Papacy in the Modern World, 1914–1978*, Burns and Oates 1981

John Macquarrie, *Twentieth-Century Religious Thought*, SCM Press 1988

A. Rhodes, *The Vatican in the Age of the Dictators, 1922–1945*, Hodder and Stoughton 1973

Klaus Scholder, *The Churches and the Third Reich*, two volumes, SCM Press and Fortress Press 1987, 1988

H. Stẹhle, *Eastern Politics of the Vatican 1917–1979*, Ohio University Press 1981

Alan Wilkinson, *Dissent or Conform*, SCM Press 1986

22

From the Second World War to the Council

1939–1958

Le Corbusier, Notre-Dame-du-Haut-Ronchamp, 1950–1955.

The Second World War had a profound effect on the Christians and churches in the countries involved in the struggle. In some countries Christians were very hard hit, and the Christian conscience in particular had difficult choices to make. The war was also a time for development and thought. Many hopes took concrete shape during the years that followed. This period of theological renewal and original experiences also saw difficulties and crises in the last years of the pontificate of Pius XII.

I · Christians in the Second World War

1. The evils of war

Christians, like all their fellow citizens, had been devastated by the consequences of war: destruction and massacres in a Europe three-quarters of which had fallen under the domination of Nazi Germany. Those with a Christian conscience were forced to make difficult choices. What should their attitude be towards the occupying powers? Ought they to submit to those put in authority over them? Could they stay passive in the face of the elimination of the Jews? Was violence justified to free one's country? Attitudes varied from country to country and even within the same country.

In the east

In the area to the west of Poland, given the name Warthegau, which had been completely annexed by Germany, the Germans who wanted to Germanize this region embarked on a persecution of the Polish church, which no longer had any legal status. Churches and monasteries were closed, all movement was forbidden, and priests were interned. Many Poles from the part of Poland annexed by the Soviet Union in 1939 were expelled to the territory controlled by the general government set up by Germans in Warsaw, where their fate was hardly better. Jews were crammed into the Warsaw ghetto. Polish Catholics appealed to the pope, who feared that the fate of these poor wretches would be even worse if he spoke out. Poland lost six million of her people. One of the victims of Auschwitz, Fr Maximilian Kolbe (1894–1941), was canonized.

In Russia the progress of the German armies gave rise to a religious revival and the formation of churches which declared themselves to be separated from Moscow. The Ukrainian Uniates with links to Rome reorganized themselves. At the same time the Soviet government built on traditional Russian feeling to strengthen patriotism in the face of the German invasion. By 1943 there was again a patriarch in Moscow, Sergius, to be followed by Alexis. The end of the war brought about a reversal of the situation and the persecutions began again.

Slovakia and Croatia

In the spring of 1939 Hitler, having annexed Bohemia, offered independent status to Slovakia, the eastern part of the state of Czechoslovakia. The head of the Slovak government was a prelate, Mgr Tiso, who had to align himself not only with the foreign policy of Germany but also with its racial policy, by taking part in the elimination of the Jews. Mgr Tiso combined Christian views with totalitarian views.

The pseudo-independence of Croatia under the direction of Ante Pavelitch was seen by a great many Catholics as revenge on Serbian Orthodoxy. It was the pretext for outrages against the Orthodox and an atrocious civil war. Mgr Stepinac, Bishop of Zagreb, was torn between his patriotism as a Croat and his desire to protest against the violation of human rights.

Norway, Holland and Belgium

The Lutheran bishop Eivind Berggrav, at first non-violent and a pacifist, then opted for resistance to Nazism which, using the Quisling government as its tool, sought to subdue the national church. A provisional instruction from the church protested against the persecution of the Jews, the conscription of labour and the recruitment of young people.

In the Netherlands in 1941 the bishops forbade Catholics to belong to Dutch Nazi movements. Catholics and Protestants joined forces to protest against the deportation of Jews during 1942–43. In retaliation the Germans extended the arrests to Christians of Jewish origin: among the victims was the Carmelite and philosopher, Edith Stein. The bishops called on Dutch officials not to collaborate over the deportation of Jews and workers. In Belgium, Cardinal Van Roey sought to be a realist: to rescue what could be rescued without too much official protest. He opposed both the Belgian Nazis and the violent resistance. He tried to take action against the deportation of Jews.

France

There were many who saw the defeat of 1940 as divine punishment for the secularization of France. Marshal Pétain appeared as a new Joan of Arc. The régime was favourable to the church: monks and nuns could resume their habits; the host imprisoned in the tabernacle could be brought out on the streets for saints' day processions. The number of pilgrimages increased: to Our Lady of Le Puy, the Great Return of Our Lady of Boulogne, etc. Schools were grant-aided. For the most part the French bishops, who were usually veterans of the 1914–1918 war, were very well disposed towards the Vichy regime, which they recognized as the legitimate power and therefore willed by God.

Racist measures were taken very soon, even in unoccupied France. There was hardly any official reaction from Christian authorities until July 1942, at the time of the round-up from Vel' d'Hiv' and the systematic deportation of Jews from France to Germany. Mgr Saliège, Bishop of Toulouse, and Mgr Théas, Bishop of Montauban, expressed the indignant protest of the Christian conscience: all men, Aryan and non-Aryan, were brothers because they were created by God; all men, regardless of race or religion, had the right to be respected by individuals and the state. Other bishops, among them Cardinal Gerlier, Archbishop of Lyons, spoke of their indignation, but remained embarrassed by their loyalty to the established power, that of Vichy, and by the distinction which they drew between morals and politics. Bishops and movements were divided over what attitude to have towards the conscription of young people to work in Germany.

The bishops were not on the whole in favour of the resistance because they disapproved of violence and insubordination to the government in control. So Christians undertook resistance work on their own responsibility, and found a voice through various clandestine publications. Protestants had made their attitude clear in the Eight Articles of Pomeyrol (Bouches du Rhône, September 1941). Starting in November 1941, the *Cahiers du Témoignage Chrétien* supported Christian resistance. Thus Christians affirmed their autonomy in the political choices that they made. In their work they met militants from all parties. Members of the Catholic Action movements and priests sacrificed their lives.

Germany

In Germany, resistance to Hitler could only be on a modest scale, because to oppose the régime was to seek the downfall of Germany. On the Protestant side, the Confessing Church very soon opposed the racial policy. Many of its members were sent to concentration camps, where several perished, including Dietrich Bonhoeffer in 1945. The most general attitude was one of timid abstention. The Catholic bishops who met periodically in the Fulda Conference could not agree to put up public resistance to these attacks on morality and human rights. They contented themselves with speaking in general terms, refusing to condemn the state directly (*The Collective Letter on the Decalogue*, September 1943). One of the rare specific statements was the condemnation in August 1941 by Bishop von Gallen of Münster of the law decreeing the euthanasia of the mentally handicapped and the sick. Some priests, including Bernhardt Lichtenberg, and militants (including the White Rose group) died for their courageous stands.

Christian resistance

The *Cahiers du Témoignage Chretien* (Notebooks of Christian Resistance) appeared from November 1941 onwards in Lyons. The title of the first was 'France, be careful not to lose your soul'. The *Cahiers* were important pamphlets of between 16 and 64 pages, with an average print-run of 30,000 copies each. In May 1943 some shorter texts appeared in a higher print-run entitled *Courrier français du Témoignage chrétien* (French Courier of Christian Witness).

Christians and the United Resistance Front

We know that attempts are going on to unite the forces of resistance effectively. These initiatives give us an occasion to specify the position of Christians with regard to a united front for the Resistance. Of course we are talking of Christians who have understood.

Speaking as Christians, we are fully aware of the transcendence of our message. It would be intolerable for Christ to be placed in a human organization on the same level as some leader or other being prepared to bring his party into a wider Christian organization. Christ transcends parties and provisional plans.

But it would be equally inadmissible if one excused oneself from involvement in the drama which is shaking the world on the pretext of the transcendence of Christianity. Christianity is transcendent, but not the Christian. The Christians of France are French. Christianity, far from giving them a dispensation from obligations which are purely French, adds to these obligations those which are peculiar to the state of being a Christian.

That is why the Christians of France can take their place in Resistance movements like all other French men and women. Moreover, we know that there are many of them. They have the duty, here as everywhere else, to make the voice of their Christian conscience heard; they have the duty, here as everywhere else, not to accept anything that runs contrary to Christianity. We say that when they are members of a particular organization (with the exception of 'Christian Witness'), they are so as French men and women and not as Christians. Since France is still at war, and no Frenchman has the right to consider himself demobilized, it is natural for them to perform their patriotic tasks in the ranks of these organizations, in the same way as others do.

Courrier français du Témoignage chrétien 2, July–August 1943.

2. The silence of Pius XII

In contrast to Benedict XV, who had been strongly criticized for his appeals for peace during the First World War, Pius XII was almost universally praised, during his lifetime, for his attitude during the 1939–1945 war. But in 1963, in a play called *The Representative*, which achieved some notoriety, a young German author, Rolf Hochhuth, accused Pius XII of not having spoken out against the extermination of the Jews by the Nazis. A bitter controversy followed. Had Pius XII been lacking in courage? Had he been sympathetic towards Nazism? Had he not known what was going on? The good thing about the affair was that it prompted the publication of documents from the archives which shed some light on things. A diplomat and secretary of state before becoming pope, Pius XII was well up in German affairs. He had signed the Concordat with Hitler in 1933 and in 1937 had shared in the drafting of the encyclical *Mit brennender Sorge*. Though he had no sympathy with the Nazis, he preferred discreet diplomatic intervention to solemn pronouncements.

The silence of Pius XII?

Here are some texts in which Pius XII referred to genocide. Subsequently they were thought to be not sufficiently explicit.

Christmas broadcast, 24 December 1942

Humanity owes this desire (for a return to peace) to the hundreds of thousands of people who, for no fault on their part, but simply because of their nationality or ethnic origin, have been condemned to death or progressive extinction.

Letter to Mgr von Preysing, Bishop of Berlin, 30 April 1943

We leave to the pastors where they work the task of estimating whether and to what degree caution must be exercised, despite reasons for intervening, in order to avoid greater evils. The declarations of bishops run the risk of leading to reprisals and pressures, and other circumstances must be taken into account, arising perhaps from the length and the psychology of the war. That is one of the reasons why we ourselves are restrained in our declarations.

Allocution to the Sacred College (the Cardinals), 2 June 1943

Our heart responds with deep and attentive concern to the prayers of those who turn to us with an attitude of anxious entreaty, tormented as they are because of their nationality or their race by great misfortunes, by the most searing and severe sufferings, and delivered over, for no fault of their own, to measures of extermination.

You will not expect us to describe here even some of what we have attempted to accomplish in order to diminish their suffering, to mitigate their moral and legal situation, to defend their inalienable religious rights and to meet their distress and their needs.

Every word on our part, addressed in this connection to the relevant authorities, every public reference on our part, has to be seriously weighed and measured, in the interest of those who suffer, so that despite us their situation is not made even more serious and intolerable.

Exhortations to peace

In 1939–1940, after striving to prevent the declaration of war, he asked Mussolini to stay out of the conflict and the European powers to sort out their problems by negotiation. Throughout the war, in a great many speeches and Christmas messages, admittedly in general terms, he kept stressing the waste of war and the advantages of negotiation and a peace based on a just balance. He formed, under the supervision of Mgr Montini, an information bureau which provided news of prisoners and missing persons. Jewish suspects and others found sanctuary in papal buildings and convents. In 1943–44, when the war reached Italy, Pius XII tried to protect Rome, pressing the king to remove Mussolini and protesting against the bombing. Rather like Benedict XV, Pius II wanted to be impartial, standing above the tumult. Was not Bolshevism as dangerous as Nazism, if not more so?

The extermination of the Jews

Even if information on the deportation and extermination of the Jews was not completely lacking and reached the Vatican quite early, it was often vague and its insane quality made it difficult to believe. In the spring of 1943, Pius XII knew where he stood. At first the pope experienced a feeling of helplessness. He referred to genocide in two public addresses, his Christmas broadcast of 1942 and a speech to the cardinals

on 2 June 1943. The allusions were very general. Neither Jews nor Germans were mentioned by name. Pius XII spoke of his fear that his intervention would rebound on those whom he sought to protect. On the other hand, he left the bishops to be judges of their own actions. In fact the result proved ambiguous. Some protests led to an increase in German oppression. By contrast, diplomatic intervention had a certain effect in Slovakia, Croatia and Hungary. Deportations of the Jews stopped for a time. In Italy, the pope remained silent at the arrest of Jews on 16 October 1943, but his discreet intervention prevented any fresh incidents.

The pope therefore said as little as possible, pursuing a policy deliberately based on diplomacy. Afterwards, many Poles would have preferred a more prophetic attitude. The pope should have had a tribunal. In 1964 in Munich Cardinal Doepfner said: 'The retrospective judgment of history has a perfect right to say that Pius XII should have made a stronger protest. Be this as it may, one has no right to doubt the absolute sincerity of his motives or the authenticity of his profound reasoning.'

II · The Religious Repercussions of Political Events in the Post-War Period

1. A new situation for Christians

The shifting of boundaries

The war resulted in tremendous losses in the countries of Eastern and Central Europe: the USSR, Poland, Yugoslavia. Poland lost almost a third of its population, many of whom were its élite (officers, university staff, priests) who were systematically wiped out by the Russians and the Germans. The Yalta agreement, made in February 1945, drew up the zone boundaries for the various allies. The USSR advanced eastwards by annexing the Baltic countries (Lithuania, Latvia, Estonia), part of the Poland of 1918 and part of

Romania (Bessarabia). Poland similarly moved westwards, recovering lands from Germany. The latter was divided into two, one zone belonging to the Soviets and the other to the West. These alterations to the frontiers resulted in the displacement of large numbers of people, particularly Germans and Poles. The religious consequences were important. Many Christians were directly or indirectly subject to Soviet oppression. In Germany, the Christian confessions were often in a diaspora situation. From then on Catholics lived in areas traditionally inhabited by Protestants, and vice versa.

Christians in politics in Western Europe

In Western Europe, Christians played an important part in politics. The wish for a juster society was born during the struggles of the Resistance. In several countries Christians formed a third force over against Communists and socialists. This was the hey-day of Christian democracy and its equivalents in Italy, Germany and Belgium. In France the preference was for a nonconfessional term. Catholics came out of the ghetto in which secularization had imprisoned them since the beginning of the century. In France this success of Christian democracy also marked the collapse of the old conservative right wing, compromised by its collaboration with the German forces of occupation.

All these Christian Democratic parties played a part in making the formerly reluctant Catholics accept democracy and a parliamentary régime. At the same time they succeeded in embodying a certain number of social and Euopean preoccupations in law. There was sometimes talk of a Vatican-dominated Europe controlled from a distance by the pope and the bishops. That was not exactly the case. These parties were for the most part formed during the Resistance at a far remove from the supervision of the bishops. Gradually, however, the fear of Communism stirred up the bishops and the pope to advise voting for Christian democracy. In France, the schools question pushed Catholics towards the Popular Republican Movement, which rapidly receded in favour of a reformed right wing. A very small minority of left-wing Christians called all confessional parties into question.

2. The consequences of the Cold War

In the two years which followed the victory of 1945, the old allies began to disagree. The USSR showed its intention of ruling in the area under its control. Within a few years in the countries of Eastern Europe the minority Communist parties succeeded, through various manoevres supported by the USSR, in taking over the controls. In the Western countries, the powerful Communist parties, particularly in France and Italy, also tried to impose themselves by means of a general strike. In 1949, the whole of China fell into Communist hands under Mao Tse Tung. If one adds to that in subsequent years the seizure of power by the Communists in Vietnam (1954 and then 1975) and Cuba (1959), the result was a Communist block of 1300 million people threatening the rest of the world by its expansionary drive.

Behind the iron curtain which separated the two Europes, persecution broke out on Christians. It differed in form and intensity depending on the country. In the USSR the fight against religion was particularly violent in the Baltic countries. In Lithuania, the priests kept up a resistance to Soviet domination which continued until 1952, resulting in the extermination of a large section of the clergy. The Uniate Christians of Ukraine led by the imprisoned Cardinal Slipyi were also gravely persecuted. But the Orthodox were not spared, in spite of the apparent submission of the officials of the Russian church. In all the Eastern countries, the state obstructed the Catholic authorities, who were accused of communicating in code, of compromising with the enemy, and so on: Cardinal Mindszenty in Hungary (1949), Mgr Beran in Czechoslovakia, Mgr Stepinac in Yugoslavia and Cardinal Wyszeynski in Poland. From 1956 onwards de-Stalinization improved the lot of Christians in certain countries like Poland (with the liberation of Cardinal Wyszynski), but worsened it in others like Hungary, where Cardinal Mindszenty remained imprisoned for fifteen years in the US legation in Budapest.

The Western countries formed another bloc around the United States and NATO (North Atlantic Treaty Organization, 1949). The Communist parties in these countries were regarded as accomplices of what went on behind the Iron Curtain, and so were distrusted. In 1949 a decree from the Holy See forbade Catholics to collaborate in any way with Communists. But the Communist parties also attracted the most underprivileged, those who dreamed of a juster society. There followed some crises of conscience for Christians which are at the heart of the social problems of their time.

3. Decolonization and the young churches

In the twenty years following the war, all the colonial empires which the European powers had built up over four or five centuries, but particularly in the nineteenth, broke up. The colonized peoples achieved their independence. Christianity seemed to be the religion of the colonizers imported from Europe. Nationalism restored to favour the ancient cultures, an often idealized past to which colonization and Christianity had dealt a blow. Had not the idea of the people's right to arrange their own affairs come from the colonizers themselves? In the end the nation states found support from the USSR, and some of them were inspired by Marxism. The class struggle evolved into the struggle of people subjected by foreign political, economic and religious domination. All this perhaps explains an opposition to Christians in those countries which were struggling for independence.

From 1949 Communist China required Christians to free themselves from foreign influence by acquiring a triple autonomy: in matters of government (by having no links with the Vatican); administration and finance (no funds from Europe); and preaching (no foreign missionaries). All foreign missionaries were very quickly expelled, and religious leaders who continued to remain faithful to Rome were imprisoned or executed. A national church was founded without links with Rome. The fight against religion reached a climax with the cultural revolution of 1966–1968, but has calmed down somewhat since.

As the colonized countries achieved independence, they contributed towards forming the Third World, which gradually became aware of its strength and blamed the West, and Christians in particular, for its poverty.

The development of the young churches

Church leaders are usually anxious to distinguish between evangelization and colonization. In his Christmas message for 1945, Pius XII asserted that the church was above nationalism, that it was not an empire linked to Europe. The pope expressed his fear of Communism, which was unjustly accusing the church of colonialism. On many occasions the bishops of the colonized countries affirmed the legitimacy of claiming independence: for example, the bishops of the Cameroons in 1955 and those of the Belgian Congo and Ruana Burundi in 1956. The European colonizers accused them of being opportunists seeking to safeguard the interests of the church and of working against their native countries.

European bishops were increasingly replaced by indigenous bishops. The mission areas,

The church in Communist China

To separate the Chinese Catholics from Rome, the Chinese Communist Party launched a campaign for triple autonomy (government, finance, personal) over against the West. Those who did not accept this were either eliminated physically or expelled. At the same time the party pressurized or forced the Catholics to form patriotic associations which designated their own bishops.

(276) The martyr's choice

The Communist armies entered Shanghai on 24 May 1949. Though prudent, Fr Bede Tsang, Rector of St Ignatius College at Zikawei, was not afraid to expose himself to danger when this was called for in defence of the young people for whom he was responsible. In the spring of 1951 he had to take part in a congress of private schools in eastern China arranged by the Department of Education. At the end of the session the members of the congress were asked to approve a joint declaration committing them to promoting the movement of triple independence among their Catholic pupils. Fr Tsang, followed by four other delegates, rose to signify his refusal. He clearly expounded some basic points of Catholic doctrine, explained the true conception of the autonomy of the church in each country, and appealed for the government's understanding. He ended by showing the natural foundation that love of country finds in Christian faith . . . The delegates applauded him and then stopped uneasily. The motion had to be withdrawn. However, Fr Tsang had just condemned himself.

On 9 August 1951, about 1 pm., they came for him; the police wanted to 'chat' with him. In prison it seems to have been suggested that the Father should become head of the separatist church in Shanghai. When he refused, they tried to break his will in order to use him in spite of himself. There followed long nights of interrogation in which insomnia and inner tension combined to drain him of his last resistance. Prisoners heard Fr Tsang say: 'Jesus, Mary, Joseph, save me.'

The guards went even further, and Fr Tsang sank into a coma. In an attempt to catch a victim who was slipping from their grasp, they transferred him to the prison hospital on 30 October. On 11 November 1951, at eight in the morning, Fr Tsang escaped them for ever.

Jean Monsterleet, *Les martyrs de Chine parlent*, 1953.

A patriotic bishop

On 17 December 1957 the Diocesan Congress of Chentu elected Li Hsi-Ying 'Bishop of Chentu with ordinary powers'. The newly-elected bishop took an oath on the Bible. One must be careful not to pass judgment too hastily on the choice of a certain number of Catholics who doubtless wanted to save what could still be saved.

Since the voice of the people is the voice of God, I must organize myself and take responsibility for the diocese. From today I wish to train the priests and the forty thousand faithful of the diocese to move under the direction of the Communist Party along the route of Socialism, to oppose all interference and meddling on the part of the Vatican and to make themselves completely independent in religious affairs. As to what doctrines to belief and what rules to observe, we shall maintain relations with the Vatican, but on the essential condition that neither the dignity of our country nor the interests of the Chinese people are infringed.

which depended directly on Rome through the vicars apostolic, became dioceses covering wholly or in part the same areas as the dioceses of the old European churches. Decolonization gave rise to young churches which were truly autonomous. It must be emphasized that this

The church and the independence of the peoples

The bishops of the Cameroons recognized the legitimacy of aspirations towards independence, but they were wary of the parties inspired by Marxism.

The church can only recognize as just and well-founded the desires of the people of the Cameroons to take the direction of their country into their own hands and to lead it towards a free, honest and prosperous life. It must encourage them, provided that the great laws of the gospel – truth, justice, prudence and charity – are observed. It is necessary for Christians to recognize the indisputable signs of the parties which claim to lead them. Some are opposed to truth, charity, justice and prudence. Catholics must recognize the principles and the methods of the movements into which they cannot now hurl themselves.

We must not be deceived or led astray. Unless it repudiates its very principles and no longer merits its name, Marxism is the current danger in our civilization.

Joint letter by the Episcopate of the Cameroons, 10 April 1957.

autonomy had begun much earlier in the Protestant churches overseas, which were less centralized on Europe than was the case with Catholicism.

In the encyclical *Fidei donum* (1957), Pius XII pointed out that evangelization was not solely the province of a specialized individual but that all the bishops had responsibility for it. They could acknowledge this responsibility by sending some of their diocesan priests to be of temporary assistance to the young churches (priests *fidei donum*).

Catholics generally reflect the attitudes of their times. But it seems that the positions taken up by the various leaders of the churches and by Christian organizations, like the actions of militants, had contributed to the acceptance by Christian and national opinion of the independence of the old colonies.

The bishops are responsible in solidarity for the evangelization of the world

United by a closer bond both to Christ and to his Vicar, my venerable brothers (the bishops), you will want to play your part in a spirit of lively charity, in this care for all the churches which weighs on our shoulders (II Corinthians 11.28). You who are constrained by the love of Christ (II Corinthians 5.14) will want to feel deeply along with us the imperative duty to propagate the gospel and to found the church through the entire world.

However, another form of support, which is without doubt more onerous, is given by many bishops who authorize some of their priests, albeit at some sacrifice, to put themselves for a limited period at the disposition of the Ordinaries (bishops) of Africa. By doing that they render them an irreplacable service.

Pius XII, Encyclical *Fidei donum*, 21 April 1957.

III · Pastoral and Theological Dynamism

1. Theology and ecumenism

The rediscovery of the Bible by Catholics

With the encyclical *Divino afflante* (1943), Catholics were given much greater freedom to study the scriptures. A burgeoning of translations, the most important being the Jerusalem Bible, witnessed to what amounted to a real discovery of the Bible in Catholic circles. The scriptures were studied for themselves as the word of God, and not just as the source of quotations to support theological opinions. In France the collection *Lectio divina* brought together the writings of Catholic exegetes. Many historical works in various collections (*Unam Sanctam, Théologie*) showed that theology is not timeless. Many source texts from the liturgy and the church fathers (*Sources chrétiennes*) were published in critical editions and translations.

Christology and ecclesiology

Theology underwent a renewal both christologically and ecclesiologically. The Jesuit Pierre Teilhard de Chardin (1881–1955) had no official recognition during his lifetime and was not permitted to publish anything. His book *The Phenomenon of Man*, which had been circulated in private, proved to be a best-seller when it was published after his death. People have spoken, following him, of panchristism, cosmic mysticism or cosmic christocentricity. Matter contains a spiritual power behind which Christ reveals himself. The cosmos is converging on the omega

Excavations at Qumran.

Teilhard de Chardin in 1931 during the 'Yellow Expedition'.

The panchristism of Teilhard de Chardin

The writings of Teilhard de Chardin (1881–1955), which circulated underground for a long period, were published only after his death.

With the origin of things, there began an advent of recollection and work in the course of which the forces of determinism, obediently and lovingly, lent themselves and directed themselves in the preparation of a Fruit which exceeded all hope and yet was awaited. The world's energies and substances – so harmoniously adapted and controlled that the supreme Transcendent would seem to germinate entirely from their immanence – concentrated and were purified in the stock of Jesse; from their accumulated and distilled treasures they produced the glittering gem of matter, the Pearl of the Cosmos, and the link with the incarnate personal Absolute – the Blessed Virgin Mary, Queen and Mother of all things, the true Demeter . . . and when the day of the Virgin came to pass, then the final purpose of the universe, deep-rooted and gratuitous, was suddenly made clear: since the days when the first breath of individualization passed over the expanse of the Supreme Centre here below so that in it could be seen the ripple of the smile of the original monads, all things were moving towards the Child born of Woman.

And since Christ was born, and ceased to grow, and died, everything has continued in motion because he has not yet attained the fullness of his form.

Pierre Teilhard de Chardin, *The Future of Man*, Fount Paperbacks 1982, 319f.

point, the return of Christ. Other writers also bore witness to a recentring of Christian existence on Christ. The development of ecclesiology which had begun between the wars was carried on. Congar, De Lubac and many other French theologians tried to root the theology of the church in history and to present the church not so much as the perfect society of which Christ had foretold all the detailed organization but as the mystery of grace and the place where Christ is encountered. This return to the sources and the attention paid to history favoured the coming together of Christians of different confessions.

The progress of ecumenism

The shared hardships of war had given the opportunity for encounter. Various associations had united Christians in the service of refugees and Jews. In 1948 the World Council of Churches was founded in Amsterdam, and this gradually integrated the different ecumenical movements: Faith and Order, Life and Work, the International Missionary Council, all of which nevertheless retained their individual meetings. Any church could join the World Council on the basis of a profession of faith in Jesus Christ as Lord and Saviour. The World Council was not a superchurch, but a forum and a listening place, an expectant community. At regular intervals it organized general assemblies on a particular theme: at Evanston in 1954, New Delhi in 1961, Nairobi in 1975, Vancouver in 1984.

Catholics continued to hold back over ecumenism. There is always a tension between the supporters of unionism, i.e. the return of separated brethren or dissidents to the true church, the Church of Rome, and those of ecumenism, i.e. a dialogue between equal partners. In the context of the formation of the World Council of Churches in 1948 Rome not only refused to take part but prohibited mixed marriages (Catholics and non-Catholics) for religious purposes and any participation by Catholics in the eucharistic worship of another confession (1948). However, in March 1950 an instruction of the Holy Office recognized the ecumenical movement as 'magnificent work' and the fruit of the Spirit. The bishops were authorized to allow inter-confessional meetings. Catholics were allowed to say the Our Father with non-Catholics. In the last years of his life Fr Couturier, who died in 1953, developed the spiritual ecumenism which he called 'invisible monasticism'.

2. Tensions and crises

The last years of the pontificate of Pius XII saw a series of tensions and crises which were interrelated. They were the result of a certain amount of misunderstanding and fear, but also an indication that in several areas limits and inevitable difficulties had been reached.

Theology

In August 1950 Pius XII published the encyclical *Humani Generis* 'on certain false views which threaten to undermine the foundations of Catholic doctrine'. The pope challenged what has sometimes been called the 'new theology', a theological meditation on contemporary humankind, which takes history very much into account. The pope called for a return to Thomist orthodoxy in the realms of philosophy and theology. In the matter of relations between Christians, the encyclical was concerned about a rash eirenism which would sacrifice doctrine to unity. No individual was named, no list of errors

The career of a worker priest

Several worker priests of the Mission de Paris recalled their careers for Mgr Feltin, the new archbishop of Paris, in October 1949. Here are some extracts from the testimony of a young priest who began by being a caster in a foundry.

When I arrived at the Compteurs de Montrouge, I had twelve uninterrupted years of seminary life behind me. I went to the working class with what I thought were indispensable riches: culture, a balanced personality, enthusiasm and so on.

I believed in personal influence. I valued contacts. I loved discussions. I hoped that my knowledge would impress people. I wanted to give God. And, more seriously, I lived and acted by dissociating my personal faith in God from the world to which the church had sent me. This world of which I knew nothing.

This spell of two months at the Compteurs de Montrouge made me lose my illusions. Leaving the factory to be more available to the Paris districts of Kremlin-Bicetre and Gentilly, I retained the conviction that I had to lose all my culture, my mentality, my inner attitudes, in order to allow myself to be taken over by the work and hopes of the working class.

I came to know the everyday difficulties of mothers: I encountered homes in which ten people were crowded into two small rooms. Above all, I discovered a more or less conscious rebellion, underlying but nevertheless real, on the part of these working-class families against the inhuman conditions that were imposed on them. So in the mission that had been entrusted to me, only one orientation was possible: my priesthood would be their priesthood, or it would not be a priesthood at all.

The people who surrounded me, whom I met in the street, with whom I unloaded a truck, whose life and work I shared in the market place where I was a fitter for almost two years, did not expect either advice or service from me. They could only be aware of one thing: we had the same life and were subject to the same destiny.

In *Les Prêtres-Ouvriers*, Editions de Minuit 1954.

rehearsed, but just below the surface it was possible to detect the theologies and theologians condemned. The incompatibility of polygenism (several human beings at the beginning of humankind) with the doctrine of creation and original sin was aimed at Teilhard de Chardin. Debates about nature and supernature, history and dogma were aimed at the Jesuit theologians who bore the brunt of the encyclical; some of them had to stop teaching and undertake not to publish. In 1954, at the time of the worker priests affair and in connection with it, Dominican theologians like Congar and Chenu were forbidden to teach.

The definition of the Dogma of the Assumption on 1 November 1950 delighted the great majority of Catholics, but led to unease in ecumenical circles among Protestants and Orthodox.

The worker priest affair

In France, concern for the evangelization of the poor could not ignore the fact that a large section of the working class belonged to the Communist movement, trade unions and the Party. Catholics thought that by showing solidarity they could work alongside the Communist party and form a Union of Progressive Christians. The worker priests joined the trade union movement. But the Holy Office banned all collaboration with the Communists. Anxiety was very soon felt in Rome over the life-style and activities of the worker priests. The pope thought that the worker priest was no longer a spiritual person, and that his role cast doubts on the specific features of being a lay person. The worker priest was laicizing himself, and Pius XII wanted to safeguard the integrity of the priesthood. In spite of the efforts of the French cardinals, on 1 March 1954 worker priests had to give up full-time factory work. Out of a hundred or so worker priests, about half submitted, while the others went on, feeling themselves bound to the working class in which the church seemed disinterested. The affair had profound repercussions. The reorganization of the seminary of the Mission de France and the creation of the Mission Ouvrière, a co-ordination of pastoral work (between priests and Catholic Action), was intended to indicate that the Church of France had not abandoned its original perspectives.

281

And there were other crises, not just in France, several of them centred on the catechism.

At the end of a pontificate rich in initiatives, a certain number of blockages had thus appeared. A new pontificate and the announcement of the Council were to allow these post-war efforts to come to full fruition.

For further reading

Trevor Beeson, *Discretion and Valour. Religious Conditions in Russia and Eastern Europe*, rev. ed. Fount Books and Fortress Press 1982

Owen Chadwick, *Britain and the Vatican during the Second World War*, Cambridge University Press 1986

John S. Conway, *The Nazi Persecution of the Churches*, Weidenfeld and Nicolson 1968

Harold E. Fey (ed.), *A History of the Ecumenical Movement. 1948–1968*, SPCK 1970, reissued World Council of Churches 1986

Adrian Hastings, *A History of English Christianity 1920–1985*, Fount Books 1987

J. A. Coleman, *The Evolution of Dutch Catholicism 1958–1974*, University of California Press 1979

E. E. Y. Hales, *Pope John and his Revolution*, Eyre and Spottiswoode 1965

23
The Church of Vatican II
1958–1980

The recent past is always difficult to write about. There is a lack of perspective on events, which have not yet shown all their consequences. Inevitably, different interpretations are given to explain certain developments. Here we can only single out a few significant events of the last decades. The Second Vatican Council seemed to be both the culmination of twenty years of pastoral and theological research and a kind of break with the church which had grown out of the Council of Trent. In acknowledging that in a world that was continually developing, the church had to keep abreast of things, the council raised great hopes. The misunderstanding between the church and the world seemed to be evaporating. However, other difficulties arose. The council encouraged freedom of speech, and a general crisis in civilization could not fail to have consequences for the church.

I · Vatican II

1. The lead-up

Pope John XXIII

On 28 October 1958 Pius XII was succeeded by Cardinal Roncalli, who took the name John XXIII. The new pope was seventy-seven years old and it was thought that he would be a caretaker pope. Of peasant stock, he had had a varied diplomatic career. He had been patriarch of Venice since 1953 and had the reputation of being a courageous man. Having lived in several different countries, he had grasped that the world had moved on a good deal and that the church played no part in many areas of life. In the spirit of the gospel, John XXIII wanted to 'simplify complicated things'. He adopted a new pontifical style. The first pope to leave the Vatican since 1870, he visited the prison in Rome and made pilgrimages to Loretto and Assisi. But in certain respects he remained a complete traditionalist.

The announcement of the Council

Many people were in a state of expectancy over the pope when the announcement that a council was to be convened caused surprise all round. On 25 January 1959, John XXIII announced his threefold intention: of calling a synod for the diocese of Rome, of reforming canon law, and of calling a council for the universal church. He is remembered above all for the last. Pius XI and Pius XII had more or less dreamed of this, but it was thought that the era of councils had terminated with the proclamation of papal infallibility and the ease of communication with Rome.

Without having any precise idea of what the council would be about, John XXIII gave it two very broad aims: an adaption (*aggiornamento*, updating) of the church and the apostolate to a world that was constantly changing, and a return to Christian unity, which the pope seemed to envisage happening in a very short space of time – a little like the first Christians' attitude to the *parousia*! For the church, it was less a question of fighting enemies than of finding a means of expression for the world in which it was living and which it ignored. The imperial power of the church had to be shaken.

Preparations for the Council

A general consultation was organized with the bishops and the universities. Twelve preparatory commissions were set up, nine of which corresponded to the Roman congregations (ministries). Right up to the last minute it could be thought that the Roman offices were organizing and directing the Council. But there were some original aspects: a Commission for the Apostolate of the Laity; a Secretariat for Christian Unity under the direction of Cardinal Bea;

and the introduction of theologians and bishops from a variety of countries into the preparatory commissions. These commissions drew up seventy schemata as the basis for the work of the Council. A ruling provided for three kinds of sessions: the commissions (bishops and theological experts) prepared and presented the texts which had been proposed; in general congregations (all the bishops) any bishop could take the floor (for ten minutes in Latin!). The public congregations, presided over by the pope, gave final approval to a text.

2. The course of the Council

The first session (autumn 1962): the Council of John XXIII

Of the 2800 Fathers who were invited (bishops and the superiors of male orders), about 2400 were present. It was the first Catholic assembly to be truly world-wide. All continents and races were represented, but many of the bishops from the Communist countries were unable to come. The spectacular innovation in comparison with previous councils was the invitation, sent at John XXIII's request, to observers of other Christian confessions: Orthodox, Anglicans, Old Catholics, Protestants. Their number grew from thirty-one at the opening of the Council to ninety-three at the end. In the following sessions there were also thirty-six lay observers, seven of them women.

At the solemn opening on 11 October 1962 John XXIII warned the assembly against the temptation to be pessimistic and integrist. On 13 October Cardinal Tisserand, who presided over the general assembly, called for the election of new commissions of the Council. This amounted to reconvening the preparatory commissions and suggested that the Council was to be directed by the Roman administration, by remote control. Cardinal Liénart, against the wishes of the president, spoke and asked for the vote to be adjourned so that the bishops could take counsel together and make their choice freely and in full possession of the facts. The national bishops were therefore able to propose candidates who were representative of the deep feelings of the Council. Two attitudes became clear. Following the vision of John XXIII the majority were concerned to adapt the church to the world, to engage in ecumenical dialogue and to return to scriptural sources; a minority, often members of the Roman Curia and the bishops of the countries of Christendom (e.g. Italy, Spain) were more concerned for the stability of the church and the safeguarding of traditional faith. Throughout the Council a way had to be negotiated through these two positions. This sometimes made for better drafting but also led to the weakening of certain texts.

The first session did not produce any definitive text. It was realized that it was impossible to work through seventy schemata and so a decision was made to reduce them to twenty. At all events, the Council seemed more like an assembly of free people and not a place where previously formulated texts were rubber-stamped.

The death of John XXIII and the ascession of Paul VI

In April 1963 John XXIII's encyclical *Pacem in Terris* had widespread repercussions because the pope addressed himself to 'all men of good will' and no longer only to Christians. Shortly afterwards, the whole world watched with emotion the slow agony of John XXIII, who died on 3 June 1963. On 21 June Cardinal Mantini was elected pope and took the name of Paul VI. Archbishop of Milan since 1954, he had previously been pursuing his career at the Vatican in the Secretariat of State. Somewhat timid, with a brilliant intellect, a very hard worker and a mystic, Paul VI was a contrast to John XXIII and gave the impression of fragility. He made an immediate decision to continue the Council.

The Encyclical *Pacem in Terris* of John XXIII (11 April 1963)

To Our Venerable Brothers, the Patriarchs, Primates, Archbishops, Bishops and Other Local Ordinaries in Peace and Communion with the Apostolic See . . . to the Clergy and Faithful of the Whole World . . .

The progress of learning and the inventions of technology clearly show that, both in living things and in the forces of nature, an astonishing order reigns, and they all bear witness to the greatness of man, who can understand that order and create suitable instruments to harness those forces of nature and use them to his benefit.

Every human being has the right of life, to bodily integrity, and to the means which are necessary and suitable for the proper development of life. These means are primarily food, clothing, shelter, rest, medical care, and finally the necessary social services.

Every human being has the right to honour God according to the dictates of an upright conscience, and the right to profess his religion privately and publicly. Human beings have, in addition, the right to choose freely the state of life which they prefer . . . Human beings have the natural right to free initiative in the economic field and the right to work.

An act of the highest importance performed by the United Nations was the Universal Declaration of Human Rights, approved in the General Assembly on December 10, 1948. It is our earnest prayer that the United Nations – in its structure and in its means – may become ever more equal to the magnitude and nobility of its tasks. May the day come as quickly as possible when every human being will find therein an effective safeguard for the rights which derive directly from his dignity as a person, and which are therefore universal, inviolable and inalienable rights.

There is an immense task incumbent on all men of good will, namely the task of restoring the relations of the human family in truth, in justice, in love and in freedom – the relations between individual human beings; between citizens and their respective political communities; between political communities themselves; between individuals, families, intermediate associations and political communities on the one hand, and the world community on the other. This is a most exalted task, all will agree, for it is the task of bringing about true peace in the order established by God.

The Council of Paul VI

The second session in the autumn of 1963 touched on various themes such as episcopal collegiality, ecumenism and religious freedom, and promulgated the Constitution on the Liturgy and the Decree on Social Communications.

In January 1964 Paul VI travelled to the Holy Land. It was a long time since a pope had left Italy. His journey was a pilgrimage to the sources and an ecumenical gesture; he met the Patriarch of Constantinople, Athenagoras. In May the Secretariat for non-Christians was formed. The number of schemata was reduced to seventeen.

During the third session, in the autumn of 1964, the Fathers faced up to the question of religious freedom. Several texts were voted on and promulgated; on the church (*Lumen gentium*), on ecumenism, and on the Eastern churches. The Council proposed the establishment of a Synod of bishops which the pope would consult from time to time. In December, on a journey to Bombay, the pope made contact with the Third World.

The fourth and last session, from September to December 1965, ended in a vote and the promulgation of all the texts previously discussed. On 4 October Paul VI went to New York to attend the General Assembly of the United Nations, where his exhortation 'No more war, ever', made a strong impact. On 4 December, in a communal celebration, the first of its kind for a pope, the Council bid its farewells to the non-Catholic observers. On 7 December, in St Peter's,

Rome, Paul VI and the patriarch Athenagoras lifted the mutual excommunications pronounced in 1054 between Rome and Constantinople (see Vol.1, p.133). This gesture was an important step along the road to unity. 8 December 1965 saw the solemn closing of the Council, which was carried out with a great feeling of hope.

3. The great openings made by the Council

In a general way the Council was intended to be a pastoral council which sought to speak to contemporary men and women. While being deeply doctrinal, it had not proposed any definitions or condemnations. It did not fulminate with anathemas, as did the councils of the past.

A theology returning to its sources

The Constitution on Revelation stresses the unity of revelation, a living tradition in which an artificial distinction is not to be made between scripture and oral tradition. Revelation is not set rigidly in a text but nurtured in the believing people, who constantly discover new riches in it. The return to the Word of God allowed a value to be put again in the Catholic Church on traditional aspects which had been somewhat forgot-

Vatican II

(283) Declaration on Religious Liberty

2. The Vatican Council declares that the human person has a right to religious freedom. Freedom of this kind means that all men should be immune from coercion on the part of individuals, social groups and every human power so that, within due limits, nobody is forced to act against his convictions nor is anyone to be restrained from acting in accordance with his convictions in religious matters in private or in public, alone or in association with others. The Council further declares that the right to religious freedom is based on the very dignity of the human person as known through the revealed word of God and by reason itself. This right of the human person to religious freedom must be given such recognition in the constitutional order of society as will make it a civil right.

Declaration on the Relation of the Church to Non-Christian Religions

[1] All men form but one community. This is so because all stem from the one stock which God created to people the entire earth; and also because all share a common destiny, namely God. His providence, evident goodness and saving designs extend to all men against the day when the elect are gathered together in the holy city which is illuminated by the glory of God and in whose splendour all peoples will walk.

Men look to their different religions for an answer to the unsolved riddles of human existence. The problems that weigh heavily on the hearts of men are the same today as in the ages past. What is man? What is the meaning and purpose of life? What is upright behaviour, and what is sinful? Where does suffering originate, and what end does it serve? How can genuine happiness be found? What happens at death? What is judgment? What reward follows death? And finally, what is the ultimate mystery, beyond human explanation, which embraces our entire existence, from which we take our origin and towards which we tend? . . . The Catholic Church rejects nothing of what is true and holy in these religions.

ten because of anti-Protestant or anti-Orthodox polemics: the priesthood of all believers, the church as people of God rather than as a legal organization, and episcopal collegiality. What is meant by the latter is that around the Bishop of Rome the bishops bear collective responsibility for the Christian people.

Openness to other Christians and other religions

The Declaration on Religious Liberty was one of the most difficult texts to work out, because the polemic of the past weighed heavily. As formerly in the time of Gregory XVI, a minority of the council sought to start from the defence of the truth and from Catholicism as the one true faith. The majority, rejecting this impasse, wanted to start from the human being and his or her inalienable rights, among which is the right freely to strive for the truth as one's own conscience sees it. Freedom, something of universal value, could not be claimed only by Catholics when they were a persecuted minority. It was equally valid for non-Catholics when surrounded by Catholics.

The Decree on Ecumenism asks that the different Christian confessions should consider first of all what they have in common, Christ and the gospel. Non-Catholic Christians should not be accused of the sin of schism. Catholics should also be aware of their deficiencies and their historical responsibilities during the schisms. This was the substance of the declaration by Paul VI and Athenagoras on 7 December 1965 (see Volume 1, p.101).

The Declaration on Non-Christian Religions was one of the most innovative texts of the Council. The Council endeavoured to discover

Vatican II

Dogmatic Constitution on the Church, *Lumen gentium*

Chapter II The People of God

9. God has willed to make men whole and save them, not as individuals without any bond or link between them, but rather to make them into a people who might acknowledge him and serve him in holiness . . . Christ called a race made up of Jews and Gentiles which would be one, not according to the flesh, but in the Spirit, and this race would be the new people of God. For those who believe in Christ, who are reborn, not from a corruptible seed, but from an incorruptible one through the word of the living God (I Peter 1.23), not from flesh but from water and the Holy Spirit (John 3.5–6), are finally established as 'A chosen race, a royal priesthood, a holy nation . . . who in times past were not a people, but now are the People of God' (I Peter 2.9–10).

That messianic people, although it does not actually include all men, and at times may appear as a small flock, is, however, a most sure seed of unity, hope and salvation for the whole human race. Established by Christ as a communion of life, love and truth, it is taken up by him also as the instrument for the salvation of all; as the light of the world and the salt of the earth (cf. Matt. 5.13–16) it is sent forth into the whole world.

Destined to extend to all regions of the earth, it enters into human history, though it transcends at once all times and all racial boundaries. Advancing through trials and tribulations, the Church is strengthened by God's grace, promised to her by the Lord so that she may not waver from perfect fidelity, but remain the worthy bride of the Lord, ceaselessly renewing herself through the action of the Holy Spirit until, through the cross, she may attain to that light which knows no setting.

that part of the knowledge of God hidden in all religion, from those known as primitive right up to the heirs of monotheistic revelation, Judaism and Islam. 'The church deplores hatred, persecution and all manifestations of antisemitism which, at whatever time and by whomsoever, have been directed against Jews.' This passage has been difficult to implement in the heated context of Middle Eastern disputes.

A church in dialogue with the modern world

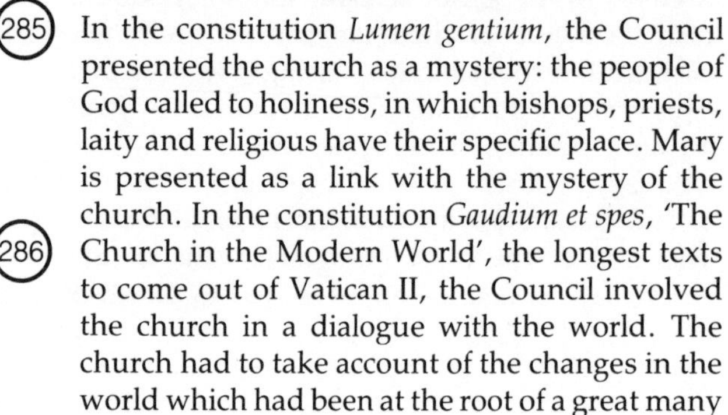

(285) In the constitution *Lumen gentium*, the Council presented the church as a mystery: the people of God called to holiness, in which bishops, priests, laity and religious have their specific place. Mary is presented as a link with the mystery of the church. In the constitution *Gaudium et spes*, 'The (286) Church in the Modern World', the longest texts to come out of Vatican II, the Council involved the church in a dialogue with the world. The church had to take account of the changes in the world which had been at the root of a great many conflicts and mistakes in the past. Atheism had to be considered objectively, and its causes searched out. Several current problems in particular were put under the microscope; marriage and the family, culture, the economy, politics and the building up of peace. The Secretariat for Non-Believers set up in April 1965 responded to these preoccupations.

A new era

Many people shared the impression that a new era was beginning for the church. Vatican II had ended the period begun by the Council of Trent. From this time on people talked of 'before the Council' and 'after the Council'. Some people thought that the church, which had lived for four centuries on the basis of the Council of Trent, was going to live for many years on the basis of Vatican II. One only had to put the texts into practice! In reality, things did not happen like that at all. The calling into question of the Council, together with the crisis of civilization, showed the fragility of a church in which differences were expressed more freely.

Vatican II

Pastoral Constitution on the Church in the Modern World
(*Gaudium et spes*)

The joy and hope, the grief and anguish of the men of our time, especially of those who are poor or afflicted in any way, are the joy and hope, the grief and anguish of the followers of Christ as well. Nothing that is genuinely human fails to find an echo in their hearts.

Whatever truth, goodness, and justice is to be found in past or present human institutions is held in high esteem by the Council. In addition, the Council declares that the church is anxious to help and foster these institutions in so far as it depends on it and is compatible with its mission . . .

The Council exhorts Christians, as citizens of both cities, to perform their duties faithfully in the spirit of the gospel. It is a mistake to think that, because we may immerse ourselves in earthly activities as if these latter were utterly foreign to religion, and religion were nothing more than the fulfilment of acts of worship and the observance of a few moral obligations. One of the gravest errors of our times is the dichotomy between the faith which many profess and the practice of their daily lives.

Preface, 42, 43

The Vocabulary of Vatican II

I The Course of the Council

SESSIONS: Periods during which the Council met.
The First Session was from 12 October to 8 December 1962; the Second Session from 29 September to 4 December 1963; the Third Session was from 14 September to 7 December 1965.

GENERAL CONGREGATIONS: daily meetings of the Council: there were 168 of them, attended by Fathers, observers and auditors.

PUBLIC CONGREGATIONS: solemn meetings open to all (the opening and the promulgation).

II The Members

FATHERS: all the bishops and superiors of male religious orders.

OBSERVERS: delegates from non-Catholic churches and confessions.

AUDITORS: from the Second Session on, representatives of the laity and religious.

EXPERTS (PERITI): theologians invited to help the commissions or chosen by particular bishops.

III The Running of the Council

PRESIDENTS: ten cardinals nominated by the pope to lead the debates at the First Session.

MODERATORS: four cardinals who guided the debates from the Second Session onwards (Suenens, Döpfner, Lercaro, Agagianian).

SECRETARIAT: secretary (Felici) and 5 sub-secretaries (Villot, etc.) entrusted with the organization.

IV The Votes

Indicated by PLACET (= yes), NON PLACET (= no), PLACET JUXTA MODUM (=yes subject to amendment).
The amendments were examined by the commissions responsible for the schemata. When a schema had been accepted 'in general' by the Council, only those amendments were accepted which were along the lines of the text.

V The Commissions

Ten of these were elected at the beginning of the Council. They comprised sixteen members elected by the Fathers and nine nominated by the pope, together with a cardinal who had been nominated beforehand. The number of participants rose to thirty at the end of the second session. The Secretariat for Unity was regarded as a commission. The commissions designated one or more reporters to present a schema.

The mixed commissions were composed of delegates from two or more commissions, charged with working out a schema. The commissions could divide themselves into sub-commissions for particular work.

VI The Texts

SCHEMA: any text under discussion which had not been definitively adopted.

CONSTITUTION: a term reserved for four essential documents of the Council:
1. Liturgy
2. Revelation
3. The Church (*Lumen gentium*)
4. The Church in the Modern World (*Gaudium et spes*)

DECREE: texts which appeared as the application of principles laid down by the constitutions:
1. Ecumenism
2. The Catholic Eastern Churches
3. The Means of Social Communication
4. The Pastoral Office of Bishops
5. The Training of Priests
6. The Ministry and Life of Priests
7. The Up-to-date Renewal of Religious Life
8. The Apostolate of Lay People
9. The Missionary Activity of the Church

DECLARATION: principles and guidelines expressing the thought of the Church:
1. The Relation of the Church to Non-Christian Religions
2. Religious Liberty
3. Christian Education

II · The More or Less Unforeseen Results of the Council

1. The voices of yesterday

The institutions foreseen by the council texts came about rapidly in the years which followed. Episcopal conferences, one of the marks of collegiality, were formed in all countries. It was sometimes a matter of adjusting groups which were already in existence. In France, the Conference of Bishops from 1966 onwards got into the habit of meeting together at Lourdes. The bishops divided themselves into a certain number of commissions which met together several times a year.

Another aspect of collegiality, the Synod of Bishops which surrounded the pope to help in the government of the church universal, met for the first time in October 1967. It consisted of 197 members, two-thirds of whom were elected by the episcopal conference. It was a kind of running-in session, and the programme was fairly vague; the evils threatening the faith, atheism, mixed marriages, the reform of seminaries and of canon law.

Often with much difficulty, councils of priests were set up in the diocese. Members of religious orders updated their constitutions and life-styles in accordance with the Decree on the Renewal and Adaptation of the Religious Life.

The Constitution on the Liturgy was the starting point for liturgical reform: the use of the vernacular, the possibility of communion in two kinds, the revival of the liturgy of the word, concelebration, etc. In 1967 the whole liturgy could be celebrated in the vernacular. These changes were generally warmly welcomed, but those who hankered after Latin launched their first attacks in pamphlet form. The pope had to defend Cardinal Lercaro, who was responsible for the reform.

2. A church speaking to the world

The church seemed to have discovered a worldwide dimension by taking a serious part in the major problems of the world. The travels, meetings and actions of the pope earned him the esteem not only of Christians but of nonChristians. He went to New York in 1965, to Portugal and Istanbul, where he met the Patriarch Athenagoras in 1967; to Latin America in 1968; to Geneva and Uganda in 1969; to the Far East in 1970. In 1966 he met the Archbishop of Canterbury. He made the central government of the church (the Roman Curia) international. From then on Italian cardinals were in the minority.

(287)

In the encyclical *Populorum progressio*, 'On the development of peoples' (1967), the pope affirmed that 'the social question has become a world-wide one'. Development had to be integral and bear on all aspects, economic, cultural and spiritual. There was a need to act on international commercial relations in order to protect the weak countries from unfair competition. The encyclical had an important influence on the episcopal conferences and on the 1971 Synod of Bishops. The Christians of the northern hemisphere were questioning the consumer society and the plundering of world resources.

3. The tensions of 1968

With hindsight, the year 1968 can be seen as a turning point, not only in French society but in the post-Vatican church.

May 1968 in the church and elsewhere

The disturbances of May 1968, which began in the university, extended into the factories and finally reached the whole of society including the church. Church institutions were put in question. Christians spoke out in the churches. 'The street is in the church'; 'the Holy Spirit is on the barricades'. Mgr Marty, Archbishop of Paris, proclaimed that 'God is not conservative'. The priests met together in a forum. The faith took on the role of protest in society. At the same time the church was accused of giving its backing to the established order.

For some people the decisions of the Council were not being put into practice quickly enough. Matters had to be brought to a head. At Pentecost 1968 Christians, priests and pastors celebrated the eucharist together to hasten on the unity of the churches. More and more priests left the church out of a concern to reintegrate the priesthood into the human condition through marriage, work, political activity.

The encyclical *Humanae vitae*

The Fathers at the Council had not considered the issue of birth control. The pope had postponed the question. He had entrusted the study of it to a commission which was increasingly coming down in favour of an alteration to the church's traditional position on the matter of contraception. The pope did not follow the advice of the commission, and in the encyclical *Humanae vitae* (July 1968) rejected all forms of unnatural birth control. The encyclical was badly received, not only by non-Catholics but also by many Catholics in the developed countries. It was more warmly welcomed in the Third World.

There were various aspects to the dispute. Many people saw the encyclical as an exercise of non-collegial authority on the part of the church. All subjects of a delicate nature such as birth control, pastoral work with the divorced, the celibacy of priests, had been removed from the discussions of the Council and the exercise of collegiality. Some of the bishops, like Cardinal Suenens, expressed their reservations.

The document was criticized for not starting from a personal standpoint but from a biological one. The idea of nature, which was fundamental to the pope's position, seemed ambiguous. Was not humankind continually transforming its nature, often fighting against it (natural calamities, illnesses, death)? As a result, many Catholics did not feel themselves bound by the encyclical. This marked a great step backwards for papal authority. Christians, and with far greater justification non-Christians, had increasing difficulty in accepting control over their behaviour by an extreme authority. Some questioned the right of 'old celibates' to speak about what did not concern them.

Medellin and the birth of liberation theology

In August 1968, Paul VI went to Colombia (Bogota and Medellin) for the Conference of Latin American Bishops (CELAM). The pope proclaimed: 'Development must be peaceful'. He rejected the violence of the liberation movements. Now for many Latin Americans the idea of development was not a good thing. It only favoured the capitalism of multinationals who had their headquarters in North America and were supported by the military régimes of Latin America. The church was often accused of conservatism and solidarity with the latter. In 1966 the Colombian priest Camilo Torres was killed in the bush in the liberation fighting. The opinion of liberation theologians was that Christians should take part in this fighting to bring justice to the most deprived. The fighting was not limited

Development and Liberation

Paul VI in the Encyclical *Populorum progressio*: On the Development of Peoples (26 March 1967)

Today the principal fact that we must all recognize is that the social question has become world-wide . . . There are certainly situations whose injustice cries to heaven. When whole populations destitute of necessities live in a state of dependence barring them from all initiative and responsibility . . . recourse to violence, as a means to right these wrongs to human dignity, is a grave temptation.

Development cannot be limited to mere economic growth. In order to be authentic, it must be complete: integral, that is, it has to promote the good of every man and the whole man . . . It is a question of building a world where every man, no matter what his race, religion or nationality, can live a fully human life, freed from servitude imposed on him by other men or by natural forces over which he has not sufficient control . . . If the new name for peace is development, who would not wish to labour for it with all his powers?

Paul VI to the peasants of Colombia, 23 August 1968

We shall continue to denounce the unjust economic inequalities between rich and poor, the abuses of authority and administration which are to your detriment and to the detriment of all. We shall continue to encourage resolutions and programmes in favour of developing peoples . . .

We exhort you not to put your trust in violence and revolution; it is contrary to the Christian spirit, and can also delay, rather then help, the social elevation to which you rightly aspire.

Final Document of the Conference of Latin American Bishops at Medellin (August–September 1968)

We are on the threshold of a new era in the history of our continent, an era which holds the promise of total emancipation, of freedom from all servitude, of personal growth and collective integration.

Just as Israel, the ancient people, once felt the saving presence of God when he freed them from the oppression of Egypt, so we, the new people of God, cannot fail to feel his saving passage in matters of true development. This is the passage for each and all from less human conditions of life to more human conditions of life.

to armed combat, but if there was violence, it was imposed by political and economic structures.

As an indirect consequence, these disputes prompted reactions from the conservatives and integrists, who held the Council responsible for all this unrest. Paul VI was badly affected by this. In the years that followed he constantly expressed himself along the lines of 'Renewal, yes; change, no.' 'Although we might have expected the days after the Council to be days of sunshine, what we have are clouds, storms and shadow' (1972).

The theology of liberation according to Gustavo Gutiérrez

The issue of development does in fact find its true place in the more universal, profound and radical perspective of liberation. It is only within this framework that development finds its true meaning and possibilities of accomplishing something worthwhile . . .

Humankind is seen as assuming conscious responsibilty for its own destiny . . . In this perspective the unfolding of all the dimensions of humanness is demanded – persons who make themselves throughout their life and throughout history . . .

Finally, the word development to a certain extent limits and obscures the theological problems implied in the process designated by this term. On the contrary the word liberation allows for another approach leading to the biblical sources which inspire the presence and action of man in history. In the Bible, Christ is presented as the one who brings us liberation. Christ the saviour liberates from sin, which is the ultimate root of all disruption of friendship and of all injustice and oppression. Christ makes humankind truly free, that is to say, he enables us to live in communion with him; and this is the basis for all human fellowship . . .

To speak about a theology of liberation is to seek an answer to the following question: what relation is there between salvation and the historical process of human liberation?

A Theology of Liberation, Orbis Books and SCM Press [2] 1988, 24f., 29.

Ernesto 'Che' Guevara, who had been close to Fidel Castro, died in the fight for liberation in Bolivia in 1967. Georges Casalis compares him with Jesus:

Nothing more resembles the life and death of Jesus than that of 'Che' Guevara, who did not consider it a privilege to cling to being equal to Fidel, to live happily with his family as a minister in the 'first free country of America' but who willingly humbled himself by going into exile in a foreign and hostile land. In all things he became like to the anonymous partisans struggling for the liberation of their people. He shared without reserve or hesitation in all the circumstances of their perilous life until he met with death in the Bolivian forests, betrayed by his friends, pursued by the armed forces of imperialism . . .

III · Disillusionment and Hope

1. The decline of religion and the return of the religious

One might have thought that the Council would have made the church more attractive. However, in the years that followed a clear recession in religious observance was evident, together with a decline in Christian influence on behaviour, at least in the Western world. All countries saw a decline in church attendance, a reduction in the number of men offering themselves for ordination or seeking to join religious orders. There were declines in the numbers of those being baptized, and even more substantial declines in the numbers of those undergoing catechesis. Fewer marriages were performed in church, and the divorce rate climbed sharply. The practice of living together also marked a disappearance of traditional Christian customs.

Conflict of interpretation

Although all this was accepted, interpretation of the trend was disputed. Religious sociology, on which work had been begun well before the Council, saw the decline of religion as an acceleration of the phenomenon of secularization, which went back to the nineteenth century. The church had not come to grips with the new society which had been shaped out of it. The last bricks were crumbling, but it was possible to build again on the ruins. At the opposite extreme, others wanted to date the rapid decline from the 1960s. The crisis was the result of an unfortunate initiative in the shape of the council. The church had been disturbed by influential minorities who thought themselves to be enlightened: theologians, liturgists, lay people from Catholic Action. Ordinary people had lost confidence in a church which complicated access to the sacraments, which suppressed solemn communion, which replaced the time-hallowed liturgy of the past with the imaginings of intellectuals. And in turn the enlightened minorities condemned these reactions from good people. It was concluded that the masses were less de-Christianized than 'ex-Christianized', i.e. excluded from the church.

Beyond question there is a wide range of positions. Integrism, of the type practised by Mgr Lefebvre, absolutely refused to recognize the Council and saw the crisis in the church as being merely an internal affair, self-destruction, which had no connection with the general problems of contemporary society. Other people, often the theologians who had been active in the Council, said that the Council had been wrongly interpreted and asked for it to be received properly, while still recognizing that the church was suffering the repercussions of a world-wide crisis of Western civilization. Certainly the church had lost some of its grip on society – Vatican II, in allowing freedom of speech, had encouraged the development within the church of movements which had come into being elsewhere. 'What the pre-conciliar institutions maintained through fear, as masters in the art of applying moral pressure, the post-conciliar church has not succeeded in maintaining by the force of its inner convictions.' Perhaps the conciliar institutions had been set up too quickly and in too authoritarian a manner for Christians who had not been adequately prepared. The lack of perspective does not permit a final judgment. This crisis was an unprecedented one.

The return of the religious

Side by side with the contraction of official religion, a return to the sacred and the religious became apparent in the 1970s. 1968 had been the start of the 'great airing of ideas': science, philosophy and especially Marxism, and politics, if only because the official churches were not giving satisfactory replies to human questions and anxieties. And so religion made a comeback, but in a somewhat ambiguous way. It was often an irrational affair, a kind of holiness far removed from the Christian religion. The customers for these para-religious products – clairvoyance, astrology, the esoteric, occultism – were numerous. The multiplication of sects has to be seen in this context.

Some people looked for an opportunity for Christianity in this return to religion. The Jesus movement, built entirely around Jesus, was formed without any link with the churches and gave rise to rock operas on Jesus like *Jesus Christ Superstar* and *Godspell* (1972): there were many stickers and slogans: 'Jesus saves', 'Jesus loves you'.

Within the framework of the church there was the development of Protestant Pentecostalism which in Catholic circles became known as the charismatic movement: it appeared in the United States in 1967 and in Europe in 1971. Sentiment and affectivity took precedence over intellect and politics. Extraordinary phenomena like speaking in tongues, healings, the presence of Satan, all returned in force. In a slightly different way the Taizé community brought together a host of young people from all countries under the auspices of the Council of Youth (1974). The contemplative monastic orders attracted followers, even if they could only come to monasteries for brief stays. A European enquiry showed that religion remained a social fact in all the developed countries. The importance of religious personalities – Martin Luther King, Mother Teresa, JohnPaul II – to the media was taken to be a sign of this. Folk religion provided a new theme for the sociologists. Pilgrimages, which were sometimes a form of pious tourism, attracted crowds of people. Did this return of the religious compensate for the contraction described above? It is difficult to say.

2. Along the paths marked out by the Council

Openness to the world

In New York Paul VI had called himself an 'expert in humanity'. The pope showed his interest in world problems by his travels, by his defence of human rights and justice: the national sections of the Commission on Justice and Peace set up in 1967 worked on all these problems. The concern on the part of Christians to be present and act in all these sectors of life was expressed by their political and social involvement. The corollary of these many involvements was often tension among Christians. Political and social divisions entered the heart of the church; the distinction between spiritual and temporal did not always seem adequate. The Catholic Action movements wanted to take a definite political stand. All this fostered fresh controversies.

John XXIII had caused a sensation by receiving Kruschchev's son-in-law. In this way he had opened up a channel to the East which Paul VI followed up by entrusting the work to Mgr Casaroli. Diplomatic relations were re-established with Yugoslavia in 1970. The Mindszenty affair was settled in 1971. On several occasions Paul VI received Soviet leaders. During his stop-over in Hong Kong in 1970 he greeted the Chinese 'for whom, also, Christ is a saving redeemer'. The overtures resulted in an improvement in the fate of Catholics in Eastern countries, where the pope was able to nominate bishops once again. But these laborious compromises often had to be limited to freedom of worship.

Ecumenism

The Council had to a great extent paved the way to ecumenism for Catholics. Paul VI met a number of the leaders of the Christian churches: the Patriarch of Constantinople, the Coptic Pope, the Archbishop of Canterbury. Catholic legislation on mixed marriages was relaxed. The non-Catholic partner was no longer given the impression of being humiliated, as previously. Without belonging to the World Council of Churches, the Catholic Church sent observers to its General Assemblies, whose workings it followed attentively. The problems of the World Council of Churches were often similar to those of Catholics. The WCC, which supported people fighting for their freedom (as in South Africa), was accused of being political; some of its members left. It also experienced the challenge from young people at Uppsala in 1968: less paper and talk, more action.

The churches have managed to produce many common texts and statements in many countries. A notable achievement in the Englishspeaking world has been the establishment of an International Commission on English Texts (ICET), which without the Commission creating or aiming to create complete standardization, has produced a happy convergence in the many new liturgical texts which a variety of churches have produced. Statements on Church Order and doctrine have emerged from a variety of combinations of the mainstream churches; for instance, the series of reports from the Anglican-Roman Catholic International Commission (ARCIC) provides some prospect of healing one of the most complicated and ambiguous breaches in the Western church. Perhaps the most impressive evidence of the wish to find a common understanding of doctrines which proved so divisive in the sixteenth century Reformation came with the WCC Statement issued at Lima in 1982: *Baptism, Eucharist and Ministry*. What was so significant about this was that churches of the Reformation were able to come to a mind on these foundation doctrines of the faith in company with representatives of the Eastern Orthodox tradition. Yet perhaps actions speak louder than words: the most impressive evidence of ecumenical progress comes from localities where the churches are genuinely working together as partners. In England, one of the best examples is in Liverpool on Merseyside, where Catholic archbishop, Anglican bishop and Free Church leaders have come to find an enviable unity of purpose in facing the problems of a great city.

On the other hand, it is only right to point out that the drive towards ecumenism has faced numerous setbacks. In the Western churches outside the Roman obedience, the only successful unions between churches of episcopal and non-espiscopal traditions have been in the Indian sub-continent, starting with the Church of South India (1947): subsequent attempts elsewhere have usually run into objections from Anglicans of Anglo-Catholic background, and have had to go ahead without Anglican participation. In England, these include a succession of schemes between 1965 and 1972 to reunite the Church of England and English Methodism, and an abortive Covenant for Unity between Anglicans and Free Churches in 1982. In Scotland, on the other hand, it has been Presbyterian fears which have been the main obstacle to any progress in union between the Church of Scotland and Anglicans. The British Council of Churches, founded in 1942, has never included the Roman Catholic Church in Great Britain except as an observer; however, the statements emerging from the Conference of representatives of British Churches at Swanwick, entitled 'Not Strangers but Pilgrims' (1987), suggest that an entirely new phase of initiative may be beginning which may abandon the old structures of the BCC in order to make possible a much greater share for the Catholic Church. Perhaps too much was expected too soon after the first post-War achievements and the changes of Vatican II; now the churches may learn from past failures.

Evangelization

The synod of bishops which met in 1974 had as its theme 'The Evangelization of the World Today'. There were plenty of ways of approaching this. The bishops of the developed countries concentrated on the problems of secularization, of de-Christianization and atheism: those of Africa and Asia were concerned with the spread of the gospel to non-Christians in a language which took account of their cultures; and those of Latin America tried to make the connection between evangelization and economic and political liberation. The task of evangelization came up against the difficulty of a much greater extension of Christianity in many countries.

The synod did not synthesize its deliberations and entrusted the pope with this task. So in December 1975 Paul VI published the apostolic exhortation *Evangelii nuntiandi*, 'to proclaim the gospel to contemporary men and women'. In referring to the documents of the council, the tenth anniversary of which was being celebrated, and basing himself on the deliberations of the bishops, the pope, sometimes in rather tightly-packed wording, touched on all the aspects of evangelization in the modern world; the task of evangelizing in spite of a certain discouragement and without failing to respect freedom; an evangelization which took account of indigenous culture (the inculturation of Christianity): the link between evangelization and liberation; the role of the small communities known as basic communities. 'The church of the twentieth century had to be made even fitter to proclaim the gospel to the humanity of the twentieth century . . . Evangelization is a joy even when the sowing has to be done in tears.'

3. The church universal, the local church and the Roman Church

The crises and the hopes of the church today are inexhaustible. But there is a key which allows us to understand them. There is a certain tension between the universality of the church and the message of the gospel on the one hand and the local churches on the other. The 1974 synod grasped this clearly. The speed of communications and the growth of the media might appear to facilitate a universal language in the church as in the world. Often this is not the case. Particularities (perhaps they are best called original local features) increasingly assert themselves, above all when there is a suspicion that the universal language is that of the dominant West.

The geographical displacement of the church

The Western church has tended to lose the dominant position which it has had since the beginning. As the twentieth century draws to a close, the focus of the church is simultaneously shifting towards the south, the east and the west. The demographic thrust of Africa has given it a place of increasing importance in the church. But above all, more than fifty per cent of Catholics are to be found in Latin America. Brazil is now the premier Catholic country in the world. In the East, Poland with its vast numbers of practising Catholics and its pope indicates a kind of church which is called to play an increasingly important role in Catholicism.

Different centres of interest

Every major sector of the church has its own particular focus of interest and its priorities. The Western church is concerned with the problems of secularization, the search for a system of values, moral reform. Poverty, economic exploitation and social revolution are challenges to the church in Latin America. The conflicts in speculative theology are only of marginal interest to the Christians of Latin America. The theologies of liberation do not transpose well into Europe. In the West, secularization has been largely accepted and the sacred is distrusted. In Poland, clericalization and the encouragement of the sacred are the basis of the church system, as a condition of survival. A Polish church which functioned like a French one would be swept away in a few years. A Church of France drawn up along the lines of the Polish system would revive the anti-clericalism of the early twentieth century. Other contrasts could be noted. Relations between different religious groups are usually courteous in the West, but synonymous with intolerance and civil war in the Middle East and Northern Ireland. The West has other intolerances to cope with!

If we add the internal theological and political tensions of the local churches, the difficulty of agreeing on a single voice for the universal church can be understood. If religious leaders keep to a spiritual, dogmatic or pious language which is acceptable to everyone, it is then thought inadequate as a response to specific situations.

The renewal of the central government of the church

Reforms in the Roman administration of the church have attempted to respond to these problems, at least partially. In 1968 the basic law of the church defined the principles of a central government. The internationalization of the cardinals has already been mentioned. More important would seem to be the internationalization of church government itself so that the members are no longer only Italians who co-opt one another. Cardinals of all countries have the highest responsibilities. The vocabulary is being improved. The Holy Office or the Inquisition has become the Congregation for the Doctrine of Faith. The age limits put on holding office stress their aspect of service. The exercise of collegiality by episcopal conferences and the synod of bishops, which has met seven times, limits and balances Roman centralization. However, some people feel disappointed. The Roman system can take over collegial institutions again, and non-Italians who have come to Rome to govern the church have soon become Romanized.

All these features of church life marked the end of the pontificate of Paul VI, who in his last years often expressed his disquiet and sometimes his sadness. This context explains the two successive elections of John-Paul I and John-Paul II (1978). In John-Paul I the cardinals chose a man of reconciliation, a pastor concerned for the poor, someone who was not a member of the Curia but still an Italian, more independent towards the two blocks. The election of Cardinal Woytyla is a consequence of the internationalization of the cardinals. It marks a concern to distance the church from Italian politics and the Western churches. But for the history of his pontificate you should turn to your daily paper.

A course of twenty centuries

There is no conclusion or final point to a history of the church, as there can be to a history of the dynasties of ancient Egypt or the French monarchy. What began at Pentecost in the year 39 is continuing. We have journeyed with a host of Christians. We have been aware of the courage of some and the compromises of others. We have felt the drama of certain situations. Fidelity to the gospel of Jesus, the work of the Spirit at Pentecost, allows Christians today to grasp again the living tradition and to transmit the heritage that they have received in new forms in a changing world. Christians of old have faced the difficulties of the hour; those of today can do the same thing.

For further reading

W. M. Abbott (ed.), *The Documents of Vatican II*, US Catholic Publications 1966

Anthony Archer, *The Two Catholic Churches*, SCM Press 1986

Trevor Beeson, *Vision of Hope. The Churches in Latin America*, Fount Books 1984

Y. Congar, *Diversity and Communion*, SCM Press 1984

John Coventry, *Reconciling*, SCM Press 1985

P. Hebblethwaite, *The Year of the Three Popes*, Fount Books 1978

Anton Houtepen, *People of God. A Plea for the Church*, SCM Press 1984

Peter Nichols, *The Pope's Divisions. The Roman Catholic Church Today*, Faber 1981

CHRONOLOGICAL TABLES

EVENTS		FOUNDERS AND WRITERS	POPES	RULERS
				England
The Bible printed by Gutenberg at Mainz	1455	ERASMUS (1469–1536)		HENRY VIII
The establishment of the Spanish Inquisition	1478		ALEXANDER VI	(1509–1547)
The baptism of the king of the Congo by the Portuguese	1491	MICHELANGELO (1475–1564)	(1492–1503)	EDWARD VI
Capture of Granada by the Catholic kings; discovery of America by	1492	THOMAS MORE (1478–1535)		(1547–1553)
Christopher Columbus				MARY
Alexander VI divides the world between Spain and Portugal	1493			(1534–1558)
The Portuguese reach the Indies (Vasco da Gama)	1498	ZWINGLI (1484–1531)	JULIUS II	ELIZABETH I
			(1503–1513)	(1558–1603)
Discovery of Brazil by the Portuguese	1500			JAMES I
The building of St Peter's, Rome, begins	1506	THOMAS MUNTZER (1489–1525)		(1603–1625)
Erasmus' *In Praise of Folly*	1511		LEO X	
Erasmus' *New Testament*; Thomas More's *Utopia*;		CRANMER (1489–1556)	(1513–1521)	*France*
The Concordat of Bologna between the pope and France	1516			FRANCIS I
End of the Fifth Lateran Council: Luther's Ninety-five Theses	1517	IGNATIUS LOYOLA (1491–1556)		(1515–1547)
Capture of Mexico by Cortes; Magellan's circumnavigation of the	1519			HENRY II
world				(1547–1559)
Luther's great Reformation writings	1520			HENRY III
Excommunication of Luther; the Diet of Worms	1521		HADRIAN VI	(1574–1589)
The Peasants' War in Germany	1524	MELANCHTHON (1497–1560)	(1522–1523)	HENRY VI
Müntzer's death; Luther's marriage	1525		CLEMENT VII	(1509–1547)
The supporters of the Protestant Reformation at Speyer	1529		(1523–1534)	
The Augsburg Confession	1530	FRANCIS XAVIER (1506–1552)		*Spain*
The Anabaptists of Münster; Ignatius Loyola's vow of Montmartre;	1534		PAUL III	FERDINAND
the English Act of Supremacy; the martyrdom of St Thomas More	1535		(1534–1549)	and ISABELLA
Calvin's *Christian Institutions*	1536	CALVIN (1509–1564)		(1497–1516)
Calvin finally in Geneva	1541			CHARLES I (V)
The Holy Office in Rome; Francis Xavier in India	1542			(1516–1556)
The beginning of the Council of Trent	1545	JOHN KNOX (1513–1572)		PHILIP II
Francis Xavier in Japan	1549		JULIUS III	(1556–1598)
Second period of the Council of Trent	1551	TERESA OF AVILA (1515–1582)	(1550–1555)	
The religious peace of Augsburg	1555		PAUL IV	*Empire*
The Portuguese in Macao	1557		(1555–1559)	CHARLES V
The Act of Uniformity in England	1559	PHILIP NERI (1515–1595)	PIUS IV	(1516–1556)
The beginning of the Wars of Religion in France	1562		(1559–1565)	FERDINAND I
End of the Council of Trent	1563			(1556–1564)
The Roman Catechism	1566	PETER CANISIUS (1521–1597)	PIUS V	RUDOLPH II
The Roman Missal	1570		(1566–1572)	(1576–1612)
The victory at Lepanto over the Turks	1571	ST JOHN OF THE CROSS		
The Massacre of St Bartholomew	1572	(1542–1591)	GREGORY XIII	*Russia*
The Jesuit Matteo Ricci in China	1582	ROBERT BELLARMINE	(1572–1585)	IVAN III
The Edict of Nantes	1598	(1542–1621)		(1462–1505)
				IVAN III
The burning of Giordano Bruno	1600		SIXTUS QUINTUS	(THE TERRIBLE
The colony of Virginia established	1607	FRANCOIS DE SALES (1567–1622)	(1585–1590)	(1533–1584)
Francois de Sales' *Introduction to the Devout Life*; founding of	1608			BORIS GODUNO
Quebec			PAUL V	(1588–1605)
The first 'reductions' in Paraguay	1610	WILLIAM LAUD (1573–1645)	(1605–1621)	
Reception of the Council of Trent in France	1615			

EVENTS		FOUNDERS AND WRITERS	POPES	RULERS
				England
st trial of Galileo	1616			CHARLES I
ginning of the Thirty Years' War	1618	VINCENT DE PAUL (1581–1660)		(1625–1649)
e foundation of the Congregation of the Propaganda	1622		URBAN VIII	CROMWELL
cond trial of Galileo	1623		(1623–1644)	(1649–1658)
nsen's *Augustinus*	1640		INNOCENT X	CHARLES II
e treaties of Westphalia	1648	PASCAL (1623–1662)	(1644–1655)	(1660–1685)
e condemnation of the Five Propositions	1653		ALEXANDER VII	GEORGE II
eation of vicars apostolic	1659		(1655–1667)	(1760–1820)
undation of the Paris Foreign Mission	1663	JOHN BUNYAN (1628–1688)		GEORGE III
mon's *Critical History of the Old Testament*	1678		INNOCENT XI	(1820–1830)
hn Sobieski saves Vienna from the Turks	1683		(1676–1689)	WILLIAM IV
vocation of the Edict of Nantes	1685	RICHARD SIMON (1638–1712)		(1830–1837)
e Glorious Revolution	1688		CLEMENT XI	
lem Witch Trials	1692	WILLIAM PENN (1644–1718)	(1700–1721)	*France*
				LOUIS XIV
e bull *Unigenitus*	1713	LEIBNIZ (1646–1716)		(1715–1774)
st Masonic lodge in London	1717			LOUIS XV
nsenist schism of Utrecht	1723	JEANNE GUYON (1648–1717)		(1715–1774)
e Moravian Brethren reconstituted by Zinzendorf	1727	FENELON (1651–1715)	BENEDICT XIV	LOUIS XVI
e 'conversion' of John Wesley	1738		(1740–1758)	(1774–1792)
eaty of limits in Paraguay	1750			FIRST REPUBLIC
ginning of the publication of the Encyclopaedia	1751			(1792–1799)
sbon earthquake	1755			NAPOLEON I
e Jesuits expelled from Portugal by Pombal	1759	VOLTAIRE (1694–1778)		CONSULATE
e treaty of Paris: France outside Canada	1763		CLEMENT XIV	(1799–1814)
ppression of the Society of Jesus by the pope	1773	ALPHONSUS LIGUORI	(1769–1774)	
dependence of the United States of America	1776	(1696–1787)		*Spain*
ynod of Pistola	1786		PIUS VI	CHARLES II
ginning of the French Revolution	1789	ZINZENDORF (1700–1760)	(1775–1799)	(1661–1700)
vil Constitution of the clergy	1790			PHILIP V
anco-Austrian war: September massacres	1792			(1700–1740)
rror and de-Christianization	1793	JOHN WESLEY (1703–1791)		
paration of church and state in France	1795		PIUS VII	*Austrian Empire*
			(1800–1823)	LEOPOLD I
oncordat between France and the Holy See	1801			(1658–1705)
apoleon crowned by Pius VII in Paris	1804	ROUSSEAU (1712–1778)		MARIA-THERESA
ccupation of Rome by the French, arrest of Pius VII	1808–9			(1741–1780)
dication of Napoleon; reinstatement of Pius VII	1814			JOSEPH II
atholic Emancipation in England	1829	LAMENNAIS (1782–1854)	LEO XII	(1780–1790)
evolution in France; Lamennais' *L'Avenir*	1830		(1823–1829)	
ncyclical *Mirari vos* of Gregory XVII	1832		PIUS VIII	*Prussia*
eble preaches 'Assize Sermon': Oxford Movement begins	1833	MIGNE (1800–1875)	(1829–1830)	FREDERICK II
F. Strauss' *Life of Jesus*	1836		GREGORY XVI	(1740–1786)
eginning of Nangking Treaties in China	1842		(1831–1846)	PETER THE GREAT
				(1682–1725)
				CATHERINE II
				(1762–1796)

EVENTS		FOUNDERS AND WRITERS	POPES	RULERS
				England
Famine in Ireland; Newman becomes a Catholic	1845	NEWMAN (1801–1890)		VICTORIA
Revolutions in Europe; June days in Paris; the pope flees to Rome	1848		PIUS IX	(1837–1901)
Roman republic	1849	LACORDAIRE (1802–1861)	(1846–1878)	EDWARD VI
Plenary Council of Baltimore	1852			(1901–1910)
Crimean War; dogma of the Immaculate Conception	1854			
Appearances at Lourdes	1858	MANNING (1806–1892)		*France*
Darwin's *The Origin of Species*	1859			LOUIS-PHILIP
Amputation of the Papal States and unification of Italy	1860			(1830–1848)
Polish revolt; Renan's *Life of Jesus*	1863			SECOND REPUB
First Workers' International; the *Syllabus*	1864	KARL MARX (1818–1883)		(1848–1852)
Austro-Prussian War	1866			NAPOLEON I
Karl Marx's *Das Kapital*	1867			(1852–1870)
The Meiji era in Japan	1868	RENAN (1823–1892)		THIRD REPUBL
Opening of First Vatican Council	1869			(1870–1940)
Definition of Infallibility; Franco-Prussian War; end of Papal States	1870			
Commune of Paris: Old Catholics	1871	GIBBONS (1834–1921)		*Austria*
Beginning of the Kulturkampf	1873			FRANZ-JOSEF
French laws authorizing trade unions and divorce	1884		LEO XIII	(1848–1916)
Colonial division of Africa (Berlin Congress)	1885	IRELAND (1836–1918)	(1878–1903)	
Toast of Algiers; founding of Ecole Biblique in Jerusalem	1890			*Prussia-Germa*
Encyclical *Rerum novarum*	1891			FRIEDRICH-WILHE
Au milieu des sollicitudes; 'rallying'	1892	LOISY (1857–1940)		(1840–1861)
Anglican ordinations declared invalid	1896			WILHELM I
Dreyfus affair; foundation of Action Francaise	1898			(1861–1888)
				WILHELM II
Boxer Revolt in Peking	1900	C. DE FOUCAULD (1858–1916)		(1888–1918)
Loisy's *The Gospel and the Church*	1902			
Separation of church and state in France	1905		PIUS X	*Russia*
Lamentabili, Pascendi; condemnation of Modernism	1907	M. BLONDEL (1861–1949)	(1903–1914)	NICHOLAS I
Anti-modernist oath; Edinburgh Missionary Conference	1910			(1825–1855)
Beginning of First World War	1914		BENEDICT XV	ALEXANDER
Armenian genocide in Turkey	1915	ST THERESE (1873–1897)	(1914–1922)	(1855–1881)
Russian revolution; Benedict XV's peace propositions	1917			ALEXANDER
Encyclical *Maximum illud*	1919			(1881–1894)

EVENTS		FOUNDERS AND WRITERS	POPES	RULERS
				England
tockholm meeting of Life and Work	1925	A. SCHWEITZER (1857–1965)	PIUS XI	GEORGE V
ausanne meeting of 'Faith and Order'	1927		(1922–1939)	(1910–1935)
ateran accords: economic crisis in the USA	1929			GEORGE VI
uadragesimo anno; Non abbiamo bisogno	1931	J. MARITAIN (1882–1973)		(1936–1952)
itler gains power: Concordat with Germany	1933			ELIZABETH II
opular Front in France; Civil War in Spain	1936			(1952–)
lit brennender Sorge; Divini Redemptoris	1937	R. BULTMANN (1884–1976)		*USA*
eginning of the Second World War	1939		PIUS XII	ROOSEVELT (1933–1945)
enocide of Jews	1943		(1939–1958)	KENNEDY (1961–1963)
iroshima; end of the war	1945	R. GUARDINI (1885–1968)		*Germany*
Vorld Council of Churches; Iron Curtain	1948			WEIMAR REPUBLIC
an on collaboration with the Communists	1949			(1919–1933)
People's Republic of China		F. MAURIAC (1885–1970)		HITLER
umani generis; Dogma of the Assumption	1950			(1933–1945)
uspension of the worker priests	1954			*USSR*
e-stalinization; Hungarian revolt	1956	K. BARTH (1886–1968)	JOHN XXIII	STALIN
later et Magistra	1961		(1958–1963)	(1924–1953)
dependence of Algeria; Beginning of Vatican II	1962	P. TILLICH (1886–1965)	PAUL VI	*Spain*
acem in Terris	1963		(1963–1978)	FRANCO
nd of Vatican II	1965	D. BONNHOEFFER (1906–1945)	JOHN-PAUL I	(1938–1975)
opulorum progressio; Synod of Bishops	1967		(1978)	*China*
lay movements; *Humanae vitae*; Medellin	1968	MARTIN L. KING (1929–1968)	JOHN-PAUL II	MAO TSE TUNG
he year of the three popes	1978		(1978–)	(1949–1976)